EMPLOYEE DISCIPLINE

Policies and Practices

EMPLOYEE DISCIPLINE

Policies and Practices

James R. Redeker

The Bureau of National Affairs, Inc., Washington, D.C.

Copyright © 1989
The Bureau of National Affairs, Inc.
Washington, D.C. 20037

Fifth Printing, July 1997

Library of Congress Cataloging-in-Publication Data

Redeker, James R., 1941–
  Employee discipline : policies and practices / James R. Redeker.
  p.   cm.
  Includes index.
  ISBN 0-87179-595-7
  1. Labor discipline—Law and legislation—United States.
2. Arbitration, Industrial—United States.   3. Labor discipline—
United States.   I. Title.
KF3540.R43   1989
344.73'012598—dc19
[347.30412598]   88-38546
                                                              CIP

Printed in the United States of America
International Standard Book Number: 0-87179-595-7

To Nancy, Rebecca,
Eric, and Tricia

Preface

My first book, published in 1984 (*Discipline: Policies and Procedures*), was born out of frustration. This book, which draws large portions from the first, is a product of success.

By 1980 I had already spent over ten years as a labor lawyer advising employers in matters relating to employment law and collective bargaining agreements. A significant part of that practice had centered on the problems created by employees who could not or would not conform to the rules set by employers to govern behavior. As a natural outcome of this, of course, was the trial of over a hundred arbitrations under the just cause provision of labor contracts.

What frustrated me was that many of the arbitrations involved the same companies, the same supervisors, and, often, the same issues. It seemed that no matter how many cases I handled for these clients, their supervisors continued to make the same mistakes. As a result, arbitrations were being lost, in whole or in part, because supervisors did not provide me with adequate facts or a record with which to work.

At that stage of my career, there was nothing more important than winning. If a client discharged an employee, I wanted—and was hired to ensure—that the employee stayed discharged. Orders to reinstate an employee without back pay were especially distasteful. For this reason, the education of supervisors on developing and preserving essential facts to justify the discipline or discharge of an employee became a consuming passion for me.

What I first developed were checklists for supervisors. These checklists described the elements of each cause for discipline and compelled supervisors to document numerous facts before taking action against an employee. They proved to be essential tools for winning discipline and discharge arbitrations. Indeed, by using the checklists, clients were assured to the degree possible that when an employee was penalized for poor conduct or unacceptable productivity, the penalty stuck.

When I discovered nonclients using the checklists, I decided to make them the basis for a desk book for supervisors. The result was Part II of the first book (Part III of this book). When used as training materials and as an ongoing reference for supervisors, Part III of this book will serve the original purpose of the checklists—making sure that the discipline or discharge of an employee for one of the sixteen causes for nonsummary action will be sustained as "for just cause" in most cases.

The checklists, however, needed to be placed in context and, as a result, Part I of my first book (substantially Part II of this book) was written as a general discussion of discipline systems and the principles which seemed to govern the reasoning of arbitrators in discipline or discharge cases. While struggling with the policy issues raised by the theoretical discussion of employee discipline and the structure of discipline systems that satisfy arbitral standards, I realized that traditional progressive discipline systems apparently were not achieving the broader purposes of employee discipline: creating disciplined employees. Clients using the checklists were satisfied because their win/loss ratio of discipline or discharge arbitrations had improved, but they continued to have employee conduct and performance problems. It was obvious also from the volume of discipline or discharge cases taken to arbitration that other employers were having the same experience. There seemed to be a great deal of disciplining but little discipline.

Curiously, even though traditional progressive discipline systems provided employees with what arbitrators were finding to be essential due process, they did not create a disciplined work force. They only provided the formula by which a company could get rid of someone perceived as a bad employee and be sustained in arbitration. In fact, it seemed accidental if the work force became disciplined as a result of the discipline activity.

This realization made me very insecure. Here I was making an excellent living from the effects of a system which really did not work, if "work" were defined in terms of creating a responsible and committed work force. What if someone figured out a new system which did work and the need for disciplining employees in the traditional sense disappeared or was largely eliminated? I would be out of a major source of my business.

Rather than wait for this to happen, I decided to see if I could design a better system: A system that would produce a disciplined work force rather than supervisors with expertise in disciplining employees. This effort produced the chapter in *Discipline: Policies and Procedure* titled "Affirmative Discipline." In this current book, I use the generic term "Nonpunitive Discipline."

Since 1984 and the publication of the material on affirmative discipline, I have designed and implemented nonpunitive systems and have seen them at work. The results have been dramatic and largely as I had suspected they would be. The initial disciplinary events continue without much decrease in volume. Indeed, if you count supervisor-employee contacts prior to the first step of formal discipline, the number of events increases. The number of discharges, however, is substantially reduced and the number of discipline or discharge arbitrations is eliminated almost entirely. Even with nonunion employers, the number of wrongful discharge suits and discrimination complaints appear fewer with nonpunitive discipline systems than for employers with traditional progressive systems. As a bonus, employers with nonpunitive systems also report less use of sick leave, lower absenteeism, and higher employee morale and productivity.

By compelling early supervisory intervention and positive problem solving without the negative effects of punishment, nonpunitive discipline turns the objective of discipline away from a process of employee elimination to one of employee retention. As a result, nonpunitive discipline reduces employee turnover. As noted, however, it does not significantly reduce (in fact, may increase) the time a supervisor must spend in the process itself. Nor does it necessarily produce a more disciplined work force. To be sure, employees who work under a nonpunitive system seem, in time, to become more disciplined. However, getting them to that state continues, in my opinion, to take too long and is too expensive.

I have concluded now that the reason why even employers with nonpunitive discipline systems still spend too much time dealing with problem employees is that too little time is spent in the selection and orientation process. Too many employees are hired with the thought that they either will become disciplined workers or will be eliminated from the work force through the discipline system, that is, "we'll give them a try and weed out the bad ones in the probation period." This philosophy is inane and wasteful. Employers who want a disciplined work force should recognize the importance of selecting the right individuals for employment at the outset. The common saying of computer people ("garbage in, garbage out") does not transfer well into this context. Taking in poorly selected employees into the work force is easy. Getting them out is very expensive, economically and emotionally—substantially more expensive than cleansing a computer program.

This book, therefore, reflects my belief that the selection and orientation of employees is as much a part of creating a disciplined work force as the discipline system itself. When employers consult with me now concerning what they perceive to be a lack of discipline in their employees, the first thing I examine is the employer's selection and orientation system. When that system is repaired, we can turn to other issues, such as supervisory training and the development of a discipline system, whether punitive or nonpunitive. First things first.

Finally, this book expands my earlier discussion of the other elements of a Workplace Due Process System, that is, employee representation and dispute resolution. I firmly believe that until employee expectations of fair and impartial treatment are fulfilled through systems they can understand and trust, employers will be plagued by wrongful discharge lawsuits, equal employment charges, and union organizing. The elimination of informal open door policies and of employer-employee distrust is a first step. For the most part, I conclude, employees want to fulfill legitimate employer expectations, do a good job, and have peers who will do their fair share. Employers need to do a better job of defining expectations and of permitting employees to have a share in creating the type of place in which they wish to work. The systems outlined in this book will help this to become a reality. These systems also are in the forefront of employment law, that is, the potential binding effect of internal dispute resolution programs in discrimination and wrongful discharge lawsuits.

I am convinced that the intelligent use of the systems described in this book will result in more committed and responsible employees with high morale, high productivity, and low turnover: a disciplined work force.

James R. Redeker
Wolf, Block, Schorr and
   Solis-Cohen
Philadelphia, Pa.
November 1988

Contents

Preface   vii

Part I. Employee Discipline: Program

1. The Context for Discipline   3
2. Employee Selection and Orientation   6
   Initial Qualifier   7
   Background Checks   8
   Multiple Step Procedure   14
   Skilled Interviewing   15
   Pre-Employment Testing   15
   Orientation   16
3. Employer/Employee Expectations   20
   Due Process Guidelines   25
   Summary   35
4. Supervisor Selection and Training   40
   The Roles and Character of Supervisors   43

Part II. Employee Discipline: Policies

5. Progressive Discipline   51
   Due Process   54
   Equal Treatment   68
   Summary   69
6. Punitive and Nonpunitive Discipline:
   A Comparison   72
   Punitive Discipline   72
   Nonpunitive Discipline   80
   Summary   92
7. Discipline Systems for Nonunion Employees   94
   Fragile Systems   95
   Employment at Will   97

The Components of a Due Process System   106
Establishing Due Process in the Workplace   124
Summary   129

Part III. Employee Discipline: Practices

8. Poor Attendance: Absenteeism/Tardiness   135

9. Abusive, Profane, or Obscene Language   154

10. Alcohol and Alcohol-Related Conduct   170

11. Poor Attitude or Disloyalty   192

12. Carelessness or Negligence   204

13. Dishonesty or Falsification of Company
        Records   215

14. Dress or Grooming   231

15. Drugs: Use or Possession   246

16. Gambling   265

17. Insubordination   279

18. Medical Disability   292

19. Misconduct, Horseplay, and Fighting   305

20. Moonlighting   328

21. Poor Performance   335

22. Work Slowdowns and Stoppages   346

23. Union Activity/Steward Abuse   359

Appendix   373

Table of Cases   383

Index   403

About the Author   413

Part I

Employee Discipline: Program

1

The Context for Discipline

Nowhere is the nature of the relationship between an employer and an employee so dependent on clear understandings than in matters having to do with discipline. It is through discipline that the employer forcefully establishes the limits of its expectations and reacts to what it believes are failures of the employees to conduct themselves in accordance with those expectations. By the same token, the employees' response to discipline gives the employer certain knowledge of the employees' beliefs as to the extent and nature of their rights and responsibilities and of their willingness to fulfill the employer's expectations. It is in this atmosphere of action and reaction that employers and employees define for each other the nature of their relationship. Where a written statement of expectations in the form of a handbook or contract does not exist, the process of definition may be confused and erratic and the resulting confusion may breed a nonproductive antagonistic workforce. The primary action tool for an employer is discipline. How it is used may determine whether the employment relationship will be positive or negative.

In his classic work *Employee Discipline*, Lawrence Stessin stated:

> Employee discipline is the real drama of labor relations. It is the panorama of industrial conflict. It is the nerve center of a network of interrelationships between management and employee. Here are no small issues. . . . On a broader canvas employee discipline is a process of control. It is a method for the maintenance of authority by management. . . . A reprimand, a layoff or a discharge are the prerogatives which management uses as a control to keep these objectives in focus. . . .[1]

3

At first glance, Stessin's view of employee discipline and its place in the employment relationship is as relevant to today's workplace as it may have been in 1960, when the statement was written. However, I believe that Stessin's understanding of employee discipline was too limited and, largely, wrong. Moreover, perceiving employee discipline in the way advanced by Stessin is more than part of the reason why employers continue to find employee discipline so perplexing and unsuccessful; it is the reason.

As Stessin used it and as it has been used traditionally in the American workplace, "discipline" is what an employer does to an employee to force a change in, or to control, behavior or performance. That is, when an employee behaves or performs below an established standard set by the employer, the employee is disciplined. In the employment context, therefore, the word "discipline" is used exclusively as a transitive verb conveying an act to an object ("I disciplined him") or as a noun giving a name to an act which has taken or will take place ("you will be subject to discipline").

My experience has been that employers who have achieved a productive work force with a high level of employee retention have come to use the word "discipline" as an adjective to describe the state-of-being of the work force or the character of the work environment. "The work force or employee is disciplined." Instead of viewing discipline as a means to an end, it is the end (objective) itself. The subtle difference between "I will discipline you" and "I expect you to be disciplined" is remarkable and focuses on the reason why traditional employee discipline systems often do not work.

When "discipline" is understood and used only as a means of achieving compliance with rules or preset standards, the employer is likely to receive from the employees only one part of what is necessary for the enterprise, submission to authority and control. When "discipline" is understood as an objective, however, the meaning of the word is forced into a broader context which includes self-control, character, responsibility and efficiency, as well as orderliness.

When being disciplined in this broad sense is the objective, the means for achieving the objective likewise must be broadened to include activities and methods not normally associated with employee discipline. An employer's discipline system can no longer be restricted to warnings and suspensions. It must include as well hiring, orientation, training, grievance and dispute resolution systems as integrated parts of a single program with a single objective: the creation and maintenance of a disciplined work force.

Where the primary objective of an employer's hiring program is to recruit bodies to do the work, and the orientation program consists essentially of "here are the tools, there is the bathroom, and quitting time is not until 5 p.m.," they are not seen as related to employee discipline. Rather, employee discipline systems are understood to be independent of all other activities in the workplace and intended only to correct unacceptable behavior or to get rid of unacceptable employees.

Where all of the activities of the employer, however, are aimed at obtaining, creating, and retaining disciplined employees, the activities become purposeful and the result is achieved by design, not by chance.

In my experience, the absence of a disciplined work force is due to one or more of the following five reasons:

1. Poor employee selection and orientation procedures
2. Poorly defined employer expectations
3. Poorly understood or satisfied employee expectations
4. Poorly selected and trained supervisors
5. Incorrect philosophy of discipline

The first four of these will be discussed in this Part. The fifth will be discussed in Part II in conjunction with discipline policies.

Notes to Chapter 1

1. Stessin, Employee Discipline (Washington, D.C.: BNA Books, 1960), p. viii.

2

Employee Selection and Orientation

Employee selection techniques, the hiring process, is not strictly within the narrow purview of this book. Yet, the subject cannot be left with the simple truism, "you hire a problem and you will have to fire the problem." If we view employee discipline as an objective and not as a means, the hiring process is, or should be, a critical element in the procedure by which an employer achieves a disciplined work force.

Employers will want to take a close look at their recruitment, selection, and placement activities if they observe some of the following trends among their employees:

- They have increasing difficulty attracting high-quality job applicants.
- They are selecting a higher ratio of employees from a dwindling pool of applicants.
- Recruiting and hiring is done more often on a "crisis" basis because of unforeseen personnel changes.
- They are working at full throttle just to replace employees who are transferred, retire, or otherwise leave the organization.
- Some recent hires are not interested in advancement or do not have the potential to advance into jobs that require greater skills.
- The rate of turnover, especially among new hires, is increasing.
- The quality of work and employee satisfaction is beginning to drop.
- The organization has a growing number of nonperforming or incompetent employees.

- Employees are increasingly bored with their jobs and complain about not knowing what is expected of them.

All too often when a client asks me to review and repair its discipline system because of a perception that the work force is "out-of-control" or lacks productivity, the source of the problem is more in the process by which employees are hired and oriented than in the discipline system itself. Employees are allowed to enter the work force without any examination of their prior work records or analysis of their predispositions. Employers rely primarily on screening employees during their initial period of employment. Employers who hire with the belief that they can weed out poor employees during a probationary or initial period of employment not only lose a significant opportunity to have a quality work force but misuse the essential purpose of the initial 30–120 days of employment—training and indoctrination.

Every hiring program should have the following components:

Initial Qualifier

Employers who wait to qualify potential new employees until the need to hire arises risk decisions based on the need for a body, any body. Companies ought not to hire "bodies," but people who will fit their type of operation and philosophy of work. Consequently, it makes sense to be in the employment market at all times and to develop a pool of potential employees from which the company can draw to provide candidates for final consideration. This appears to be even more necessary now that the effects of the birth dearth are beginning to be felt and it's becoming more difficult to find new employees.

Some projections are that American employers will experience a shortfall of five million employees by the year 2000.[1] As a result, when a "help wanted" sign goes up, there will be fewer responses than in the past when the baby boom pumped an excess of new employees into the marketplace every year. Blessed with a seller's market for the next 15 years, employees will move from job to job rather than from unemployment to a job. New employees will have to be induced to leave other jobs and those who need jobs will be suspect.

A seeker-pool system enables the employer to do better

background checks and qualification studies of potential employees. In developing a seeker pool, the employer has time to do a complete review of an applicant's employment application and to perform the necessary background checks. Based on this information, the applicant either does or does not qualify to take a place in the candidate pool. By drawing from a pool of initially qualified applicants, the employer may better fit an individual to an open job and reduce training costs.

Background Checks

Applicants come with backgrounds that are probative predictors of future behavior. However, many employers, overreacting to potential defamation lawsuits, have cut off the flow of information regarding an employee's work record. This is unfortunate, if not unexpected, in light of the increase of litigation surrounding the employer/employee relationship in recent years. Although the problem of potential liability for unfavorable references is not entirely solvable, it is largely illusory. It is hoped that by better understanding the futility of "name, rank, and serial number" policies and the potential risks of withholding relevant information about a former employee, fewer employers will resort to this policy.

Defamation/Malice

There are two principal bases for liability against employers arising out of disclosures of employee work records: defamation and malice.

Defamation occurs when there is an unprotected communication of a false fact.* Essential to this tort is that the fact being communicated be false. Consequently, where the referring employer communicates a true fact to an inquiring employer, there should be no basis for defamation liability unless the fact is communicated for a malicious purpose. For example, if an employee had a marginal attendance record (true fact), but was otherwise a satisfactory employee, a referral that volunteers the attendance information for the purpose of injuring the employee and interfering with the

---

*Throughout this discussion "false fact" and "true fact" are used to distinguish between isolated pieces of information, each of which can be the basis for legal action.

employee's prospective employment may result in the liability of the referring employer (or individual giving the referral), even though the fact is true.

Many states also recognize a conditional privilege for referring employers so that, unless the privilege is destroyed through malice or, in some states, negligence, the referring employer is protected from liability for a good-faith communication, even if the fact communicated is technically false. In states that recognize a conditional privilege, there is little to justify an employer's "name, rank, and serial number" policy. Conditional privilege recognizes that good-faith referrals cannot unreasonably interfere with the prospective contract rights of the former employee.

Most employers with a policy of giving out no qualitative information about a former employee base this policy not on a judgment that there is no conditional privilege covering the situation under the controlling state law or the possibility of malice but on a misperception of the value of "non-communication." This reasoning centers on the requirement for this tort that before a false fact can be defamatory, it must be communicated. Consequently, referring employers believe that if no possibly false fact is communicated about a former or present employee, they cannot be held liable for defamation. Of all the justifications for a "no comment" policy, this is the most porous and least reliable (although seemingly the one most relied upon). In fact, the emerging doctrine of "compelled self-defamation" has developed precisely in reaction to the "no comment" referral policies. The purpose of the doctrine is to supply the necessary element of communication for the tort of defamation in employment cases.

For example, assume an employee is discharged for poor performance in a situation where the real cause is a refusal to comply with the sexual demands of a supervisor. When the employee applies for a new job and is required by the new employer to state why she was discharged by the former employer, the employee, to be truthful, must communicate the official cause, poor performance. This "compelled" communication supplies the very element of the tort that employers hope to avoid by a "no comment" policy, thus evaporating the purpose of that policy.

The remedy to the dilemma created by compelled self-defamation would appear to be not telling a discharged employee the reason for the discharge. In such a case, the employee could not communicate a potentially defamatory statement. However, the employer virtually invites a wrongful discharge lawsuit because of the confusion and hurt of the employee who is discharged for no stated reason. Further, the act of discharge, itself, may be considered defamatory in some states, if based on false facts.

The bottom line is that employers cannot effectively protect themselves from liability simply by refusing to release relevant information about the work performance of a former employee. The only real protection is that which comes from truth, the good faith and non-negligent acquisition of facts, and the absence of malice.

Releases

Occasionally, employers attempt to protect themselves through statements or waivers signed by employees releasing them from liability for communicating facts about the employee's work record. Releases and waivers have limited value in this context. First, a release executed at the time of employment when the employee has no knowledge of the information to be communicated later has questionable, if any, legal effect. Second, since liability occurs only when a false fact is communicated or a true fact is communicated maliciously, even if the release is executed at the time employment is severed, the release must make clear that the employee recognizes the possibility that the employer may communicate false facts or true facts maliciously. That is, a court must be able to conclude that the employee intended that the employer would not be liable for the damages caused by these types of communication. A general release would not likely be found to have this meaning nor the releasor this intent. Consequently, unless the release clearly specifies these possibilities, it will offer no protection against just the kind of liability employers wish to avoid.

There can be value to a general release, however, if it can be found to have destroyed the employee's expectation, if any, of privacy concerning the work record. Eliminating the expectation of privacy would be an effective protection against subsequent claims of tortious intrusion upon seclusion (civil invasion of privacy). However, a release is not necessary for this kind of protection, since a simple and clear notice by the employer that it will release information concerning an employee's work record to potential new employers would be sufficient.

This leaves as the single value of a general release the psychological effect on an employee who may otherwise contemplate a lawsuit against the referring employer. This value may be worth the exercise, even though the employer realizes that all other generally perceived purposes are largely illusory.

One exception to this conclusion may be where an employer and employee agree to the specific information that will be communicated to prospective employers. It is unlikely in these situations, however, that the employee will agree to the communication of facts which would be the basis for liability, i.e., false or irrelevant facts.

The value of a release, particularly one signed at the time of employment, therefore, is not in its effectiveness as a release but as evidence of notice to the employee that performance evaluations will occur and, most important, will be provided to those with a need to know and others as may be specified in the release. In some states and under the Restatement of Torts, this kind of notice is sufficient to invoke the principle of absolute privilege.

In Pennsylvania, for instance, an employer's communications about an employee is protected by a conditional privilege. This privilege can be destroyed as to the public and all others without a need to know by malice or negligence.[2] However, to those with a valid business need to know, the privilege is absolute.[3] Also, a conditional privilege will become an absolute privilege whenever an employee consents to the publication of an evaluation, even when the evaluation contains defamatory material. These employer evaluations of an employee are deemed to be consented to by the employee and "consent is an absolute privilege."[4]

In response to the plaintiff's argument in *Baker v. Lafayette College* that his consent to the evaluation and its publication to those with a need to know was limited only to "honest findings of the investigators," the Pennsylvania Superior Court[5] stated:

> We also believe as a matter of policy that the consent privilege should be absolute. The person who agrees to submit his work to criticism or evaluation assumes the risk that the criticism may be unfavorable. Therefore when that person consents to a publication of the evaluation he has reason to know that the publication may be defamatory and should not be heard to complain if that is in fact the case. *See* Comment (d) to §583 of the Restatement.

We therefore agree with the well-reasoned decisions of our sister states. The existence of malice, recklessness or negligence does not defeat a privilege based on consent, because such privilege is absolute.

A referring employer's best protection against defamation lawsuits by former employees, however, is provided by the following safeguards:

- Internal policies and supervisory training programs designed to ensure complete and fair investigations of facts concerning employee behavior,
- Honest and unbiased evaluations of employee performance, and
- Effective due process systems.

These policies and programs, when coupled with a notice to employees that destroys any expectation of privacy and that implies their consent to publication of their work record evaluations, will shield an employer from liability, except in the most bizarre circumstances.

Liability to Future Employers

Prospective employers may also have a claim against a referring employer with a "no comment" policy. An employer who conceals relevant facts concerning an employee's prior record may find itself, in serious cases, liable to the new employer. For example, assume a hospital terminates a physician for incompetence and conceals the cause for the termination under the guise that the physician resigned. The physician now obtains employment with another hospital which had sought information from the first and had been told only that the physician had resigned. If the physician commits malpractice while employed by the second hospital and it can be shown that the physician would not have been hired if the truth had not been concealed, the first hospital should have some share in the liability for the damages. This principle can be extended to theft and other criminal behavior in the workplace. Certainly, there seems to be a general duty not to actively conceal facts of criminal or other behavior that could create serious health and safety problems. Whether the principle might be extended to poor performance or productivity, however, is doubtful at this stage in the development of the law.

Criminal Records

In a growing number of industries, a criminal record examination is also mandatory. These industries are not limited to those related to security or law enforcement and include any work where an employee would be placed in a position to repeat the kind of crime documented in his or her criminal record. Maintenance employees in apartment houses with access to the apartments, for instance, should not have a record of conviction for theft or rape. Discovering this record would seem well within the duty owed by a landlord to a tenant.

The refusal of employment based on the examination of criminal records is fraught with potential problems, however. Arrest records cannot be used because they may be evidence of invidious discrimination and do not establish criminal behavior. As a result, employers are restricted to examining conviction records. Unfortunately, some jurisdictions respond to requests for criminal records by indicating both arrests and convictions on a consolidated report. In those situations, wise employers will have someone who is not involved in the hiring decision separate arrests from convictions and deliver to the decision maker only the conviction record.

Further, various jurisdictions have statutes restricting the use of criminal conviction records as a basis for employment decisions.[6] Under these restrictions, crimes for which the applicant was convicted must be reasonably related to conduct relevant to the workplace. Although it is difficult to imagine a crime which cannot be made relevant to the workplace on some theory, this public policy statement can be the basis for an exception to the employment-at-will principle in many jurisdictions, if the statute itself does not contain a remedy.[7]

Former Supervisors and Peers

Sometimes an effective and useful method for obtaining information concerning an applicant's work record is to obtain the names of the employee's former supervisors and co-employees. Although these individuals may themselves risk liability for defamation, intrusion on seclusion, and intentional interference with prospective contractual relations, they may prove to be the best sources for information. All too often, employers do not take the time to contact these individuals as part of an employment screen.

Despite the difficulties of doing background checks, the effort is well worth it. The time and trouble, however, argue in favor of a seeker-pool system, since completing an adequate background check will be impossible when the need for an employee is immediate.

Multiple Step Procedure

A technique of significant value is the use of multiple steps in the hiring process. Running an applicant through all of the hiring process steps during a single visit is efficient, but an employer may lose an important opportunity to judge an applicant's dependability and character. Separating the hiring process into a series of steps is an invaluable technique. An applicant, once qualified through an initial seeker evaluation and placed in the applicant pool, should be required to report at different times and places for the remainder of the process. For instance, an initial interview should be on one day at an assigned time with subsequent interviews requiring the applicant to be at different places for appointments on different days. If pre-employment physicals or drug screens are used, they also should be scheduled at other times, and not consolidated into one visit.

By structuring a hiring program in this fashion, the employer can observe whether applicants can be punctual and responsible at a time when these qualities are crucial to the individuals themselves. If they fail this simple test at this time, serious questions are raised about their dependability after employment, when their dependability will be crucial to the employer.

Assume that an employer calls an applicant and schedules an interview with the personnel department for 8 a.m. on Monday. The applicant is then scheduled for an interview the following day with the hiring department at 2 p.m. The pre-employment physical is scheduled in a doctor's office for the following morning and the final interview for 4 p.m., back at the plant, on the same day. The applicant is required to find three different places and to be punctual four times. The applicant who fails this simple test may not be the person the employer is looking for.

Skilled Interviewing

Interviewing is a specialized skill often overlooked by employers. My experience has been that applicant interviewing is frequently left to those who lack these skills. As a result, significant questions are not asked and answers given to interview questions which are not evaluated properly. Rarely are these skills displayed by the first-line supervisor who needs to fill a vacancy. To depend on the supervisor's judgment, except in the last stage of the hiring process, is, therefore, risky. Employers should recognize the value of interviewing skills in their organizations and they should take steps to develop that specialty and to provide some interview training to all their supervisors. A set of guidelines which can be used to train interviewers appears in the Appendix.

Pre-Employment Testing

Pre-employment tests fall into four general categories: medical, substance, skills, psychological. All of these tests must be reasonably related to the job for which the applicant is applying and must be qualified as free of potential disparate impact on protected minorities. General medical and substance testing, and, to some degree, psychological testing, all carry special burdens of confidentiality since the information discovered, even if true, can be the basis for liability if revealed to others than those with a strict need-to-know.

Establishing baselines for medical and workers' compensation plans is an insufficient justification for a broad-based pre-employment physical and should be left to post-employment examinations. Pre-employment medical examinations should be only in those areas directly related to an applicant's physical ability to perform the specific job, after reasonable accommodation for any disability or handicap.

Substance testing, while growing in popularity and presenting fewer risks than similar testing during employment, also carries a heightened risk, especially in areas of defamation due to the communication of false positives, intrusion on seclusion, battery, and the malicious publication of a true fact. For these reasons, expert assistance must be obtained in designing these programs in all cases.[8]

Tests for skills, both general and specific, abound from

several private companies and employer groups. The risk in using these tests is that they may not be justifiably related to the job for which the applicant is applying, and they may have a disparate impact on protected groups. Employers should monitor closely the effect of these tests on hiring and measure for themselves the impact on various protected groups. A test can be sold as "qualified," but it may have a disparate impact in a particular application. However, by changing a test or developing a training program, an employer can improve its hiring record for one or more protected groups.

Psychological testing also has enjoyed an increase in popularity. These tests purport to measure everything from honesty and dependability to propensity for concerted action or methods for problem solving. They often are paper and pencil tests—since polygraphs are illegal in most situations—and can either be scored and interpreted by the employer or by the company selling the test. Feelings about psychological testing as valid predictors of behavior and as violators of an applicant's privacy run high. Many employers use them, and there is certainly no shortage of psychological test sellers and their related services. There is nothing per se illegal about these tests, but their quality and intent vary significantly and employers should not use them without expert guidance and a clear understanding of the risks involved.[9]

Orientation

An employer should include the following elements in its orientation program:

- Welcome to the employee and introduction to fellow employees;
- Tour of the work area and facility;
- Tour of company plants, facilities, products and/or services;
- Review of work schedules, work assignments, pay policies, performance appraisal programs;
- Description of the company's organizational structure;
- Review of company history, philosophy, policies, and practices;
- Explanation of employee responsibilities to the company;
- Description of company responsibilities to employees;
- Description of company code of conduct;

- Review and summary of benefits;
- Description of training opportunities;
- Training in safety practices.

New employees require orientation that goes beyond the rudiments of the job and job schedule. These initial weeks are vital to the development of a committed and responsible employee. Time and effort invested during this period to acquaint the employee with all aspects of the workplace culture and the employer's expectations will, in my experience, pay huge dividends. A well-designed orientation program should include not only job-related education but also a full explanation of the company's due process system, how the employee's job relates to or affects the operation as a whole, the history of the company and its position in the industry, and the employee's responsibility to the company and to other employees. The objective of the orientation is to bring the employee into the organization as a member of both a micro and macro team and to get the employee to "buy into" the company's philosophy. The orientation process should be spread over several weeks to ensure assimilation, and refresher courses should be offered for all employees in an organized fashion.

All too often, I suspect, the scenario for a new employee goes as follows:

Manager at chance meeting with employee:
Manager: Hello. Are you new?
Employee: Sort of. I started a month ago.
Manager: Well, welcome. I am the manager.
Employee: Hello. I am Fred Jones.
Manager: Well, Fred, I hope you enjoy working here at Ajax.
Employee: Yes sir.
Manager: I am sure by now you have had a chance to read the employee manual. If you have any questions, do not hesitate to call on me or someone in the personnel department. We want all your questions answered. Open the door, your know.
Employee: Well, thank you. Actually, I was told the manual is being revised and not available for awhile.
Manager: Oh. I thought that the revision had been done six months ago—at least I was told it was in the process at that time.
Employee: Maybe.

Manager: Well, anyway, I am sure that one of our personnel people has briefed you on the important stuff.

Employee: Not really. I was supposed to have a meeting, but production was tight and my supervisor had to have it postponed. I guess they will get to it—sometime.

Manager: A month, huh? You have qualified for benefits then, and made it through probation. Good.

Employee: I don't know. I guess so.

Manager: Well, you had your thirty-day review, I assume.

Employee: Postponed.

Manager: Oh. Well have a nice day. Remember, my door is always open.

Employee: Thanks . . . ah, Mr. Manager.

Really building loyalty and commitment! On the way to a disciplined work force!

Notes to Chapter 2

1. *See generally* Johnston, *Workforce 2000* (Indianapolis: Hudson Institute, 1987).

2. *See Banas v. Matthews Int'l Corp.*, 502 A.2d 637, 121 LRRM 2515 (Pa. Super. Ct. 1985).

3. *Agriss v. Roadway Express*, 334 Pa. Super. 295, 483 A.2d 956 (1984).

4. *Sobel v. Wingard*, 531 A.2d 520 (Pa. Super. Ct. 1987). *See also Baker v. Lafayette College*, 504 A.2d 247 (Pa. Super. Ct. 1987), *aff'd*, 532 A.2d 399.

5. *Baker, supra* note 4, at 250. *See also DeLuca v. Reader*, 227 Pa. Super. 392, 323 A.2d 309 (1974); *Royer v. Steinberg*, 153 Cal. Rptr. 499 (1979); *Dominquez v. Babcock*, 696 P.2d 338, 339 (Colo. App. 1985), *cert. granted*, 727 P.2d 362 (Colo. 1986); *Gengler v. Phelps*, 589 P.2d 1056 (N.M. 1978); *Ernst v. Indiana Bell Tel. Co.*, 475 N.E.2d 351 (Ind. 1985); *Johnson v. City of Buckner*, 610 S.W.2d 406 (Mo. Ct. App. 1980).

6. *See* 18 Pa. Stat. 9125.

7. *See Hunter v. Port Auth. of Allegheny County*, 277 Pa. Super. 419 (1980) and *Cisco v. UPS*, 476 A.2d 1340 (Pa. Super. Ct. 1984).

8. For a complete discussion of the risks of substance testing, see Redeker & Segal, *Practical Lawyer* (April 1987) p. 26 *et seq.*

9. Pre-employment testing is an extremely complex and fluid area of the law and employers interested in using this selection tool must consult legal counsel with skill in these areas. All such tests are governed by federal and state statutes and their relevant reg-

ulations prohibiting discrimination in employment. In addition, the Uniform Guidelines on Employee Selection Procedures (43 Fed. Reg. 38290) must be understood and applied. Hundreds of court cases have considered this issue, and guidance must be obtained concerning their effect on particular situations, especially as they relate to validation studies and procedures.

3

Employer/Employee Expectations

Management personnel, for the most part, have an acute sense of the employer's rights and expectations in connection with employees. This sense may be either conscious or unconscious, developed or instinctive. When employees either disregard these perceived employer rights or fail to fulfill the employer's expectations, then management personnel react. This reaction is most often in the form of what management calls discipline. The extent to which the employer's rights and expectations have been consciously and intelligently developed and defined may often be reflected in the type of reaction or discipline which occurs. Where the sense of employer rights is instinctive, the disciplinary reaction probably will also be instinctive. The system of discipline, if it can be called that, will have logic and internal consistency only by chance.

Similarly, employees develop a sense of their own rights and expectations. They react, rationally or irrationally, to what they perceive to be employer failures. Moreover, the extent to which employee rights and expectations have been defined and intelligently developed may well dictate the nature of the employees' response to these perceived employer shortcomings. Employee reactions may be as ill-considered and irrational as some employer discipline.

Unfortunately, many employers and employees have little more than the most primitive understanding of their own responsibilities toward each other. Yet, an understanding of their mutual responsibilities may be more important to labor peace than all the laws heretofore devised to govern the employment relationship. Indeed, employment contracts and collective bargaining agreements are frequently no more nor less than written statements of these understandings. For this reason, the most successful leaders of business and labor often seem to be those who recognize the responsibilities as well as the rights of both management and labor and who strive to maintain a balance to ensure that the expectations of each are fulfilled.

In this respect, it can be argued that the extent to which employers and employees each perceive the efforts of the other to fulfill expectations and honor the rights of the other is in direct relation to the productivity of the business enterprise and the existence of labor peace. It is noteworthy that the perception of the labor/management effort may be more important than the actual fulfillment of any expectations. Consequently, much of what will be discussed later will have to do with the perceptions, as well as the realities, involved in the labor/management relationship.

While the nature of the industry, the area in which the company is located, and the type of person who is employed may result in the emphasis of one element over another, the basic categories of rights, responsibilities, and expectations of labor and management remain fairly constant.

Management has the right to expect employees to be on time; to attend regularly; to put in a full day's work; to be physically and mentally prepared for the tasks to be performed; to respond positively to direction; to learn the job at hand, as well as new jobs; to adjust to change; to get along with fellow employees; and to know and to follow the rules and regulations of the plant. In short, the employer has the right to expect responsible conduct and a good-faith effort.

Employees have the right to expect sound management of the business to ensure the continued existence of employment; information concerning the performance of the business; safe and healthful working conditions; fair and predictable treatment; responsible and humane supervision; decent pay for work performed; appreciation for services; fair promotion and transfer procedures; and adequate job training and orientation. Most of all, they have a right to be treated as people of dignity and substantial worth, with responsibilities that extend beyond the workplace.

When an employer offers work for pay and an employee accepts pay for work, a contract is established which consists of the perceptions of each of the other's rights and expectations and an acceptance of the responsibility to fulfill those expectations. If the commitment or understanding of either party is lacking, mistaken, or incomplete, the contract is destined for breach, and an unproductive and antagonistic atmosphere is almost a certainty. For example, if an employer expects that a responsible employee will always work unlimited overtime with little or no notice, but the employee defines "responsible" in some fashion short of the employer's expectation, the failure of the employer to define the requirements of the job will result in both employer and employee dissatisfaction and an ultimate severance of the employment relationship. Also, if an employee defines fair treatment as no overtime work even in the face of a clear necessity but has not told that to the employer at the outset, the relationship will be breached at some point.

The problem is that the parties, by not defining their expectations at the time of initial employment or during the orientation period, depend on haphazard events to define their relationship. While this is occurring, one, and usually both, parties may become so disgruntled that the relationship's destruction becomes self-fulfilling long before either the employer, out of kindness or fear of liability, or the employee, because of economic loss, decides to sever the relationship. In these cases, each concludes that the other has failed to fulfill legitimate expectations. These conclusions cause resentment, anger and, often, a desire for revenge. Supervisors who can't wait to get the "goods" on the employee lie in wait and employees play the game by displaying a defiant attitude and disrespect for legitimate rules.

Consequently, the establishment of a harmonious and productive relationship would seem to depend, in the first instance, upon the conscious awareness of each party of the expectations, responsibilities, and rights of the other. Such an awareness is produced most frequently by the clear statement and delineation of these rights and responsibilities in either written company policies or a negotiated labor agreement. The absence of such writing leaves to chance the true nature of the bargain struck at the time the employee is hired.

The employer clearly has the right to discipline and discharge employees to achieve employee cooperation in the performance of their responsibilities. To be sure, that right is limited by laws protecting employees in various specified classes from discipline or discharge due to membership in the class (race, religion, national origin, sex, or non-job-related handicaps) or engaging in concerted activities. Where a collective bargaining agreement is in force, that right may be further limited by a clause permitting discipline or discharge, where just cause exists. Generally, the law does not require just cause to exist prior to the exercise of the employer's right to discipline employees.[1] In the absence of a contract and so long as the discipline is not administered for an unlawful reason or contrary to a stated public policy, the employer is free to exercise this right at will. Moreover, the exercise of this right to sever the employment relationship is unilateral and, in most circumstances, is without loss or damage to the employer except for the costs of finding and training a replacement. Generally, there is no legal requirement that there be a cause for the discharge or a statement of the reason. Although some state and federal courts are attempting to force changes in this essential concept, the general rule continues to prevail in most cases that employers have almost complete control over the continuation of the employment relationship without incurring risk for its termination.

While the employer has extensive and unilateral rights to discipline or discharge an employee, the employee has a right to react to discipline that is perceived as unjust by withholding his or her services, either individually or in concert with other employees. An employee who withholds services may choose to resign or to strike. Employees who choose to strike can be permanently replaced. The result is the same; the employment relationship is severed. An employee who terminates employment also exercises a unilateral right.

There is a difference, however, between an employer's unilateral act and an employee's. The action of the employee damages the employee far more severely than it does the employer. As a result, an employee's withholding of services in protest over unfair treatment, for example, is neither an adequate nor acceptable act for most employees. Consequently, employee reactions to unjust discipline tend to be of a lesser magnitude and are calculated to disrupt harmony in the plant and/or to reduce productivity. Employees decrease their productivity, take advantage of sick leave, are mildly insubordinate, are tardy or absent, and engage in a number of behavioral difficulties. These reactions are in the nature of protests, but not always consciously so. Deliberate or not, they are perceived by the employer as acts of unsatisfactory employees who must be disciplined. The result is often a self-fulfilling prophecy, and the employer exercises its unilateral right to sever the employment relationship. Under these circumstances, the potential for a lawsuit by a terminated employee is high.

From my vantage point as a practicing labor lawyer serving clients in virtually all industries, I have discerned several trends that are relevant to employee resignation or employee termination of employment. In industries plagued by employee shortages, even bad employers seem to have few workplace problems, other than unacceptably high turnover. The reason for this seems to be that employees do not experience serious economic loss by severing their employment. New jobs with new employers are readily available. For example, the high-tech industry experienced little union organizing for many years. Jobs were plentiful and, rather than fighting to improve working conditions, employees simply quit. As that industry has begun to sort itself out, the number of available jobs has decreased in relation to the available pool of workers. Union organizing and wrongful-discharge litigation, therefore, have increased dramatically in this industry as employees are forced to keep jobs with employers who fail to meet their expectations. Employees have no choice.

Further, within a single industry, some employers constantly struggle with employee relations problems resulting from low productivity and other behavior-related conduct while others, making the same product in the same way with similar employees, enjoy markedly different employee relations. The only apparent difference between the two employers is the employer itself.

In these settings, I usually find a great deal of discipline being imposed but little employee discipline. Obviously, something is broken. One employer could not have the continuing bad luck of always getting problem employees, while the other has the continuing good luck of getting problem-free employees. I suggest that the troubled employers rarely have problem employees but have employees with problems and that these are often created by the employer. Moreover, these conditions tend to worsen as employees in these circumstances act out their dissatisfaction with the employer's conduct or attitude. Frequently, by failing to understand or refusing to fulfill these employee expectations, employers stimulate reactions that are perceived as behavioral problems, quelled only by discipline.

Recognizing the importance of fulfilling legitimate employee expectations is the employer's first step in breaking the problem spiral. The next step is identifying those expectations. In doing this, the employer must avoid the seduction of defining employee expectations based only on what is legally enforceable. Most employees have a very imperfect understanding of what the law requires or provides. Their reactions are not based on legal principles, but on what they believe is fair and just. Consequently, structuring employee policies and procedures based on "legal rights" is not only too limiting but also wrong. Owners of unproductive plants find no comfort when told they are doing nothing illegal when they fire another "problem" employee. Their product is not being converted to revenue because their work force lacks discipline.

Central to creating a productive, problem-free work force is the recognition that employees believe they have a right to a fair and appropriate discipline system. Employees further expect that this right will be fulfilled, even though a lawyer may opine that they have no legal right to either fairness or equity. A successful manager forgets the strict legal rule and sets out to construct a system that fulfills reasonable employee expectations. In doing this, employers must be ready to relinquish some of their inherent legal managerial rights. How to relinquish some elements of control without losing the ability to manage the operation is discussed in Chapter 7, "Discipline Systems for Nonunion Employees." Chapter 7 also brings together all the elements of a "Workplace Due Process" system and discusses how such a system can be developed. However, we must first identify those rights that employees expect to be fulfilled.

Due Process Guidelines

The following principles contain the realistic, if not the legal, expectations of employees and the responsibilities of management. These principles, or rights, comprise what will be termed in this book, "due process."

- *Employees have a right to know what is expected of them and what the consequences of not fulfilling those expectations will be.*

One of the most frequent inquiries of labor arbitrators deciding discipline cases is whether the employee actually knew that what he or she did fell short of what the employer expected.[2]

To be sure, certain offenses are so clearly contrary to acceptable conduct that discipline is readily accepted or justified upon review regardless of whether there was any prior communication or warning to the employee. These acts are few, however. They include theft, intentional destruction of company property, total refusal to perform safe work, and gross or intentional endangerment of the safety of coworkers. All other acts normally demand some kind of prior notice before terminal discipline will be viewed as justified. The seriousness of the act, however, will often determine the kind of notice required. Occasionally, the nature of the act may be so egregious that even though the offense would normally call for some notice prior to discharge, summary action may be appropriate.

For instance, excessive absenteeism may be just cause for discharge only after a series of lesser penalties or other types of notices have been used to impress on the employee the unacceptability of his or her conduct and to warn the employee that continued similar conduct will result in the termination of employment. On the other hand, gross insubordination may warrant discharge after only a single warning, or in an extreme case, it may even justify summary discharge.

Various methods of notice are available to employers and the one chosen may vary according to the sophistication of the employee involved. At one end of the spectrum is a simple clause in the contract that employees will be disciplined only for just cause, or in a policy manual that the employer expects employees to act responsibly. This type of notice carries added responsibilities for management, because it must further define what is "just cause" or "responsibly" for that plant. Since "just cause" and "responsible" defy definition in a vacuum, these concepts must evolve on a case-by-case basis, as instances demanding discipline arise.

In this manner, a code of conduct gradually emerges. However, the code will only develop to the extent that specific cases occur, and the employer's response and concept of appropriate behavior is communicated to the employees. The extent to which a single disciplined employee is actually aware of a specific rule, therefore, depends upon the employee's personal experience. The extent to which the employees in general are aware of the employer's expectations depends upon what they have observed of the employer and upon the folklore of the workplace.

Obviously, while giving the employer great flexibility, this method also presents the greatest possibilities for misunderstanding and employee resentment. It also creates difficult evidentiary problems when the discipline must be justified to an arbitrator or to an employee.

At the other end of the spectrum is the contract or policy manual which details at great length the twenty-five or so common acts which will result in discipline, replete with specific punishments for each. Carried to the extreme, there will be gradations of punishments depending on established variables. While having the advantage of complete notice, this technique locks the employer into rigid rules which must be applied regardless of the personal circumstances of the employee, and the system lends an aura of a military camp to the workplace.

Obviously, a system which provides adequate notice to employees, but still maintains employer flexibility, is preferred and will generally lie somewhere between the two extremes. Precisely where on the continuum the proper balance will be achieved depends on the nature of the employer, the employees, and the workplace in general. The various types of notice and their implementation will be described in detail in a later chapter. For the moment, it is sufficient to mention that some kind of notice of employer expectations must exist prior to discipline, if the employees are to receive due process and if the system is to have widespread employee acceptance.

● *The employee has a right to consistent and predictable employer responses to violations of rules.*

Almost as important to the employee as knowing that a particular act may result in discipline is the certainty that the discipline will actually take place. Arbitrator Dallas M. Young stated this principle as follows:

> When a man's job is involved; when a company's investment in the employee is about to be lost; when the future relationship between a management and its employees is at a stake—a supervisor is dealing with an extremely serious matter. Arbitrators and Arbitration Boards have consistently held that essential to making discharges stand up are: (1) very clear instructions; and (2) even more explicit statements about the penalty for failure to comply.[3]

If discipline is to have its desired effect, it must be both rehabilitative and a deterrent.[4] The deterrent value increases as the predictability increases. Consistency and predictability do not preclude the individuality of the discipline. However, even in individualizing discipline there must appear to be a consistency in the principles of application. Above all, the employees in the plant must readily perceive that the employer is dispensing discipline according to some defined policy and that the employees are treated the same, according to their individual circumstances.[5] Consistency in discipline requires that obviously similar employees be treated in obviously the same manner. Predictability in discipline requires that the employer always react in the same fashion when presented with the same stimulus.

For instance, an employer may be consistent in its discipline even though a junior employee with a record of disruptive behavior is given a suspension for insubordination, while a senior employee with an unblemished record is merely warned. However, when two junior employees with similar records are given different types of discipline for the same offense, the employer will be viewed as erratic and possibly vindictive. Fear of the unknown will then breed resentment, distrust, and disharmony. The result of this employee reaction is often an unproductive atmosphere.

• *The employee has a right to fair discipline based on facts.*

Nothing is more vital to an effective discipline system than the process of gathering facts before judgments are made.[6] Employees appear to be quick to perceive or imagine ulterior motives. Also, they are as quick to accept a decision based on recognized facts. Employees are often more knowledgeable of what really happened in a given situation than they are given credit for. Rarely do they come forward and reveal those facts when the employment of another is at stake. Most employees appear to want justice done and dislike those among them who do not perform in accordance with their responsibilities. However, the revered American tradition that an authority must prove its case without the aid of the accused, and to a great extent the general citizenry, also pervades the workplace. The law of the shop seems to be consistent in that the employer commonly must discover the facts in any given case without the aid of the rank and file. The degree to which the employer is able to ascertain these facts, in spite of the "conspiracy of silence," may often be the measure of the employees' esteem and respect for management.

To operate an effective discipline system, then, the employer must establish methods for fact-finding which are dependable and free from personal prejudices. To a great extent, this depends upon well-trained supervisors. Supervisors are most often the only direct source of information regarding employee conduct. They must be schooled in methods of ascertaining the facts necessary to permit the employer to make and substantiate conclusions upon which discipline decisions depend. Countless discharge and discipline cases have been reversed or modified by an arbitrator simply because management's judgment was based on supposition, assumptions, wishful thinking, or unwarranted jumps in logic. Clearly, an employer must train all first line supervisors to recognize and to obtain all of the elements of an employee's offense before discipline can fairly follow from the facts.

The most important element in the process of fact-finding is a detailed record keeping system. Discipline for absenteeism; tardiness; falsification of records or excuses; or for repeated offenses of the same kind, all depend upon the ability of the employer to document the violations. These records must be more than mere notations of occurrences. They should include enough description of the events to assure that anyone reading the record can conclude that the offense occurred or reoccurred. As sad as it may seem, the employer must maintain records on every employee, as if it will some day have to justify the employee's discharge.

If the employees are aware that whenever discipline is administered the employer can establish that a violation occurred and that the employee disciplined was the proper person, confidence and trust are established in the absoluteness of the employer's system, as well as an awareness that the employer is not to be abused.

Of course, all this may be of little value if the discipline administered is not appropriate for the offense or for the circumstances. Appropriateness is relative. What may be shockingly severe to one group of employees may be routine to others. As stated earlier, the key to employee acceptance appears to be consistency. While many cases can be cited where an arbitrator has modified discipline for being too severe, there are none where an employer presented evidence that the same offense resulted in comparable discipline in other cases and an arbitrator modified the disciplinary action. In fact, such an action by an arbitrator might be cause for overturning an arbitrator's award.[7]

The importance with which arbitrators view comparable treatment is demonstrated by the fact that they will rarely, if ever, reduce the penalty of an employee, where it is proven that the degree of discipline given was the same as that given other employees on prior occasions for the same cause. This will be true even where the arbitrator may believe the punishment was too severe. In *Rohn Industries*, for instance, an employee was discharged for sleeping on the job. The arbitrator, clearly affected by the union's argument that the penalty was too severe, nevertheless sustained the discharge, because the employer had discharged up to eight other employees previously for the same reason.[8] The arbitrator quoted Arbitrator Whitley P. McCoy, in *Stockham Pipe Fittings Co.*, as follows:

> Where an employee has violated a rule or engaged in conduct meriting disciplinary action, it is primarily the function of management to decide upon the proper penalty. If management acts in good faith upon a fair investigation and fixes a penalty not inconsistent with that imposed in other like cases, an arbitrator should not disturb it. The mere fact that management has imposed a somewhat different penalty or a somewhat more severe penalty than the arbitrator would have, if he had had the decision to make originally, is no justification for changing it.[9]

There is now a trend alluded to earlier which makes gathering and documenting facts even more important—defamation lawsuits—especially in jurisdictions where the concepts of good faith and fair dealing have not taken hold. Employees are arguing that a negligent investigation by an employer has resulted in a negative action based on a false fact and that the action, impugning the employee's capabilities, caused defamation. Based on this premise, individual supervisors would also be liable.

In *Banas v. Matthews International*,[10] for instance, the appellate court sustained defamation damages against the employer in a situation where the employer's investigation of an alleged misappropriation of company property was negligently conducted and resulted in the discharge of an employee for theft based upon a false conclusion. As the law is developing, it is likely that the supervisor who conducted the investigation could have been successfully joined as a defendant.

- *The employee has a right to question the facts and to present a defense.*

In great measure, the plant is a microcosm of our society, and many of the rights employees believe to be theirs are drawn directly from the principles by which our society operates. It is, perhaps, for this reason that many theoreticians in this field speak in terms of the constitutional concepts of due process.

Arbitrator Carroll R. Daugherty eloquently stated this proposition as follows:

> Every accused employee in an industrial democracy has the right of "due process of law" and the right to be heard before discipline is administered. These rights are precious to all free men and are not lightly or hastily to be disregarded or denied. The Arbitrator is mindful of the Company's need for, equity in, and right to require careful, safe, efficient performance by its employees. But before the Company can discipline an employee for failure to meet said requirement, the Company must take the pains to establish such failure. Maybe X was guilty as hell; maybe also there are many gangsters who go free because of legal technicalities. And this is doubtless unfortunate. But company and government prosecutors must understand that the legal technicalities exist also to protect the innocent from unjust, unwarranted punishment. Society is willing to let the presumably guilty go free on technical grounds in order that free, innocent men can be secure from arbitrary, capricious action. (2) The Arbitrator then has only two alternatives: (a) reinstate X with pay for all time lost; and (b) reinstate him without such pay. (3) In the light of all the instant facts, the Arbitrator is of the opinion that the proper decision here is to reinstate X as of the date of his discharge but without back pay. The company is now so directed.[11]

Unfortunately, many academicians, and some arbitrators, confuse these noble principles with the economic realities of plant operations: A company is not a precise mirror image of our society, because it is not fashioned as a democracy, or even a limited democracy. Such ivory tower thinking is in the forefront of the movement toward the conversion of economic entities into social entities, with the result that American businesses are being crippled by the massive amounts of non-productive time required to meet government regulations. Nevertheless, the concepts of self-worth and dignity are carried into the shop, even if self-determiniation may not be. Star-Chamber proceedings simply do not work. Employees believe that they have a right to a "day in court," and they react strongly when this is denied.

While it is debatable in the practical world of a production facility whether an employee's right to defend himself or herself arises before or after the employee has been disciplined,[12] the right itself is not open to question. Arbitrator Theodore K. High stated the right in this fashion:

> I find it completely unacceptable that the Company feels
> it adequate to simply take disciplinary action and then wait for
> the employee to file a grievance before getting the employee's
> side of the story. The whole purpose of an investigation and
> giving an employee an opportunity to present his case is so that
> it will have an effect upon the Company's disciplinary action,
> if any, which it finds appropriate under the circumstances. In
> other circumstances, I would find that this failure to provide
> sufficient due process to Grievant would be sufficient to nullify
> the Company's disciplinary action.[13]

The central role of industrial due process is to provide an
effective opportunity for an employee to be heard and to mount
a defense. While widely recognized, this employee right is one
which can be satisfied at various times in the procedure. A
denial at an early stage will not void otherwise appropriate
discipline, where the right is granted at sometime prior to the
administration of the disciplinary action. This precise issue
was raised in *University of Missouri*.[14] In that case, the grievant argued that a denial of an evidentiary hearing before
termination was a denial of due process, which should void
the discharge. Arbitrator Yarowsky, in refusing to give cre-
dence to the argument, stated:

> He is entitled to these protections [substantive and procedural
> due process] in any case and independent of the University's
> Grievance Procedure. But the Board finds that C___ was not
> denied due process of law because he has no guarantee of a full
> due process hearing before termination. [Citing *Arnett v. Ken-
> nedy*, 414 U.S. 632, 6 FEP Cases 1253 (1974)] C___ does not
> question whether he has been afforded a full due process hear-
> ing before this board. Such a claim would not be plausible from
> any perspective in view of the fact that the hearing before this
> Board was totally adversarial, witnesses were sworn, exami-
> nation and cross-examination of witnesses were fully and freely
> permitted and a recording of the two-day trial was made, tran-
> scribed and made available to both parties. "As an untainted
> trial *de novo*, the proceedings before the Joint Council (this
> Board of Arbitration) cured any prior deprivation of appellants'
> (Grievant's right to a full and fair hearing)." *Perry v. Milk
> Drivers' Union*, 656 F.2d 536, 108 LRRM 2570 (9th Cir. 1981).[15]

In the context of the workplace, the right to substantive
and procedural due process includes the employee's right to
know the charges and to be presented with the facts substan-
tiating those charges. It also takes into account the uneven-
ness of the odds. Managers, no matter how benevolent, may
overlook the truly threatened atmosphere of a meeting between employer and employee. The employee, often alone, is

faced with a judge and jury, all in one. Even if the discipline given is eminently fair, the employee may be left with feelings of being alone and intimidated—feelings which sometimes are expressed by obstinate resentment. If discipline, short of discharge, is to have a beneficial effect, the process must avoid those things which can cause this kind of reaction. A right does not exist unless it is effective.[16]

One example of how proper discipline had a negative result is the recent case of a pro-company employee who for years had voted in several representation elections against the petitioning union. After changing his vote in the last election, he felt obligated to explain his about-face. In a conference with the personnel director, he recalled an instance several months before in which he had been disciplined for negligent work performance. He admitted that the discipline had been fair and deserved. However, he added that when he was called into the personnel director's office for his hearing, he was met, not only by the director, but also by his foreman, the second line supervisor, the production manager, and a secretary to take notes. Five to one. While treated fairly, he felt so completely outnumbered that he decided he had to do something to even the odds.

Clearly, if the discipline system is to achieve its purpose of producing a responsive and productive workplace, it cannot emasculate the employee, and the employee must have the right to effectively make a defense. In unorganized plants this may take the form of simply evening the numerical odds or of having another rank-and-file employee present to assist the accused either as an ombudsman or as a friend.[17] (Several types of representation systems for nonunion employees are discussed in the Chapter 7, "Discipline Systems for Nonunion Employees.") In an organized plant, this function is performed by the shop steward. Either way, not only must the employee be given the chance to defend herself or himself, but an atmosphere and opportunity to mount an effective defense must exist. Absent that element, the employee may feel railroaded and oppressed and may react by voluntarily, or unconsciously, holding back.

- *The employee has the right to appeal the disciplinary decision.*

Our system of society has established a healthy distrust of single, no-recourse proceedings, and this, too, carries into the plant. The initial proceeding, which results in the administration of the disciplinary action, has too much chance of being colored by personal bias and by the feelings of the moment. Besides, the confrontation is simply over too soon to leave the employee with any confidence in its objectivity. Even if not used, the employee should know that, if he or she believes the treatment to have been unfair, there is a possibility that some person in greater authority will examine the facts and make a dispassionate decision removed from the effects of the moment and the personalities involved.

The basic right of appeal is often difficult to transform into a reality. In an organized plant it is easy, inasmuch as an arbitration process is built into most contracts. Yet even unorganized plants can attain some of this type of security. However, the unorganized plant must always prove to its employees that the appeal process is, in fact, fair and honest. This is a heavy burden to satisfy.

Various methods for satisfying this burden are discussed in Chapter 7, "Discipline Systems for Nonunion Employees."

- *The employee has the right to progressive discipline.*

Another frequent inquiry of arbitrators is whether the employee was given a chance to improve his or her performance or behavior before discipline was administered. Except in the few cases enumerated earlier which will justify a summary discharge, arbitrators and employees believe in second, third, and sometimes, fourth chances. It is seen as essentially unfair to summarily discipline someone—to take away his or her livelihood—without giving the employee prior opportunities to conform to the expectations of the employer or to correct a mistake. Indeed, a recent study by Professor Malinowski concludes that a large majority of the employees who have been reinstated by arbitrators have continued in their employment satisfactorily.[18]

Consequently, the concept of "another chance" appears to be founded in fact, and its use as a management tool is justified, not only to preserve the employment of a worker, but also to preserve the employer's training investment.

Progressive discipline systems will be discussed later in detail. Essentially, such systems demand warnings of progressive forcefulness and provide assistance to cure errant conduct as well as an opportunity to clear the record of offenses which are too old to be useful in determining the pattern of an employee's conduct. The employee must be given the opportunity to pay his or her debt to the employer, to be punished, and to be done with it. An employer's overly long memory exists as a destructive cloud over employees, which destroys their confidence in the fairness of the employer and which can cause resentments to build.

- *The employee has a right to be considered as an individual.*

As noted earlier, consistency in discipline does not require that the employee's personal circumstances be ignored. Any effective discipline system must consider what is appropriate for that particular employee. As stated by Arbitrator Roger I. Abrams, "A system which accounts for individual differences and considers each case of discipline fairly, on its individual merits, is not unreasonable."[19] The employee's prior service, performance, discipline record, and even his or her psychological state are, therefore, all proper conditions to be considered in determining whether the employee should be disciplined and, if so, to what degree.

In its early stages, discipline in the workplace exists to bring about future conformance to the rules. Discipline that fits the violation but not the individual may be counterproductive. While caution must be exercised to avoid wide disparities in treatment that others may view as discrimination, an employee's prior records and performance must be considered when fashioning a fitting discipline. When disparate treatment of employees is based on demonstrable considerations, such distinctions are rarely protested with much vigor. Here, too, the value of well-maintained records is utmost.

Summary

While discipline is often viewed only as a negative tool by which conduct is conformed to pre-determined standards, successful mangement uses discipline as an affirmative tool by which discipline is achieved. Properly constructed and administered, the discipline system can produce trust and reliance on the good faith and strength of the employer. Discipline systems are accepted by employees as necessary to maintain order in the plant. Most employees welcome a system that will eliminate or rehabilitate employees who will not or cannot fulfill their responsibilities either to the employer or to their co-workers. If the system is designed and operated in a manner which incorporates the rights of employees as detailed here, the discipline system becomes a constructive instrument to enhance productivity rather than a purely negative tool of control.

One of the best summaries of these principles is that of Arbitrator Carroll R. Daugherty and his opinion is worth extensive quotation.[20]

> Test Applicable for Learning Whether Employer Had
> Just and Proper Cause for Disciplining an Employee

> Few if any union-management agreements contain a definition of "just cause." Nevertheless, over the years the opinions of arbitrators in innumerable discipline cases have developed a sort of "common law" definition thereof. This definition consists of a set of guidelines or criteria that are to be applied to the facts of any one case, and said criteria are set forth below in the form of questions.

> A "no" answer to any one or more of the following questions normally signifies that just and proper cause did not exist. In other words, such "no" means that the employer's disciplinary decision contained one or more elements of arbitrary, capricious, unreasonable, and/or discriminatory action to such an extent that said decision constituted an abuse of managerial discretion warranting the arbitrator to substitute his judgment for that of the employer.

> The answers to the questions in any particular case are to be found in the evidence presented to the arbitrator at the hearing thereon. Frequently, of course, the facts are such that the guidelines cannot be applied with slide-rule precision.

> The Questions

> 1. Did the company give to the employee forewarning or foreknowledge of the possible or probable disciplinary consequences of the employee's conduct?
>> *Note 1*: Said forewarning or foreknowledge may properly have been given orally by management or in writing through the medium of typed or printed sheets or books of shop rules and of penalties for violation thereof.
>> *Note 2*: There must have been actual oral or written communication of the rules and penalties to the employee.
>> *Note 3*: A finding of lack of such communication does not in all cases require a "no" answer to Question No. 1. This is because certain offenses such as insubordination, coming to work intoxicated, drinking intoxicating beverages on the job, or theft of the property of the company or of fellow employees are so serious that any employee in the industrial society may properly be expected to know already that such conduct is offensive and heavily punishable.

Note 4: Absent any contractual prohibition or restriction, the company has the right unilaterally to promulgate reasonable rules and give reasonable orders; and same need not have been negotiated with the union.

2. Was the company's rule or managerial order reasonably related to the orderly, efficient, and safe operation of the company's business?

Note: If an employee believes that said rule or order is unreasonable, he must nevertheless obey same (in which case he may file a grievance thereover) unless he sincerely feels that to obey the rule or order would seriously and immediately jeopardize his personal safety and/or integrity. Given a firm finding to the latter effect, the employee may properly be said to have had justification for his disobedience.

3. Did the company, before administering discipline to an employee, make an effort to discover whether the employee did in fact violate or disobey a rule or order of management?

Note 1: This is the employee's "day in court" principle. An employee has the right to know with reasonable precision the offenses with which he is being charged and to defend his behavior.

Note 2: The company's investigation must normally be made before its disciplinary decision is made. If the company fails to do so, its failure may not normally be excused on the ground that the employee will get his day in court through the grievance procedure after the exaction of discipline. By that time there has usually been too much hardening of positions.

Note 3: There may of course be circumstances under which management must react immediately to the employee's behavior. In such cases the normally proper action is to suspend the employee pending investigation, with the understanding that (a) the final disciplinary decision will be made after the investigation and (b) if the employee is found innocent after the investigation, he will be restored to his job with full pay for time lost.

4. Was the company's investigation conducted fairly and objectively?

Note: At said investigation the management official may be both "prosecutor" and "judge," but he may not also be a witness against the employee.

5. At the investigation did the "judge" obtain substantial evidence or proof that the employee was guilty as charged?

Note: It is not required that the evidence be preponderant, conclusive or "beyond reasonable doubt." But the evidence must be truly substantial and not flimsy.

6. Has the company applied its rules, orders, and penalities evenhandedly and without discrimination to all employees?

Note 1: A "no" answer to the question requires a finding of discrimination and warrants negation or modification of the discipline imposed.

Note 2: If the company has been lax in enforcing its rules and orders and decides henceforth to apply them rigorously, the company may avoid a finding of discrimination by telling all employees beforehand of its intent to enforce hereafter all rules as written.

7. Was the degree of discipline administered by the company in a particular case reasonably related to (a) the seriousness of the employee's proven offense and (b) the record of the employee in his service with the company?

Note 1: A trivial proven offense does not merit harsh discipline unless the employee has properly been found guilty of the same or other offenses a number of times in the past. (There is no rule as to what number of previous offenses constitutes a "good," a "fair," or a "bad" record. Reasonable judgment thereon must be used.)

Note 2: An employee's record of previous offenses may never be used to discover whether he was guilty of the immediate or latest one. The only proper use of his record is to help determine the severity of discipline once he has properly been found guilty of the immediate offense.

Note 3: Given the same proven offense for two or more employees, their respective records provide the only proper basis for "discriminating" among them in the administration of discipline for said offense. Thus, if employee A's record is significantly better than those of employees B, C, and D, the company may properly give A lighter punishment than it gives the others for the same offense; and this does not constitute true discrimination.

While excellent as a "cookbook" summary of the disciplinary process, Arbitrator Daugherty's focus is too narrow. Disciplinary processes should be understood primarily as tools by which employers strive to keep employees and to create a committed and responsible work force. They are not tools to eliminate bad actors, even though they have significant utility for that purpose.

As is shown in later chapters, a well-designed and well-implemented discipline system demands supervisory intervention before a problem actually develops. The key is to train supervisors to know when that intervention should take place and how it should occur.

Notes to Chapter 3

1. *But see* the discussion of the erosion of this concept in Chapter 7, Part II of this book.

2. *See General Elec. Co.* (Abrams), 74 LA 847; *New Castle Hosp.* (Witney), 74 LA 365; *Prismo-William Armstrong Smith Co.* (Jedel), 73 LA 581.

3. *Arco Precision Gear & Mach. Corp.* (Young), 31 LA 575, at 579-560. *See also Babcock & Wilcox Co.* (Dworkin), 41 LA 862.

4. *See* Alexander, "Concepts of Industrial Discipline," *Management Rights and the Arbitration Process*, Proceedings of the Ninth Annual Meeting of the National Academy of Arbitrators (Washington, D.C.: BNA Books, 1956), pp. 76, 79–81.

5. *See General Elec. Co., supra,* note 2.

6. *See Grief Bros. Cooperage Corp.* (Daugherty), 42 LA 555; *Decor Corp.* (Kates), 44 LA 389; *Wolf Mach. Co.* (High), 72 LA 510.

7. *See Norfolk Shipbldg. & Drydock Corp. v. Local No. 684,* 671 F.2d 797, 109 LRRM 2329 (CA 4, 1982).

8. *Rohn Indus.* (Sabo), 78 LA 978.

9. *Stockham Pipe Fittings Co.* (McCoy), 1 LA 160.

10. *Banas v. Matthews Int'l Corp.,* 502 A.2d 637, 121 LRRM 2515 (Pa. Super. Ct. 1985).

11. *Grief Bros. Cooperage Corp., supra,* note 6, at 557.

12. *Compare* Summers, "Individual Protection Against Unjust Dismissal: Time for a Statute," 62 VA. L. REV. 481, 504 (1976), which concludes that arbitrators have generally held that the "employee is not entitled to a hearing before discipline is imposed . . . ," with the opposite finding in, Jennings & Wolters, "Discharge Cases Reconsidered," 31 ARB. J. 164, 178 (1976).

13. *Wolf Mach. Co., supra,* note 6.

14. *University of Mo.* (Yarowsky), 78 LA 417.

15. *Id.,* at 421.

16. *See also Plantation Patterns* (Dallas), 78 LA 647.

17. Littrell, "Grievances Procedure and Arbitration in a Nonunion Environment: The Northrop Experience," *Arbitration Issues for the 1980's,* Proceedings of the Thirty-Fourth Annual Meeting of the National Academy of Arbitrators (Washington, D.C.: BNA Books, 1982).

18. *See* Malinowski, "An Empirical Analysis of Discharge Cases and the Work History of Employees Reinstated by Labor Arbitrations," 36 ARB. J. 31 (1981).

19. *General Elec. Co., supra,* note 2, at 850.

20. *Grief Bros. Cooperage Corp., supra,* note 6, at 557-559.

4

Supervisor Selection and Training

It is commonly held that first- and second-line supervisors are the key to effective and positive employee relations. This is pure hokey. The key to effective and positive employee relations is the chief executive officer. The corporate culture and deployment of assets emanates from that office and that office alone. So long as the CEO is preoccupied with short term gains and seduced by numbers and capital acquisitions, the basis for positive employee relations will be absent.

One of the most remarkable and tragic statements made to me in recent years was by an MBA candidate at one of the leading business schools in the country. I asked him how many personnel oriented courses were required as part of his curriculum. His reply was, "none; they are all electives and only the women take them." This comment rivals that of a CEO who asked me, after reviewing my recommendation for a supervisory development program, "but if the supervisors have to do all of those things the program covers, when will they have time to work?"

I suspect that American business, although constantly losing ground to foreign competitors in terms of real productivity, has managed to avoid total disaster despite its de-emphasis on employee welfare partly because of the surplus of workers entering the job market. But those days are gone now and, what used to be a dead-end track in corporate America—human resources—will find itself at the center of the struggle to survive as employers seek to overcome a shortage of available employees in critical areas and a surplus of middle managers who desire to fulfill their career objectives but have nowhere to go. CEOs and CFOs must recognize that significant resources must be dedicated to human development if their enterprises are to survive. Employees in the past were encouraged to retire early or to resign. Employees now must be stimulated to stay and learn new jobs out of necessity. There just will not be anyone to take their job if they leave. An employer's program to attract and to keep employees must include creative and credible methods for satisfying employee needs, not the least of which is due process in the workplace.

If first- and second-line supervisors do not do their jobs, any employee-management system, no matter how well designed, will fail. But supervisors are developed, not born, and the development of an effective supervisor requires commitment from senior management. Without this commitment, good supervisors will occur only by chance.

The ability to handle people and stimulate them to excellence is a special skill distinct from the ability to plan production schedules or to produce a flawless product. Consequently, an employer must develop programs that will identify individuals who have the potential to develop supervisory skills. This may require a dramatic restructuring of current compensation systems that now reward technical excellence or productivity with a promotion to a supervisory position. Involving rank and file employees in the development of employee-handling systems is one method of discerning potential supervisors. Including some rank and file employees in supervisory development programs is another. Most important, however, is the conscious selection of supervisors based on their ability to handle people as well as on their technical excellence. Technical excellence without people skills should be rewarded in some fashion other than a supervisory promotion.

Supervisory training cannot be limited to seminars and lectures. It must include doing and creating. All too often, supervisors do not want to supervise, they resort to the "they made me do it" syndrome when it comes to discipline. Typically, a supervisor is handed a discipline system and told to implement it. The supervisor did not participate in creating the system, may misunderstand it, and, probably has little or no belief in its philosophy. The imposed system may be viewed solely as a series of required steps to be taken before "they" will let the supervisor get rid of a behavior problem.

If supervisors have to implement and use a discipline system, it should be one they understand and believe in. Codes of conduct, problem solving procedures, and discipline programs should never be created and imposed downward by a personnel department, even with the "input" of supervisors who are asked to comment on them. Systems are organic and should be created and periodically adjusted by supervisors themselves. In this way, supervisors "buy into" the success of the program. Most of all, they must be encouraged to use the discipline system as a means to keep, not get rid of, employees.

If keeping employees is the expressed objective of the systems, supervisors should be required to operate them to achieve that objective. How well that objective is met by a supervisor should be central to his or her own performance evaluation. Part of every supervisor's training, of course, is how to evaluate employee performance. Just as important, however, are the training and experience gained by supervisors when they participate in the development of a performance review system for their peers. While effective employee evaluations depend on identifying objective criteria for measurement, the supervisor's evaluation should measure his or her success in retaining employees, establishing positive contacts with employees, and developing employee responsibility. When these latter criteria become central to the supervisor's own performance evaluation, their importance will not be lost or be made incidental.

Finally, time must be taken for supervisory interaction. Group problem solving and discussion of personnel related issues are invaluable means of learning from the experiences of others. Often supervisors are forced to operate in a vacuum, and they develop a belief that their problems are unique. They are denied the opportunity to benefit from their peers because the employer does not think the time spent is "worth it."

Perhaps the best system I have seen in operation is one in which groups of six first-line supervisors met on a weekly basis for one to two hours of employee problem solving. At these sessions, each supervisor was expected to bring at least one issue for group discussion. The issues were not limited to traditional behavioral problems of specific employees and much of the time was devoted to how to recognize good performance. The employer understood that reacting to positive employee efforts was sometimes as difficult as reacting to substandard performance. Consequently, supervisors were encouraged to discuss the types of positive contacts they had with employees during the prior week as well as the corrective actions taken. The supervisors involved in these "problem solvers" were intentially rotated so that every supervisor met at some time with every other supervisor to discuss employee-handling issues. The technique not only provided a forum for supervisors to explore their problems, but also impressed upon them that their problems were not unique. In addition, the frequency of the meetings required supervisors to be alert to issues within their area of responsibility, and it encouraged them to bring issues to the group before they became subject to steps of formal discipline. The absence of second-line supervisors at these meetings reduced tension and created more of a work group atmosphere.

The process of creating a disciplined work force takes time, energy, and commitment. This is the essence of management's discipline.

The Roles and Character of Supervisors

At all levels of management, supervisors must understand their various roles and develop leadership characteristics if a disciplined work force is to be achieved. Without this knowledge, supervisors are left to grope for techniques that will encourage appropriate employee responses. Unfortunately, the empirical trial-and-error methods imposed on most first-line supervisors often result in employee confusion and resentment. Equally unfortunate is that most supervisory training programs I have examined concentrate almost exclusively on treating symptoms of poor discipline and do not help supervisors to understand their power bases and how to use them to maximum effects. As a result, there is often little method or forethought to a supervisor's approach to employee problems.

Supervisors play three distinct roles within their organizations: interpersonal, informational and decisional.[1] In performing each of these roles, the supervisor has duties and functions both as the unit supervisor and as the organizational representative.

The interpersonal role played by the supervisor takes the form of leadership when directed toward the supervised unit. In this role, the supervisor is required to motivate employees to work toward achieving the goals of the organization and to establish a beneficial work atmosphere. In connection with the organization as a whole, the supervisor is a liaison who obtains necessary information or other resources needed by the unit to perform its work.

The informational role of the supervisor is one of monitoring, disseminating, and speaking. As a monitor, the supervisor collects information for the performance of the other two duties. As a disseminator, the supervisor transmits information from outside the unit to the unit's members. As a speaker, the supervisor takes the information generated within the unit and communicates it to others outside the unit.

In the decisional role, the supervisor has four tasks: entrepreneur, problem solver, allocator, and negotiator. As an entrepreneur, the supervisor effects changes within the unit to adapt or respond to changes outside the unit. As a problem solver, the supervisor handles disturbances within the unit. As an allocator of resources, the supervisor determines how the material and labor resources of the unit should be deployed to achieve desired results. Finally, as a negotiator, the supervisor bargains with those outside the unit to obtain what the unit requires to function.

When a particular organization is analyzed as having an undisciplined work force, it is not unusual to find that supervisors have been viewed only as allocators of resources and problem solvers. Consequently, they consistently fail to achieve the results desired by top management. Most often the fault lies with top managers who neither understand the true roles of supervisors nor provide the training to fulfill these roles successfully.

Supervisors (and top management) must also understand the sources of their power and how and when to use their various types of power. Unfortunately, supervisors often view their power as one- and possibly two-dimensional only. This makes it impossible to manage effectively through the use of power from all sources, as the situation requires. Various kinds of power naturally exist for the supervisor:

1. The right to lead conferred by position (legitimate power);
2. The ability to give rewards (reward power);
3. The ability to punish (coercive power); and
4. The knowledge necessary for the achievement of unit goals (expert power).[2]

Legitimate power exists solely because supervisors are accorded the power of the organization. Where power is not clearly conferred, supervisors may be denied its effective use. Consequently, where management denies their supervisors one or more of their roles or denies them the necessary support to exercise their inherent powers, the power emanating from their position is not legitimatized and they are viewed by subordinates as weak and ineffectual.

The use of legitimate power also requires some finesse by supervisors. Supervisors cannot display their status difference by being rude or authoritarian. They must lead confidently and convey by their enthusiasm the importance of tasks. Their requests must not only appear legitimate for a business purpose, but also must be clear, since subordinates cannot perform if they do not understand what is required of them. In this respect, supervisors must remember to check that subordinates comprehend their requests. More important, supervisors must explain the reasons for their requests and cannot assume that the reasons are obvious. Once a request is communicated, supervisors cannot rely on subordinate implementation, they must insist on compliance and verify performance. Also, if supervisors expect and demand appropriate subordinate responses, they, themselves, must respect the authority over them and utilize established channels of communication and decision making. Finally, they must be responsive to their subordinates' concerns. By doing these things, supervisors establish and reinforce the credibility of the legitimate power inherent in their position.

Reward power implies the existence of rewards to confer. Most often, rewards are defined in monetary or time-off terms. These rewards are supplied by top management to supervisors for disposition to their employees. Their existence, therefore, is normally not within a supervisor's control. Another form of reward, wholly within the control of supervisors not only to give but also to create, is that of recognition. (This form of reward is discussed in Chapter 6 under nonpunitive discipline.) Reward by recognition is the most powerful for supervisors and, in my view, exceeds the power of other forms of reward.[3] To use this kind of power, supervisors must be shown its value and effectiveness. Top managers must require its use and base supervisory evaluations on its employment.

The effective use of reward power requires supervisors to verify compliance with their requests. Levels of behavior or performance that will result in a reward must be feasible for the employees. Further, the reward must be attractive and desirable to the achiever. Thus, awarding time off to an employee who wants overtime is an ineffective reward. (Absence of punishment is not considered an attractive reward.) The supervisor also must be viewed as the source of the reward decisions if the appropriate relationship is to develop between the supervisor and the employee. Finally, the reward must be for a legitimate purpose, not a bribe for responsible conduct. For this reason, managers should examine carefully the appropriateness of monetary rewards for acceptable attendance or non-use of sick time. What kind of message does such a bribe convey regarding other employer expectations and standards?

Coercive power is traditionally associated with discipline. Because the use of coercive power and the preconditions for its use (notice, consistency, promptness, predictability, accuracy of facts, and appropriateness of response) are treated elsewhere, this power is not discussed here. However, it is interesting to note that industrial psychologists determined long ago that the use of coercive power will not create long term behavioral changes but only short term compliance with rules. This failure of purpose is discussed more completely in Chapter 7.[4]

Expert power is that which comes from the knowledge necessary to achieve unit goals. Using this kind of power requires the supervisor not only to possess special expertise but also to promote the image of expertise. To maintain credibility, supervisors must avoid careless statements or lies and act confidently and decisively in times of crisis. Moreover, supervisors must keep informed and maintain their technical edge, since their knowledge is the basis for power. In dealing with subordinates, a supervisor must relate his or her expertise to the needs of the unit and not threaten the self-esteem of those supervised by using knowledge to make others seem ignorant.

Understanding the role, the source, and the use of supervisory powers is vitally important for successful unit management. For the most part, these elements must be taught to supervisors. Top managers do a disservice to their organization when they reward employees by making them supervisors—based on their ability to exercise expert power, for instance—and then expect them to exercise the other powers or to fulfill all of the roles of a supervisor without training in these areas. Good supervisors then emerge only by accident.

Good supervisors must also have certain inherent character traits; these cannot be developed through training. Most important is the motivation to manage. This trait is discernible in certain ways. Supervisors with the motivation to manage are able to obtain the support of their superiors and will have a positive attitude toward them. Also, because resources are limited, these supervisors have a will to compete to get those things that enable their unit to achieve desired results. They will have an active and assertive nature that enables them to take charge and engage in disciplinary actions. They must feel comfortable using both rewards and punishment and must have a desire to learn which of their powers should be used in various circumstances. Their willingness to attend to administrative details displays a positive supervisory character trait. For this reason, I view supervisory resistance to maintaining performance records or to completing disciplinary notices as a major character flaw, and I question the appropriateness of selecting that individual in the first place. When I discover such resistance, during any analysis of the root causes of an undisciplined work force, I wonder "who made this person a supervisor?" Finally, a good supervisor desires visibility and invites attention and criticism. Good supervisors are not afraid to be creative or assertive within appropriate channels.[5]

Notes to Chapter 4

1. *See generally* Mintzberg, *The Nature of Managerial Work* (Englewood Cliffs, N.J.: Prentice Hall, 1980).

2. *See generally* French & Raven, "The Bases of Social Power," *Studies in Social Power*, Cartwright, ed. (Ann Arbor: Institute for Social Research, Univ. of Michigan, 1959).

3. *See generally* B.F. Skinner's discussions of operant conditioning in *Science and Human Behavior* (New York: Macmillan, 1953) and *Cumulative Record* (New York: Appleton-Century-Crofts, 1959).

4. *See generally* Yukl, *Leadership in Organizations* (Englewood Cliffs, N.J.: Prentice Hall, 1981) pp. 47–58 and Saal & Knight, *Industrial/Organizational Psychology* (Monterey, Calif.: Brooks/Cole Pub. Co., 1988), pp. 337–347.

5. For a detailed discussion of managerial motivation, *see* Miner, "Twenty Years of Research on Role-Motivation Theory of Managerial Effectiveness," *Personnel Psychology*, 1978. Subsequent observations have not improved on Miner's work.

Part II

Employee Discipline: Policies

5

Progressive Discipline

Although not required by any law, the baseline for all nonsummary disciplinary action is that it must be progressive.[1] Without this element, a discharge for a nonsummary offense would be without due process and would be voided by a labor arbitrator or otherwise be perceived as unfair. In this connection, the failure of due process is often expressed in terms of result: the failure to have just cause for the action.

As stated previously, a progressive discipline system is one that provides to employees, prior to termination of employment, one or more warnings of unacceptable conduct. The progressive nature is usually twofold: (1) the system "progresses" through a series of warning steps and (2) each step in the process contains some added element, which is calculated to impress on the employee the growing urgency of compliance and risk of termination.

In theory, when an employee finally demonstrates that he or she is no longer an acceptable member of the workforce through repeated refusals or failures to adhere to established and reasonable standards, the employer is justified in terminating the employment. Arbitrator Harry J. Dworkin, in *Babcock & Wilcox Co.*, described this approach to discipline in a case involving a discharge for excessive absenteeism as follows:

> The arbitrator acknowledges that an employee may be subject to discipline, including discharge, for chronic absenteeism where he has failed to respond to more moderate disciplinary procedures. Where the company issues warnings and suspensions, which prove to be ineffectual, management is then free under proper circumstances to consider termination of employment. Where an employee continues to disregard his attendance obligations, just cause may be presented for discharge. The

51

employer has the right to anticipate that its employees will observe the regular scheduled hours of work, and dereliction in these respects may present just cause.

Employers generally will utilize other available methods for correcting chronic absenteeism before discharge penalty is invoked. Discharge is warranted only in such cases where corrective measures appear to be futile. In the instant case, the arbitrator does not feel that the grievant was accorded the proper corrective disciplinary procedures.

The arbitrator subscribes to the principle of progressive discipline. This concept is referred to by Professor Lawrence Stessen in *Employee Discipline*, page 142, citing *Bell Aircraft Corp.*, 17 LA 230 (Arbitrator Joseph Shister): ". . . What progressive discipline does mean is that progressively more severe penalties may be imposed on each given employee each time any given offense is repeated. Progressive discipline also means that after a specified number of offenses, regardless of whether the offenses are identical or not, the company may have the right to discharge the given employee. Both of these latter interpretations of progressive discipline avoid the inequitable meting out of discipline, and at the same time serve the dual purpose of progressive discipline, namely, the discouragement of repeated offenses by employees and the protection of the right of the company to sever completely its relationship with any employee who by his total behavior shows himself to be irresponsible."[2]

For any discipline system to have credibility, the standards of conduct or performance must be clearly established so that all employees are, at least theoretically, aware of the employer's expectations. Discipline, then, is used to achieve employer expectations by compelling or encouraging compliance with company rules.[3] As we shall see, some discipline systems seek to compel compliance through progressively increasing penalties or through a series of threats of penalties or punishment. These are classified here as punitive systems. Other systems seek to encourage compliance through a matrix of counselings without penalties. These are classified here as nonpunitive systems. These two types of systems are discussed in detail below. Regardless of whether the employer chooses to use the more traditional punitive system or a nonpunitive system, the baseline for satisfying the requirement of due process is that progressive steps must be taken which provide the employee a notice that certain conduct is below the employer's expected standard, an opportunity to bring the conduct into compliance with the standard, and a communication of an increasing likelihood of termination.

The punitive approach to discipline, to correct behavior through progressively more severe penalties, has developed into a fairly set formula. This formula consists of a series of steps, one or more of which may be eliminated or added. However, it is rare for the number of steps to be fewer than three or more than five. The following four steps are involved most frequently:

1. An employee who has committed an infraction is verbally warned and told that if the same infraction occurs again within some specified period the degree of disciplinary action will be increased.
2. If the employee again commits the same or a similar violation within the specified period, the employee will be given a written warning which will be placed in his or her personnel file. The employee will be told that, if his or her conduct is repeated within a specified period, the employee will be disciplined again, but more severely.
3. If the employee again transgresses in the same manner and within the specified period, he or she will be suspended from employment for a period of time without pay and will be given a final warning. This warning will clearly specify discharge as the result of another such infraction within a stated time.
4. If the employee again violates the same rule within the specified time, the employee will be discharged.

Because the system progresses through ever-increasing levels of severity, it is assumed that the employee will learn what type of conduct is acceptable and will be given an opportunity, or be compelled, to conform.

Nontraditional discipline systems, or nonpunitive systems, also consist of a series of warnings (steps). These steps are similar to those in the traditional punitive system except that the penalties of the punitive system are replaced by other forms of enforcement. For instance, in a nonpunitive system the first step continues to be a verbal warning and the second step continues to be a written warning. The third step, however, eliminates the economic detriment to the employee (unpaid suspension) and replaces it with a forcefully worded, final written warning. Chapter 6 explores the various devices used to enhance the urgency of the third step in a nonpunitive system.

Both punitive and nonpunitive systems, however, must contain two additional and essential elements. Without them, an arbitrator may still find the discipline to have been unfair. These elements can be stated briefly as follows:

1. The system must provide all essential elements of due process to the employee;
2. All employees must be treated equally or advanced through the steps of the system in the same fashion without discrimination.

Due Process

The concept of due process is as elusive in employee-employer relations as it is in the law. The primary elements of employee due process were described in Chapter 3 and include procedures in a macro sense beyond those traditionally found within the four corners of what generally is called a discipline system. The focus here is micro in the sense that we will examine more precisely the elements of due process which must exist within a discipline system itself. In doing this, I refer to what arbitrators perceive as necessary. In this respect, I am using arbitrators as mirrors of perceptions of fairness and just cause. Nonunion employers who do not consider arbitration as the forum for dispute resolution should read "arbitrators" as meaning other employees or judges and juries in wrongful discharge cases.

Essentially, arbitrators appear to conclude that due process exists where the employee is made aware of the nature of his or her violation of company rules or standards; the employee is not punished unless the violation is shown by the weight of credible evidence; the employee is allowed to know all of the facts supporting a finding of a violation; and, the employee is given an opportunity to defend himself or herself. In addition, arbitrators often find that employers must have forfeited the element of surprise prior to their implementing disciplinary action. That is, an employee must know that certain acts, if committed or continued, will result in some kind of punishment, usually the kind actually administered. Indeed, industrial due process is inextricably involved in the similarly evasive concept of just cause. This was recognized by the U.S. Court of Appeals for the Eighth Circuit in *Local 878 v. Coca-Cola Bottling Co.*, as follows:

arbitrators have long been applying notions of "industrial due process" to "just cause" discharge cases. As Professor Summers noted, "[o]n the bare words 'just cause' arbitrators have built a comprehensive and relatively stable body of both substantive and procedural law." Summers, *Individual Protection Against Unjust Dismissal: Time for a Statute*, 62 Va. L. Rev. 481, 500 (1976) (footnote deleted). Professor Summers also commented that the retention of the bare "just cause" language in newly negotiated agreements is an indication of the widespread acceptance of arbitrators' due process interpretations. Id. at 505. To a similar effect are the comments of Professor Getman:

> To enhance its chances of winning at arbitration, a company needs to establish careful disciplinary procedures consistent with arbitration awards defining the concept of just cause. Arbitrators generally insist on equal punishment for the same offense, and they require that employees be given advance notice of company rules *and a chance to explain their behavior before they are disciplined*. Getman, Labor Arbitration and Dispute Resolution, 88 Yale L.J. 916, 921 (1979) (footnote deleted, emphasis added). *See also Combustion Engineering, Inc.*, 42 Lab. Arb. 806 (1964) (Daugherty, Ar.).[4]

Notice of Standards

Where an employee's defense is built upon proven surprise or lack of knowledge, discipline is rarely found to be appropriate.[5] Consequently, the first, and perhaps the most important, element which must be shown to exist in any discipline case is that the employee knew, or should have known, that his or her conduct would produce a disciplinary response. In fact, the progressive or corrective discipline system is built upon the principle of employee awareness, thereby eliminating any element of surprise. As employees move through each step, they receive actual notice that their behavior is in violation of specific rules or standards. For this reason, some personnel directors refer to the operation of the system as an employee's self-discipline. That is, employees who knowingly subject themselves to punishments of increasing severity are, in effect, disciplining themselves. The obvious key, here, is the word "knowingly." If an employee is unaware of a rule or does not know that specific conduct will violate a rule, the employee can hardly be found to have knowingly subjected himself or herself to discipline.

A corollary to this principle is that an employee does not receive the benefits of progressive discipline when an employer administers increasing degrees of punishment regardless of the nature of the rule which has been violated. For instance, an employee who is warned for excessive absenteeism, suspended for carelessness, and discharged for abusive language may not be found to have had due process. Satisfactory movement through the steps of the progressive discipline system only occurs when that movement is occasioned by repeated violations of the same rule or type of rule. The exception is when the employee has been previously warned about the "bundling" of offenses.

For adequate notice to have been made to employees, however, two things must exist: (1) a publication of standards of conduct and (2) a publication of the discipline system itself.

Such publications should be of two kinds in all cases, general and specific. Although arbitrators rarely overturn otherwise appropriate discipline because of the absence of a general publication, they will almost always find that a specific publication must exist, particularly in cases involving discharge or suspension. A general publication occurs when the employer distributes to all employees a standard set of rules and regulations. Distribution can be achieved by incorporating the publication into a union contract or an employee handbook or by posting the document on a bulletin board. A publication is general if it is distributed to all the employees in the same manner at a time not directly associated with any specific event.

A specific publication usually is written in response to a particular event or situation, is addressed to an individual employee or to a group of employees smaller than the entire workforce, and is intended to communicate a rule of management. This type of publication usually is written during the course of the discipline, and its contents are communicated when the individual employee is told the nature of the unacceptable conduct, why it was unacceptable, and what will result from continued actions of the same kind. Specific publication is essential to a finding of due process where the discipline is of an advanced degree. Arbitrators have found specific publications to be acceptable where: (1) an employee admits to specific knowledge of the allegedly broken rule; (2) an employee admits to being aware of the degree of discipline required by the discipline system for the particular infraction; and, (3) the employer can document the transmittal of this information.

To sustain discipline which will cause an employee to suffer some economic loss, therefore, employers are frequently required to document, or otherwise prove by the weight of the credible evidence, that the employee received specific publication of the rule and that his or her act was in violation of that rule. In addition, an important issue to arbitrators seems to be whether the employee was able to predict what the results of his or her actions would be prior to the disciplinary action.[6] The element of predictability in the discipline system is discussed in Chapter 3.

Four recent cases demonstrate various aspects of the notice requirement. In *Montague Machine Co.*, an employee was discharged for poor work performance.[7] The company presented evidence that several warnings had been given to the employee prior to the event which precipitated the discharge. One of these warnings had been in writing. The arbitrator found that the verbal warnings could be best characterized as "casual conversations," and since they could not have been perceived by the employee as warnings, the verbal warnings should be disregarded as ineffective. The written warning, while effective as a warning for poor work performance, did not state that a future similar occurrence would result in discharge. Consequently, the arbitrator held that the employee had not been given adequate notice of the seriousness of the situation and should not have been discharged. By failing to give the employee adequate notice of the consequence of his continued poor performance, the employer was perceived as not really trying to rehabilitate the employee.

In *Watauga Industries*, an employee was discharged for smoking marijuana on the employer's premises in violation of a specific company rule.[8] Finding that the employer had condoned the possession and smoking of marijuana in the past, the arbitrator reinstated the employee. The arbitrator's reasoning was that the employee had not been given notice that the rule against the possession and the use of marijuana in the plant was going to be enforced.

In a somewhat similar case, *Gill Studios*, the employee was also reinstated for lack of adequate, specific notice.[9] In that case, the employee had been discharged for having received three reprimands in six months. Although the rule had been generally publicized, the employer had not told the employee after his second reprimand that another, within a specified period of time, would result in discharge. This employer, also was found to have made an inadequate effort to rehabilitate the employee.

By way of contrast, the arbitrator in *Lucky Stores* sus-

tained the action taken against an employee who had been
discharged following an absence for a concededly legitimate
illness.[10] In that case, the employee had received prior warnings and had been suspended once for chronic absenteeism.
The suspension letter threatened the employee with discharge
for any further absences, regardless of the reason for the absence. The discharge was sustained, even though the employee's record had improved and the absence was caused by a
legitimate illness. The arbitrator found that the absenteeism,
although improved, was still excessive and that the employee
had been given adequate notice that his next absence, regardless of cause, would result in discharge.

Notice of Effect of Violating Standard

It is essential, therefore, that the employee know, and the
discipline system provide, that uncorrected behavior will result in the termination of employment. This effect must be
clear and unequivocal; there can be no confusion. The importance of the lack of confusion cannot be overemphasized. Three
unreported (private) arbitration cases, discussed below, illustrate what I believe are common problems.

In one case, the employer gave the employee a "final warning" that any further infraction of the work rules would result
in discharge. The employee proceeded to violate work rules
and received no less than 20 additional warnings. The twenty-
first violation occurred when, in a fit of rage, the employee
slammed his locker door, breaking it off its hinges. The employer fired the employee and raised the "final warning" as
satisfying the due process requirement. Not surprisingly, the
arbitrator held that the final warning had been diluted into
meaninglessness and the employee did not have adequate notice that the next or any future rule infraction would result
in his discharge.

The problem is obvious: when an employer provides notice
that something will occur if the employee does not change,
that something must occur or all future notices will become
suspect. The solution to the problem, however, is not quite so
easy.

Assume an employee has an absenteeism problem. The
employer gives the employee a final warning that any further
absences will result in discharge. Obviously, an absence in
the next week will justify—if not require—discharge. But,
what if the employee has a perfect record for six months and

then has an absence? Is discharge warranted? What if the perfect record extends for a year, two years? At some point, effecting the threatened discharge will become unfair and unenforceable.

In this example, the employer could have reduced the problem by stating in the warning notice that the employee would be discharged if he resumed an unacceptable pattern of absences within the next year. This "time limit" in the notice would eliminate the most obvious defect in the example. However, the solution is rarely adequate if all it involves is the simple limitation on the effective period of the notice. The issue is, by its nature, a continuum. As the time increases, the severity of the new infraction must also increase. The longer the time period between the date of notice and the end of "probation," the more likely the possibility that the employee will do something that may not qualify as justifiable discharge, but which will dilute or destroy the effectiveness of the notice if some action is not taken.

For instance, if an employee is given a final warning that another negligent act within 12 months will result in his discharge and, within a week, the employee allows a truck to roll back into a platform dock which results in a broken taillight, there is little question that he should be discharged, even though the damage was slight. However, the same event occurring in the ninth month of the effective period, and after eight months of negligence-free work, hardly seems to warrant a discharge.

The solutions are: (1) avoid the temptation of prolonged probation periods and, (2) when minor infractions occur for which a discharge is inappropriate because of the passage of time or lack of seriousness of the offense, a second notice should explain to the employee that the failure to discharge under the circumstances does not eliminate or alter the effectiveness of the final warning. In this fashion, the time limit is begun again.

For instance, in the negligence case above, what if the employer had given the following notice to the employee:

> On June 15, 1987, you were given notice that any act of negligence in the next 12 months would result in your discharge. On February 20, 1988, when releasing the brake of a truck you allowed it to roll back into the platform and broke one of its taillights. Until then your conduct had been negligence free. After reviewing your work record since June 15, and, considering the minor nature of the occurrence, you will

not be discharged. However, any act of negligence—even of a minor nature—during the balance of the effective period of this notice, will result in your discharge.

The effect of this notice would be to start the clock again so that the seriousness of any new act of negligence would be viewed from the date of this last notice. Further, the notice does not indicate toleration and does not risk the loss of the effectiveness of the initial final warning. Consequently, the employee cannot argue later that he had been confused, or lulled into a sense of security.

In another case, a suspension was voided based on a finding that there had been an insufficient prior warning and, consequently, an absence of a necessary precondition to the second disciplinary step. In that case, the first-line supervisor had been promoted up from the ranks. Overnight he went from co-worker to boss. As Murphy's Law would predict, one of his close friends became his first problem. The friend had become chronically tardy. The supervisor, obviously uncomfortable about disciplining his friend, waited until the problem could no longer be ignored. Over a beer after work one day he said, "Sam, you have to get to work on time regularly or I will be forced to write you up. I do not want it to get to that point." The problem did not abate, and the supervisor suspended the employee for three days, as the next step required by the discipline policy after a verbal warning. The employee argued at the arbitration that he had not taken the conversation in the bar as a warning, only as a casual statement by a friend. Consequently, he had not been given the first step of discipline. The arbitrator agreed.

The problem is apparent on the surface, as is the solution: the supervisor must ensure that the employee understands that what is happening is part of the formal discipline process. The underlying problem, which is far more difficult to solve, is that the employer had failed its supervisor by changing his status without appropriate training. The supervisor was expected to go through a complete role change with virtually no help. As a result, he was in an untenable position. The outcome was the absence of clear and unequivocal notice to the employee of the problem.

The final case illustrates confusion due to an incomplete communication in the notice. In this case, the employee had been given a final warning and suspension for absenteeism.

The notice warned that any continuation or resumption of unsatisfactory attendance within the next 12 months would result in termination of employment. Less than one month later the employee was negligent. The employer discharged the employee, but the employee argued that the final warning was limited to absenteeism and provided no notice that an infraction of the code of conduct would result in discharge. The employee was reinstated.

The bundling of offenses always creates problems unless the discipline system itself anticipates and solves the problem before the fact. It is patently absurd to limit an employer's ability to terminate an employee except in cases where the employee is guilty of repeatedly violating the same rule. Followed to its extreme, an employee, governed by a four-step procedure and a code of conduct containing 16 rules, can have 48 rule violations in any rolling 12-month period and still avoid discharge.

The solution to this problem is to reorient the process and recognize the primary issue involved. The issue is whether the employee can, or is willing to fulfill the employer's expectations that he assume responsibility, as it is defined in that workplace. In the case discussed above, absenteeism was not the problem, but only a symptom of the problem. The question was not whether the employee could improve his attendance but whether he could be responsible. Therefore, had the final notice clearly stated that the employee would be required to be responsible (i.e., free of all rule infractions) for the stated period, a sufficient specific notice would have preceded his negligent act. The final notice should have read:

> Based on the above review, your attendance record is clearly less than acceptable. This creates a serious question concerning whether you can or want to be sufficiently responsible to continue your employment. This is your final notice than any conduct within the next 12 months that violates any of the rules of conduct, or, otherwise indicates a lack of responsibility— including a continuation or resumption of unacceptable attendance—will result in your discharge.

Training this supervisor to view subordinate behavior in terms of total responsibility rather than isolated behavioral acts would have averted the entire problem.

Factual Accuracy of Basis for Discipline

Whereas the first requisite of due process is notice of the standards set by the employer and the effects of violating them, the second requisite of due process is that the charge be factually accurate. Often, this depends on documentation. Without proof of each of the essential elements of the offense, an arbitrator cannot and will not sustain the discipline. Nowhere is this more obvious, and most often lacking, than in "accumulation" cases. A common query of employers is whether disciplinary action taken against an employee will be sustained upon challenge, where the violative act of the employee is claimed to have been "the last straw." Upon close examination, however, the other "straws" rarely exist, except in some supervisor's vague memory. Other than the fact that the discipline would be extremely hard to justify to an arbitrator because of the absence of proof, it could be nearly as difficult to justify it to the employee involved and to the employee's coworkers. This latter consideration is especially important where the employees are not represented by a union and where the propriety of the discipline may be important to many more people than the union's business agent and an arbitrator.

In this regard, a common misconception, which appears to lead many employers astray, is that verbal warnings need not be recorded or written. When a verbal warning is not recorded, a supervisor must depend exclusively on memory, a notoriously defective disciplinary device. Moreover, the memory involved is not only the supervisor's but the employee's as well. The supervisor's memory may always be accurate, but the supervisor can assume that the employee's will always be defective. The arbitrator will not know whom to believe. For this reason, many employers have found it advisable to abandon the traditional rubric of initiating disciplinary action with a verbal warning, replacing it with a procedure involving a first and a second written warning. Whatever the system's formal requirement may be, the first warning must at all times be recorded in some fashion to ensure that the event is documented and becomes a part of the employee's record.

As noted above, the value of documentation is most critical in cases of cumulative causes for discipline, such as absenteeism, tardiness, negligence, or poor production. The most reliable source for this type of documentation is frequently the foreman's or supervisor's log book in which all facts which may be, or may become, relevant to the operation of the department are recorded on a daily basis. In this respect, most supervisors must face the unpleasant reality that, no matter how good employees may seem, the supervisor must be prepared to keep records to be able to justify any disciplinary action which may be required at some time in the future.

Employee Knowledge of the Facts

The third requisite of due process is that the employee be allowed to know all of the facts of the charge against him or her. Arbitrators attach an importance to the use which an employer makes of the evidence upon which the discipline has been based. Whether a union is involved or not, this evidence cannot be held in secret but must be shown to the employee for examination. It is only after the employee has had a full and free opportunity to examine the case that the employee can be expected to acknowledge and learn from his or her mistake or to mount a legitimate defense. Even if the employee does not seek to examine the evidence but appears to acquiesce to the disciplinary action, the employer should take steps to ensure that a recital of the facts is documented and placed in the employee's file. Only then will both the employee and the employer be assured that the discipline given is appropriate under circumstances where the employee's work history may be relevant.

Opportunity to Defend

Due process also requires that employees have an opportunity to defend themselves in an established review procedure. Discipline in a vacuum is rarely found to be appropriate, because it is inherently suspect. An opportunity to defend means more than some *pro forma* meeting at which a supervisor politely listens to an employee's excuses. Again, records are important to document the fact that the employee was shown the evidence upon which the discipline was based and that opportunity was given for the employee to provide explanations or to prepare a defense. The employee's defense should be examined carefully and any factual disputes resolved before the discipline becomes final or before the next step in the appeals process is engaged. Just as the employee can make a mistake, so also can the supervisor.

In the progressive discipline system, natural plateaus exist, at which opportunities are presented for employees to mount a defense. These occasions change in character as the discipline increases in severity. For instance, at the warning stage, meetings with the first and second line supervisors and the employee are held. At these meetings, the facts are revealed and discussed; for an initial disciplinary measure, this is usually sufficient. However, at the suspension and discharge levels when an employee is about to suffer more tangible economic loss, the conference with the employer usually assumes a more formal atmosphere, like that of a hearing. Usually present at these hearings are the employee, the immediate and second line supervisors, as well as the manager of industrial relations, or some other similarly placed individual in authority.

Surprisingly, it is often in the hearing aspect of the discipline system that due process is denied. This is due primarily to the fact that supervisors are rarely given the training necessary to handle disciplinary meetings: Notes are not kept; things are left unsaid; facts are not revealed, or sometimes, are concealed; and employees are not given an adequate opportunity to tell their side of the story. Often, what results from these meetings is a failure to give adequate specific notice, a loss of a valuable opportunity to effect a real rehabilitation, and an employee who may be confused, embarrassed, and resentful rather than one who has been helped. This is unfortunate, since the disciplinary conference may well be the single most important element in the system's operation. Indeed, it is the disciplinary conference which is central to the affirmative system emphasized and discussed in Chapter 6.

In *Plantation Patterns*, for example, the discharge of an employee for dishonest misrepresentation was reduced to a suspension solely because the employer had denied the employee due process.[11] In this case, the employee had requested his supervisor to falsify his time card to allow payment for time away from the job. The employer's grievance system provided for an evidentiary hearing with the employee and, subsequently, a third step grievance meeting. While the evidentiary hearing was conducted, the employee was not allowed representation, and the third step meeting was not held. After reviewing the evidence, the arbitrator stated:

> So where are we? Where we are is at a juncture wherein the arbitrator is abundantly satisfied that D____ was guilty of dishonest misrepresentation designed to defraud the Company.
> However, the story doesn't end here. The Union charges correctly that the grievant was denied Union representation at the *one* meeting that was held after his escapade. This was a meeting of three Company officials, *i.e.*, Kathie Shirah, Donnie Lowe, and Rocky Stiff and the grievant. This presumably was an investigation, but this is not the way to conduct an investigation. First of all, the Company should have asked D____ if

he wanted Union representation, it should not have been denied him. Also, common decency dictates that you don't "tape" the proceedings of such a tribunal without the knowledge and the express approval of the accused. This was not done.

In addition, there never was a convening of the parties via the grievance procedure. Shortly after the convening of what the Union describes as a Kangaroo Court the Company discharged the grievant. Section 2, Article XVI of the labor contract specifies that if a non-probationary employee files a grievance within a five day period, "the matter *shall* be taken up at a meeting of the Grievance Committee as provided in Step Three of the Grievance Procedure, which meeting shall be held within five (5) working days of the suspension." [Emphasis added.] Obviously, there was no third step meeting in this case, although it was mandated.

What we have here is a case where an employee is clearly guilty of a serious misdeed, but in his defense, the Company has blatantly and illegally subverted the due process rights of the aggrieved.

What is the arbitrator to do? Well clearly, the grievant should not be applauded and made scotfree for his excesses. But equally seriously, the Company should be rebuked for its behavior.

Award

The discharge of the grievant is reduced from discharge to a suspension without pay for two months. He shall be reinstated to his former or equal position, his seniority shall be restored, and he shall be made whole for that portion of his unemployment which the arbitrator has found to be improper.

The arbitrator retains jurisdiction in this matter for the purposes of the remedy.[12]

Another example is found in *Texas International Airlines*.[10] The employee had been discharged for sleeping on the job. Apparently, the employee had pulled two chairs together in the employee lunchroom during his lunch period and had covered them with a blanket; he had then proceeded to fall asleep. This had been noted by a supervisor, who allowed the employee to continue to sleep past the time he was due to report back to work. When the employee failed to return to his work station, the supervisor discharged him. The arbitrator noted that the employee had not been allowed to give his side of the story or otherwise defend himself and found that the company had denied him due process. The discharge was overturned, and the employer was ordered to reinstate the employee with full backpay. As in *Gill Studios*, central to the arbitrator's reasoning was the concept that the employer is obligated to make reasonable efforts to rehabilitate an employee and to assist the employee in avoiding future acts which will result in discipline.[14]

Effective Defense

The fourth requisite of due process involves an employee's ability to raise a defense at a hearing. An adequate defense may depend on the presence of another person, a steward, an ombudsman, or an appointed supervisor who can speak on the employee's behalf. This is apparent from the list of participants in the disciplinary meetings described above. Unless represented by some other person, the lone employee in this situation is expected to face three or four managerial personnel in a closed hearing. In this kind of atmosphere, it would be impossible for most rank-and-file employees not to feel intimidated, let alone mount an effective defense. Nevertheless, the opportunity and ability to respond effectively to charges and to raise mitigating circumstances is essential to industrial due process. Due process cannot be denied in fact, or in effect, if the discipline is to be positive rather than negative and if the process is to provide apparent fairness. The progressive discipline system presents several opportunities to employers to satisfy this perceived right, and they must make special efforts to develop and to realize these opportunities.

Of all the due process elements which must be incorporated into the progressive discipline system, the ability of an employee to effectively defend himself is the one most often lacking. It is one element that is not a self-activating principle of the discipline system itself, but requires direct and effective action by the employer. Notice, for example, usually occurs as a natural consequence of the progression of the system, as does the increasing severity of penalties. The content and value of disciplinary conferences, however, are totally dependent on the human element. The give-and-take required in conferences cannot be formulated in an office or satisfied with written procedures. Effective management of conferences can only be achieved through the training and retraining of supervisors. I am convinced, however, that the absence of a proper philosophy of discipline in the workplace, which stiffles productive discussion, is a good part of the problem. In most traditional punitive systems, the purpose of a disciplinary conference is less interactive than dictatorial. The supervisor is delivering a message, and any questioning or confrontation is not only unwanted but feared.

The basic unfairness of a discipline system which denies an employee the right to have someone speak for and defend him or her was the central issue in *Fort Wayne Community Schools*.[15] In that case, an employee's request for representation in the hearings preceding her discharge was denied. This denial was held by the arbitrator as a denial of due process, and the employee was ordered reinstated with backpay, even though she had been found to have committed the acts upon which the discharge was premised.

In unionized settings, of course, the availability of an employee representative is assured by the National Labor Relations Act in the person of a union steward or business agent. Satisfying this element of due process in a nonunion workplace requires substantial ingenuity and employer maturity. Some methods by which this right can be satisfied without creating a de facto union or unreasonably diminishing managerial control over the enterprise are discussed in Chapter 7, "Discipline Systems for Nonunion Employees."

Grievance Procedures

Another integral part of the discipline system is a credible grievance or dispute resolution procedure. In unionized workplaces, grievance procedures are developed as part of the union's right and obligation to represent its members. In nonunion workplaces, the employer must establish a credible method for discussing and contesting disciplinary events if employees are to receive due process. Various types of grievance procedures for nonunion employees are discussed in the Chapter 7, "Discipline Systems for Nonunion Employees."

Right to Appeal

Finally, due process requires that employees have the right to appeal disciplinary actions to an impartial decision maker or body. This is especially true when employment is severed. Again, most unionized workplaces are covered by contracts that require binding arbitration as the forum for such disputes, and it is out of these proceedings that much of the law of workplace due process has developed. For their own protection, nonunion employers must also recognize that they, too, are "obligated" to provide their employees with some similar method for impartial review. A failure to provide a credible appeal system simply pushes employees to obtain that review outside the workplace—in courts or before civil rights agencies. Designing and implementing a credible appellate review system with a nonunion workplace, however, requires skill and sensitivity. The emphasis here must be on what the employees will perceive as credible. Various types of appeal systems for nonunion employees also are discussed in Chapter 7.

Equal Treatment

Probably the most troublesome element in any discipline system, particularly one based on the traditional concept of punishment, is that of equal treatment. The difficulty lies in the shifting sands of employee perceptions of equality and the inevitable question of what constitutes sameness. The standards and the punishment can be absolutely equal as written, but employees are never equal. Each employee's work record, background, and psychological make-up is different, and the struggle frequently comes over the fact that the same treatment, mechanically applied to all employees, is often unfair. Nevertheless, any discipline system that is effective must maintain the appearance of fairness to all. Absolute, quantifiable equality in treatment, however, is not necessary, except in the most restrictive and battle-torn workplaces. In such places, employers are forced into a mechanical application of the rules, regardless of the special circumstances of employees, and in the name of equal treatment employers must dispense periodic injustices.

Nevertheless, the standardization of expectations and discipline is essential to the employer's ability to sustain penalties for just cause.[16] Within this standardization there may be room for the exercise of judgment and for individual treatment. However, whenever these judgments deviate from the norm to such an extent that the appearance of fairness is called into question, the system is in danger of collapse. While the employer may believe it is constructive to treat employees as individuals, the employees will, in fact, suspect favoritism or discrimination. Consequently, unless the basis for any specialized treatment outside the general rules of the system is readily apparent to all employees, the employer is at risk.

The key to maintaining equality in the administration of a discipline system is, again, record keeping. An employer can only be assured that discipline cases will conform to the desired pattern by keeping track of the specific causes for disciplinary actions. This is especially true when the degree of punishment to be administered is involved. Because no system, however detailed, can take into account every fact-mix, it is impossible to prescribe precise penalties for all cases. Moreover, to attempt to do so would result in a many-paged document reminiscent of a prison camp. Often, the best way to develop sensible patterns for reacting to behavioral problems is simply to allow them to evolve—all previous, similar cases should be taken into account, and the employer's reactions should be appropriate to each case.

Employees are less likely to feel that a discipline system is being operated unfairly if the only differences from case to case are in the severity of the penalty, not in its occurrence. This is most frequently seen in discussions over what is called mitigation of the penalty.[17] For example, an employee's tardiness, even though caused by an extremely difficult home situation, must still be disciplined. The employer may take the employee's special circumstance into account when determining the severity of the discipline.

The traditional, punishment-oriented systems allow little flexibility for individual treatment of employees. This may not be a fatal defect, however. The inherent danger of allowing individual judgment or discretion to enter into the discipline system is that any such allowances will be perceived by other employees as favoritism or unfairness. In a work environment where all subjective decisions are disputed, the employer often has to resort to complex and mechanical rules, which may produce more suffering and injustice in the long run, but which are still acceptable to the employees.

Summary

Although perhaps the oldest and most widespread of contemporary discipline systems, progressive discipline continues to be often misunderstood and misapplied by employers, with the result that employee due process is often denied. The beauty of the system is to be found in the ease with which it can be understood and communicated and the almost automatic manner in which it can operate. Its failings are to be found in those areas which rely on the affirmative exercise of human judgment and participation. The frequency of its failures is due to the fact that many employers do not understand that the system is not entirely self-effecting and that supervisors must be trained in its operation. Unless supervisors are schooled in the objectives and procedures of disciplinary conferences, the elements involved in various types of rule violations, and in the differences between equal and same treatment, the progressive system can be just as oppressive and destructive of a productive work environment as having no system at all.

Some of the technical elements of workplace due process are inherent in progressive discipline, e.g., notice, opportunity to improve. Other elements, such as a credible dispute resolution program, must be introduced deliberately, especially in nonunion settings. Moreover, some progressive discipline systems—especially those based on a punitive philosophy—actually deny due process as they degenerate into little more than steps to be followed by a supervisor who intends to fire a troublesome employee. When a discipline system is designed with a primary goal of getting rid of people, due process will almost always be absent.

Notes to Chapter 5

1. Situations such as theft, assaulting a supervisor, intoxication on the job, etc. which call for summary discharges and are considered serious enough that the employer is relieved of any responsibility to attempt corrective discipline, have been excluded from this discussion.

2. *Babcock & Wilcox Co.* (Dworkin), 41 LA 862, at 866.

3. Presumably the company rules are reasonably related to the expectations of the employer. Irrelevant, confusing, or unnecessarily complicated rules are destructive to the credibility of the entire personnel program.

4. *Local 878 v. Coca-Cola Bottling Co.* (1980), 613 F.2d 716, 103 LRRM 2380, at 2383. *See also Rochester Methodist Hosp.* (Heneman), 72 LA 276.

5. *See Werner-Continental* (LeWinter), 72 LA 1; *General Elec. Co.* (MacDonald), 72 LA 809; *Wilson Paper Co.* (Rose), 73 LA 1167; *A.P. Green Refractories Co.* (Williams), 64 LA 885; *Canron Inc.* (Marcus), 72 LA 1310; *City of Toledo* (Heinsz), 70 LA 216.

6. *See, e.g., Bethlehem Steel Co.* (Fishgold), 74 LA 507; *Witco Chem. Co.* (Light), 71 LA 919; *Alameda-Contra Costa Transit Dist.* (Koven), 76 LA 770; *Pickands Mather & Co.* (Witt), 76 LA 676; *Northrop Worldwide Aircraft Serv.* (Mewhinney), 75 LA 1059. *But see, e.g., City of Detroit* (Coyle), 75 LA 1045; *Dravo Doyle Co.* (Jones), 73 LA 649.

7. *Montague Mach. Co.* (Bornstein), 78 LA 172.

8. *Watauga Indus.* (Galambos), 78 LA 697.

9. *Gill Studios* (Goetz), 78 LA 915.

10. *Lucky Stores* (Darrow), 78 LA 233.

11. *Plantation Patterns* (Dallas), 78 LA 647.

12. *Id.*, at 649.

13. *Texas Int'l Airlines* (Dunn), 78 LA 893.

14. *Gill Studios, supra*, note 9.

15. *Fort Wayne Community Schools* (Deitsch), 78 LA 928.

16. *See, e.g., Arkansas Glass Container Corp.* (Teple), 76 LA 841; *Carborundum Co.* (Millious), 71 LA 828; *Niles, Shepard Crane & Hoist Corp.* (Alutto), 71 LA 828; *Sun Furniture Co.* (Szollosi) 71 LA 929; *General Mills Fun Group* (Martin), 72 LA 1285; *Boise Cascade Corp.* (Richardson), 66 LA 1302.

17. *See, e.g., Varbros Tool & Die Co.* (Kabaker), 42 LA 440; *Johns-Manville Perlite Corp.* (Traynor), 67 LA 1255; *Menasha Corp.* (Roumell), 71 LA 653; *Safeway Stores* (Winograd), 75 LA 430.

6

Punitive and Nonpunitive Discipline: A Comparison

Punitive Discipline

As noted in Chapter 5, the traditional or punitive approach to discipline is a system of ever-increasing penalties. An employee knows that what he or she is doing is contrary to acceptable levels of conduct, and is given multiple opportunities to conform to the company's rules. Each time the employee fails, he or she is warned and ultimately punished through the loss of pay, with the hope that, chastised, he or she will conform. Consequently, the punitive discipline system's hallmark is punishment, and in this, it closely parallels the discipline of children in the home. Progressive punitive discipline is recommended by arbitrators and in most human resources textbooks as the best, if not the only, way to effective discipline in the workplace. However, these authorities seem to ignore the need to discipline white-collar as well as blue-collar employees and the obvious inappropriateness of a disciplinary suspension without pay for a secretary or a bookkeeper. In spite of its shortcomings, progressive punitive discipline has dominated American industry as the accepted method of disciplining all employees for over half a century. Nevertheless, we continue to have undisciplined work forces.

Over the 20 years of my practice as a labor lawyer, countless employers with punitive discipline systems have complained that, in spite of a great deal of disciplining, employee productivity and morale continue to be low; absenteeism, tardiness, and turnover are high; and supervisors resist supervising either because they do not know what to do or do not like doing it. Their employees resist change, lack commitment to the operation, and resent almost all efforts to correct problems. In seeking a solution, however, many of these employers almost completely overlooked their discipline system as a cause. Rather, they (as I for much of my career) saw the solution to be a tougher and more stringent discipline system. The improvements we achieved resulted from better defining codes of conduct and training supervisors as effective enforcers. The improvements were achieved through compelling compliance with rules. Rarely was the workplace made a better place to work. Almost never were there quantum leaps in productivity or morale. At best, we cleaned out bad performers and kept those employees who functioned well, in spite of us. I discovered, however, that our efforts never resolved the essential problem: Why, even in unionized settings with employee representation, impartial dispute resolution, and the other basic elements of due process, does the discipline system not produce a disciplined work force?

The answer is that punitive discipline is flawed in both philosophy and design and, thus, in operation. It may be traditional and it may have historic dignity, but it is wrong conceptually and, if it works at all, it works only by accident.

Wrong Object[1]

The first problem with traditional punitive discipline is that its object is too limited or just plain wrong. The punitive system's goal is to force employees to comply with the employer's rules and policies. In and of itself, this is not a bad objective, but it is not the best one, either. Certainly, all employers want compliant employees who do not violate rules. As an object of a discipline system, however, this goal is too shallow. Rather, the employer should develop employees who have a sense of their own responsibilities and who attempt to fulfill them, and should consider rule compliance as a by-product only. The result may be the same, but the objects of these two views are vastly different.

The punitive system produces, at best, an employee mentality of having to comply with rules to avoid trouble. This psychology does not stimulate a desire to achieve. Staying out of trouble is not a positive value. A proper system should get employees to fulfill their responsibilities; rule compliance should be an incidental result.

Wrong-Issue Focus

Punitive systems also focus on the wrong issue. As operated, most of these systems spotlight the problem employee, an employee who has violated a rule. This employee was wrong, perhaps even bad and, like a child, deserves punishment. The system threatens the bad employee to force him or her to stop doing bad things.

Unfortunately, a system thus focused is intimidating and destructive to the employee's feelings of self-worth. His or her outward appearance may be one of contrition, belligerence, or passivity. But the inward reaction is one of hurt, anger, and resentment about being seen and dealt with as a problem or bad person, and the employee's thoughts may turn to denial, defensiveness, and antagonism. These employee reactions occur because the system focuses on them—they are identified with, and so become, the problem. As a result, they cannot deal with the problem dispassionately. Because it does not distinguish between the employee and the problem, the system is threatening and painful to the employee.

While the system calls for counseling that may be valuable in and of itself, its positive impact is limited by psychological blocks employees put up in defense against what they see as a personal attack. They react negatively; counseling brings up mixed desires to strike back and to run away. The discipline, while theoretically achieving its purpose, is destructive.

Wrong-Time Focus

The time focus of traditional punitive systems is also wrong. The sequence of the counseling discussion is usually as follows:

> **Supervisor:** John, last Tuesday you were late for the third time this month. This is excessive, and I warn you that if this keeps up you will be suspended without pay for three days according to our policy.
>
> **John:** If you say so.
>
> **Supervisor:** I say so and the company says so.

The focus of the discussion is entirely on John's past conduct. "You broke the rules. If you do that again, you will have something bad done to you." Not one positive note is struck during the entire counseling session—yet according to the tenets of punitive discipline, it could not be faulted, and every labor arbitrator would find that it satisfied the warning-step requirement of due process.

But, because the time and issue focuses were wrong, the supervisor lost an opportunity to create a productive employee-employer relationship. There was no look at the future, except as it involved an absence of the past. No hint was given about what could be done in the future to solve the problem. There was only a threat of what will happen if the past events are repeated.

In all likelihood, John is not a problem employee, but an employee with a problem. The time focus combined with the issue focus clouds this fact, and the employee is left alone and resentful with a threat hanging over him unless he solves the problem.

Wrong Rationale

The rationale behind progressive discipline systems is also incorrect. The primary tool of all punitive discipline systems is the threat and actuality of punishment. For some reason, employers believe that an employee who has violated a rule should be punished for this act.

But the employer gets no mileage out of punishment. All it does is create anger and resentment. Except for some possible psychic pleasure that the employer could derive, punishment serves no valid business purpose. The object of discipline should be rehabilitating employees who have violated expectations and making them productive members of the work force. Does punishment produce in employees the desire to do a better job?

Suspension without pay, as a form of punishment, is an ultimate absurdity. Almost all traditional punitive systems have a suspension-without-pay procedure as the final step before discharge. In fact, some labor arbitrators seem to imply that unless an employee is given a suspension as a last-ditch attempt to correct bad behavior, progressive discipline has not been implemented. Suspensions without pay, however, are neither theoretically necessary nor practically useful in any situation. The have the same effect and benefit as shooting yourself in the foot.

Indeed, many arbitrators have held that the absence of a disciplinary suspension does not result in the loss of due process where the final notice sufficiently informs the employee of the precariousness of his or her situation.[2] In addition, numerous unpublished awards involving Positive Discipline®[3] are also to this effect.

Consider the situation of a female employee who has a history of excessive absenteeism. This absenteeism has created significant disruptions in the company operations. Employees must be temporarily transferred or must work overtime to cover the absent worker. The bad employee is warned twice that unless she improves her attendance, she will be disciplined further. Nevertheless, her record does not improve. Under the punitive discipline system, the employee is suspended without pay for three days.

The results are that the employee is punished by the loss of wages and given more time off; the company has disrupted its own operations, incurred the extra overtime expense, and further penalized itself by losing the profit it could have made from the employee's labor. It is questionable whether the employee or the employer suffered the greater punishment. The punishment produces understandable employee resentment, but that resentment is nothing compared with the employer's resentment. Thus the natural desire on the part of the company and the supervisor, whose schedule was disrupted, is to move to the last step in the system and to get rid of the employee as quickly as possible.

Three arguments are usually given in favor of disciplinary suspensions as a necessary and valuable part of punitive discipline. First, the employee is given a forceful notice through a loss of income that his or her conduct must improve, and the loss of income ensures that the message gets across. Second, the employee is punished for poor conduct and, because of the punishment, will remember that the conduct is not acceptable. Third, assuming the loss of income is substantial enough (three days or more) to affect the home budget, the employee's spouse is drawn into the process, putting the employee under additional pressure to reform.

Only the third reason makes any sense at all. However, a strong, clearly written warning can accomplish the same purpose; it is sufficient to give the employee notice of his or her precarious condition and, if sent to the employee's home, it will most likely be seen by the spouse as well. A suspension creates nothing but resentment. Of course, sending the notice into the home carries with it other risks, especially when the cause for the discipline is excessive absenteeism. Usually the spouse demands some explanation of where the employee was when he or she was supposed to be at work.

Because the basic logic of a punitive discipline system is based on the premise that "the worse I treat you the better you will be," it is generally a failure. I suggest that, at a minimum, the disciplinary suspension be eliminated entirely and replaced with some other device for giving an emphasized final notice.

Wrong Dynamic

Punitive discipline systems also fail because their dynamic is adversarial. The supervisor is pitted against the employee, who is locked in a struggle with the faceless employer. The supervisor believes that the employee's conduct is creating trouble in the production unit and, as a result, the supervisor's life is miserable. Perhaps the supervisor is also in trouble; the employee is damaging the job performance of the supervisor as well as his or her own. It is in the supervisor's best interest to move the bad employee out as quickly as possible. At the very least, the employee is a bad element to be neutralized.

The employee, on the other hand, comes to the disciplinary encounter with all the American worker's baggage of resentment and suspicion of authority figures. Stimulated by the supervisor's attitude, the employee realizes that he or she is in a struggle for economic survival. The employee must prove to the supervisor that the facts are wrong, that the application of the policy is unfair, or that some special consideration should be given to individual circumstance. The employee also believes—perhaps correctly—that the supervisor's passion is to get rid of him or her. The employee thinks, "it's him against me, and he has the power and will not give me a break."

The stage is set from the beginning, and maneuvering for advantage starts immediately:

Supervisor: John, you have been late three times in the last two weeks and . . .

John: Wait a minute. Just when was I late?

Supervisor: My attendance card shows you were late on Wednesday, the twenty-third . . .

John: That may be what your card says, but ask anyone on the floor. I was not late last Wednesday. In fact, ask Joe. We came in together. Did Joe get marked late? Check it out. I'll bet he wasn't marked late.

Supervisor: Joe isn't the issue. You are. I know you were late on Wednesday because I personally saw you by the coffee machine at starting time and you didn't start work until ten minutes into the shift.

John: I was in the plant, wasn't I? I punched in on time, didn't I? How could I be late? Look at my time card. I bet it shows I punched in on time.

Supervisor: The policy says you must be at your work station ready to work at the beginning of the shift, and you were not, regardless of the time you punched in.

John: If that's the policy, I've never seen it. Besides, what were you doing watching me drinking coffee? If I was going to be late, why didn't you have the decency to tell me about the policy then? I could have a broken watch. Instead, you wanted to get me into trouble. You're the one at fault. You should be disciplined, not me.

Supervisor: John, it's not my responsibility to remind you of every policy all the time. You have a set of the rules. You should know what the policy is.

John: Lots of people get coffee when they come in. They don't get into trouble. Just watch Mary. You're singling me out.

Supervisor: Now, damn it, John. I've had enough of you . . . [and on . . . and on . . . and on].

If anything of real value is to be accomplished, obviously the combative, adversarial nature of counseling must be defused.

Wrong Direction

The hypothetical dialogue also illustrates another failing in the traditional discipline system. The direction is all wrong. It is downward, in the mode of parent to child. The employment relationship should be horizontal, adult to adult. So long as employees are treated like children, they will act like children—testing, pushing, trying to get away with whatever they can. When the entire disciplinary experience changes, allowing supervisor and employee to deal with each other as mature individuals, the greatest potential exists for employees to assume their responsibilities.

Insufficient Actors

In traditional punitive discipline systems, the responsibility for solving the problem is solely on the employee: "You must stop being absent excessively"; "You must not use obscene language"; or "You must be more productive."

While the counseling session has defined the problem and has made painfully clear the consequences of not solving it, the employee is essentially left alone with his or her dilemma. Hostile, angry, and ashamed, the employee must turn it around fast. No one will help, but everyone will be watching to see if a solution is found. Sometimes, because the solution is relatively simple, the employee succeeds. But even if the employee does succeed, he or she still has negative and antiproductive feelings and resentment.

Lack of Reward

But what if an employee succeeds in solving the problem? What if he or she steps up production, learns to come to work on time, or stops playing around and begins working? What does the employee get? Under the traditional system, the only reward lies in not being subjected to more discipline. Clearly, all rewards for solving a discipline problem under a traditional punitive system are negative. While it is true that some good supervisors go beyond the system and are supportive to employees who are turning it around, the system itself does not require this kind of behavior. The system stops too short to be truly successful.

The Supervisor's Role

Any one of the eight defects described here would be enough to justify the modification, if not outright scrapping, of any punitive discipline system. Yet this system grinds on as the dominant method of disciplining employees. The system does not work well, as a general rule, and when it does work, it is usually because supervisors have consciously or unconsciously overcome inherent flaws and gone beyond the system in practice.

In my experience, there is one additional reason why punitive discipline does not work. The reason—not a defect in the system *per se*—is that supervisors know progressive discipline doesn't work well, dislike using it and, as a result, use it only as a last resort.

Without question, discipline is one of the supervisor's hardest tasks. The difficulty increases when the supervisor has been promoted from within and is supervising employees who, perhaps the day before, were peers. For this reason, supervisors frequently do not discipline employees soon enough, let things slide, and overlook trouble signs. A discipline system that is demeaning and intimidating is bound to be the last resort—and then it is usually too late.

Nowhere is the failure of the traditional system more apparent than in white-collar environments. Because white-collar employees appear to be too sophisticated or responsible to be threatened with punishment, supervisors stuck with traditional punitive systems do not discipline at all. They feel demeaned by the process. This is also why many employers have no discipline policy for white-collar workers. The personnel director feels that the traditional system is inappropriate but does not know why and simply does without any system. Consequently, problems go unsolved until they cannot be ignored. At those times, employees are suddenly disciplined or even discharged. The actions taken confuse and frustrate employees. This is the environment that creates lawsuits alleging discrimination and abusive or wrongful discharge.

Nonpunitive Discipline

If the only difference between punitive and nonpunitive discipline were the deletion in the nonpunitive system of the suspension without pay as a final step prior to discharge, there would be no reason to devote more than a sentence or two to the subject. Superficially, their structures are deceptively similar, except for the disciplinary suspension step, but, in fact, their differences are dramatic and profound. Indeed, nonpunitive discipline is so different from punitive discipline that I caution against the design and implementation of such a system without assistance from someone or some organization with extensive experience working with it. Otherwise it will deteriorate into a punitive system with nontraditional labels.

While punitive discipline can be implemented with relative ease by mechanically following prescribed steps, the nonpunitive system demands much more. It requires a substantial change in the way a company views its employees. Moreover, it requires a change in the employer's traditional attitude toward supervisors. Nonpunitive discipline requires an alteration to the entire corporate culture. When properly designed and implemented, productivity increases and the need for disciplinary action decreases.[4] Although nonpunitive discipline requires supervisors to be much more than technical problem solvers and work schedulers (pushers), it makes it easier for supervisors to supervise. Supervisors using nonpunitive discipline are more willing and able to deal with employee problems before they become a basis for termination. Companies using nonpunitive discipline, such as AT&T, General Electric, Union Carbide, Shell Oil, Exxon, Northern States Power, Amoco, and Prince George Pulp and Paper Company, all report that the system produces a decline in disciplinary events and terminations, while improving employee morale and commitment to the enterprise. The reasons why nonpunitive discipline creates a positive work atmosphere are interesting.

The Object

While the punitive system seeks only to achieve employee compliance with rules, nonpunitive discipline's objective is to have employees take responsibility. From the date of hire, repeated emphasis is placed on employer-employee responsibilities. Everyone is told and reminded regularly that different parts of the operation must perform their special tasks if the company is to succeed and if employment is to be secure. The idea of responsibility becomes part of "shop talk." In fact, some employers believe that having employees sign a statement upon hire, which says they understand that to keep their jobs they must perform responsibly, is particularly helpful. Instead of giving employees a list of rules and regulations—which they are told not to violate to avoid trouble—the employer gives out the same list, but emphasizes that unacceptable conduct is a threat to the overall success of the enterprise. This distinction is the essence of the entire system. Consequently, when employees violate any of these rules, they act irresponsibly and fail to live up to their end of the bargain.

Although the object of discipline changes in a nonpunitive system, the need to define employer expectations does not. To ensure due process, the employer cannot simply tell employees that they are expected to be responsible and leave it at that. A published list of unacceptable acts would be virtually the same with a nonpunitive as with a punitive system. The difference is that in nonpunitive systems, the rules are called employee responsibilities. And the employer publicizes that one of its responsibilities is to make sure that its expectations are clearly defined. This method, by its nature, is an affirmative and not a negative act.

The Focus

If an employee fails in one of his or her responsibilities, the nonpunitive approach focuses attention not on the employee and his or her problem but on the problem and its solution. In this way, the employee is removed as the central issue. Not being threatened, the employee is thus more ready to dispassionately discuss and try to solve the problem. In a very literal sense, the employee is treated as someone who has a problem requiring a solution, not as a problem employee who has to be subjugated. The employee is still "OK."

Although the problem must be defined as part of the resolution process, even in nonpunitive discipline, the primary focus is on finding a solution. If an employee has a tardiness problem, the supervisor and employee discuss why. Does he or she have transportation problems, domestic problems, or chores that create difficulties in the morning? Whatever the cause, the supervisor and employee together develop a solution. The solution may be restructuring the early morning regimen or using a different mode of transportation. Perhaps the solution is no more than encouraging the employee to go to an employee assistance program for help. Retraining in some aspect of the job might be another option. Whatever the solution, its achievement becomes a new part of the employee's responsibilities so that he or she can aim for a specified goal. Effecting the mutually developed solution, however, is up to the employee.

Essential to refocusing the process in nonpunitive discipline is changing the time focus from the past to the future. Once the problem has been defined, all supervisory and employee efforts are directed toward the future. "What can we do to ensure the performance of your responsibilities in the future?" is the important question. The employee is not haunted by continual reflections on past misconduct. The focus is affirmative rather than condemnatory. The joint development of a method to correct problems does not leave employees floundering with a difficulty they already have demonstrated an inability to resolve. Moreover, employees are convinced in most cases that supervisors are not trying to get rid of them, but are finding ways of helping them keep their jobs.

The Method

Nonpunitive discipline replaces threats and punishment with encouragement. Certainly, the ultimate result of failed discipline is termination, even in this system. However, employment termination after the use of nonpunitive discipline is caused by repeated failures to successfully implement agreed-upon solutions. Thus, termination is not the ultimate punishment, but the result of a failure of the discipline system. Job retention rather than termination is the focus of discipline.

Instead of treating employees more harshly with the intent of making them better, nonpunitive discipline encourages employees to perform defined responsibilities through intermediate and compassionate goal setting. If an employee must be terminated, it is because he or she cannot perform those responsibilities satisfactorily, not because the employee is a bad person who deserves punishment.

The Dynamic

By now it is obvious that the dynamic of nonpunitive discipline is cooperation, not combat. Since the process focuses on what can be done in the future to solve a problem, and the method uses encouragement to achieve the fulfillment of responsibilities, the dynamic must be cooperation. The employer is working with the employee to solve a problem. Neither is attempting to force his or her will on the other; thus they have a common goal.

The Direction

The direction of the employer-employee relationship is horizontal—adult-to-adult—not downward as in a parent and child relationship. As adults, the supervisor and employee discuss the problem and its effects on the workplace, develop a solution to the problem, and agree to its implementation. Nothing is imposed; conclusions and decisions are mutual. Incrimination and recrimination that demean the employee and cause psychological blockage do not take place in these interactions.

The Actors

Critical to this process is the joint creation of the solution. The employee is never left alone to find a remedy. The supervisor also has a stake in the outcome. It is their joint responsibility to see to it that the employee fully performs all obligations.

In this respect, some supervisors must refocus their attitudes and goals. Their job is not to identify troublesome employees and quickly get rid of them, but to run a stable, productive unit. Eliminating employees is costly; the employer loses its training investment. A supervisor with high turnover is failing the employer by not fulfilling his or her responsibility. Consequently, supervisors must understand that they have a real stake in solving employees' problems. The solution must be realistic and, while the employee may be the primary actor, the supervisor, as coach, must play a very active role.

Nonpunitive discipline puts emphasis on recognizing the efforts and successes of employees on the mend. Some supervisors, unfortunately, see no reason to commend employees for doing what the employees are expected to do. This attitude is simply wrong. Employees who solve personal work problems should be recognized for their effort and success with, at least, a word indicating that the change has been noticed. Giving encouragement to an employee having trouble implementing a solution to a problem is also important. This is part of the joint effort by employee and supervisor and part of the reward. Not being subjected to further discipline is a negative reward—or no reward at all. Positive reinforcement through recognition is a vital part of nonpunitive discipline.

Implementation

Theory may be interesting, but it is without value unless it can be put into a workable system. The chart below sets out the procedures of a nonpunitive system in practice.[5]

The first conference should not be the first time a supervisor has noted and discussed a problem with an employee. Few causes for nonsummary discipline occur suddenly. Absenteeism, poor production, poor attitude, carelessness, all develop over time. A good supervisor working with this system has had several informal conversations with the employee about what may be a developing problem. If these conversations do not have their intended effect or if the violative con-

Nonpunitive Discipline

First Conference	Second Conference	Decision Day
• Verbal solution and affirmation • Note to file • Follow-through	• Written solution and affirmation • Follow-through	• Written affirmation and final solution • Follow through

```
        └─unsolved─┘      └─unsolved─┘          │
            │                 │                 │
  solved            solved             solved
    │                 │                 │
    ↓                 ↓                 ↓
```

Recognition and Reinforcement (R & R)

duct appears without warning, the supervisor uses a more structured approach, as necessary.

First Conference

At the first conference, the supervisor presents the facts as evidence of violative conduct. He or she defines the problem and then asks the employee whether the facts—not the conclusions drawn from the facts—are accurate. If a significant dispute exists, further investigation would be warranted, and the conference would be adjourned. Once the facts are agreed on, the supervisor and employee discuss why these create difficulty in the workplace and show a failure in performing employee responsibilities. This entire discussion should be very short and in as few sentences as possible. The reason for brevity is that the focus at this point is on the past and, therefore, negative, and the purpose of the conference is to create an affirmative feeling and result.

After defining the problem, the discussion shifts to its main purpose: development of a constructive solution. The problem is broken into parts, and the supervisor and employee discuss how to resolve the problem. Since it is important that implementation be a joint effort, the supervisor should consider what he or she can do to participate in the process. The supervisor's role should be an apparent part of the solution.

After the solution is developed, a timetable for its implementation is set. Both the solution and the timetable are agreed on by supervisor and employee. After discussion, the supervisor records what took place, including the solution and timetable, in memorandum to the employee's file. A copy of this memo is given to the employee.

A Case Study

The following case study illustrates the way in which nonpunitive discipline works.

> Note to File: First Conference
> Re: John Smith; Excessive Absenteeism
> On October 16, 1987, I had a first conference with John Smith concerning an attendance problem.
> Facts: Between August 1, 1987 and October 13, 1987, John was absent or tardy six times: August 1, tardy (30 minutes); August 16, absent; September 10, absent; September 21, absent; October 6, tardy (20 minutes); October 13, absent.
> Explanation: John explained that all absences were caused by illnesses, usually what seemed to be viruses. One lateness was caused by a late bus. Another lateness occurred when John got into a discussion with Hank Snow in the canteen and got to his desk twenty minutes late.
> Further investigation was not warranted. The only question was whether John was late on October 6, even though he was in the building. Since he admitted that he was not "at work" on time, he was late under our rules.
> Solution: John and I agreed that part of his responsibility as an employee was to have regular attendance. Four absences and two latenesses in ten weeks is not regular attendance and causes problems in the department because of our work load. John agreed that he had to take better care of himself and that a possible solution would be more sleep. John also agreed to be at the bus stop early enough to anticipate late buses and said he was cutting it too close. We reviewed the absenteeism policy that allows one absence or lateness per month. John agreed to get a bus schedule and discuss with me which bus should be taken to ensure his being on time under most circumstances. Finally, John agreed that he had to be at his desk ready for work at 9 a.m. Conversation with other employees should be limited to nonwork time.
>
> Peter Brown, Supervisor

After the first conference, the supervisor should follow up by asking John if he got a copy of the bus schedule and if his plan to leave earlier in the morning is working out. The employee must know that the supervisor is working with him and that he is not alone. The supervisor adds a note to the memorandum of the first conference that explains when he completed the follow-through. It must be noted that the burden to execute the solution is on the employee. The supervisor cannot assume any of the responsibility (such as getting the bus schedule), or the employee will develop a dependence and subsequent excuses for nonperformance, such as "I thought he would do it."

If the solution developed in the first conference is successful, the employee is put into Recognition and Reinforcement (R&R). When the timetable has been met, the supervisor recognizes the employee's accomplishment and then notes it in his file. Periodically, the supervisor reinforces continued good performance by complimenting the employee.

Second Conference

If the conference did not produce the desired result, a second conference is called to determine why the first solution did not work. At this meeting, the facts are reviewed briefly; then the reason for failure is analyzed. Once this analysis is concluded, a new solution is developed with a new timetable. But this time, the solution is written down and signed by the employee. The signed agreement or affirmation also contains a statement that the performance of responsibilities is an essential condition for retaining employment. The agreement would be as follows:

Note to File: Second Conference
Re: Understanding and Affirmation, John Smith; Excessive Absenteeism

On January 15, 1988, I had a second conference with John Smith about attendance.

Facts: John had a first conference on October 16, 1987. Since then, John was absent three more times (November 10, December 15, and January 13) and late once (January 5, 25 minutes).

Explanation: John explained that his absences on November 10 and January 13 were due to colds. His absence on December 15 was caused by the illness of his wife and his need to care for their child. The lateness on January 5 was caused by John's taking a late bus.

Further investigation was not warranted.

Solution: John and I agreed that he had to get his health problem under control. I suggested that he consult the company doctor to see if he needed some preventive treatment. John and I also agreed that we would set up a method for care of his son in the event his wife gets sick again. John thinks his mother can come over. If his mother can't babysit, I will help him find some other solution. John also agreed to get up 30 minutes earlier each day to make sure he would get the earlier bus.

Peter Brown, Supervisor

I agree to this solution and agree to be at work regularly and to be on time. I understand that if I have three more attendance violations before August 1, 1988, I will be terminating my employment.

John Smith

Once more, the supervisor must follow through and record results:

Note to File, January 22, 1988
Re: Follow-through on John Smith's attendance problem.

On January 22, 1988, I met with John about the solution we had developed to his attendance problem. He saw Dr. Jones on January 18, after work. The doctor told him he was in good health and recommended more sleep and vitamins to stay healthy. John said he was following the doctor's advice. John told me he had talked to his mother about taking care of his child in the event his wife is ill again, and she refused. I said he could take a personal holiday if his wife got sick again and if he called in before the start of the shift. I told him that using personal holidays for this purpose could not be a long-term solution. John agreed to check with his wife's friends for substitute child care.

Decision Day

If the solution is successful and the timetable met, the employee would go into R&R. But let's assume that our employee continues to have a problem. At this point there is a serious question about his willingness or ability to fulfill his responsibilities as an employee. Under the traditional system, he would have received his written warnings, and his continued unacceptable conduct would have resulted in a disciplinary suspension without pay. With nonpunitive discipline, however, the disciplinary suspension is eliminated. Instead, the employee is given time to consider whether he wishes to continue his employment.

The purpose of the decision time is to require the employee to focus on his or her dilemma. The employer is ready to terminate the employment unless he or she becomes responsible, as responsible is defined by the employer—not the employee. To keep the job, therefore, the employee must decide whether to conform or not. The decision is the employee's, not the employer's. The employer's decision has already been made—if you want to work here you must be responsible in the way I expect you to be. Because of all the notices the employee has received, the employee knows exactly what the employer expects.

The time given the employee to make this decision varies from one implementation to another. Some employers give the time between one work day and another. Some prefer to allow a weekend. Others give the employee the next day off with pay. The question, however, is always the same: Do you want to work here and conform to what I expect from an employee?

The concept of giving a day off with pay instead of the usual suspension without pay is usually received by employers being introduced to nonpunitive discipline with derision and shock. Certainly, it sounds like a holiday. More than that, it sounds like a reward for good conduct, not the final step in a discipline system. But consider the supervisor's objective and what he or she wants to accomplish.

The object is to avoid the cost of employee turnover and develop responsible employees. Without question, the cost of one day's pay is far less than the cost of having to replace the employee. Moreover, the cost of dealing with angry and resentful employees is infinitely higher than a day's pay. One lawsuit, one charge, one arbitration, or one union campaign would dwarf the cost of all decision days a company might have over several years. Finally, the bookkeeping department's headaches over calculating and deducting a day's pay from a salaried employee are not worth the money. Obviously, taking away a day's pay from the employee is not done to save money. Then why do it?

To punish? Punishment may satisfy a supervisor's psychic need for revenge, but it breeds anger and resentment in the employee. In addition, it creates an "I've paid my debt" mentality. Punishment has too many negative side-effects to be a useful tool. To drive home a point? While this may be praiseworthy, to drive that point home with punishment neutralizes, if not negates, the intended purpose.

The decision day off with pay achieves the objective without any of the negative side effects. In fact, it enhances the positive effect the employer is trying to achieve.

During the decision-day conference, the supervisor or, if appropriate, the director of personnel initially reviews the problem and the failed solutions. This review is not accusatory but explanatory: The employer is concerned that the employee may be unwilling or unable to be responsible. Since solutions were jointly developed and implemented, their lack of success indicates that perhaps no solution will work. Consequently, John must determine how committed he really is to working for this particular company. Does he really want to be employed by a company with these expectations? Perhaps he is better suited to work elsewhere. This question must be answered by the employee alone. He must be compelled to commit himself and to understand the importance of the decision.

His sense of the urgency and the finality of his decision, however, must be heightened. At the same time, he cannot be permitted to redirect his feelings in a negative or defensive way against the employer. The essential dilemma of his situation must be clearly before him: If employment is to continue, he must perform his responsibilities and fulfill the employer's expectations; if he cannot or will not commit himself, his employment will be terminated. The choice is his. The employer is not doing anything to him. The ultimate demonstration of the employer's good will is that the employee is given time off without loss of pay to consider his decision. The employee has nothing to resent except, possibly, the employer's insistence that he fulfill expectations. In the decision-day conference, the supervisor says:

> Supervisor: John, we have talked about the fact that the solutions we had developed haven't worked. You continue to be late and absent. I have a serious concern about whether you want to continue to work here. I don't want

your commitment now. I want you to stay away from work tomorrow. You will be paid, so you don't have to worry about that. I just want you to consider whether you want to work here. When you come back the next day, I will want your answer. If you decide that you cannot or do not want to continue, fine. I will make the termination as easy as possible. If you decide you want to continue, great. However, I will want a firm commitment from you that you will fulfill all of your responsibilities, including coming to work regularly and on time. If you do not, then we have both failed and your employment will be ended.

Because the time off inflicts no pain other than that involved in making a decision, the employee has nothing in the way of his coming to grips with his situation. Moreover, the stark reality of the employer's ability to actually take away his job is driven home with objective force.

After the Decision Day

When the employee comes back, he will be required to commit himself. If he decides to keep his job, he and the supervisor analyze why earlier solutions did not work. The focus is on creating a new solution—one that must work. Together they try, one more time, to solve the problem. Once a solution is developed, the employee signs it and affirms his intent to live up to all of the employer's expectations. This final stage of nonpunitive discipline would appear in the record as follows:

Note to File: March 24, 1988
Re: Decision and Affirmation, John Smith; Excessive Absenteeism

Facts: On March 23, 1988, John Smith was given a decision day off with pay. John had conferences on October 16, 1987 and January 15, 1988 for excessive absenteeism. Solutions to his problem were agreed to at each conference. Nevertheless, on February 16 and on March 21 John was again absent. John's explanation for both absences was the flu. The decision day was given so John could decide whether he wanted to continue as an employee of the company. Twelve attendance violations in less than seven months is unacceptable.

Peter Brown, Supervisor
Decision and Affirmation: I have decided to keep my job. I understand, however, that to keep my job it is my

responsibility to take care of myself and come to work on time. I know that one more attendance violation before August 1, 1988, will result in the termination of my employment. After that date I must continue to have an acceptable attendance record to keep my job. I understand that I must perform all of my responsibilities as an employee and that my violation of any rule of conduct within the next 12 months will result in termination of my employment.

John Smith

Again, the supervisor should follow up to encourage the employee and help him through any difficulty. Although the supervisor's participation is now limited, his role as a coach continues, and the project remains a joint effort.

The Final Outcome

Of course, nonpunitive discipline can fail. Some individuals will never be able to reach an acceptable level of performance. The speed with which nonpunitive discipline identifies these types and moves them on to other employers is no slower than that with progressive systems and, because supervisors are more alert to their responsibilities, can be much faster. The value of nonpunitive discipline, however, is the high probability of success. If an employee can be stimulated into productivity and responsibility, this system will do it. In the process, employees view themselves, their jobs, and their employer positively.

One of the greatest positive outcomes of nonpunitive discipline is its effect on supervisors. With proper training, supervisors experience a community with their employees. Moreover, supervisors lose their fear of discipline and employee encounters. They are no longer reluctant to supervise, because the process is nonthreatening and nonpunitive. As a result, the system is used, and used much earlier as a problem solver than the traditional progressive system. Moreover, because nonpunitive discipline is not demeaning, it may be the only employee enhancement and control system that will work for white- and pink-collar employees.

Summary

Essential to the success of the nonpunitive (or punitive) system is the continuing role of the supervisor as a counselor.

The supervisor acts not only as an early warning for employees to avoid the need for formal discipline but also, between steps, encourages and supports the employee's struggle to solve a problem. Assuming a good hiring and orientation program that produces employees with realistic potential for long-term employment, supervisors must be charged with ensuring that the potential is realized. A discharge is a failure, of course. The failure should be due to the employee's unwillingness or inability to be responsible and committed to the enterprise, not to the supervisor's failure to supervise properly. Assessment of this dynamic should be the central and most important part of the evaluation of the supervisor's job performance.

Notes to Chapter 6

1. Portions of the following discussion were originally published articles by this author in *Personnel*, the magazine of the American Management Association in October and November, 1985.

2. See *National Supermkts.* (Ross), 79 LA 523; *Montague Mach. Co.* (Bornstein), 78 LA 172; *Wolf Mach. Co.* (High), 72 LA 510; *Pete Pasquinelli Co.* (Jones), 68 LA 1068; *Pretty Prods.* (Stouffer), 51 LA 688.

3. See note 4, *infra.*

4. The most refined system of nonpunitive discipline is that marketed under the trade name "Positive Discipline®" by Performance Systems Corporation of Dallas, Texas. This company has tracked the effects of nonpunitive discipline on productivity and other "bottom-line" measures, the most complete study being that of General Electric.

5. The structure of the nonpunitive system described here is generic and not intended to be, nor is, descriptive of any proprietary system. The structure of a "Positive Discipline" system is unique and is similar to the structure described here only in a generic sense.

7

Discipline Systems for Nonunion Employees

One of the more complex problems faced by a company with employees not represented by a union has been to develop a credible due process discipline system. The system must be credible in the sense that employees feel secure that discipline will occur only when justified and necessary and that it will be free from personal biases. Employee insecurity increases when there is no effective means of testing the justification and necessity of disciplinary action. In this regard, unions, attempting to organize employees, frequently find that their arguments based upon protection from unfair treatment and advocacy within the discipline system are the most difficult for employers to combat. Loud employer pronouncements of fairness cannot overcome a single instance of discipline that employees perceive to have been unjust, even though the discipline may, in fact, have been warranted.

The reason for the complexity of this problem lies in the nature of discipline itself. Discipline systems involve the confluence and accommodation or resolution of conflicting rights. Moreover, the rights are largely perceived; they are not codified by any statute. Nevertheless, they are rights about which the parties feel very strongly. Consequently, the stage of discipline on which these battles are fought is highly charged with feelings of rights not recognized as often as rights denied. Where the struggle demands a winner and loser, the potential for turbulence in the workplace is great and the desire of employees to join together and enlist the aid of an outsider to tip the scales in their favor inevitable. Where the drama requires no winners and losers but cooperative problem solving, the issue of rights has been resolved before the curtain goes up and the action involves only the implementing of agreed principles. The complexities often arise most at the time the employer realizes that the recognition of employee rights requires some concession from traditional managerial power.

In the most simplistic sense, the manager of a company is theoretically concerned first and foremost with the operation of the enterprise in a profitable manner. In this context, labor is nothing more than a tool of production, entitled only to those things necessary to enable it to function. What those necessary things may be are subject to great variance in interpretation. Serious problems develop when an employer, with a limited sense of what employees need, is confronted with a work force which demands, subtly or not, its desire for rights the employer may not even be prepared to consider. (Many employers would never concede that some of the rights discussed in Chapter 3 apply to their employees.) For these employers, a "living" wage and "reasonable" benefits totally fulfill their employer obligations. In return, the employees are expected to work hard in docile submissiveness. Protesters and complainers are viewed as troublemakers with bad attitudes and are eventually discharged. After all, the reasoning goes, the company does belong to the employer, and its representatives should have the unrestricted right to run it as they see fit. If the employees do not like it, they can quit. Wages and benefits will be kept at those levels absolutely necessary to keep employees with the requisite skills.

Any suggested diminution of the employer's total authority and flexibility is met with great resentment and, often, skepticism.

Fragile Systems

While the consummate industrial capitalist is portrayed here only to make a point, it is remarkable how frequently such employers are encountered, even in today's world. They zealously guard their private domains and resist any change which requires them to consider anything which cannot be immediately quantified. However, either as a means of increasing employee satisfaction for the purpose of enhancing productivity or as a means of avoiding unionization, employers find it necessary to yield some of their absolute authority. It is in the area of discipline and due process that concessions are most frequently required and the most productive. In doing so, however, these employers resist any material infringement upon their discretion and insist that it is vital to the operation of the plant that they maintain ultimate control. Consequently, discipline systems in unorganized companies frequently do not satisfy all of the employees' rights. The result is a fragile system that will only work as long as there is widespread acceptance of the actions of the employer. Any mistake or unpopular decision may totally fracture the credibility of the system and, with it, the security of the employees. As noted earlier, employee insecurity creates innumerable problems for the employer and, ultimately, produces union activity.

Nevertheless, many employers of unorganized workers appear willing to operate in this uncertain atmosphere. They take their chances on always being right, and they have faith that, even if a mistake is made, their goodwill among the employees will overcome temporary unpleasantness. As evidence of their recognition of the fragility of the employee relations, disciplinary discussions are timid or tentative, and discipline is often confused and incomplete. As a result, employees are not well controlled and take advantage of the employer's hesitancy. The operation acquires a country club atmosphere, and supervisors are reduced to leadmen and referees.

In this respect, one company with whom I have had contact with about 250 employees had fought off 10 union drives in 13 years. There had been tie votes, one- and two-vote margins, and lost elections, which had been subsequently overturned and won. The plant's management and supervisors had become so concerned about the effect of every decision on the employees and whether any degree of constraint or unpopularity would shift the delicate balance of votes that the operation of the plant became extremely difficult, and overall productivity was low. Finally, when the union returned for its nearly annual drive, the supervisors simply refused to campaign, believing that the union would actually make it easier to deal with the employees. The company lost the election. Part of the problem was the employer's discipline system, which depended on the employer's discretion. The employees had been able to use the employer's fears that its actions would be perceived as unfair to obtain inappropriate liberties.

Certainly, increasing or maintaining high productivity levels and avoiding union organization are two principal reasons for any employer of unorganized employees to have a credible discipline system. These reasons are not the only reasons, however, and perhaps, are no longer the most important.

Employment at Will

A strong trend has developed toward making it a requirement of law that employees can be discharged only for just cause after having been accorded due process. This trend has matured in several states. In other states it is only in its gestation stage, but the signs are that it will continue to grow and emerge kicking and screaming into the employment world. Consequently, it is clear now that we are seeing the beginning of the end of employment at will as even a general proposition.[1]

Actually, the concept of employment at will has been chipped away at for many years, and, having taken off the easy pieces, the sculptors are turning to the foundation itself. Under the banner of developing laws, the present attack is against what are being called "abusive" discharges. The intent is to have state legislatures and courts declare that no employee can be discharged except for just cause, whatever that may turn out to be. Discharges would then be litigated before an arbitrator or in a court as a matter of law, not as the result of an agreement.[2]

Although first popularly espoused during the Industrial Revolution, the courts in most jurisdictions in the United States to this day have persistently held to the common law view that a written or verbal contract for employment for an indefinite period is terminable at the will of the employer for good, bad, or no cause whatsoever. Indeed, this principle was declared by the Supreme Court in *Adair v. United States* and has been actually codified in Georgia.[3]

Over the last forty years, however, various federal and state laws have circumscribed and limited this general rule. The Labor Management Relations Act, or the Taft-Hartley Act, prohibits discharges or discipline for participating in concerted activities. Title VII of the Civil Rights Act of 1964 prohibits discipline or discharges based upon an employee's race, color, religion, sex, or national origin. The Rehabilitation Act of 1973 prohibits discipline or discharges due to non-job related handicaps and disabilities. The Age Discrimination Act of 1967, as amended, prohibits the disciplining or discharge of an employee between the ages of 40 and 70 because of his or her age. In addition, several statutes, e.g., the Fair Labor Standards Act and the Occupational Safety and Health Act, prohibit the discharge or disciplining of an employee for exercising rights given by these laws.

Several states have added to these limitations as well by restricting the employer's right to discipline or discharge employees for conviction of certain crimes or for refusing to submit to polygraph tests. Nevertheless, neither the federal government nor any state has passed any legislation which destroys the basic principle of employment at will. Some state legislatures,[4] however, have just such legislation pending, and it is not beyond belief that someday one of these proposed laws will be enacted, opening a new era in employer/employee relations. The arguments are being made in a most eloquent and learned fashion, and they are not without substantial popular appeal.[5]

While up to this time legislatures appear reluctant to eliminate the basic principle of employment at will altogether, courts have been presented with an ever-increasing assault.[6] The theories used by former employees and their creative lawyers can be separated into three large groups: implied contract, public policy, and tort.[7]

Implied Contract

The implied contract attack is two-pronged. The first prong is that an obligation of good faith and fair dealing should exist as implied in every employment relationship. As with certain commercial contracts, the parties to a contract of employment[8] must deal with each other fairly and in good faith. Good faith and fair dealing, of course, are argued to include concepts of due process and just cause. Consequently, employers in states (such as California and Montana) that have adopted this concept as implied in every employment arrangement have a special reason to ensure that their internal policies and procedures will satisfy these rights. Of course, the effect of adopting this implied obligation is that every termination decision (and, theoretically, every disciplinary decision that threatens ultimate termination or denies or retards promotion) becomes subject to scrutiny and decision by a court or jury. Needless to say, juries are more likely to be made up of a majority of employees rather than employers. The object of every former employee-plaintiff is to get past pretrial motions and to the jury where the potential for a favorable verdict is high.

The second prong of the implied contract theory is that the employer should be bound by its representations to employees. These representations, it is argued, constitute enforceable elements of the contract between the parties. Representations can be both oral and written. As a result, statements by an employer that it will treat employees fairly or, even, that an employee will be employed until retirement, may be binding and enforced against the employer. The meaning and effect of such statements may end up before a jury for decision. It is not surprising, therefore, that employees are winning many of these lawsuits and obtaining verdicts in six figures.

A fruitful source for employer representations has been employee manuals and policy statements, although retirement plan documents and employment ads and other discharge materials have been used. Of the bases for finding contractual commitments to enhanced employment security, these documents are the most easily controlled. Several elementary principles can be followed to avoid this kind of liability:

1. The employer should never make representations, oral or in writing, concerning any type of employment security beyond that of an employment at will prior to the applicant's actual employment unless it is prepared to be bound by them. In most situations, applicants are looking for work and the company to which they are applying seems just fine. They do not have to be sold on the employer. Nevertheless, inexperienced interviewers often make the mistake of puffing about their workplace as a wonderful place to work. On occasion, the policy manual is even displayed. Under these circumstances, whatever is said or presented in writing prior to employment may well be argued later as the basis for an employee's decision to accept employment and an integral part of the bargain. Later written disclaimers by an employer to the effect that employment is at-will may not be sufficient to overcome the strength of the pre-employment representations. In one case, for instance, an employee was able to establish that promises of employment security were made to him to induce a move from California to New York. Documents subsequently executed by him stating that his employment was at-will did not rebut these representations.[9]

2. Employment application forms and other documents involved in the employment process should contain statements that the employment is at-will. In most cases, these statements have been held to be adequate to establish that the employee accepted employment with the clear understanding that employment is at-will and, therefore, cannot later claim another employment status. The Sears, Roebuck and Co., for instance, includes the following as part of its employment application:

> In consideration of my employment, I agree to conform to the rules and regulations of Sears, Roebuck and Company and my employment and compensation can be terminated with or without cause, and with or without notice, at any time, at the option of either the company or myself. I understand that no store manager or representative of Sears, Roebuck and Company, other than the president or vice president of the company, has any authority to enter into any agreement for employment for any specified period of time or to make any agreement contrary to the foregoing.

This disclaimer has been held to be effective as establishing an at-will relationship.[10]

The key to successfully using a disclaimer is that it actually communicates to the employee that he or she can be terminated for any (or no) reason and without due process. In these cases, it is arguable that a simple statement that employment is at-will adequately communicates that message effectively unless the statement is further clarified as in the Sears statement. An employee may easily argue that the phrase "at-will" meant nothing to him or her at the time. Another form of disclaimer is as follows:

> I understand and agree that, if employed, my employment will not be covered by any contract for a specific term and that my relationship with the company can be terminated by the company at any time without prior notice or warning.

As the damage awards have accumulated, fewer employers object to language this strong in an application, choosing to lose an occasional applicant rather than risk the expense of being a defendant.

3. Employee manuals should state clearly that employment is at-will or can be terminated at any time, that no

supervisor can modify policies, and that policies can be changed at any time. Certainly, these statements may appear to contradict the purposes of other policy statements and procedures that apply to due process for employees. They need not actually do this, however, and the two can co-exist very well.

It is impossible in a code of conduct, for instance, to list all possible ways an employee may fail to act responsibly. Consequently, as a general proposition, no code of conduct should purport to be complete. It is, therefore, consistent for an employer to state that the code of conduct is illustrative only and is to be understood by the employee as a guide only. This recognizes the possibility that something justifying discipline could arise that was not anticipated when the code was constructed.

The same is true of grievance and appeal systems. Although an employer hopes that all eventualities will be covered by its policies and procedures, there is always the possibility that an unanticipated situation will have to be handled outside the system. For this reason, unless the employer is prepared to be bound to policies as written, policies should be prefaced with a statement that they will govern most cases but that there may be circumstances in which the procedures may not be followed. While I encourage employers to act as if bound, I would suggest that the problem of being bound should not create much concern. Supervisors can make mistakes and it may be very important, in the face of some of these, to be able to argue that the employer was not bound by the language of the policy itself.

Employer concern that employees may not take policies seriously because they are not all-inclusive should be satisfied by a prefatory statement similar to the following:

> [*Employer*] believes that each employee is an individual who deserves to be treated as an individual. Consequently, it is impossible to develop a policy that will govern or control every situation. The following policies were created to apply in most situations that may occur; however, where [Employer] believes that the individual needs or circumstances of an employee need to be honored or require special consideration, the policies may not be followed or used in every respect.

In essence, an employer seeking to avoid a finding in a court of law that an employee manual or other similar document is a contract should use various disclaimers to indicate that the manual is not intended to be a contract and is not a complete statement of potential employer actions. Specifically, the employer should destroy the elements of a common law contract by stating that policies are unilaterally created by the employer and can be changed at any time, and by ensuring that policy statements form no part of the pre-employment process.

Public Policy

Many courts have been carving out exceptions to the employment-at-will principle on the basis of public policy. In certain circumstances, courts are finding that a discharge violates some significant policy for the public good and, therefore, should be invalidated, even though employment was at the will of the employer. As a general rule, the public policy exception requires an explicit statement of a public policy; it cannot be implied. Consequently, most courts look for legislative expression of public policies and will not inject one into a case when none can be found.

Just cause or fairness, for instance, generally will not be implied as a public policy. A prohibition against terminating an employee for filing a workers' compensation claim,[11] or serving on a jury,[12] or exercising political free speech,[13] or refusing to commit perjury or some other illegal act,[14] however, will be enforced because the court can find a legislative expression of that policy in a statute.

Statutes that contain their own enforcement provisions cannot be a source for a separate cause of action based upon the public policy statement within that statute. Consequently, there is no independent cause of action where the alleged cause for discharge was sexual harassment,[15] age,[16] handicap,[17] or any other reason prohibited by statute and remedied through a civil rights agency, department of labor, or labor board procedure, as set out by the statute.

Attorneys representing former employees, of course, will encourage courts to find public policy statments embodied in legislative pronouncements almost anywhere. The most potentially fruitful ground, yet largely untilled, is that of state and federal constitutions. Although these documents were originally intended to define the rights of a citizen vis-à-vis the state or federal government, broad expressions of due process and similar rights within those documents are tempting. The broadest interpretation to date is the Court of Appeals for the Third Circuit holding in *Novosel v. Nationwide Insurance Co.*[18] In that case an employee's discharge for refusing to support his employer's position on pending legislation was held to have violated the public policy embodied in the first amendment's protection of political free speech. Whether more courts will reach into state and federal constitutions for statements of public policy in private employment situations is unknown, but it is a real possibility. It is a fairly short jump from the first to the fourth and fifth amendments to read due process into an employment relationship. All a court need do is find that a job is "property." This is already a fact in many European countries.

Torts

Former employees who sue employers following a discharge often seek to include various torts as causes of action in addition to their claims for breach of implied contract or violation of public policy. This is partly because liability under a public policy or implied contract theory rarely will award damages beyond the loss of compensation. Tort damages, on the other hand, may award psychic (pain and suffering) and penalty damages. These damages are based on what a jury believes to be necessary to either compensate a former employee for damages to his or her general well-being or to punish the employer for having committed a grievous wrong with the idea that the employer will never repeat the act. Damage awards from this type of case can be as high as the $19 million award against Sears, Roebuck and Co. for the demeaning fashion in which a store manager was terminated.[19]

Typical tort claims include intentional infliction of emotional distress, defamation, intrusion on seclusion, publicity given to private life, publicity placing a person in a false light, negligence, fraud, and interference with present or future contract advantages. In essence, where a court concludes that there may be some facts that would lead a jury to find a tortious discharge in one of these categories and a jury concludes that the discharge was somehow unfair, there are many ways for the jury to find a basis for substantial liability on the employer's part.

Any person doubting that courts (and juries, if the case goes to a jury) strain to "interpret" the law to reach a conclusion in favor of an employee where the facts indicate the employee was treated unfairly need only read such cases as

Garibaldi v. Lucky Food Stores,[20] *Toussaint v. Blue Cross &
Blue Shield of Michigan*,[21] *Green v. Oliver Realty*,[22] and *Novosel v. Nationwide Insurance Co.*[23]

In *Garibaldi*, an employee was fired for refusing to deliver
a load of spoiled milk and, instead, reporting the spoilage to
the local health department. Even though an arbitrator—in
"final and binding" arbitration pursuant to a Teamster contract—found the employee had been properly discharged, the
court permitted the case to be submitted to a jury based on
public policy exception to the employment-at-will principle.
The public policy was found in the health laws.

In *Toussaint*, the Michigan Supreme Court held that Blue
Cross and Blue Shield of Michigan breached an employment
contract with Toussaint, which had been created at his employment interview, by telling him he would be employed "as
long as he did his job." This oral assurance of job security was
enhanced by Toussaint's subsequent receipt of a personnel
policy manual that set forth disciplinary procedures for all
employees following their probationary period. It further contained a just cause provision. In finding a breach of contract,
the court held:

> employer's statement of policy, such as the Blue Cross Super-
> visory Manual and Guidelines, can give rise to contractual rights
> in employees without evidence that the parties mutually agreed
> that the policy statements would create contractual rights in
> the employee . . . although the statement of policy is signed by
> neither party, can be unilaterally amended by the employer
> without notice to the employee, and contains no reference to a
> specific employee, his job description or compensation, and *al-
> though no reference was made to the policy statement in pre-
> employment interviews and the employee does not learn of its
> existence until after his hiring.*[24] (Emphasis added)

Consequently, the Michigan court indicated that it would
find an implied contract even without any of the common law
requirements of the existence of a contract, such as negotiations, a bargain, a meeting of the minds, and the possibility
that one party may unilaterally change the terms of the agreement.

In *Green*, the court enforced against a successor employer
an alleged oral promise of employment for life by the prede-
cessor where, when the employee brought the alleged promise
to the attention of the successor, he was immediately fired.

In *Novosel*, the Third Circuit read into the employment
of an insurance agent the public policy of right of political free

speech, using the first amendment of the United States Constitution as the source for that policy even though the first amendment is clearly intended only to protect the rights of a citizen against the tyranny of the government.

The old saying, "Bad facts make bad law," is relevant to this subject. In this context, I believe there is one extremely important conclusion upon which all employee relations must be built, if American industry is to survive into the 21st century: there is no case reported where a former employee received elemental due process and was treated fairly and, nevertheless, was successful in a lawsuit against an employer. Also, I have read many cases where the treatment of the employee shocked my conscience more than the degree to which the court prostituted the law to provide relief to the employee.

This reality is not much different from that seen in both civil rights and unfair labor practice cases. Even though the administrative agencies should not be concerned with concepts such as fairness or due process, when those elements are not found in a case, the possibility that an employee will be held to have been discharged because of his or her membership in a protected class increases to nearly 100 percent. Frequently, the reverse can be said as well.

Moreover, I believe it is often true that when employees believe that they have received due process and have been treated fairly, they rarely file complaints alleging wrongful discharge or discrimination. For one thing, if a former employee who has received due process tells a story that even approximates the actual facts, no lawyer possessing any degree of good judgment would take the case. Unfortunately, many former employees do not believe they have been treated properly, lie to lawyers, or manage to find a lawyer who lacks good judgment. As a result, these cases are being filed and employers must rely on the judgments of administrative agents, judges, and juries to avoid liability. These judgments, as stated earlier, are usually based on perceptions that the employee was or was not treated fairly and did or did not receive elemental due process. The law is forced to justify these judgments.

Consequently, it is absolutely vital that an employer who wishes to avoid litigation and, if sued, wishes to avoid liability, have in place an internal policy to ensure that an employee will receive due process and as a result, fair treatment.

In addition to avoiding union organization and liability for either violation of civil rights laws or wrongful discharge, employers need to keep and attract employees who could just as well go to another employer. The shortfall of five million available workers by the year 2,000 means that competition for employees will become increasingly fierce.[25] Employers who are able to keep their employees and attract new ones from less satisfactory workplace cultures will win this competition and survive.

There are, then, four reasons why employers must develop effective due process and discipline systems for their nonunion employees.

1. To create a productive, responsible work force committed to the enterprise;
2. To avoid union organization;
3. To avoid litigation and liability arising from allegations of violations of the civil rights laws, wrongful discharge, or torts committed in connection with employment termination; and
4. To stimulate current employees to stay and employees of other employers to come.

In review, we have already concluded that due process in the workplace requires clear notice to employees of the employer's expectations and a fair system of progressive discipline, preferably nonpunitive. Both of these elements have been discussed in earlier chapters in detail and, as they relate to both union and nonunion employers, other elements such as a credible dispute resolution program also have been mentioned.

As to nonunion employees (regardless of whether all or only some employees are unionized), employers have special problems when it comes to the three remaining elements of due process in the workplace. These elements include the following:

1. a credible grievance procedure;
2. a credible dispute resolution program; and
3. an employee representation system.

The Components of a Due Process System

The remainder of this chapter discusses various methods by which employers of nonunion employees can satisfy employee expectations without significantly diminishing their managerial prerogatives and ability to control the enterprise.

Also explored are possible means by which these methods can be effectively designed and implemented.

Grievance Procedures

For this discussion, grievance procedure refers to all systems by which an employee may question or appeal a supervisor's decision that affects job security short of submitting the problem to a final decision maker. The submission of problems to a final decision maker is treated later in the discussion of credible appeal systems. Grievance systems are given myriad names by employers to distinguish them from "union" systems. They may be called problem resolution procedures, problem-solving, communication systems, or even opinion exchanges. For our purposes, they are referred to generically as grievance procedures.

Grievance procedures for nonunion employees can be informal or formal. The point at which an informal system becomes formal is blurred.

Informal Systems

Informal grievance systems do not specify steps within set time limits to achieve final disposition of a problem and have a minimum "paper trail," if any. An informal grievance procedure simply invites the employee to discuss the problem with members of management with an unspoken interest in achieving a resolution. At one extreme is a grievance provision that merely states:

> Employees are encouraged to discuss any problem with their supervisors or any member of management, including the president of the company. All doors are open to all employees at all times.

At the other extreme is a provision containing some minimal restrictions or steps:

> Employees are encouraged to discuss any problem with their immediate supervisor. If the problem is not resolved to your satisfaction at that level, you should speak to the director of personnel. If the problem is not resolved at that level, the door of the president of the company is open to you.

Although an informal grievance system works well in some situations, it carries the risk that employees will not use it because they do not believe that problems handled informally will be taken seriously and resolved fairly. The psychology is similar to our belief in an acquaintance's statement, "we should have lunch sometime." The invitation is too vague. A more credible invitation would be, "I have next Thursday free; are you available then for lunch?"

The informality of the system, while least threatening is also least inviting. Implicit in the informality is a message not to use it. The more informal a system, the more confusing it is to employees because they don't know to whom they should refer their problems. Assisting employees with problems is not a clearly defined responsibility of anyone beyond the first-line supervisor. Since the supervisor may be part or all of the problem, the employee must choose the path to resolution. This creates a risk in the employee's mind that his or her choice may be wrong, and the person approached may respond by denying responsibility for a resolution or by discussing the problem inappropriately with others. The informality, therefore, can convey to the employee that whomever else the employee may involve in the process will not know what they can or cannot do because these powers and responsibilities are not defined in the policy statement.

For these reasons, informal open door policies often do not work and the symptom of their ineffectiveness is their non-use. Employees simply do not believe that a general invitation to walk through the open door for assistance has any meaning beyond a general "we should have lunch sometime." The effectiveness of all due process systems, if they are to achieve their multiple purposes, depends on their credibility. It seems, therefore, that employers who depend on informal grievance systems create an incredible burden of affirmatively overcoming the inherent problems of such a system.

Formal Systems

Formal grievance systems, although differing in their degree of formality, define grievance procedures by specifying each step and the person responsible for taking action at each of these steps. In establishing such systems, employers must determine the number of steps, the identity of the supervisory or managerial employee who will deal with the problem at each step, and the time period for proceeding to the next step. Some employers are reluctant to specify these procedures because their formality resembles a union contract. However, the presence of established steps lends credibility since it implies that the employer wishes its employees to use the process and is prepared to deal honestly with the problem. The formality implies seriousness and accountability.

A formal grievance procedure may appear as follows:

We believe that all problems or questions which you may have with or about your work or any decision regarding your employment should be discussed and resolved as soon as possible. Unresolved problems or questions cause confusion and reduce the potential for a good work experience. In this connection, all supervisors are aware that all issues may not always be resolved to your satisfaction and, in that case, you may wish and should talk to someone else. At the same time, we believe that the best way to handle your concerns effectively is to allow those who are closest to the issue to have an opportunity to be involved under most circumstances. However, if you wish to skip any of the steps of this procedure and refer your question or problem to anyone in the procedure, you may do so. The important thing is that the problem is resolved or the question is answered. If you do not use this procedure, we assume that you understand and agree with the answer or action of your supervisor. The procedure is as follows:

First Step: If you have a problem or question, we urge you to speak with your immediate supervisor. Sometimes it may be helpful to put your problem or question in writing to make sure that both you and your supervisor understand the issue involved.

Second Step: If you have trouble understanding your immediate supervisor's answer or wish to discuss any action he or she has taken regarding your employment, you are encouraged to discuss it with your department head or shift foreman. These people will explore with you the issue and the facts and have the ability to correct your supervisor. Again, it will be very helpful to put your question or problem in writing, although this is not necessary. Your department head or foreman will help you do this, if you wish.

Third Step: If you still wish to discuss the answer given you or the action taken, you are encouraged to discuss it with the director of personnel. The director of personnel will assist you in putting your question or problem in writing as an aid to making sure that everyone understands the issue. The director of personnel may wish to consult with your supervisor and foreman or department head as well and has the ability to correct their answers or actions.

Several things are worth noting about this policy. First, there are no time limits placed on moving from one step to the next. This is done because, whatever the time frame, the employee should be permitted access to the procedure. The failure to move promptly may affect the action taken by the decision maker, but it should not preclude the employee from using the procedure. There is only one exception to this recommendation: discharge.

It is especially important in discharge cases that the employer have closure on the matter. Further, if the employer wishes to argue later in litigation that the employee is barred from challenging the discharge because he or she failed to use the internal procedure, the employee must have been obligated to use it. Such an obligation must not only be clearly stated in the policy, but time requirements should be explicit to avoid the possibility that an employee could "cure" the defect later. For this reason, it is recommended that a separate discharge grievance procedure, or statement modifying the general procedure, be used, such as the following:

There may be times when it is in the best interest of the Company that an employee be separated from employment. In such cases, the discharged employee is required to use the grievance procedure if he or she wishes to contest the discharge decision. If an employee does not contest the decision through the grievance procedure, he or she is presumed to be in agreement with the action.

In discharge cases, the discharged employee must notify the personnel director of his or her contest of the decision before the close of regular business on the day after the discharge occurs. If the discharged employee does not do this, he or she is presumed to be in agreement with the action and will be bound by it. If the discharged employee gives notice of his or her contest of the decision within the time requirement, the personnel director will interview the employee and do an investigation. The personnel director's decision will be made as soon after the completion of the investigation as possible.

The second thing to note about the general procedure is that the employee is offered the opportunity to use any of the steps at any time but is encouraged to proceed from one step to the next. This flexibility is meant to overcome any reluctance to using the procedure because of perceived personality problems.

Third, note that the employee is only encouraged to put things in writing to avoid, again, any psychological bar to using the procedure. However, the employee is clearly on notice that the personnel director will put the question or problem in writing so that when this occurs the employee is not alarmed.

Appeal Procedures

Although many nonunion dispute resolution systems treat the final review stage as nothing more than the last step in a grievance procedure, the final appeal should be viewed as a distinct process. By separating the final appeal process, the employer is implicitly recognizing that it has special significance to the employee. It is, in fact, the special step taken by an employee when all normal procedures have failed to produce an acceptable result. To an employee who feels unjustly treated, a final appeal lends credibility not only to the process but also to the employer's stated commitment to principles of fairness.

Appeal procedures, like grievance procedures, can differ in the degree of formality, but, consistent with the degree of seriousness that should be accorded the process, the differences are less extreme. The process should have a degree of formality at least equal to the importance placed upon it.

Common issues exist for all types of appeal procedures and employers should resolve these issues prior to selecting any particular model. Throughout this decision-making process, employers should keep in mind that their actions are unilateral and, therefore, wholly within their control. Although they are giving up some of their managerial discretion, they are doing it to achieve protection from employee rights litigation and union organization. In addition, they are striving to build increased employee responsibility and commitment. If the employer is unwilling to relinquish any of its traditional management prerogatives and designs a system which is illusory or capable of arbitrary management decisions, these purposes will not be achieved and there is no reason even to begin the process. On the other hand, the desired benefits can and must be achieved without loss of managerial control over essential issues. Finding the appropriate balance between employee rights and managerial control is the most difficult exercise in developing an effective dispute resolution system and rarely can be done by an employer without the assistance of expert advice.

One of the most interesting issues is whether an appeal procedure unilaterally implemented by an employer for nonunion employees can provide the same degree of protection against a wrongful discharge lawsuit and/or statutory litigation, as would an arbitration pursuant to a labor agreement with a union. Unlike the union contract situation, where the binding effect of an arbitration as the exclusive remedy for the covered employee is well established, the binding effect of an appeal procedure in a nonunion setting is largely undetermined in American jurisprudence.

Where an ex-employee files a lawsuit alleging a breach of contract and the court rules that a prior procedure was fair and has already determined the issue, the courts will usually defer to the prior decision and will not permit a de novo review. The reasoning of the courts is relatively simple: if an employee claims that his or her discharge violated an expressed contract with an implied term, such as an employee handbook, and the handbook (or other employment document) establishes a fair method for resolving the dispute brought before the court, the employee must be bound by that procedure. That is, an employee cannot seek to take advantage of only part of an alleged contract.

In *Toussaint v. Blue Cross & Blue Shield*,[26] the Supreme Court of Michigan suggested that

> the employer can avoid the perils of jury assessment by providing for an alternative method of dispute resolution. A written agreement for a definite or indefinite term to discharge only for cause could, for example, provide for binding arbitration on the issues of cause and damages.

This decision was followed by *Khalifa v. Henry Ford Hospital*.[27] In that case, the appellate court noted that an internal appeal procedure established to determine the issue of just cause would be binding on an employee, so long as the procedure satisfies the requirements of elemental fairness and due process. The court found that the procedure was consideration for the just cause criteria. In this particular situation, an employee complained that the appeal procedure set up by an employee handbook was unfair and should not be binding on him. The appeal procedure ended with a hearing before a grievance council made up of elected nonsupervisory employees. The council could uphold, overturn, or modify the employee's discharge. The handbook stated that the council's decisions were final and binding.

The court stated that procedural fairness in private dispute resolution procedures do not require constitutional due process but only adequate notice of the time and place of the hearing, a reasonable time for preparation, an opportunity to present evidence and argument. In this case, the court held that the plaintiff had been accorded a fair hearing and, therefore, he was bound by the council's decision.[28]

At least one court has also held that an employee must exhaust the available remedies in an employee handbook. In *Schnelting v. Coors Distributing Co.*,[29] a former employer sued the company for wrongful discharge, relying on the just cause provision in the employee handbook. The company argued that the plaintiff's case should be dismissed because he did not first attempt to use the procedures in the handbook for resolving disputes. The court agreed, stating

> it has long been the rule in Missouri that the aggrieved employee must exhaust the remedies provided in the agreement before resorting to the court for redress! ... This principle is no less applicable where the rights asserted by plaintiff are contained in an employee handbook.[30]

As noted earlier, however, most wrongful discharge cases also contain allegations of numerous torts. Assuming, as I believe we can, that an appeal procedure can be provided by an employer for nonunion employees which can preclude subsequent court cases brought on the basis of a breach of contract, will the same procedure be effective in precluding related tort claims? In this respect, it is well to remember that employers seeking to establish the preclusive effect of their nonunion dispute resolution system must argue by analogy to the body of law developed in connection with arbitration under the union contract.

In *Allis-Chalmers Corp. v. Lueck*[31] the United States Supreme Court held that Section 301 of the Labor Management Relations Act[32] precludes an employee covered by a union contract from bringing a state tort claim if the claim depends upon a substantive analysis of the terms of the contract. Rather, the employee must exhaust his contract remedy. Under Section 301, the contract dispute resolution procedure must be used if the claim depends on a substantive analysis of the contract, arises from or derives from rights created by the contract, and if the claim is "inextricably intertwined" with the provisions of the contract.[33]

However, this analogy is not exact because Section 301 preempts only cases involving union contracts or other agreements with labor organizations.[34] Consequently, an employer should also seek help in these cases by analogizing to the Federal Arbitration Act.[35] Using both of these analogies, employers can construct formidable arguments in favor of precluding ex-employees from relitigating tort, as well as contract claims where the same claim—or the substantive facts—have been previously tried in a fair internal dispute resolution proceeding.

While engaged in the designing of a dispute resolution program for clients which we hope will have preclusive effects in the event of wrongful discharge litigation, questions invariably arise concerning whether statutory claims (usually those involving claims of employment discrimination) can be precluded as well. *Alexander v. Gardner-Denver*[36] established the principle that federal discrimination statutes, particularly Title VII, involve a public policy too important to be resolved in an arbitration. Consequently, an individual is entitled to have a court resolve these issues, even if they had been previously submitted to arbitration. However, in stating this principle, people often overlook the fact that the Supreme Court did not say that prior arbitration decisions should be totally disregarded. Rather, these decisions are to be given such weight as the court deems appropriate:

> We adopt no standards as to the weight to be accorded an arbitral decision, since this must be determined in the court's discretion with regard to the facts and circumstances of each case. Relevant factors include the existence of provisions in the collective-bargaining agreement that conform substantially with Title VII, the degree of procedural fairness in the arbitral forum, adequacy of the record with respect to the issue of discrimination, and the special competence of particular arbitrators. Where an arbitral determination gives full consideration to an employee's Title VII rights, a court may properly accord it great weight. This is especially true where the issue is solely one of fact, specifically addressed by the parties and decided by the arbitrator on the basis of an adequate record.[37]

Accordingly, there may be substantial value to having statutory claims determined by an internal dispute procedure, even though the decision may not be preclusive. Indeed, there is some indication that the Supreme Court may be ready to relax the principle in *Alexander v. Gardner-Denver*. In *Mitsubishi Motors Corp. v. Soler Chrysler-Plymouth*,[38] the Supreme Court held that Sherman Act claims could be arbitrated. Also, in *Shearson/American Express v. McMahon*,[39] the Supreme Court required the arbitration of an antifraud claim under Section 10-b(5) of the Securities Exchange Act. In *Mitsubishi*, the Court stated:

> Having permitted the arbitration to go forward, the national courts of the United States will have the opportunity at the award-enforcement stage to ensure that the legitimate interest in the enforcement of the antitrust laws has been addressed. . . . While the efficacy of the arbitral process requires that substantive review at the award-enforcement stage remain minimal, it would not require intrusive inquiry to ascertain that the tribunal took cognizance of the antitrust claims and actually decided them.[40]

Several lower courts, relying on holdings in *Mitsubishi*, *Cone Memorial Hospital*, and *Shearson*, have required or given binding effect to the arbitration decisions in employment discrimination cases.[41] Consequently, a properly designed internal dispute resolution procedure may have significant value even in cases that involve statutory claims.

The difficulty with mandatory systems designed to provide employers with a "failure to exhaust" defense, from an employer's point of view, is that a process which is binding on an employee must also be binding on the employer and must contain some guarantees that the employee received due process. If the process can be overridden by managerial fiat or does not provide actual due process, the employee can successfully argue that exhaustion of that remedy would have been futile or was illusory.

Consequently, an employer seeking maximum protection against employee rights litigation by having a mandatory appeal process must be prepared to give up its unilateral discretion to make ultimate decisions. It must adopt a system that accords the basic elements of due process, that is, the right to mount an effective defense (including the right to examine documents and witnesses and to be represented), the right to a hearing, and the right to a binding decision by an impartial body or person.

In providing these elements, however, an employer may retain some limitations or control. For instance, the employer may limit the kind of issue that can be appealed. One common limitation is that only issues involving discharge or job security can be subjected to the process. By doing this, the employer stipulates that only in those cases with the highest risk for lawsuits will it be willing to subordinate its traditional managerial discretion to a binding neutral process.

A further limitation would be that the employee can challenge only the application of a rule and that the neutral party cannot alter or invalidate a rule as unreasonable. This limitation is greater than that which is usually applied to typical arbitrators under union contracts and is less expansive than a usual just cause standard. In addition, it preserves the employer's right to establish its own rules of conduct. Where those rules are clear and are adequately communicated, a court that finds an implied contract in the publication of the process would not be able to modify the terms of that contract. Indeed, if a union contract were to limit the arbitrator's power in the same fashion, an arbitrator's decision that went beyond this limitation would be reversible in a district court as beyond the arbitrator's authority. Because this decision would follow the completion of due process, the employee could not successfully argue that the discharge had been abusive or wrongful since he or she was aware of the standard of conduct demanded by the employer and a fair process had concluded that the employee had violated the standard which mandated discharge.

Having resolved these threshold issues, the employer is ready to consider which of the available appeal models it believes will work best for it and its employees.

Designated Officer

Probably the most common approach, but the least likely to pass muster before a court as guaranteeing a fair and impartial result (due process), is the designated officer model. This system has as the final appeal some designated individual who will review the employee's case and make a decision. The identity of the individual may vary widely from employer to employer. In one case, the individual may be the personnel manager; in another, the company president; in another, the plant manager; in another, some officer off the premises, such as a corporate or divisional manager or, even, the corporate president.

As a rule, the closer the designated officer is to the employee's chain of supervisory command the more risk there is of losing credibility. In the employee's mind, at least, there is a suspicion that the reviewing officer will be inclined to support the supervisor and, by definition, will be prejudiced. Consequently, the system's success may depend on the employees' perception of the officer's character. Unfortunately, the employees' view of a designated officer's fairness and neutrality is rarely equivalent to the officer's own view (or fantasy) of his or her neutrality. Let's face it, when on the last judgment day all of humanity stands before the throne of God and some are told to go to the right and some are told to go to the left, those told to go a direction they do not like will claim that God was unfair. And that was God! Is a designated officer entitled to more credibility?

Such systems, therefore, are fragile. The greatest chance of success is offered where the reviewing officer is off the premises and separated by distance and authority from the actual, day-to-day supervision of the employee. Even in these circumstances, employee suspicion will severely attack the system's credibility. Moreover, the use of a designated officer will most likely be viewed with the greatest suspicion by a judge or administrative agent as having delivered due process.

Chosen Officer

The chosen officer model allows the employee to select which officer will review his or her case. Credibility is enhanced because the employee is able to avoid those individuals he or she believes may harbor some prejudice or predisposition. Frequently, the employer will limit the list of review officers from which the employee may select. Typically, the choices are restricted only to officers of vice president rank or above or to some similar classification. In addition, the restriction may exclude officers who lack management's confidence as skilled in personnel areas. The restrictions on that basis must be very few, and it is recommended that all officers above a certain level be made available to the employee.

The employer's risk in such a system is that some officers may deal with employee problem issues from the heart and without sensitivity to the needs of the enterprise. For instance, the vice president in charge of sales may make a decision wholly inconsistent with good personnel sense simply because he or she is insensitive to the personnel needs of the organization. Of course, the opposite may also be true and the officer may be insensitive to the rights of the employee.

Rather than gerrymandering the selection list, the employer choosing this kind of model should train the officers prior to their use of the system. However, my experience has been that many officers are almost untrainable when it comes to personnel matters. Their positions of authority seem to increase resistance to learning from those they feel are subordinates. As with all appeal programs, but especially this one, the employer must recognize that the enterprise can withstand an occasional bad decision for the benefit of the process. Further, a bad decision by an officer may be a significant tip-off that the officer is not handling his or her own subordinates in a fashion consistent with the employer's philosophy.

Officer Review Panel

This model utilizes a panel (usually an uneven number) of officers appointed by the employer or, in whole or in part, selected by the employee. For instance, an employer may provide that the review and decision will be by an panel of three, consisting of the president, the vice president of personnel and the vice president in charge of the employee's area of work. Or, the employer may provide some other mix of officers who are unassociated with the employee's normal chain of command. On the other hand, the process may allow the employee to choose one or more of the officer reviewers, may provide for chance selection, or for some combination of those methods.

The purpose of a panel is to increase the potential for a fair and objective hearing and decision. Giving the employee some control over who will be on the panel increases its credibility. Choice by lot or some other mechanical process has a similar effect. The defect is that it increases the man hours devoted to an issue and that scheduling may be a significant problem, especially since the cancellation of an appeal hearing can have a severe impact on the system's credibility. In addition, it is often difficult to get a group of officers together for any reason, let alone dealing with a rank-and-file employee's grievance. Even when these meetings are finally scheduled, they are often cancelled because of other concerns that officers perceive as more important. The effects of such cancellations can be fatal to the purpose and effect of the process.

Peer Review

Another model, which is gaining increased acceptance and popularity, uses a panel consisting, in whole or in part, of the employee's peers. Although the number and mix of reviewers may vary, the most common has two uninvolved supervisors and three peers, with the personnel director serving as a nonvoting facilitator.

As a means of increasing the reviewer's responsibility, employers may limit the eligible peers to those who have seniority above a certain level. In addition, the employer may stipulate that only those employees who have completed a special training course may be in the pool of peers. As with peer representatives, the employer has an opportunity through the training program to enhance employee attitudes concerning its commitment to fairness and due process. These trained employees, then, form a powerful core of advocates in the employer's favor in the event of a union organizational drive.

Typically, the grieving employee is presented with a container filled with the names of eligible peer reviewers from which he or she pulls five names. After reading the five names, the employee may eliminate two. The three remaining constitute the peer members of the panel. The employee repeats the process with a container of names of uninvolved supervisors, drawing three and discarding one. The panel then assembles to review the documents and hear all witnesses. The panel's vote can be limited to a simple "yes" or "no." Some employers permit the panel to modify the discipline or discharge to a lesser penalty. The panel must never be permitted to modify the rule itself, or the rule making process will be effectively taken away from the employer and given to ad hoc panels. A panel should be limited to affirming or denying the application of the rule to the facts as it finds them. After the panel members vote, the personnel director reads each ballot and when there are three of the same, the counting stops. Unless it is necessary to count all five to get three alike, the panel and the employee do not know whether the vote was split or unanimous.[42]

Employee Arbitrator

Similar to an ombudsperson, the employee arbitrator functions only to review and decide employee disputes. This model is available only to large employers, usually with multiple locations. Generally located in a central corporate office, these employee arbitrators travel from location to location to hear employee appeals. The same risks concerning credibility exist as with ombudspersons, including the difficulty encountered whenever it becomes necessary to terminate the employee arbitrator or even when one quits for unrelated reasons. Their leaving always involves questions concerning whether their decisions may have led to their exit from the company.

Commercial Resource

Some employers have felt it wise to maximize the protections that a due process appeal system can provide by establishing a system whereby an employee can have his or her case heard by an outside neutral, such as a professional labor arbitrator or private court. While providing the highest degree of unassailable neutrality, this system also presents risks and costs many employers find unacceptable, at least at present. Perhaps, if employee rights litigation continues to increase at its current rate, this assessment may change and the voluntary use of commercial resources will increase.

Some companies feel it is a risk to introduce an outsider into their employment culture. For the most part, this is a false risk. The identity of a professional arbitrator can be controlled through designation in the document establishing the procedure. This method, however, may prove very unsatisfactory, since excellent arbitrators usually have full calendars and a speedy hearing from a single designated arbitrator, or even a panel of designated arbitrators, may be difficult. For this reason, employers with this type of system may opt for an expedited process available through the American Arbitration Association. This process provides a labor arbitrator at the employment site on short notice for a one-day hearing and bench decision. Control over the identity of the arbitrator, however, is limited.

Another alternative is the use of one of the private courts which are developing in most major metropolitan areas. These courts are usually staffed with retired or former judges or other trained professionals who, for a fee, will hear and decide any civil matter brought before them. The process is swift and relatively inexpensive, especially when compared to the cost of litigation. It is questionable, at this stage of infancy in this new industry, how expert the judges may be in workplace issues.

A common problem exists in the establishment of these

systems: how do you handle the cost? Some employers will choose to pay the entire cost of the professional. This will normally average about $500, in addition to the related costs of representation and time lost in assembling all parties for a single formal hearing. Others require that the employee, when filing for the appeal, deposit one-half or some other portion of the arbitrator's fee. The purpose is often to discourage frivolous appeals. The employee's deposit may or may not be returnable to the employee if he or she wins, depending on what the employer provides in the program document.

Employee Representation

Whether the resolution process is in the preliminary or final stage, employees take great comfort in not having to face the employer alone. Having a representative evens the odds or prevents "ganging up"; it adds credibility to the system because the employer permits an employee witness so there can be nothing hidden. Unions satisfy this need through union stewards or business agents. It makes sense for employers seeking to avoid unionization or lawsuits, therefore, to establish a process by which employees can secure some form or representation in both the grievance and the appeal process. In this respect, it is worth reflecting that while employees may not understand or appreciate the concepts of the *Wein-garten* rights or their unavailability to nonunion employees as a technical application of the law, they have learned all about the *Miranda* rights and, probably, believe that there is some basic American right to a representative in all circumstances. At least, the denial of this right would be viewed very negatively.

Moreover, if the desire of an employer is to use its due process system as a shield against wrongful discharge and civil rights complaints, the availability of a representative of the employee during the disciplinary process for employee assistance and advocacy is critical.

Several models for representation programs have emerged in recent years. Which model is suitable for an individual employer depends on several factors: the culture of the employees, the environment the employer desires for the workplace, the amount of effort the employer wishes to expend in training, the sophistication and maturity of the employer's supervisors, and the extent to which the employer is prepared to voluntarily give up some of its inherent power. Consequently, choosing a particular program must be preceded by a systematic process of definition and self-examination.

Ombudsperson

One of the oldest models is that of the ombudsperson. With this system, a person is employed outside the normal personnel administration chain to meet with and counsel employees with problems. Although the ombudsperson is an employee and subject to the employer's pleasure, the ombudsperson is expected to act aggressively on behalf of other employees to insure that they are being treated fairly by those above them in the supervisory chain.

The primary concern with this model, as with all elements in due process systems, is that of credibility. The system is successful only to the extent that the employees have faith in the system as the means of achieving fair treatment. To enhance the credibility of the ombudsperson, the employer should take care to keep that person independent of the personnel department, reporting only to the highest authority in the organization, preferably outside the local plant or facility, and maintaining files which are secure against inspection by all other supervisory and managerial employees. Further, the ombudsperson must be above suspicion of being in conspiracy with anyone in the employee's authority chain. For that reason, private meetings with supervisors and managers should not occur and in all other respects the ombudsperson should conduct business with the same degree of confidentiality and fidelity as does an attorney with a client. The most successful of these programs are those in which the ombudsperson does not act as a judge but as an advocate, not as a member of management but as the employee's peer.

Uninvolved Peers

The hallmark of the peer model is that an employee is given the ability to choose an uninvolved co-worker to participate in the grievance and/or appeal process as his or her representative. Although this system's risks may be significant, some employers have found that the risks can be minimized, if not eliminated. The primary risk is that a single or a few employees may be chosen repeatedly as representatives with the result that they achieve a status in the workplace which can be troublesome or abused. If left uncontrolled, the most militant and unreasonable employee may become a de facto union steward and acquire a level of notoriety that may preclude justifiable discipline of that individual. Moreover, the risk is increased that the employee will become the kind of leader who, when not given his or her way, would align with a union and become a substantial force favoring organization.

To minimize this risk, an employer may choose to limit the number of employees who may serve as representatives and the number of times an individual may serve within a stated time period. Typically, employers use seniority as the basis for limiting the number of available representatives. Presumably, by providing that only employees with, for example, five or more years of seniority can be selected as representatives, the employer is assured that the individual chosen will have a sense of loyalty to the organization. By restricting the number of times an individual can serve, such as only once in a 12-month period, no person can achieve a stature so great as to become a de facto employee leader.

Probably the best program is one that permits development of a pool of representatives from employees of a certain seniority level. The pool is made up of volunteers. The volunteers must first qualify for the pool by successfully completing a training program. The employer uses the training program to teach the volunteers the extent of their responsibilities and rights. An intelligent employer also uses the program to communicate to employees its commitment to a good organization where everyone can work in harmony. Once the pool is developed, employees seeking representation may choose any individual, although time restrictions can still be imposed. One advantage of this system is that it creates a number of people in the work force who have been given the responsibility of a steward in a controlled fashion. Any union seeking to organize the workforce, therefore, must face an employee group who will be thinking or saying, "do you mean that I cannot perform my responsibility adequately?"

Uninvolved Supervisor

The system that uses uninvolved supervisors as representatives avoids the risk of developing leaders within the ranks of organizable employees. It also provides the best quality representation, since, at least theoretically, supervisors are the most articulate in the workplace. In addition, supervisors, by being involved in discipline situations that have been created by another supervisor's response to their employees' conduct, have an opportunity to see first hand how another supervisor is handling a workplace problem. This opportunity helps in the training of the representative-supervisor. It also increases consistency in handling disciplinary issues.

The problems with this kind of system are credibility and supervisory antagonism. Employees tending toward suspicion and mistrust easily find supervisory conspiracy in everything that does not go precisely as they wish. Consequently, employers with this kind of system must take special care to train supervisors to perform their duties responsibly on behalf of the employee and not in concert with the other supervisor. Again, confidentiality and the absence of private (ex parte) meetings are essential.

Supervisory antagonism can only be avoided through maturity enhanced by training. Recognizing that supervisors do not want other supervisors to criticize their handling of a problem or, for that matter, to observe how they perform their job, supervisors must subordinate their own feelings to the objectives of the program. This is achieved only through training and frequent stroking by the personnel department. When operating well, the uninvolved supervisor program has the greatest potential for providing the best employee representation. It promotes consistency in handling discipline and builds a true *esprit de corps*.

Nonemployee

Nonemployee representatives are rare and generally not advisable. Such a representative may be anyone from the community: clergyman, politician, attorney, or union leader seeking to gain employee acceptance.

Nonemployees are not recommended for several reasons. Many bring issues into the process that are irrelevant to the workplace and attempt to put pressure on the supervisor. The focus of the issue may be changed for the benefit of the representative and to the employee's prejudice. Outside involvement may stimulate the publication of the matter to the general community, raising issues of defamation and bad public relations. Further, if an employee is permitted professional representation, such as by an attorney, the supervisor may be outmatched and intimidated into avoiding problems rather than solving them.

Establishing Due Process in the Workplace

Workplace due process programs contain many elements in addition to dispute resolution. However, no element is more important than that which enables employees to effectively have their job security questions determined. This aspect of the program reflects some of the most significant employee expectations which, if unsatisifed, will lead workers to seek more credible forums, e.g., union representation, civil rights agencies, and the courts. I believe that most American workers respond negatively to any system that denies them an opportunity to mount an effective defense and to appeal their arguments to an impartial third party. To be effective, therefore, a Workplace Due Process program must satisfy these needs.

Developing a System

There is no pat formula for providing the elements of due process in the workplace that is appropriate for all companies or employees. A single company may find that different policies and procedures would be appropriate for different employee groups within the same enterprise. Development of a system for any company must be preceded by careful study of available alternatives and, usually, must involve the guidance of an expert and, on a controlled basis, the significant input of employees. The structure of the system is not nearly as important as the employees' belief in its fairness. A purchased or "canned" system risks irrelevance and unsuitability to the specific workplace. For this reason Workplace Due Process is a matrix of possibilities developed in a facilitated and controlled environment.

After dealing with hundreds of different companies in connection with their employee discipline problems and witnessing how various systems achieve or fail to achieve their objectives, I have become convinced that the only system which stands a reasonable chance of success is one that is not constructed by top management or human resource professionals and then imposed on supervisors and their subordinates. Supervisors required to "punish" or "write up" an employee are tempted to apologize for having to take the action and blame administrators above them. They hide behind the fact that a system created by someone else (impliedly someone who has no idea of what really goes on) forces an action. They often mistakenly believe that they retain credibility with the employee. Unfortunately, this type of supervisory conduct reduces the system's credibility.

A second reason supervisors fail is that they do not understand either the theory or the intent of the system they are required to use. I never cease to be amazed by the number of times I have encountered supervisors who have been "trained" through hours of classroom-style instruction and who do not really understand the objectives of a disciplinary system. As a result, they do the easy thing—follow the steps to avoid getting into trouble and that is all they remember from their training.

Finally, supervisors often do not understand the code of conduct they are required to enforce. They do not know why some acts are summary offenses and some require progressive discipline. Worse yet, they do not know the elements of the specific offenses so that they take actions unsupported by necessary facts and that must be subsequently reversed.

A remedy to these problems is to place the development of the disciplinary system, code of conduct, grievance procedure, employee representation system, and appeal program in the hands of those who must work with them, supervisors. The supervisors are then compelled to examine all issues related to these systems, to achieve a finer understanding of their structure and to distinguish why the systems require some types of action rather than others. Most important, the systems are theirs and they feel a heightened sense of responsibility for their success in implementation.

Turning over the development of these critical systems to "nonprofessionals" requires employers to give up some of their managerial prerogatives. In addition, they must ensure that the systems developed do not incorporate inherent defects unforeseen by those inexperienced in human relations. In this respect, the most basic rule is that the employer must retain sufficient control over the process so that the supervisors will develop quality systems that are consistent with, and acceptable to, the employer's philosophy. This is accomplished through the use of a qualified facilitator. This facilitator must be someone who thoroughly understands the values, structures, and pitfalls of systems and programs in each of the due process categories. The facilitator guides the supervisors' work socratically and, then, controls the drafting of the language incorporating the desires of the supervisors. To avoid the worst possible situation—the creation of systems that are unacceptable to the employer—the facilitator should first meet and discuss with the employer's senior executives all possible options and establish general guidelines for the panels. Part of this process is to obtain a commitment from these executives that the company will accept any system constructed within these guidelines.

For instance, the executive control group must discuss and resolve the following issues:

1. *Discipline System*:
   a. Will either a punitive or nonpunitive system be unacceptable?
   b. Will a paid decision day be unacceptable?

2. *Code of Conduct*:
   a. Will an undefined, broad statement of responsibility, without more, be unacceptable?
   b. Will a very detailed list of prohibited acts be unacceptable?
   c. Will a separation of conduct, performance, and attendance problems into separate codes be unacceptable?
   d. Concerning attendance problems, will either an excuse-based or a no-fault absenteeism control policy be unacceptable?
   e. Concerning attendance problems, will the quantification of excessive conduct be unacceptable?
   f. What offenses must be summary? Are there any offenses which cannot be summary?

3. *Grievance Procedure*:
   a. Is either a formal or informal system unacceptable?
   b. Is the treatment of discharge grievances separate from other grievances unacceptable?

4. *Employee Representation*:
   a. Is an employee representation system unacceptable?
   b. Are any of the following unacceptable as a potential employee representative: peers, supervisors, managers, non-employees, ombudsperson?

5. *Appeal Procedure*:
   a. Are any of the following unacceptable as a final appellate officer or body: designated corporate officer, chosen corporate officer, corporate officer panel, all peer panel, all supervisor panel, mixed peer and supervisor panel, professional arbitrator, private court, any other nonemployee, designated employee?

b. Is access to the procedure for any of the following issues unacceptable: discipline short of discharge, discharge, evaluations, denial of merit increases, denial of promotions, denial of benefits such as leaves or seminars, claims of discrimination or harassment?

It should be noted that each of the questions is stated in the negative. That is, the executive control group defines for the facilitator what is unacceptable. Whatever is not stated as unacceptable is within the range of acceptability.

After the executive control group has met with the facilitator and set the general guidelines, the facilitator and a managerial project director meet to establish supervisory panels or work groups. In some cases, employees may be included in the panels as well. By unilaterally naming those supervisors and, if wished, those employees who will constitute the panels, the employer is also controlling the process. The project director (usually the director of human resources) should have sufficient acquaintance with the potential panel members to ensure the correct chemistry for each. For instance, the panels should be made up of a mixture of experienced and inexperienced personnel who have demonstrated some likely skill in the subject matter of the particular panel. Each panel should consist of at least six and no more than ten people. The panels should be of even numbers to ensure decisions by consensus rather than by vote.

There would be separate panels for each element in the due process program. In addition, there should be a communication panel. The communication panel would be charged with the responsibility of determining how the development process, as well as the product itself, will be communicated to the employees and what kind of training will be needed during the implementation period. Curiously, the communication panel may well become one of the most exciting as the members create ways to get the message across, including the use of video tapes, for example.

Once the panel members are chosen, all involved personnel meet with the facilitator, project manager, and CEO or other high officials to become oriented to their tasks and the company's philosophy. The communication panel then receives its first assignment: produce a communique to all employees describing what is taking place. Each panel convenes to discuss and develop their specific program pieces. The facilitator not only guides its deliberations and structures its product development but serves as the liaison to other panels, ensuring consistency.

When the panels have produced their working plans, each presents their products to a general meeting of all involved personnel for critique. The panels then reconvene to finalize their products. When all pieces are constructed, they are presented to the executive control group for its adoption. Following adoption of the various elements of the due process program, the communication panel can implement its communication and training program.

Summary

The stakes are high. Because of the shift in our economy from smokestack (blue collar) to service (white collar), unions, to survive, must organize workers who traditionally have been nonunion. What unions sell most effectively is due process. Wrongful discharge lawsuits have reached epidemic proportions and judgments often reach six figures. The success or failure of these lawsuits depends on the presence of workplace due process. Keeping and attracting employees depends in large measure on the quality of the company's worklife. Much of that quality is created by due process. American industry must be more productive if it is to compete successfully with foreign businesses. Employee commitment, responsibility, and productivity is related to how employees are treated. Workplace Due Process is more than a defensive tool, it stimulates positive qualities.

Due process in the workplace can be a reality only when there is a reasonable definition of employer expectations and credible discipline, employee representation, grievance, and appeal systems. In addition, supervisors must understand the philosophy and intent of these systems and want to make them work. They will do that best if they have developed them and have a stake in their success.

Notes to Chapter 7

1. For an authoritative discussion of the origins of the employment-at-will doctrine and its progress toward demise, *see* Perritt, *Employee Dismissal Law and Practice*, 2d ed. (New York: John Wiley & Sons, 1987).

2. *See* Summers, "Individual Protection Against Unjust Dismissal: Time for a Statute," 62 VA. L. REV. 481 (1976); Stieber, "The

Case for Protection of Unorganized Employees Against Unjust Discharge," *Proceedings of the 32nd Annual Meeting*, Industrial Relations Research Association (Madison, Wis.: IRRA, 1980), p. 155; Peck, "Unjust Discharges From Employment: A Necessary Change in the Law," 400 OHIO ST. L.J. 1 (1979); Howlett, "Due Process for Nonunionized Employees: A Practical Proposal," *Proceedings of the 32nd Annual Meeting*. Industrial Relations Research Association (Madison, Wis.: IRRA, 1980), p. 164; Blumrosen, "Strangers No More: All Workers Are Entitled to 'Just Cause' Protection Under Title VII," 2 INDUS. RELS. L.J. 519 (1978); Aaron, "Constitutional Protections Against Unjust Dismissals from Employment: Some Reflections," *New Techniques in Labor Dispute Resolution* (Washington, D.C.: The Bureau of National Affairs, Inc., 1976), p. 13; Blades, "Employment at Will vs. Individual Freedom: Of Limiting the Abusive Exercise of Employer Power," 67 COLUM. L. REV. 1404 (1967); St. Antoine, "Protection Against Unjust Discipline: An Idea Whose Time Has Long Since Come," *Arbitration Issues for the 1980s*, Proceedings of the Thirty-Fourth Annual Meeting of the National Academy of Arbitrators (Washington, D.C.: BNA Books, 1982), p. 43.

3. *Adair v. United States*, 208 U.S. 161 (1908); Ga. Code Ann. §§66–101.

4. Curiously, proposed legislation that will codify an employee's right to just cause and due process in discharge decisions frequently had languished for lack of powerful support. Employers do not support it and unions, seeing much of the justification for their existence being shifted to courts and alternative arbitration systems, do not either. See the history and apparent demise of Pennsylvania's effort with H.B. 1742, Pa. Gen. Assembly, 1981 Session.

5. *See* Summers, *supra*, and other articles listed in note 2.

6. *See generally* Madison, "The Employee's Emerging Right to Sue for Arbitrary or Unfair Discharge," 6 EMPLOYEE RELATIONS L.J. 422 (1980–81) and Perritt, *supra*, note 1.

7. Since the attack on the employment-at-will principle involves the laws of individual states and the cases being decided are so many and frequent, this discussion will not attempt to cite individual cases. The reader is referred to the *Individual Employee Rights* service of the Bureau of National Affairs, Inc. for the specific cases within relevant jurisdictions.

8. There is no argument that employment is not contractual. The argument centers, rather, on the elements and duration of the contract. When an employer offers an individual employment for which consideration in the form of wages and benefits is given and an employee accepts the offer by performing the work, a contract exists. The rights of the parties to sever or terminate that contract are at issue in the context of employment at will. The employer asserts that it has the unlimited right to terminate the contract for any reason not prohibited by a specific law. The employee asserts

that the employer's right is limited by either a condition which can be implied into the contract or by public policy.

9. *Ohanian v. Avis Rent A Car Sys.*, 779 F.2d 101, 121 LRRM 2169, *modified*, 121 LRRM 2229 (2d Cir. 1985).

10. *Reid v. Sears, Roebuck & Co.*, 790 F.2d 453, 122 LRRM 2153 (6th Cir. 1986).

11. *Rettinger v. American Can Co.*, 574 F. Supp. 806, 115 LRRM 2011 (W.D. Pa. 1983).

12. *Reuther v. Fowler & Williams*, 255 Pa. Super. 28, 386 A.2d 119, 115 LRRM 4690 (1978).

13. *Novosel v. Nationwide Ins. Co.*, 721 F.2d 894, 114 LRRM 3105, *reh'g denied en banc*, 115 LRRM 2426 (3d Cir. 1983), *on remand*, 118 LRRM 2779 (W.D. Pa. 1985).

14. *Callahan v. Scott Paper Co.*, 541 F. Supp. 550 (E.D. Pa. 1982); *Kalman v. Grand Union Co.*, 183 N.J. Super. 153, 443 A.2d 728, 115 LRRM 4803 (1982); *Stanley v. Sewell Coal Co.*, 285 S.E.2d 679 (W. Va. 1981); *Tameny v. Atlantic Richfield Co.*, 27 Cal. 3d 167, 610 P.2d 1330, 115 LRRM 3119 (1980); *O'Sullivan v. Mallon*, 390 A.2d 149, 115 LRRM 5064 (N.J. Super. 1978); *Trombetta v. Detroit, Toledo & Ironton R.R.*, 81 Mich. App. 489, 265 N.W.2d 385, 115 LRRM 4361 (1978); *Peterman v. Teamsters Local 396*, 174 Cal. App. 2d 184, 344 P.2d 25, 44 LRRM 2968 (1959).

15. *Wolk v. Saks Fifth Ave.*, 728 F.2d 221, 115 LRRM 3064 (3d Cir. 1984).

16. *Murray v. Commercial Union Ins. Co.*, 782 F.2d 432, 121 LRRM 3073 (3d Cir. 1986).

17. *Bruffett v. Warner Communications*, 692 F.2d 910, 115 LRRM 4117 (3d Cir. 1982).

18. *Supra*, note 13.

19. *Rawson v. Sears, Roebuck & Co.*, 615 F. Supp. 1546, 38 FEP 1392 (D. Colo. 1985).

20. *Garibaldi v. Lucky Food Stores*, 726 F.2d 1367, 115 LRRM 3089 (9th Cir. 1984), *cert. denied*, 471 U.S. 1099, 119 LRRM 2248 (1985).

21. *Toussaint v. Blue Cross & Blue Shield of Mich.*, 408 Mich. 579, 292 N.W. 2d 880, 115 LRRM 4708 (1980).

22. *Green v. Oliver Realty*, 526 A.2d 1192 (Pa. Super. Ct. 1987).

23. *Supra*, note 13.

24. *Supra*, note 21, 115 LRRM at 4716.

25. For a general analysis of the effect of the birth dearth on employment, *see* Johnston, *Workforce 2000* (Indianapolis: Hudson Institute, 1987).

26. *Supra*, note 21, 115 LRRM at 4720.

27. *Khalifa v. Henry Ford Hosp.*, 401 N.W.2d 884 (1986), *appeal denied*, June 3, 1987.

28. *See also Vander Toorn v. City of Grand Rapids*, 348 N.W.2d 697 (1984), *appeal denied*, Feb. 25, 1986.

29. *Schnelting v. Coors Distrib. Co.*, 729 S.W.2d 212, 125 LRRM 3367 (Mo. Ct. App. 1987).

30. *Id.* at 15.

31. *Allis-Chalmers Corp. v. Lueck*, 471 U.S. 202, 118 LRRM 3345 (1985).

32. 29 U.S.C. §185.

33. *Supra*, note 31, at 220–221.

34. *See Caterpillar, Inc. v. Williams*, 482 U.S. ___, 125 LRRM 2521 (1987) holding that LMRA §301 does not apply to individual employment contracts.

35. 9 U.S.C. §1 *et. seq. See Southland Corp. v. Keating*, 465 U.S. 1 (1984).

36. *Alexander v. Gardner-Denver*, 415 U.S. 36, 7 FEP 81 (1974). *See also Steck v. Smith Barney, Harris Upham & Co.*, 661 F. Supp. 543, 43 FEP 1736 (D.N.J. 1987) (ADEA); *Wilmington v. J.I. Case Co.*, 793 F.2d 909, 40 FEP 1833 (8th Cir. 1986) (§1981); *Zipf v. American Tel. & Tel. Co.*, 799 F.2d 889 (3d Cir. 1986) (ERISA); *McDonald v. City of West Branch, Mich.*, 466 U.S. 284, 115 LRRM 3646 (1984) (42 U.S.C. §1983); *Barrentine v. Arkansas-Best Freight Sys.*, 450 U.S. 728 (1981) (FLSA).

37. *Alexander v. Gardner-Denver, supra*, note 36, at 60 n.21.

38. *Mitsubishi Motors Corp. v. Soler Chrysler-Plymouth*, 473 U.S. 614 (1985). *See also Moses Lt. Cone Memorial Hosp. v. Mercury Constr. Corp.*, 460 U.S. 1 (1983).

39. *Shearson/Am. Express v. McMahon*, 482 U.S. ___, 55 USLW 4757 (1987).

40. *Mitsubishi Motors Corp. v. Soler Chrysler-Plymouth, supra*, note 38, at 638.

41. *Steck v. Smith Barney, Harris Upham & Co., supra*, note 36; *Swenson v. CDI Corp.*, 670 F. Supp. 1438, 44 FEP 1743 (D. Minn. 1987); *Claim of Garcia*, 479 N.Y.S.2d 594, 104 A.D. 675 (N.Y. App. Div. 1984) (unemployment compensation); *Claim of Ranni*, 58 N.Y.2d 715, 444 N.E.2d 1328 (1982) (unemployment compensation). *But see Jersey City Educ. Ass'n v. Jersey City Bd. of Educ.*, 527 A.2d 84, 44 FEP 1750 (N.J. Sup. Ct. App. Div. 1987); *Admiral Merchants v. Department of Labor*, 149 Mich. App. 344, 386 N.W.2d 193 (Mich. Ct. App. 1986); *Harris v. Iannaccone*, 487 N.Y.S.2d 562, 107 A.D. 429 (N.Y. App. Div.), *aff'd*, 496 N.Y.S.2d 948 (N.Y. 1985); *Thornton v. Potamkin Chevrolet*, 44 N.J. 92, 219 A.2d 505, 43 FEP 1733 (1983) (arbitration decision is persuasive but not binding).

42. An excellent example of such a system is Peer Grievance Review™ of Performance Systems, Dallas, Texas.

Part III

Employee Discipline: Practices

8

Poor Attendance: Absenteeism/ Tardiness

Issue
Whether an employee may be discharged or otherwise disciplined for poor attendance, excessive absenteeism, and/or tardiness.

Principle
An employee may be discharged or otherwise disciplined for poor attendance where the action taken is pursuant to a reasonable rule of which the employee is actually or constructively aware and which has been consistently applied and enforced. The employee must have actual notice of the consequences of poor attendance or continued poor attendance. In addition, there must be an absence of mitigating circumstances which justify either the employee's absences or a reduction in the degree of discipline.

Considerations
1. Whether the attendance rule is reasonable and consistent with the just cause provision of the labor agreement or general company policy;
2. Whether the rule has been communicated to the employees generally or, at least, in such fashion that the employee has actual or constructive notice of the standard of attendance required;
3. Whether the employee actually knew or had reason to know that the consequence of his or her actions, or contin-

135

ued actions, would be the discipline actually given;

4. Whether the discipline given the employee is consistent in occurrence and degree with the discipline given to other employees in similar situations;

5. Whether the employee's seniority, work history, attitude, type of absences (intermittent or extended), and/or likelihood of improvement would justify a mitigation of the discipline.

Discussion　　As a general rule, discipline up to and including discharge for poor attendance will more likely be sustained if effected according to a progressive discipline system following a well-communicated, reasonable attendance rule. When such a system has functioned to counsel and warn the employee of the consequences of poor attendance and has provided the employee with the opportunity to change his or her behavior, arbitrators will find that the discipline was warranted.[1]

When the progressive discipline system has been followed, the arbitrator is more likely to favor the action taken by the employer, and the arbitrator's ability and willingness to impose his or her own punishment will be limited.[2] When the employer has not used progressive discipline or has not applied the system consistently, the arbitrator is more likely to create an ad hoc system and reinstate an employee if he or she feels that discharge was too severe in light of the previous discipline or the employee's general work record.[3] In *Niagara Machine and Tool Works*, for instance, the arbitrator reinstated an employee who had been terminated for failure to maintain acceptable attendance levels.[4] The arbitrator felt that the employee's seventeen years of seniority outweighed his excessive absenteeism and that he might have been helped by progressive discipline.

It is clear from a review of arbitrators' opinions that discipline is more readily sustained when it is pursuant to an employer's formal attendance and absenteeism/tardiness policy. Arbitrators have found, however, that even though there may not be formal policy or rule, an employer can discipline an employee for violating some generally accepted attendance standard.[5] That is, an employer has a right to expect regular attendance from its employees: "Regularity of attendance is a basic employee responsibility and an inherent employee obligation."[6] In cases where formal rules exist, however, an employee must be made aware by the employer that his or her absenteeism will result in discipline up to, and including, discharge. Arbitrators have reinstated or reduced discipline when the employer has failed to communicate to the employee the consequences of his or her continued absenteeism.[7]

Commonly, arbitrators employ a fairly systematic process in the review of discipline for poor attendance. At the outset, an arbitrator will make a determination concerning the validity of the employer's attendance rule or absenteeism policy. The review of the rule is for reasonableness and for consistency with the labor agreement. The arbitrator will then determine if the employee was made aware of the rule and whether or not the rule was consistently enforced. Failure to meet these requirements may be sufficient rationale for the lessening or voiding of the discipline imposed on an employee.

Unless restricted or curtailed by the language of the labor agreement, the creation and enforcement of an attendance policy is generally held to be part of the employer's right to manage its enterprise.[8]

An employer's absenteeism policy is considered reasonable if it has been adopted to correct and not to punish absenteeism and tardiness.[9]

Employees must receive notice of the attendance policy and any changes which may be made to it. In *Marley Cooling Tower Co.*, the arbitrator found that any changes the company made in the type of absence that did or did not count in its no-fault absentee program, (e.g., snow days, jury duty, funeral leave) should have been made known to the employees prior to the change and prior to the enforcement.[10] Arbitrators will not enforce a rule or practice of which employees are not informed or are informed of only as a consequence of their behavior.[11]

Similarly, arbitrators will not sustain discipline if the employer fails to uniformly enforce the rule.[12] In *General Mills Fun Group*, the arbitrator reduced the discipline given to the employee, because the company failed to apply the procedures of its established system of corrective discipline.[13] The arbitrator found that the company had a good discipline system that it should have used; the company had both the means and the method to penalize the employee; and the company failed to do so properly. In *Georgia Pacific Corp.*, considerable confusion existed within the company about the accuracy of the attendance records, so the absentee program was ineffectively maintained and inconsistently applied.[14] There was enough confusion present that the grievant's discharge could not be sustained. In another case reflecting the problems with record keeping and enforcement, *Dunlop Tire and Rubber Corp.*, the arbitrator found that the company could not count absences in its absenteeism program when an employee submitted a doctor's note or excuse, if the company had previously taken an inconsistent position as to whether such a note excused an absence.[15]

If the rule survives the initial level of scrutiny—that is, whether the employer uniformly enforces its attendance rule—then the arbitrator will proceed to examine how the rule was applied to the specific grievant. If the employee was aware of the rule and the discipline was a result of a consistent application and enforcement of the policy, the discipline will almost certainly be sustained.[16]

If the employee was not aware of the rule or the employer did not make the existence of the rule adequately known to the employees, the discipline will be reduced.[17]

In *Werner-Continental*, the employer had no policy requiring discharge for absenteeism.[18] The grievant was, without question, excessively absent. However, his absences primarily were due to union business and other responsibilities pursuant to the labor agreement. In addition, the company, until its decision to discharge him, had accepted his excuses without negative comment and had not discharged any other employee for absenteeism. The grievant was reinstated.

Similarly, in *General Electric Co.*, the grievant was placed in a special program due to his excessive absenteeism.[19] The grievant was not informed of his responsibilities to the program, which included his receipt of counseling services and his adherence to certain attendance standards. His discharge for a subsequent absence was not sustained, because the arbitrator found that the grievant had no reason to believe that special rules now applied to his behavior.

In *Wilson Paper Co.*, the arbitrator found that the employee was not aware of any discipline policies regarding attendance and that his attendance was no worse than that of other employees.[20] Accordingly, the discharge was not sustained.

Most arbitrators also impose a requirement that the employer must have notified the employee of the consequences of his or her continued absenteeism. If this notice requirement is satisfied, the discipline, including discharge, normally will be upheld.[21] In *Witco Chemical Corp.*, the employee was repeatedly warned and suspended for his absenteeism and, prior to his discharge, the employer sent a letter advising the employee that the next absence would result in discharge.[22] His discharge was sustained. In *Alameda-Contra Costa Transit District*, the arbitrator stated, "The necessity of putting an employee on prior notice as to the probable consequences of his misconduct is one of the hallmarks of industrial discipline; in the absence of any such notice, the grievant's discharge cannot be sustained based on his absence record alone."[23] Applying similar logic, the discharges in *Pickands Mather & Co.* and *Northrop Worldwide Aircraft Services* were not sustained.[24]

Some arbitrators, however, do not require that the employer must have given the employee specific notice of the probable consequences of his or her behavior; rather, they assign to the employee the responsibility of acting in a reasonable and responsible manner. In *City of Detroit*, the employee was required to notify specific persons of an intended absence; the employee failed to do so and was suspended.[25] In *Dravo Doyle Co.*, the employee was not warned that his next absence would result in discharge; however, the arbitrator sustained the discharge, concluding that "any reasonable person could not help but be aware that he was approaching a peril point."[26]

If there is evidence that the attendance rule was not applied consistently or was applied inconsistently toward the grievant, the discipline will be reduced.[27]

In *Carborundum Co.*, the arbitrator found that although the employer's attendance rule on its face was reasonable, its application was unclear and inconsistent.[28] There was evidence of instances when some employees could avoid punishment and others could not. The grievant was reinstated, and the discharge reduced to a suspension.

In *Sun Furniture Co.*, when management punished the employee, it went from the initial action in the progressive discipline system directly to the last step.[29] The arbitrator found this discipline too harsh and reinstated the employee.

The last part of the arbitrator's analysis is an overall review of the facts and the equities of the grievance. A determination is made whether mitigating circumstances exist that may justify either the employee's behavior or a reduction of the discipline.[30] The review of mitigating factors includes an examination of the employee's work history, length of service, absence record (e.g., whether absences were chronic or intermittent), the reason for the absence, and the likelihood of improved attendance.[31]

In *Menasha Corp.*, the arbitrator, finding that the grievant's 27 years of service warranted more than a mechanical application of the employer's policy regarding minor offenses, reinstated the employee.[32] Similar determinations were made in *St. Regis Paper Co.* and *Niagara Machine and Tool Works*.[33] In both cases, the employees' long service records served to mitigate discharges to lesser penalties.

In *Northrop Worldwide Aircraft Services*, two employees were suspended for calling in sick and then playing on the employer's basketball team the same evening.[34] The suspensions were not sustained: The arbitrator, in addition to finding that the employees were not warned of the consequences of playing, found that there was no previous record of this type of absenteeism or misrepresentation by either employee. Arbitrators do not sympathize, however, when the employee's behavior forms a pattern or is part of a continuing theme. The employee in *ITT General Controls*, for instance, was discharged for not notifying the employer during a three-day absence; he had been previously discharged for the same offense.[35]

In deciding whether a penalty should be mitigated, arbitrators may also examine the reason for the grievant's absence and the likelihood of improved attendance. In *Automotive Distributors*, the employee was chronically absent due to a sinus condition.[36] However, he had not sought treatment for the condition in the year and a half he had been troubled by it. The arbitrator balanced the employee's health problems against the employer's need to have employees available on some reasonable, regular basis; the arbitrator found the employer's need more important. Of particular importance appeared to be the improbability of improved behavior by an employee who had made no attempt to correct the condition.

Moreover, in *Safeway Stores*, when an employee's absences were attributable to industrial accidents on several occasions and a motorcycle accident on another, the arbitrator found that the absences were not sufficient justification for a discharge, because they were of such a nature, i.e., extended absences, that the company could plan and cover for the employee's absence.[37]

In *Menasha Corp.*, the employee had been absent due to an illness that doctors suspected was cancer.[38] In refusing to sustain the discharge, the arbitrator reasoned that the employee now knew that he did not have cancer and, therefore, the likelihood that the employee's attendance would improve was good. Consequently, he deserved another opportunity. Similar reasoning was employed in *Warner and Swasey*. The employee's absences were due to alcoholism; the employee was rehabilitated and was held by the arbitrator to be deserving of a second chance.[39] But, the employee in *Champion International* did not fair so well.[40] She admitted that her excessive absenteeism was due to her dislike of her job. The arbitrator refused to reinstate her, because her attendance was not likely to improve at the same job.

Often arbitrators appear to make a determination purely on the basis of some notion of fairness which is neither defined nor capable of definition. In *Morton-Norwich Products*, for instance, an employee requested two extra days of funeral leave when his father died.[41] The employer denied the request and suspended the employee when he did not show up for work on those days. The arbitrator found that the employer acted unreasonably. In *Ogden Food Service Corp.*, an employee with a poor performance record was discharged when he left work to attend to a family friend who had suffered a heart attack.[42] The arbitrator reinstated the employee, finding the employer's reaction was not fair. The arbitrator found probative that the employee had followed all the notification procedures and that the person was, in fact, a close family friend.

No general rule based upon these examples of arbitral fairness can be stated, however, because arbitrators do not always exhibit the same degree of sympathy. In *FMC Corp.*, the employee did not show up for work because he was too upset by a friend's being found murdered, shot through the head.[43] The arbitrator found that the termination was appropriate: The employee had a generally poor attendance record and, if he had taken his job seriously, he would have called his employer. Similarly, in *Boeing Services International*, an employee was terminated because he had been in jail for 10 days, during which time he failed to notify his employer.[44]

Generally, arbitrators appear to agree that mitigating circumstances, if they are to be considered, must be part of the facts prior to the discharge. In *Western Gear Corp.*, and *Johns-Manville Products Corp.*, the employees involved had problems with alcohol.[45] In *Western Gear*, a drinking problem was discovered to be the cause of the employee's absenteeism only after he had been discharged.[46] The arbitrator found the discharge to be in accordance with the company's progressive discipline system, and the discovery that the employee's absenteeism was due to a drinking problem did not present a sufficiently mitigating circumstances to require reinstatement. In *Johns-Manville*, the employee's successful rehabilitation after he had been discharged was not sufficient grounds to earn him a second chance.[47]

While arbitrators will generally consider mitigating facts only if they preceded the discharge, they will, in certain cases, review predischarge conduct and decide whether that conduct, although unacceptable, constitutes sufficient proof that an employee will not be able to meet the requirements of the job. The facts and opinion in *Knauf Fiber Glass*[48] are particularly illustrative of this arbitral approach. From the employee's record, it was clear that she had developed an attendance pattern which kept her just short of discharge under the employer's no-fault absenteeism policy. As her accumulated absenteeism points would drop due to the passage of time, she would again be absent. Rather than accepting that the employee had figured out how to "work the system," the employer reacted by creating a special probation for her with more stringent requirements. The employee completed the probation but resumed her regular pattern. The employer again placed her on a special probation, even more stringent than before. When the employee had a personal emergency that resulted in another absence, she was discharged. While variations of no-fault absenteeism policies are generally enforced by arbitrators,[49] the discharge was not sustained in this case. The arbitrator decided as follows:

> The Company based its termination of the Grievant on the fact that she failed to meet the terms of her special probation. Without a doubt, the Grievant failed to meet those terms. The question presented to the Arbitrator is whether the special probation program as applied here to the Grievant warranted her discharge under the parties' "just cause" provision.
>
> The Arbitrator need not decide in this case whether the Company can ever use special probation to deal with an employee with a chronic absenteeism problem. Serious questions were raised at the hearing by the Union concerning the Company's policy and practice. For example, what triggered the placement of an employee on special probation? On the other hand, the Company reasonably believed that there had to be a way to deal with the "high riders," those employees who were

able to avoid discharge by carefully playing the point system. It determined that stricter attendance requirements would be warranted for those employees.

. . .

As far as the Company was concerned, the incident of December 3, 1982, was the last straw. It is common in a discharge case for absenteeism under a point system to find that the final point is just one more instance of a pattern of poor attendance. But that final "point" must be found to have been warranted in order to justify a termination. In determining the just cause of the Grievant's discharge, therefore, it is important *why* the Grievant left the plant.

. . .

It is also relevant for the Arbitrator to consider mitigating circumstances in resolving the present case. The evidence shows that the employee was considered to be a good worker. She had almost ten years of service with the Company. Her attendance during her special probation had shown some marginal improvement over the prior period. Even if not working perfectly, the special probation program was working.

. . .

Considering the evidence presented as a whole, the Arbitrator concludes that L___ was not discharged for just cause. In fashioning an appropriate remedy, however, the Arbitrator cannot ignore the Grievant's absenteeism record. Putting aside the emergency of December 3, the Grievant had consciously violated her two absence allowance during November of 1982. While her discharge cannot stand, a full measure of discipline is appropriate.

At the hearing, the Union suggested in the alternative a remedial approach which the arbitrator finds has merit. The Grievant will be returned to her position with the Company with no loss of seniority, but with no back pay. The Grievant will be on special probation for a ninety day period during which she will be allowed only one unexcused absence. In addition, her points under the Company's regular attendance policy should continue as they were at the time of her discharge on December 12, 1982.

It was apparent at the hearing that L___ felt deeply about her personal obligations and responsibilities as the unwed mother of three children. While understandably her son and daughters may be of paramount importance to her, her employer can insist that she meet reasonable attendance requirements. The Grievant can meet those requirements, keep her job and support her children. If she cannot meet those requirements now and in the future, she will lose her job and her children will suffer as a result. It will require great effort on her part to merit her dual responsibilites, but it certainly is worth the effort.

. . .

For the reasons noted, the grievance is granted. L___ was not discharged for just cause. The remedy is as set forth above in the Opinion.

This case demonstrates a fairly common problem: employer dissatisfaction with a flawed system and the difficulty in correcting the flaw on an ad hoc basis. If an employer creates a system which accepts an objective level of absence, the employer will generally be held to permitting that level. For example, if a system permits 5 percent absenteeism and an employee learns to work that system by keeping his or her attendance just short of unacceptable, the system has worked. The employee's absences may be annoying, but they do not warrant discharge. Some method of achieving responsible conduct must be found other than constant threats of discharge. If the employer cannot accept the absenteeism level contemplated by its system, a uniform attendance system should be adopted that establishes a new level of responsibility.

The arbitrator's award is unsatisfactory in that it merely creates another ad hoc probation. A better remedy is simply to tell the employer to either live with the level of irresponsibility its system allows or to define a more acceptable level. If the system's limit of acceptance is, in fact, unacceptable, the employer should redefine the limit.

Key Points

1   *The attendance rule must be reasonable.*

Examples

Employee *A* was discharged following an unexcused absence. The policy which he violated provided for discharge if an employee had one unexcused absence at any time within 12 months following a disciplinary suspension for poor attendance. Previously, after six unexcused absences in one month, the employee was warned verbally; after three unexcused absences within the next two months, he was given a written warning; and, after one unexcused absence in the month following his written warning, he was given a three-day disciplinary suspension. When the employee returned to work after the suspension, his supervisor told the employee in a letter that he would be discharged if he was absent one more time in the next 12 months. The employee's next absence occurred 10 months later, and he was discharged pursuant to the notice in the supervisor's letter. The employee's defense included the fact that he had called the employer prior to his work shift and said that he would not be in due to a family emergency. The arbitrator, noting that the employee had evidenced true concern for his job by calling in and had substantially improved his record, reinstated the employee with full back pay. The arbitrator felt that the rule was unreasonable as applied to this employee, because it punished an employee who was making a good-faith effort to be a responsible employee and who was succeeding.

Employee *B* was discharged for poor attendance. The policy under which he was disciplined requires discharge if an employee demonstrates a continued pattern of excessive absenteeism at any time within 12 months following a disciplinary suspension for poor attendance. After a three-day suspension, the employee had a perfect attendance record for three months. In the fourth month, he had one unexcused absence. In the fifth month, he had another unexcused absence and was warned about redeveloping a violative pattern. In the sixth month, the employee had two unexcused absences and in the eighth, three more. His discharge followed. The arbitrator sustained the discharge, finding that the employee demonstrated a blatant lack of concern for his job.

Employee *C* had four unexcused absences and two occurrences of lateness in the month of January. He was given a verbal warning. The following month he had three unexcused absences and one lateness. He was given a written warning. He had three unexcused absences and two latenesses the following month. He was given a three-day suspension with a note stating that if he was either late or absent again in the next 12 months he would be discharged. Three months later, after no intervening absences or latenesses, *C* called his supervisor prior to the work shift and said he would not be in due to car trouble. *C* was discharged. At the hearing, the employer established that car trouble had never been accepted by the company as a valid excuse. The arbitrator reinstated the employee on the basis that the 12-month period was too long, thereby, rendering the rule unreasonable; the employee had demonstrated concern for his job and had made an effort to be dependable.

Guidelines

The attendance policy of the employer must not be too restrictive in either the length of time an employee has to demonstrate good attendance or in its definition of good attendance. The policy must be flexible enough to allow for exigencies resulting in isolated occurrences. The policy must only discipline behavior which truly demonstrates a wanton disregard for employee responsibility.

Relevant Cases

Mesker Indus. (Mikrut), 85 LA 921
Dap, Inc. (Shieber), 84 LA 459
Sanyo Mfg. Corp. (Nicholas), 84 LA 169
Shell Oil Co. (Allen), 83 LA 787
Pantasote, Inc. (Seinsheimer), 82 LA 665
Coca Cola Bottling Co. (Berger), 81 LA 56
Todd Pacific Shipyards Co. (Jones), 81 LA 1095
Ideal Electric Co. (Martin), 77 LA 123
In re Bon Secours Hospital (Feldsman), 76 LA 705
Le Blond Machine Tool (Keenan), 76 LA 827
Dravo Doyle Co. (Jones), 73 LA 649
Wilson Paper Co. (Rose), 73 LA 1167
Werner-Continental (LeWinter), 72 LA 1
Carborundum Co. (Millious), 71 LA 802
Park Poultry (Hyman), 71 LA 1

2   *There must be actual or constructive employee knowledge of the acceptable standard of conduct.*

Examples

Employee A was discharged for excessive absenteeism after an absence supported by a doctor's note for illness. The employee asserted at the arbitration that he believed a doctor's note made the absence excused and not subject to the discipline policy. The employer could not demonstrate that doctors' excuses had been considered unacceptable in the past under the attendance policy and the policy statement itself was unclear. The arbitrator, noting a lack of notice to the employee regarding acceptable conduct, reinstated the employee with back pay.

Employee *B* was discharged for excessive absenteeism after her return to work following a disciplinary suspension. She asserted at the arbitration that she was unaware that she could not be excessively absent, i.e., more than one a month, for a full six-month period following a disciplinary suspension for the same cause. Relying on the clear policy set forth in the rules distributed to all employees at the time of hire, the arbitrator sustained the discharge.

Employee *C* had a bad attendance record. In accordance with the terms of the employer's progressive discipline system, he was discharged after an absence caused by an illness which was supported by a doctor's note. The employer refused to accept the note as an excuse but did not dispute its legitimacy. The employer told *C* that the note was satisfactory to allow for the payment of sick leave benefits but not to excuse the absence for purposes of the absenteeism control policy. *C* disputed this reasoning and asserted that an excuse is an excuse for all purposes. The arbitrator sustained the discharge after the employer had demonstrated that one of the absences upon which previous discipline was based had been of the same kind and was also supported by a doctor's note. Since *C* had not complained then that the discipline was unfair, he could not complain at the time of his discharge, nor could he state that he had no knowledge of the employer's policy.

Guidelines

The policy which the employer asserts has been violated must have been actually communicated to the employee in some precise form, so the employee can be found to have had constructive notice of it. The policy communicated must be clear and the knowledge transmitted to the employee must be found to be incapable of confusion.

Relevant Cases

Cameron Iron Works (Milentz), 84 LA 936
Dap, Inc. (Shieber), 84 LA 459
Suncrete Ready Mix (Cloke), 84 LA 613
Fred Rueping Leather (Jacobowski), 83 LA 644
Weyerhaeuser Co. (Shearer), 83 LA 365

Oglebey Norton Co. (Duda), 82 LA 652
Safeguard Scientifics (Gallagher), 82 LA 945
McGraw-Edison (Role), 81 LA 403
Multiplex Co. (Smith), 81 LA 625
Southwest Forest Industries (Cromwell), 81 LA 1234
Burns International Security Services (Kelliher), 78 LA 1163
Lucky Stores (Darrow), 78 LA 233
Ludington News Co. (Platt), 78 LA 1165
Northrop Worldwide Aircraft Services (Mewhinney), 75 LA 1059
Bethlehem Steel Corp. (Fishgold), 74 LA 507
Wilson Paper Co. (Rose), 73 LA 1167
General Electric Co. (MacDonald), 72 LA 809
Marley Cooling Tower Co. (Sergent), 71 LA 306

3 *The employee must be found to have known of the probable consequences of his or her act prior to its commission.*

Examples

Employee *A* was discharged for excessive absenteeism after a continued pattern of absences following a disciplinary suspension. The notice of suspension did not contain a statement that the continuation of the violative conduct would result in discharge, although the employer's written policy clearly provided for this penalty. The employee presented evidence that the employer did not always discharge other employees in similar circumstances. The arbitrator, noting the confusion created by the employer's failure to follow its own policy, reinstated the employee without back pay, based upon the employee's otherwise good work record.

Employee *B* was discharged for excessive tardiness. The published policy of the employer is that a continued pattern of excessive tardiness after a disciplinary suspension for the same cause may result in discharge. This policy was quoted in the employee's final warning. There was no evidence of any other employee having gone this far in the discipline system. The arbitrator reinstated the employee without back pay based upon his otherwise good work record. The possibility and the uncertainty of discharge as stated in the policy allowed the arbitrator to substitute his judgment for that of the employer. Had the final warning stated to the employee that he would be discharged, the arbitrator may not have felt so much latitude.

Guidelines

The notice to the employee of the consequences of his or her continued violative behavior must be unequivocal and precise. There can be no possible room for any other result. In the absence of this clarity, arbitrators will feel free to examine other elements of the employee's work history to see if the penalty should be mitigated.

Relevant Cases

Lear Siegler, Inc. (Rothschild), 85 LA 411
Sanyo Mfg. Corp. (Kelliher), 85 LA 707
Shell Oil Co. (LeBaron), 85 LA 769
Atlantic Richfield Co. (Gibson), 84 LA 257
Cameron Iron Works (Milentz), 84 LA 936
Dap, Inc. (Shieber), 84 LA 459
Litton Microwave Cooking Products (Bognanno), 84 LA 761
Nuturn Corp. (Seidman), 84 LA 1058
Great Plains Bag Corp (Leach), 83 LA 1281
Great Midwest Mining Corp. (Mikrut), 82 LA 52
Metropolitan Transit Authority (King), 82 LA 141
Atlantic Richfield Co. (Heinsz), 81 LA 1193
Multiplex Co. (Smith), 81 LA 625
Burns International Security Services (Kelliher), 78 LA 1163
Lucky Stores (Darrow), 78 LA 233
Ludington News Co. (Platt), 78 LA 1165
Alameda-Contra Costa Transit District (Koven), 76 LA 770
Pickands Mather & Co. (Witt), 76 LA 676
City of Detroit (Coyle), 75 LA 1045
Northrup Worldwide Aircraft Services (Mewhinney), 75 LA 1059
Bethlehem Steel Corp. (Fishgold), 74 LA 507
Dravo Doyle Co. (Jones), 73 LA 649
Wilson Paper Co. (Rose), 73 LA 1167
General Electric Co. (MacDonald), 72 LA 809
Werner-Continental (LeWinter), 72 LA 1
Witco Chemical Corp. (Light), 71 LA 919

4   *The discipline must be consistent with that given to other employees in similar circumstances.*

Examples

Employee *A* was discharged for excessive tardiness following one reoccurrence after a disciplinary suspension.

At the arbitration, *A* presented evidence of another employee who, after being tardy three weeks after his suspension, was only warned by a supervisor for that behavior and told that a reoccurrence would result in discharge. The arbitrator reinstated *A* without back pay and gave him a final warning.

Employee *B* was suspended for excessive absenteeism. At the arbitration *B* presented evidence of another employee who was only given another written warning after a similar violative act. The employer countered by showing that in all similar cases, except the one cited by *B*, employees were given suspensions and there were mitigating circumstances to explain the difference raised by *B*. The arbitrator sustained the suspension.

Guidelines

Although variations in the treatment of employees will not necessarily result in the nullification of an entire system, they must be truly exceptions to a well-established and -used policy and supported by sound reasoning.

Relevant Cases

Arch of Illinois (Feldman), 84 LA 185
Shell Oil Co. (Allen), 83 LA 787
Texas City Refining (King), 83 LA 923
American Mfg. Co. (Speroff), 82 LA 36
Burns International Security Services (Kelliher), 78 LA 1163
Ludington News Co. (Platt), 78 LA 1165
Irwin-Willert Home Products Co. (Maniscalco), 77 LA 146
Arkansas Glass Container Corp. (Teple), 76 LA 841
Dunlop Tire & Rubber Corp. (Williams), 76 LA 1228
ITT General Controls (Bickner), 76 LA 1258
Monsanto Co. (Thomson), 76 LA 509
General Mills Fun Group (Martin), 72 LA 1285
Carborundum Co. (Millious), 71 LA 802
Georgia Pacific Corp. (Imundo), 71 LA 195
Shepard Niles Crane & Hoist Corp. (Alutto), 71 LA 828
Sun Furniture Co. (Szollosi), 71 LA 928

5 *The employee's work history must not create an aura of injustice.*

Examples

Employee *A* was discharged for excessive absenteeism. Her final warning had stated that continued excessive absenteeism would result in further discipline, up to, and including, discharge. The arbitrator found that neither the history of the employer's absenteeism policy nor the final warning required the employer to discharge the employee. However, because the employee had a history of barely acceptable attendance and demonstrated no significant improvement as a result of progressive discipline, the discharge was sustained.

Employee *B*, was discharged for excessive absenteeism; his final warning had indicated that a continued pattern of excessive absenteeism could result in his discharge. The arbitrator examined the employee's work history, because the employer's policy did not mandate discharge. Noting that attendance appeared to be the employee's only problem and that a prior despicable attendance record had been substantially improved as a result of progressive discipline, the arbitrator reinstated the employee without back pay.

Employee *C* had a record of 25 percent absenteeism in six months and 10 tardinesses. *C* was given a written warning. In the next month, his absenteeism dropped to 15 percent, with only one tardiness of five minutes. Still excessive, *C* was given a disciplinary suspension. In the following month, *C* had one occurrence of absenteeism for four days due to a legitimate illness. He had no other one-day absences nor tardinesses. *C* was discharged. The arbitrator reinstated the employee with back pay. Regardless of the fact that the employee technically violated the rule, the record demonstrated the success of the progressive discipline system and a conscientious effort on the part of the employee to be dependable.

Guidelines

Unless precluded from examining the judgment of the employer, arbitrators will look to an employee's work history to determine whether the employee had demonstrated sufficient disregard for his or her obligations over a significant period of time to be considered incorrigible.

Relevant Cases

AMAX Coal Co. (Kelroy), 85 LA 225
Shell Oil Co. (Allen), 83 LA 787
Southwest Detroit Hospital (Ellmann), 82 LA 491
Knauf Fiber Glass (Abrams), 81 LA 333
Burns International Security Services (Kelliher), 78 LA 1163
East Ohio Gas Co. (Michelstetter), 78 LA 71
Ludington News Co. (Platt), 78 LA 1165
Irwin-Willert Home Products Co. (Maniscalco), 77 LA 146
ITT General Controls (Bickner), 76 LA 1258
Niagara Machine & Tool Works (Grant), 76 LA 160
Northrop Worldwide Aircraft Services (Mewhinney), 75 LA 1059
Ogden Food Service Corp. (Kelman), 75 LA 805
Safeway Stores (Winograd), 75 LA 430
St. Regis Paper Co. (Andersen), 75 LA 737
FMC Corp. (Doering), 74 LA 1185
Morton-Norwich Products (Nitka), 74 LA 202
Menasha Corp. (Roumell), 71 LA 653
Warner and Swasey (Siegel), 71 LA 158

Notes to Chapter 8

1. *Armstrong Rubber Co.* (Williams), 74 LA 362; *Sharon Steel Corp.* (Klein), 71 LA 737; *Witco Chem. Corp.* (Light), 71 LA 919.
2. *Bethlehem Steel Corp.* (Fishgold), 74 LA 507; *Champion Int'l* (White), 74 LA 623; *Hawaii Transfer Co.* (Tsukiyama), 74 LA 531.
3. *Pickands Mather & Co.* (Witt), 76 LA 676; *Werner-Continental* (LeWinter), 72 LA 1.
4. *Niagara Machine & Tool Works* (Grant), 76 LA 160.
5. *Werner-Continental, supra*, note 3; *Wilson Paper Co.* (Rose), 73 LA 1167.
6. *Ideal Elec. Co.* (Martin), 77 LA 123.
7. *Werner-Continental, supra*, note 3.
8. *Werner-Continental, supra*, note 3; *Lime Register Co.* (Heinsz), 76 LA 935; *Scott Air Force Base* (Fitzsimmons), 76 LA 46.
9. *In re Bon Secours Hosp.* (Feldsman), 76 LA 705; *Le Blond Machine Tool* (Keenan), 76 LA 827; *Dravo Doyle Co.* (Jones), 73 LA 649; *Park Poultry* (Hyman), 71 LA 1.
10. *Marley Cooling Tower Co.* (Sergent), 71 LA 306.
11. *Northrop Worldwide Aircraft Servs.* (Mewhinney), 75 LA 1059; *Wilson Paper Co., supra*, note 5; *General Elec. Co.* (MacDonald), 72 LA 809.
12. *Dunlop Tire & Rubber Corp.* (Williams), 76 LA 1228; *General Mills Fun Group* (Martin), 72 LA 1285; *Carborundum Co.* (Millious), 71 LA 802; *Georgia Pacific Corp.* (Imundo), 71 LA 195; *Sun Furniture Co.* (Szollosi), 71 LA 928.
13. *General Mills, supra*, note 12.

14. *Georgia Pacific Corp., supra*, note 12.

15. *Dunlop Tire & Rubber Corp., supra*, note 12.

16. *Irwin-Willert Home Prods. Co.* (Maniscalco), 77 LA 146; *ITT General Controls* (Bickner), 76 LA 1258; *Monsanto Co.* (Thomson), 76 LA 509.

17. *Wilson Paper Co., supra*, note 5; *General Elec. Co., supra*, note 11; *Werner-Continental, supra*, note 3.

18. *Werner-Continental, supra*, note 3.

19. *General Elec. Co., supra*, note 11.

20. *Wilson Paper Co., supra*, note 5.

21. *Bethlehem Steel Corp., supra*, note 2.

22. *Witco Chem. Corp., supra*, note 1.

23. *Alameda-Contra Costa Transit Dist.* (Koven), 76 LA 770.

24. *Pickands Mather & Co., supra*, note 3; *Northrop Worldwide Aircraft Serv., supra*, note 11.

25. *City of Detroit* (Coyle), 75 LA 1045.

26. *Dravo Doyle Co., supra*, note 9.

27. *Arkansas Glass Container Corp.* (Teple), 76 LA 841; *General Mills, supra*, note 12; *Carborundum Co., supra*, note 12; *Shepard Niles Crane & Hoist Corp.* (Alutto), 71 LA 828; *Sun Furniture Co., supra*, note 12.

28. *Carborundum Co., supra*, note 12.

29. *Sun Furniture Co., supra*, note 12.

30. *Irwin-Willert Home Prods. Co., supra*, note 16.

31. *See Safeway Stores* (Winograd), 75 LA 430; *Menasha Corp.* (Roumell), 71 LA 653.

32. *Menasha Corp., supra*, note 31.

33. *Niagara Machine & Tool Works, supra*, note 4; *St. Regis Paper Co.* (Andersen), 75 LA 737.

34. *Northrop Worldwide Aircraft Servs., supra*, note 11.

35. *ITT General Controls, supra*, note 16.

36. *Automotive Distribs.* (Eisler), 76 LA 552.

37. *Safeway Stores, supra*, note 31.

38. *Menasha Corp., supra*, note 31.

39. *Warner & Swasey* (Siegel), 71 LA 158.

40. *Champion Int'l, supra*, note 2.

41. *Morton-Norwich Prods.* (Nitka), 74 LA 202.

42. *Ogden Food Serv. Corp.* (Kelman), 75 LA 805.

43. *FMC Corp.* (Doering), 74 LA 1185.

44. *Boeing Servs. Int'l* (Kramer), 75 LA 967.

45. *Western Gear Corp.* (Sabo), 74 LA 641; *Johns-Manville Prods. Corp.*, (Kates), 76 LA 845.

46. *Western Gear Corp., supra*, note 45.

47. *Johns-Manville Prods., supra*, note 45.

48. *Knauf Fiber Glass* (Abrams), 81 LA 333.

49. *Atlantic Richfield Co.* (Gibson), 84 LA 257; *Dap, Inc.* (Shieber), 84 LA 459.

9

Abusive, Profane, or Obscene Language

Issue   Whether an employee may be discharged or otherwise disciplined for abusive, profane, or obscene language.

Principle   An employee may be discharged, or otherwise disciplined, for use of abusive, profane, or obscene language where the conduct demonstrates gross disrespect or insubordination to a supervisor, is not provoked, and causes disruption in operations or among other employees. An employee may be discharged, or otherwise disciplined, for similar conduct directed at co-employees where the conduct is unprovoked and causes or is intended to cause a disruption to production or the peaceful atmosphere of the workplace.

Considerations   1. Whether language is directed at a specific person, rather than generally;
2. Whether the nature of the work environment or the workplace is such that "shop talk" is similar to or the same as the language used;
3. Whether the supervisor uses similar, or the same, language in his or her dealings with employees;
4. The nature of the specific incident, i.e., whether the language used was at a time of high tension, after provocation, or as part of an insubordinate action;
5. Whether the language used was heard by other employees, customers, or the

general public and caused a disruption to production or reflected poorly on the reputation of the employer;

6. Whether the employee's work record reveals prior warnings for similar conduct or is otherwise generally unsatisfactory.

Discussion   While it is apparent from the numerous arbitration awards concerning discipline for use of abusive, profane, and obscene language, the threshold of arbitrator sensitivity varies widely. This variance occasionally affects awards; decisions almost always depend upon elements other than the specific words used. In fact, except in extreme cases, the specific words fade into the background as the arbitrators concern themselves with why the employee deported himself or herself in the particular manner, what the employee intended to impart by his or her conduct, and the effect of the conduct on others.[1]

Consequently, in determining the type of discipline to be meted out to an employee for use of abusive, profane, or obscene language, it is suggested that the decision be based primarily on considerations other than the words used.[2] These considerations differ in emphasis depending upon whether the abusive conduct is directed at supervisors or other employees.[3]

Where abusive language is directed at supervisors, arbitrators generally look to see if the abuse is, in reality, just another form of insubordination; if the abuse is witnessed by other employees or persons, thereby, heightening the effect of the disrespect and its effect on an "orderly" shop; and/or if the abusive language is initiated by supervisory provocation.

In *Jones & Laughlin Steel Corp.*, for instance, an employee who was also a shop steward, came to the plant at a time other than his normal working hours to discuss a grievance.[4] While at the plant and on the production floor, he was informed by a supervisor of his next overtime assignment. In contesting his assignment, the employee used abusive and profane language directed toward the supervisor and, presumably, within the hearing of other employees. Finding the employee's conduct to warrant discipline, the arbitrator sustained the company's action on the basis of insubordination. The fact that the conduct occurred while the employee was "off duty" was found irrelevant, and his defense that he was conducting union business was held insufficient to justify the conduct.

In *Borg-Warner Corp.*, the discharge of an employee was sustained where he had called a female supervisor a "faggot" and had made obscene gestures toward her.[5] The arbitrator made special mention of the fact that the abusive language was within the hearing of other employees who laughed, subjecting the supervisor to derision.

In *Dobbs House, Inc.*,[6] the arbitrator reinstated the employee and commuted the discharge to a suspension without pay, when the employee's abusive conduct took place in a supervisor's lunchroom where only the union steward and supervisors were present.[7]

As a general rule, arbitrators distinguish between cases involving abusive language and gestures directed toward supervisors which occur in the presence of other employees and cases where the conduct takes place in the presence only of supervisors. For instance, an employee may be disciplined to a high degree, even discharged, where he or she abuses a supervisor on the shop floor; the employee may not be disciplined, at least to the same degree, where the same abuse occurs in a supervisor's office. The rationale is that the former is a direct assault on the supervisor's position of authority, while the latter is merely a personal attack with implications that do not go beyond their personal relationship.

The derision of a supervisor in such a place and in such a manner that the supervisor's status is damaged in the eyes of others who he or she may supervise is viewed as extremely serious and warrants severe discipline. It is a direct challenge and threat to the order of the operation. On the other hand, these elements are not as important when the confrontation takes place outside the hearing of others.

Where the abuse is directed toward nonsupervisory employees, arbitrators emphasize the issues of whether the abuse causes a subsequent altercation between employees; whether the language may be common "shop talk"; whether the conduct was provoked; and whether the abuse is of a specifically distasteful nature, e.g., racial or ethnic slurs, as well as sexual comments and actions, are treated as the most serious. In *Anaconda Copper Co.*, for instance, the discharge of an employee for "sexual harrassment" was sustained.[8] The employee had used coarse language with sexual overtones and had made obscene finger and pelvic movements toward a female employee. This conduct had continued over a substantial period of time, and the arbitrator concluded that it had created an intimidating atmosphere for the female employee. The grievant complained that he had been denied progressive discipline. The arbitrator held, however, that the verbal warning and two transfers to get him out of certain areas were sufficient notice to him that his conduct was not being condoned. The arbitrator stated that the company had no further obligation to administer any more corrective discipline.[9]

In *New Industrial Techniques*,[10] the shop steward, who was also a leadman, had made repeated obscene gestures and acts toward women that constituted sexual harassment. The company discharged him. The arbitrator found particularly relevant the facts that the employer had held educational sessions and had an articulated policy against sexual harassment. The grievant has also received both verbal and written warnings. Under these facts, the arbitrator found the company's witnesses more credible than the grievant's. Indeed, it is amazing that the employer allowed the conduct to continue for so long without taking action sooner.

In this context, it may be that the employer has no alternative but to discharge an employee for obscene conduct which creates an atmosphere offensive to female employees. Allowing such a condition to exist has been held to be a violation of Title VII of the Civil Rights Act and the basis for assessment of damages against both the employer and individual employees. In respect to labor arbitrators, therefore, the failure to stop such behavior through discipline may give rise to a grievance by the offended female alleging a violation of the contract's nondiscrimination provision.[11]

Verbal and physical abuse which provokes fighting, of course, clearly justifies discipline, although the abuse most frequently appears in cases only as a side issue to the discipline resulting from the fight. Where arbitrators are given the latitude and have the inclination to differentiate between two combatants in terms of degrees of punishment, however, the abusive conduct will be used as the basis for sustaining a higher level of discipline for one. Racial and ethnic slurs figure prominently in these cases. (For a more extended discussion of these cases, see Part III, Chapter 19.)

"Shop talk" is a frequent defense raised by grievants and presents evidentiary problems for arbitrators. It is difficult in these cases for an arbitrator to discern what is, and what is not, commonplace in the plant. The theory of the defense is simply that an employee cannot be disciplined for using language, or engaging in conduct, which is usual and ordinary in the workplace. As a rule, arbitrators make short work of this defense and appear to pay little attention to the actual words used during the incident in the case presented to them. Their focus, rightfully, is on the manner with which the words are spoken, the intent of the employee in using them, their effect on the persons in the area, and the present and future orderliness of the workplace.

In *Louisville Gas and Electric*,[12] for example, the arbitrator held that sexual harassment was not proven where an employee had pointed a metal rod at a female co-employee and asked "how she would like to have the rod stuck in her so that her temperature could be taken." The arbitrator noted that the employee had made the same threat to a male employee and that the female employee had taken both threats as a joke. The arbitrator stated:

> What may be offensive to one person is often quite all right with another. Modern mores being what they are, crude language abounds in shops and offices. This is well illustrated by P___'s reply to the remark, a four letter expletive, which coming from a lady would have shocked most people twenty years ago, but which is now, unfortunately, rather commonplace.

On the simplest level, an employee cannot be appropriately disciplined for using obscene language in a conversation with other employees or even a supervisor. No matter how coarse the language, its use is not with improper intent or adverse effect. The language may be offensive and may justify some corrective action, but it rarely justifies discipline in that context.

However, where the language is pointed and apparently intended to abuse a supervisor in such a way that it may diminish his or her effectiveness as a supervisor, it can be the basis for discipline, regardless of the general level of profanities or obscenities in the workplace. The only really significant time that a pointed use of profanity or obscene language may be successfully defended under the rubric of "shop talk" is where the supervisor engages in such language or actions. An employee who can prove that a supervisor uses profane or obscene language in his or her day-to-day treatment of employees, or in the specific instance being scrutinized, may successfully avoid the discipline. The attitude of arbitrators appears to be that the supervisor cannot be offended by conduct which is similar to or a variation of his or her own. Nor can such conduct be found to be a significant attack on the supervisor's authority.

In *Steiger Tractor*,[13] an employer was held to have improperly discharged an employee who engaged in an extended emotional outburst after his supervisor told him to stop talking and get back to work where it appeared that the outburst followed the supervisor's statement on the previous day that "he couldn't babysit each individual to do a good job" and where the employee had epilepsy-like symptoms for which he was taking medication. The arbitrator stated:

> First, at the outset, the arbitrator wishes to make very clear his finding that the conduct of the grievant on December 15 was a flagrant abuse of and challenge to the authority of supervisor Kolb. In and of itself it was a clear flagrant act of insubordination, and a cause for immediate discharge under the company's rules, unless there would be some distinct and substantial mitigation circumstance. Again, his behavior was insubordinate, disruptive, and substantial.
>
> . . .
>
> A second major consideration is the recognition that there was some contribution of fault on both sides in the immediate circumstance of the incident and the direct prior background, with some mitigation accruing to the grievant, but insufficient to excuse his behavior. While the grievant may not have liked the increased company speed up and pressure to produce more or faster, this does not justify his resentment for which he is at fault. If he had a complaint he should have discussed it and not allowed it to smoulder. The evidence indicated that other employees were subject to the same speed up and expectations. It may be that the grievant finds it more comfortable to work at a more regular pace with greater attentiveness to detail, which he may have enjoyed in the past, but if so, he may simply have to accept the necessity of accommodating to todays changing condition. The company does have the legitimate right to set standards and methods. The company has been faced with the problems of the recent poor ecomony, its effect in the farm implement industry, and the need to upgrade and improve its efficiencies and cost reduction. To the extent that the company is legitimate on such measures, it is incumbent upon the grievant to accommodate. Even if, in this context, the grievant had some basis for concern or protest, this would not justify the insubordination outburst he displayed.
>
> Continuing, the grievant's complaint of the speed up and the claim of his wish to do quality work, is contradicted by the supervisor's claim that the grievant did not maintain quality consistently, required more supervision, and where his December 14 shoddy work was inconsistent with the other employee who performed satisfactorily. On the other hand, these statements by the supervisor must be further conditioned by the fact that there was no record of a criticism or warning to the grievant of poor work performance or a notation of such in his file.

The grievant does indicate that he was conscious of personal dignity of himself and other employees, along with his concern for quality. Somewhat in contrast was the indication from the evidence that the supervisor treated the grievant in a belittling and negative antagonistic manner, both at the end of the prior day of the 14th, and the morning of the 15th. His references to not being able to babysit and provide as much supervision as in the past, to alleged prior pressures of the grievant on an earlier foreman, were provocative and demeaning. He provided further provocative fuel on the morning of the 15th by ignoring the good faith of the grievant who made it to work in spite of the bad weather, had already been actively at work, and was actually discussing the work condition with the other employee. On the other hand, in defense of the supervisor, he may have faced a hectic situation that morning, the grievant did not tell him he was discussing work with the other employee, and the supervisor did not immediately jump to suspend the grievant at his first outburst, but instead warned him and started to leave. It was the grievant who initiated the emotional outburst, and who again resumed his diatribe instead of shutting up. Admittedly, while the grievant's conduct was not an intentional refusal to work as such, but was rather more a display of abuse and challenge, it still remained insubordinate.

. . .

From these above circumstances just discussed, there is an additional factor ascertained which merits distinction. Combined with the recognition that the supervisor was abrupt and negative or antagonistic on the morning of the 15th with the grievant, is the related feature ascertained that the supervisor was apparently jumpy and arguably excessively authoritative in his style or method of supervision. By the same token, it is apparent that the supervisor could have easily avoided the confrontation or de-escalated the situation by a less provocative style or by more maturely offering some explanation or opportunity to the grievant to voice his concerns. This the supervisor did not do. Even in the face of a possible confrontation or development of a disciplinary situation, the company does have an obligation to manage properly and to help avoid or de-escalate a situation if it can be done readily and there is opportunity to do so. Such appeared to be the case here. Quite frankly, I feel the evidence indicates some basis to be critical of the supervisor's own conduct toward the grievant. If this were the only additional mitigating circumstance or factor to consider, then I would still not regard this as sufficient to overturn the discharge and to be regarded as an excusable mitigation circumstance, when added to the above factors described. However, when this particular factor is added to the additional more substantive facts of the grievant's indicated ailment, then it attains greater weight and relevance.

The third next major area to be discussed is the indicated ailment or condition of the grievant. Our starting point premise in this area is the display and conduct of the grievant on the morning of December 15, and again shortly thereafter in the early afternoon investigation meeting conducted by the company. His emotional outburst was so flagrant, extended and unwarranted, that it should have been apparent to supervision and alerted it to the likelihood that there was something wrong with the grievant at the moment. His display was akin to a seizure, and was something beyond a more conventional insubordination by an employee which arises in the usual work context. There was no evidence that he had before given forth such a display. A few hours later during the investigatory meeting, the very fact of his rambling, babbling, his inability to stick to the point, and his inability to supply a more direct coherent outline for his actions and concerns, continued to indicate that there was something wrong with him, or that he was suffering from something. It was apparent that trying to conduct a rational orderly meeting with the grievant was rather futile. Certainly when a long standing employee with a reasonably satisfactory work record evokes such a sudden unusual display, it would seem the company has some obligation to recognize it as a possible sickness or condition which is affecting the employee's behavior, and which may mitigate or reduce his personal responsibility at the moment, at least it should cause the company to be so alerted and to investigate the matter further. This the company did not apparently do.

. . .

In summary then, the arbitrator concludes and determines that the discharge was not justified While the conduct of the grievant was a flagrant insubordinate abusive challenge to the supervisor, the just cause element is substantially reduced by the mitigating circumstances. Such mitigation includes the opportunity of the supervisor to have better handled the situation and to have avoided the confrontation. But more significant is the alert the company should have recognized, that the grievant may have been experiencing some form of ailment or affliction, which is further compounded by the company's own medical records of the prior condition and medication of the grievant.

Where the abuse is directed toward, or in the presence of, a customer or other member of the public, arbitrators examine the nature of the abuse, the precipitating cause of the conduct, and most important, the effect of the conduct upon the business and reputation of the employer.[14]

In *H.E. Miller Oldsmobile*,[15] the arbitrator concluded that a mechanic cursed at a customer. The discharge of the mechanic was sustained, even though the arbitrator felt that the company had placed the mechanic in an improper position and that a suspension would have been adequate discipline. The unusually restrictive contract language effectively controlled the arbitrator's discretion nevertheless. The arbitrator's analysis is instructive:

Given the clarity of paragraph 17:26, the broad consensus that negotiation history should not be used to vary clear contract language, and the admonition in paragraph 16:01 not to subtract from the provisions of the Agreement, I cannot hold that mechanics are not covered by the provision dealing with cursing in the presence of a customer. There is ambiguity, however, as to whether cursing that is merely heard by a customer as opposed to cursing that is directed toward a customer is covered by paragraph 17:26. The admonition to avoid nonsensical results, when considered in light of the context in which the Agreement is administered and the fact that mechanics do not deal with customers on a regular basis, does indicate that paragraph 17:26 should be interpreted so that it does not lead to immediate discharge every time a mechanic curses so that he can be heard by a customer. It would not be enough to justify a discharge if a mechanic cursed to himself while performing his work and a customer just happened to hear him. At the very least, the mechanic should be speaking to a customer or speaking under circumstances that indicate that he intends for the customer to hear him. In addition, since both the Company and the Union agree that the purpose of the provision is to protect the dealer's relationship with customers, the circumstances and words used should be such that it is reasonable to assume that the mechanic's comments might be offensive to the customer. Thus the answer to the first issue is a qualified yes.

. . . I would convert the discharge to a suspension for a period of time without pay. I recognize that the Company cannot tolerate the use of insulting and offensive language to customers. But the point that this conduct is unacceptable could have been made by a suspension without pay. Prompt suspension without pay for a period of time should be enough to satisfy most customers. Moreover, I believe the Company bears some responsibility for what happened. Mechanics are not hired to deal with customers. The Company's policy is that customers should not wait in the area in which mechanics work. It is the responsibility of the service manager and assistant service manager to deal with customers and to see that they stay out of work areas. By not discharging their responsibilities fully, the service manager created unnecessary problems for the mechanics. While I recognize that the Grievant was wrong in responding to this situation in the way that he did, this problem might not have arisen if management personnel had handled this situation properly.

Arbitrators universally accept the need of an employer to maintain a good public image as something which can be enforced through employee discipline. No defense on the basis of "shop" or "street" talk will be sufficient to void discipline for abusive, profane, or obscene language or conduct directed toward a customer. Even where a customer is abusive and, perhaps, deserves a verbal thrashing, employees are expected to rise above the provocation. Under these circumstances, however, discipline penalties may be mitigated.

Abusive, profane, or obscene language or conduct—not directed at a customer, but within the hearing or presence of a customer—may also be sufficient cause for discipline. Such conduct is viewed as destructive of an atmosphere conducive to the employer's business. Accordingly, some discipline was sustained in *Washington IGA Foodline*, where the employee's profane and abusive language was directed at a store manager within the hearing of customers.[16]

Where some or all of these elements are proven to the disadvantage of the employee, evidence presented on other issues is generally discounted in some fashion. Of course, in all discipline cases the prior record of the employee and the presence, or absence, of corrective discipline is considered to be of great importance.[17]

Key Points

1   *Whether the abusive language or conduct is aimed at a specific person, particularly a supervisor.*

Examples

Employee *A* was told by his supervisor to stop loafing and to get back to work. The employee exclaimed "Oh, f___," and the words rang out through the workplace in which there were both males and females working. The supervisor discharged the employee. The arbitrator, noting that the words were used only as an exclamation and not directed toward the supervisor or any other person, reinstated the employee, commuting the discipline to a warning.

Employee *B* was told by his supervisor to stop loafing and to get back to work. The employee replied to the supervisor, "f___ you." Two other employees nearby heard the exclamation. The employee was discharged. Finding that the employee had been previously warned for insubordinate conduct toward his supervisor and that his language was directed at the supervisor, the arbitrator denied the grievance and upheld the discharge.

Guidelines

General exclamations may be cause for discipline, depending on the circumstances. However, discipline for such conduct must be modest, or it will be reversed or reduced. Abusive, obscene, or profane conduct or exclamations which are individual-specific will sustain more extreme discipline and, if coupled with other insubordinate conduct or disruption in the plant, discharge.

Relevant Cases

Fordham University (Irsay), 85 LA 293
Montebello Container Corp. (Kaufman), 85 LA 1011
Continental Fire Drum (Yaney), 83 LA 1197
Burton Manufacturing Co. (Holley), 82 LA 1228
Care Inns (Taylor), 81 LA 687
D&D Poultry (Nelson), 81 LA 553
FMC Corp. (Nicholas), 81 LA 176
General Portland, Inc. (Flannagan), 81 LA 230
Louisville Gas & Electric Co. (Stonehouse), 81 LA 730
Tempmaster Corp. (Kubie), 81 LA 371
Borg-Warner Corp. (Neas), 78 LA 985
Dobbs House (Hilgert), 78 LA 49
Jones & Laughlin Steel Corp. (Cook), 78 LA 566
Michigan Bell Telephone Co. (Dyke), 78 LA 896
Washington IGA Foodline (O'Reilly), 78 LA 391
Tenneco Oil Co. (Marlatt), 71 LA 571
FSC Paper Corp. (Marshall), 65 LA 25
E. F. Hauserman Co. (Gibson), 64 LA 1065
Bunker Ramo Corp. (Somers), 62 LA 18
Leaseway of Western N.Y. (France), 60 LA 1343
Cadillac Plastic & Chemical Corp. (Kates), 58 LA 812
New York News (Berkowitz), 58 LA 835
Dempster Brothers (Haemmel), 57 LA 1279
PPG Industries (Coburn), 57 LA 866
Eaton, Yale & Towne (Kates), 56 LA 1037
Economy Forms Corp. (Sembower), 55 LA 1039
Ekstrom, Carlson & Co. (Davis), 55 LA 764
O'Neal Steel (King), 55 LA 402
G. Heileman Brewing Co. (Solomon), 54 LA 1
Permatex Co. (Goetz), 54 LA 546
Whirlpool Corp. (Williams), 54 LA 576
Glass Container Manufacturers Institute (Dworkin), 53 LA 1266

Canteen Corp. (Keefe), 52 LA 781
Chalfant Manufacturing Co. (Nichols), 52 LA 51
Circus, Circus (Kotin), 52 LA 1071

2   *Whether the work environment, including supervisory conduct, is such that the language used is not unusual.*

Examples

Employee *A* was found by his foreman sitting down reading a newspaper. The foreman said to the employee "Get your f___ ass off the chair and go back to work." The employee replied, "f___ you." The foreman discharged the employee for disrespect. The arbitrator reinstated the employee with full back pay, stating that the supervisor's conduct stimulated, and made acceptable, the similar reaction by the employee.

Employee *B* was a clerk in a large direct mail operation and worked in an open office occupied by 50 other male and female clerks. Although talking was not encouraged, the employees generally carried on conversations as they processed orders, and the level of work noise was subdued. Employee *B* was reprimanded by the supervisor for spending too much time away from his work desk. He replied in bold tones, "Get off my back, you s ___ of-a-b__." *B* was discharged. The arbitrator sustained the discharge on the basis that the employee's response was not only a direct verbal attack on the supervisor but was heightened in effect by its contrast to the work atmosphere. Consequently, the incident constituted a serious and demeaning act against the employer which demanded a strong response.

Guidelines

Although some distinguished arbitrators refuse to accept the "shop talk" principle, most arbitrators consider the general work environment important, especially where a supervisor is responsible for some of the tone setting, and will not sustain extreme discipline in cases involving use of language common in the conversation between employees.

Relevant Cases

Rockwell International Corp. (Feldman), 85 LA 246
Indal Aluminum Gulfport (Nicholas), 84 LA 124
American Packaging Corp. (Laybourne), 83 LA 369
Interstate Brands Corp. (Richman), 83 LA 497
Meiger, Inc. (Ellmann), 83 LA 570
Michigan Bell Telephone Co. (Dyke), 78 LA 896
General Electric Co. (Bridgewater), 72 LA 654
E. F. Hauserman Co. (Gibson), 64 LA 1065
Bunker Ramo Corp. (Somers), 62 LA 18
Cadillac Plastic & Chemical Co. (Kates), 58 LA 812
Underwood Glass Co. (Hon), 58 LA 1139
Economy Forms Corp. (Sembower), 55 LA 1039
Circus, Circus (Kotin), 52 LA 1071

3 *Whether the precipitating cause for and factual circumstances surrounding the conduct make the employee's action understandable.*

Examples

Employee *A*, a black, was approached by his supervisor and told that he saw him having a drink with a white woman and that no "black b___ working for him should mess with white women." *A* responded by calling the supervisor a "s___ of-a-b___." Thereupon, the supervisor discharged the employee. The arbitrator reinstated the employee without back pay, concluding that the employee's response, while not justified, was provoked by the supervisor.

Employee *B* was reprimanded by a supervisor for poor work performance. An argument ensued, during which the employee uttered obscenities directly to the supervisor. The employee was discharged. The arbitrator sustained the discharge, refusing to find the tension caused by the argument as justification for the outburst without specific proof of serious supervisory provocation.

Guidelines

Where an employee reacts to provocation or a generally tense atmosphere, severe discipline will not be sustained. However, where the conduct of the employee occurs during a tense atmosphere caused by his or her own actions, the tension will not mitigate the conduct.

Relevant Cases

Interstate Brands Corp. (Richman), 83 LA 497
Lockheed Corp. (Taylor), 83 LA 1018
Steiger Tractor (Jacobowski), 83 LA 966
Washington Scientific Industries (Kapsch), 83 LA 824
Social Security Administration (Muessing), 81 LA 1001
Tenneco Oil Co. (Marlatt), 71 LA 571
FSC Paper Corp. (Marshall), 65 LA 25
E. F. Hauserman Co. (Gibson), 64 LA 1065
AMF Harley-Davidson Motor Co. (Christenson), 61 LA 162
Kast Metals Corp. (Moore), 61 LA 87
Leaseway of Western of N.Y. (France), 60 LA 1343
New York News (Berkowitz), 58 LA 835
PPG Industries (Coburn), 57 LA 866
University of Chicago (Scitz), 57 LA 539
Ekstrom, Carlson & Co. (Davis), 55 LA 764
Chalfant Manufacturing Co. (Nichols), 52 LA 51
Circus, Circus (Kotin), 52 LA 1071
Royal Industries Union (Johnson), 51 LA 642

4   *Whether offending language or conduct occurred in the presence or hearing of other employees, customers, or the general public.*

Examples

Employee *A* was reprimanded by his supervisor for lack of production. Later, *A* went to the office of the supervisor; and behind closed doors, an argument ensued, during which the employee made obscene remarks about the supervisor's relationship to his mother. The employee was discharged. The arbitrator reinstated the employee with minor discipline, noting that while the act of the employee was disrespectful and reprehensible, it was not so serious an attack on the supervisor's authority, or standing in the eyes of other employees, that it warranted discharge.

Employee *B* was reprimanded by his supervisor for lack of production. *B* argued with the supervisor and, within the hearing of other employees, called the supervisor a g___ d___ s___ of-a-b___. The employee was discharged. The arbitrator sustained the discharge, stating that the conduct of the employee was directed toward destroying the supervisor's authority and, therefore, justified the strongest possible discipline for the supervisor to retain his effectiveness with the other employees.

> ## Guidelines
>
> Abusive, obscene, or profane language against a supervisor in private will not support severe discipline, while the same or similar conduct before other employees, customers, or the general public will. Arbitrators reason that public displays of disrespect or objectionable conduct will cause a breakdown in plant order, disruptions, and/or damage to the good will and reputation of the employer.

Relevant Cases

Alumax Extrusions (Miller), 81 LA 722
H. E. Miller Oldsmobile (Westbrook), 81 LA 1112
Social Security Administration (Cox), 81 LA 459
Washington IGA Foodline (O'Reilly), 78 LA 391
Tenneco Oil Co. (Marlatt), 71 LA 571
FSC Paper Corp. (Marshall), 65 LA 25
City of Los Angeles (Tamoush), 64 LA 751
Leaseway of Western N.Y. (France), 60 LA 1343
Cadillac Plastic & Chemical Co. (Kates), 58 LA 812
New York News (Berkowitz), 58 LA 835
Underwood Glass Co. (Hon), 58 LA 1139
Dempster Brothers (Haemmel), 57 LA 1279
PPG Industries (Coburn), 57 LA 866
University of Chicago (Seitz), 57 LA 539
Economy Forms Corp. (Sembower), 55 LA 1039
Prophet Foods Co. (Howlett), 55 LA 288
G. Heileman Brewing Co. (Solomon), 54 LA 1
Permatex Co. (Goetz), 54 LA 546
Glass Container Manufacturers Institute (Dworkin), 53 LA 1266
Circus, Circus (Kotin), 52 LA 1071

Notes to Chaper 9

1. *See Jones & Laughlin Steel Corp.* (Cook), 78 LA 566; *Washington IGA Foodline* (O'Reilly), 78 LA 391; *Tenneco Oil Co.* (Marlatt), 71 LA 571; *Cadillac Plastic & Chem Co.* (Kates), 58 LA 812; *New York News* (Berkowitz), 58 LA 835; *Eaton, Yale & Towne* (Kates), 56 LA 1037; *Economy Forms Corp.* (Sembower), 55 LA 1039; *Glass Container Mfrs. Inst.* (Dworkin), 53 LA 1266; *Canteen Corp.* (Keefe), 52 LA 781; *Circus, Circus* (Kotin), 52 LA 1071.

2. *See E. F. Hauserman Co.* (Gibson), 64 LA 1065; *Bunker Ramo Corp.* (Somers), 62 LA 18; *Kast Metals Corp.* (Moore), 61 LA 87; *Underwood Glass Co.* (Hon), 58 LA 1139; *PPG Indus.* (Coburn), 57

LA 866; *University of Chicago* (Seitz), 57 LA 539; *Economy Forms Corp., supra,* note 1; *Royal Indus. Union* (Johnson), 51 LA 642.

3. *See Leaseway of Western N.Y.* (France), 60 LA 1343; *G. Heileman Brewing Co.* (Solomon), 54 LA 1; *Permatex Co.* (Goetz), 54 LA 546; *Whirlpool Corp.* (Williams), 54 LA 576; *Chalfant Mfg. Co.* (Nichols), 52 LA 51.

4. *Jones & Laughlin Steel Corp., supra,* note 1.

5. *Borg-Warner Corp.* (Neas), 78 LA 985.

6. *Dobbs House, Inc.* (Hilgert), 78 LA 49.

7. *See also Michigan Bell Tel. Co.* (Dyke), 78 LA 896; *Tenneco Oil Co., supra,* note 1; *Kast Metals Corp., supra,* note 2; *Cadillac Plastic & Chem Co., supra,* note 1; *Economy Forms Corp., supra,* note 1; *G. Heileman Brewing Co., supra,* note 3; *Permatex Co., supra,* note 3; *Glass Container Mfrs. Inst., supra,* note 1; *Circus, Circus, supra,* note 1.

8. *Anaconda Copper Co.* (Cohen), 78 LA 690.

9. *See also General Elec. Co.* (Bridgewater), 72 LA 654; *Bunker Ramo Corp., supra,* note 2; *Leaseway of Western N.Y., supra,* note 3; *Underwood Glass Co., supra,* note 2; *University of Chicago, supra,* note 2; *United States Steel Corp.* (McDermott), 55 LA 990; *United States Steel Corp.* (McDaniel), 53 LA 1210.

10. *New Indus. Techniques* (Gray), 84 LA 915. *See also Hyatt Hotels Palo Alto* (Oestreich), 85 LA 11; *Vernitron Pitzoelectric Div.* (Abrams), 84 LA 1315; *United Elec. Supply Co.* (Madden), 82 LA 921; *Veterans Admin. Med. Center* (Dallas), 82 LA 25; *Louisville Gas & Elec. Co.* (Stonehouse), 81 LA 730.

11. *See* Redeker, "Sexual Harassment: Facing the Problem," Delaware State Chamber of Commerce (1982); Redeker, "Sexual Harassment: Employer's Vigilance Needed," *Apparel World* 4 (January 1983), p. 42.

12. *Louisville Gas & Elec. Co., supra,* note 10.

13. *Steiger Tractor* (Jacobowski), 83 LA 966.

14. *See Washington IGA Foodline, supra,* note 1; *Briggs & Stratton Corp.* (Gundermann), 57 LA 441; *Prophet Foods Co.* (Howlett), 55 LA 288; *G. Heileman Brewing Co., supra,* note 3; *Thiokol Chem. Corp.* (Williams), 52 LA 1254.

15. *H.E. Miller Oldsmobile* (Westbrook), 81 LA 1112.

16. *Washington IGA Foodline, supra,* note 1.

17. *See Anaconda Copper Co., supra,* note 8; *International Paper Co.* (Jaffe), 56 LA 558; *Chalfant Mfg. Co., supra,* note 3.

10

Alcohol and Alcohol-Related Conduct

Issue   Whether an employee can be discharged
              or otherwise disciplined for problems re-
              lated to alcohol, alcoholism, or the use of
alcoholic beverages.

Principle   Alcoholism, itself, is not a cause for dis-
                   cipline. Alcoholism is a defense which may
                   be raised by an employee to avoid disci-
pline. The effectiveness of the alcoholism defense will depend
upon when it is raised for the first time, the acts which precipitated the decision to discipline, the willingness of the employee to enter a treatment program, the likelihood of
rehabilitation, or the proven success of the program.

The use and/or possession of alcoholic beverages at times
proximate to the employee's workday, on the job, on the employer's premises, or throughout the employee's workday are
just causes for discipline, and rules prohibiting such conduct
will be enforced as written. Such rules may also be enforced
in accordance with their intent so long as some legitimate
employer interest warrants a broader interpretation of the
rule. Where there is no rule, discipline for alcohol-related conduct will be justified when it infringes upon some employer
interest or creates a safety risk.

Considerations   Alcoholism
                     1. Whether the behavior of the alcoholic
                        while intoxicated is bizarre, aberrant,
                        or otherwise disruptive;
                     2. Whether the alcoholic's condition has

170

an adverse effect on his or her work performance and/or attendance;

3. Whether the employee is participating, or is willing to participate, in an alcohol treatment program and the reasonable likelihood of the program's success;
4. Whether the time when the defense of alcoholism is first raised is sufficiently early to give credibility to the employee's expression of intent to solve the problem.

Alcohol-Related Conduct

1. Whether the employee is drinking, or intoxicated, while working or on the premises of the employer;
2. Whether the employee is drinking at a time which is proximate to his or her worktime and appears under the influence of alcohol at the time he or she reports to work;
3. Whether the employer has a clear and communicated rule against drinking during the employee's workday, on the employer's premises, or at a time proximate to the employee's workday;
4. Whether the proof of the employee's intoxication is clear and convincing.

Discussion   There are two distinctly different, but sometimes related, alcohol problems faced by employers. The first involves employees who are *bona fide* alcoholics and probably have that disease. The second involves the discovery of employees who are drinking while on the job, who are intoxicated while on the job, or who are drinking at a time proximate to their worktime. The considerations for an employer encountering these problems are distinctly different from those encountered with alcoholism. Alcoholism is in the nature of a defense and the employer must determine the effect, if any, that should be given to that defense. This determination often requires compassion rather than the strict administration of a discipline system. Other conduct resulting from the use of alcohol requires discipline. Because these two related problems are treated so differently by arbitrators, patterns of decision can be constructively discussed only when they are taken separately.

Alcoholics and Alcoholism

In recent years, alcoholism has been perceived as a disease and has been treated similarly to other medical disabilities. (See Chapter 11.) Consequently, arbitrators, while recognizing the right of an employer to have a regular and productive workforce, demand a direct effect of the employee's condition on the workplace and rehabilitative approach by the employer, except in extreme and unusual circumstances. That is, alcoholism, as the sole criterion, will not justify discipline.

Employers usually encounter alcoholism when an employee uses it as a defense, explaining conduct and seeking to avoid discipline. Whether it will be an effective defense, or whether an employer must even consider it, will depend on the severity of the conduct for which discipline is given and the time when the defense is raised. Generally, there are two distinct classes of conduct, or effects on the workplace, which produce different arbitrator responses when an alcoholism defense is considered, i.e., aberrant behavior which would normally result in summary discharge and conduct which is commonly unacceptable, such as poor work performance or absenteeism, which would properly be subject to progressive discipline. In the former, the defense of alcoholism may be allowed to mitigate the discipline. In the latter, the defense generally will not be effective when raised for the first time in the context of a discharge. The differences in arbitral treatment seem to be based on the belief that a summary discharge offense usually involves a single, isolated event; the employee would not have revealed his or her alcoholism prior to the event; and the employee would not have had the chance to seek the employer's tolerance and assistance in obtaining treatment. On the other hand, if the employee has gone through several progressive discipline steps without revealing the nature of the problem and only does so to avoid the immediate discomfort of a summary discharge, arbitrators tend to doubt the employee's sincerity in seeking treatment.

The nature of the aberrant behavior at the workplace, however, may override an arbitrator's willingness to accept an alcoholism defense as mitigation of a summary discharge. For instance, in *Asarco, Inc.,* an employee was discharged for being intoxicated on the job.[1] The employee was a miner, and his condition placed not only himself but others in danger. The arbitrator distinguished cases in which the danger was less severe and found that the alcoholic's participation in an alcohol treatment program would not be sufficient assurance of continuing safe conduct. In *National Gypsum Co.*, the discharge of an employee was sustained, when it appeared that he was prone to seizures as a result of his alcoholism.[2]

Three additional cases demonstrate the parameters of arbitrators' decisions in this area. In *Standard Packaging Corp.*, the discharge of an employee, who had lied about the death of his mother to get time off and who had other previous disciplinary problems, was effectively reduced to a one-year suspension without pay (reinstatement without back pay).[3] Although the situation might otherwise have justified discharge, the arbitrator reduced the discipline because of the employee's alcoholism and placed the employee on six months probation, during which time he was to get control over his problem.

By contrast, in *NCR*, where an alcoholic employee vandalized his supervisor's home, the discharge was upheld, even though, as the arbitrator noted, alcoholism is a disease and the employee was in a treatment program. The conduct was too egregious and reinstatement would have undermined company discipline.[4]

Similar reasoning was applied in *Freeman United Coal Co.*[5] In that case an intoxicated employee operated a grader along a heavily traveled road, struck a berm, careened off the road, and plunged into a creek. The employee was hurt and the grader was damaged. The seriousness of the action overcame the arbitrator's sympathy for the employee and the discharge was sustained primarily as a lesson to other employees. The arbitrator stated:

> With or without rules, any reasonable Employee should know that the possession and use of intoxicants at a coal mine is prohibited. Moreover, any reasonable Employee should know that working with dangerous equipment under the influence of alcohol is dangerous and a most serious violation likely to result in discharge. It is clearly prohibited by state law.
>
> One thing distinguishes this case and places it upon an entirely different footing from any of the other cases shown in the evidence. Grievant was in an extreme state of intoxication so that he was dangerous to himself and others. Whether or not that condition was the product of disease, Grievant should have recognized his condition and the danger it presented. Grie-

vant nevertheless went ahead to operate dangerous equipment producing an immediate danger and jeopardy not only to his own life but also that of his fellow Employees. Mine roads, especially in and about well traveled areas where haul trucks, powder trucks, Employees coming to work and other traffic is present, is dangerous enough. In a state of extreme intoxication under which Grievant sought to operate under those conditions, accident and injury is almost inevitable. Indeed, in this case that precise result followed Grievant's continued operation of the grader in the condition he was in resulting in injury to himself and at least some damage to property. Clearly the accident was the result of Grievant's intoxication. The evidence disclosed that there was nothing defective about the grader and no other vehicles, fortunately, were involved. Grievant simply lost control due to his extreme state of intoxication.

Irrespective of the Company's leniency with respect to less serious alcohol related incidents in the past, any Employee must be charged with knowledge that the operation of dangerous equipment in a state of extreme intoxication is intolerable and will be dealt with severely. The Arbitrator cannot find that the Company has by policy been inconsistent in dealing with alcohol when events were known to it. While lesser incidents have involved both classified Employees and supervisors, nothing about the Company's past leniency could possibly have misled Grievant or any other Employee into believing that the operation of equipment under the influence of alcohol would be tolerated and especially the operation of dangerous equipment where the lives of others are placed in jeopardy under conditions of extreme inebriation.

Under these extreme circumstances, the Company has an unchallengable right to punish such conduct severely as a deterrent to insure that it will never happen again and the lives of its Employees will not be unduly jeopardized. Given the unusual seriousness of this occurrence and its almost wilful character, The Arbitrator simply cannot hold that the Company did not have the right to discharge Grievant under concepts of just cause. Neither can the Arbitrator hold that the Company acted discriminatorily by imposing lesser penalties where the Employee's conduct did not directly endanger life and limb.

In situations not involving egregious behavior normally subject to summary discharge, however, arbitrators frequently look to the time when the defense of alcoholism was first raised and the likelihood of rehabilitation in determining the appropriateness of the discipline. In *Greenlee Bros. & Co.*, for instance, an employee's discharge for excessive absenteeism was mitigated to a suspension on the basis of the employee's excellent work record prior to the onset of the disease and a determination by the arbitrator that the employee deserved one last chance.[6]

The time when an employee raises the defense of alcoholism is often relevant in progressive discipline situations, because it is viewed as an indication of an employee's sincerity and the likelihood of improvement. In *Armstrong Furnace Co.*, for example, the arbitrator found the defense to be insufficient when raised for the first time only after the discharge.[7] As in *Bethlehem Steel Co.*, the arbitrator restricted his authority to events that occurred before the discharge.[8]

In this respect, the employer's knowledge of the employee's condition is also relevant. Where, for instance, an employer is aware that an employee's absenteeism is a result of his or her alcoholism and the employer does nothing to encourage the employee to enter a treatment program as a condition of further employment, a discharge may be found to be without just cause. Thus, in *St. Joe Minerals Corp.*, the arbitrator voided the discharge to give the employee a chance at rehabilitation.[9] Also, in *Youngstown Hospital Association*,[10] it was held that an employer improperly discharged a nursing attendant about whom it had constructive knowledge, prior to discharge for absenteeism, that he had an alcohol-dependency problem. However, where the employee's poor record goes unabated after repeated warnings and the treatment program appears to be ineffective, a discharge will be warranted.[11]

Another major factor in discipline cases where alcoholism appears as a defense is whether the employee submits to, or is willing to submit to, a treatment program. Arbitrators usually will reduce the discipline when the employee is in an alcohol treatment program or where the employee expresses a timely willingness to enroll in such a treatment program.[12]

On the other hand, when the employee refuses treatment, does not comply with the treatment requirements of the program, or the program proves unsuccessful, arbitrators will uphold the discharge.[13]

One arbitrator has set out what appears to be the three generally accepted elements that should be met prior to disciplining an alcoholic: (1) the employee should inform the employer of his or her illness; (2) the employer should direct or encourage the employee to seek treatment; and (3) the employee must refuse, or not abide by, the conditions of the treatment.[14] While other arbitrators may not denote these criteria so clearly, they do, however, seem to apply them with one caveat, i.e., the employee cannot raise the issue of a treatment program for the first time either as a defense or as an alternative to the discipline after he has been disciplined. Rather, alcoholics must have applied for treatment before their condition hampers their work performance to the point where the degree of discipline required by the normal application of the system is discharge.

In *Bemis Co.*,[15] an employer was not required to reinstate a discharged employee after the employer permitted the employee to enter an alcoholic rehabilitation program following his discharge due to excessive absenteeism. The employee claimed that the absences were due to his alcoholism but failed to reveal this condition before his discharge, for fear of losing his job. The arbitrator held:

> There is nothing in the Working Agreement between the parties which requires the Company to ferret out employees who are indulging in alcohol or other drug abuse and to force them to enter into the Rehabilitation Program. The program is, apparently, of a strictly voluntary participation basis. While both the Company and Union representatives are obligated to assist employees in making the decision for voluntary participation, they have no *right* to force the employee to do so.
>
> Therefore, the Arbitrator must conclude from a careful analysis of all information and evidence presented to him that the Company had no obligation or legal duty in this case to require the Grievant to participate in the Rehabilitation Program as an alternative to his discharge for excessive absenteeism. There was no dispute that the excessive absenteeism was primarily due to the alcohol and/or drug abuse.
>
> However, the high degree of correlation between the use of those elements and absenteeism was not fully revealed to the Company until the hearing subsequent to the discharge. There is nothing in the Agreement between the parties exculpating an employee from his actions due to the fact that it is subsequently learned they were due to chronic alcoholism.
>
> In this case, it is undisputed that the Grievant received repeated warnings as to his excessive absenteeism. In this manner, it called to his attention the fact that disciplinary steps would probably lead to discharge unless the absenteeism was corrected. The employee had reason to believe that unless he joined and obtained rehabilitation under the Company-sponsored program, or otherwise, he would be discharged. Nevertheless, he did not choose such course until after his discharge.
>
> The action of the Company, in discharging the Grievant, was valid and for just cause. This was not changed or revoked by any subsequent knowledge or actions.

Key Points

1   *Alcoholism itself does not constitute just cause for discipline.*

TO OBTAIN BACK ISSUES OF
THE PROVIDENCE JOURNAL BY MAIL

Send a written request, along with a check or money order made payable to
The Providence Journal, to: The Providence Journal, Back Issues, 75 Fountain Street,
Providence, RI 02902. Daily newspapers are $2.50 each (including handling/postage).
Sunday newspapers are $4.50 each (including handling/postage).

Issue Date/Edition   # Copies   Amount

_____   _____   _____

_____   _____   _____

_____   _____   _____

_____   _____   _____

Total Amount Enclosed _____

DELIVER NEWSPAPERS TO:

Name_____

Address_____

City_____

State _____

Zip Code_____

Phone Number_____
                                    (DAYTIME)

Newspapers only are available **for the past 60 days** of the current publication date,
while supplies last. For further information call 401.277.7010.

Examples

Employee *A* was disciplined for excessive absenteeism on several occasions. The problem continued unabated and the employee was given a three-day suspension. At the time of this discipline, he admitted to being an alcoholic. The employer warned the employee that he must get the problem under control. After the next absence, the employee was discharged. Noting that in all prior cases of discharges for absenteeism employees had been allowed up to three additional absences after a suspension, the arbitrator reinstated the employee with full back pay, but directed a treatment program. The employer's argument that the employee's alcoholism constituted a sufficient basis for concluding that he would not conquer his attendance problem was dismissed without merit.

Employee *B*, intoxicated, entered the plant after his shift was over and proceeded to batter his machine with a metal pipe. When a supervisor and another employee tried to stop him, he attacked them with the pipe. Only after a struggle, during which *B* injured two other employees, was he subdued. At the discharge hearing, *B* argued for reinstatement, using alcoholism as his defense. The discharge notice showed alcoholism as the cause. The arbitrator, discounting the notice as inartfully drawn, sustained the discharge, basing the decision upon the egregious conduct of the employee.

Guidelines

Alcoholism as a defense may or may not be effective, depending on the circumstances of the case. The conduct or work performance which results from alcoholism is the basis for discipline, not alcoholism itself.

Relevant Cases

Eastern Airlines (Turkus), 74 LA 316
St. Joe Minerals Corp. (McDermott), 73 LA 1193
Greenlee Bros. & Co. (Wolff), 67 LA 847
Armstrong Furnace Co. (Stouffer), 63 LA 618
Bethlehem Steel Co. (Porter), 43 LA 1215

2   *Where the aberrant behavior is so severe that it would normally justify summary discharge, alcoholism will be*

*an effective defense when raised for the first time at the
discharge hearing, unless the conduct was exceptionally
damaging to the employer or constituted on extreme risk
to the safety of the employee or others.*

Examples

Employee *A* was discharged following a company picnic;
he had become intoxicated and by his generally obnoxious
behavior, was disruptive. The employer had intended the
picnic to be a family affair, and many children were present. The employee's work record was average. At the discharge hearing, the employee confessed to alcoholism and
offered to enter a treatment program to avoid the discharge. The arbitrator reasoning that the conduct, while
justifying some discipline, was not so extreme or so directed against the employer that discharge would be appropriate, reinstated the employee without back pay. The
arbitrator accepted the employee's defense of chronic alcoholism as complete but ordered treatment as a condition
of continued employment.

Employee *B* was discharged after he became intoxicated
at a company picnic and boisterously denounced the quality of the employer's product, and the company in general,
using a great deal of profanity. The picnic was a family
affair at which various customers and their families were
also present. At the time of his discharge, the employee
pleaded alcoholism, offered to enter a treatment program,
and noted that his problem with drinking was generally
known in the plant, although he had kept it in sufficient
check to avoid any serious work performance problem.
The arbitrator sustained the discharge on the basis that
the conduct was too extreme to be mitigated by an alcoholism defense first raised seriously in connection with
the discharge.

Employee *C* reported to work intoxicated. Rather than
punching in, he went to a remote place in a warehouse
and fell asleep. When discovered by a supervisor, he was
discharged. The employee raised alcoholism as a defense
at the time of discharge. The arbitrator, noting that, while
C had reported for work intoxicated, he neither attempted
to punch in nor to work. Accordingly, the arbitration ruled

that while some discipline may have been warranted, discharge was too severe. The interest of the employer had not been so abused that the same degree of discipline, i.e., summary discharge, should be given to this employee as to another who had not been drunk.

Employee *D* reported to work intoxicated. He punched in and proceeded to his work station where he immediately began to throw all his tools in the trash. He then went to his supervisor and told him to f——— himself and left the premises. The employee was discharged. In reducing the discharge to a leave of absence, the arbitrator held that the conduct warranted removal from the workplace, but not termination, until the employee had been given a reasonable time to try a rehabilitation program.

Employee *E*, a batch operator in a chemical plant, reported to work intoxicated. His condition was discovered after he had put chemicals in incorrect proportions into the batch mixer. The employee was sent to the locker room to shower and to go home. He showered with his clothes on, put on another employee's trousers, and was discovered in his car trying to start it with the other's keys. The employee revealed his alcoholism at the discharge hearing and offered to enter a treatment program, as a condition of reinstatement. Reasoning that the damage to the company's product was so great and that the danger to other employees, due to a possible reoccurrence and the volatility of the chemicals involved, was so substantial that the employer could not reasonably take a chance, the arbitrator sustained the discharge.

Guidelines

Egregious behavior normally justifying summary discharge may be mitigated by alcoholism, even when raised for the first time in connection with the discharge. Discipline will be sustained, however, if the conduct was so severe that a repetition would create a substantial safety hazard to the employee, or to his or her fellow workers, or if the conduct so shocked the conscience of the arbitrator that the discipline is viewed primarily as a punishment.

Relevant Cases

Ohio River Co. (Hewitt), 83 LA 211
Asarco, Inc. (Grooms), 76 LA 163
Standard Packaging Corp. (Fogelberg), 71 LA 445
NCR (Gundermann), 70 LA 756
Greenlee Bros. & Co. (Wolff), 67 LA 847

3   *Where the conduct would normally have justified progressive discipline, alcoholism will constitute an effective defense only if raised prior to the step calling for discharge or if the employer is actually shown to have known of the disease and has not required the employee to enter a treatment program.*

Examples

Employee *A* was discharged for poor production in accordance with the employer's progressive discipline system. At the arbitration, the employee raised the defense of alcoholism. The arbitrator found the defense insufficient to avoid the discipline of discharge, noting the numerous warnings the employee had been given and her failure to reveal her illness and seek treatment before her discharge.

Employee *B* was discharged for excessive absenteeism in accordance with the employer's progressive discipline system. The employer maintained an alcohol control program and advertised the availability of treatment to the employees. *B* had not volunteered for the program. At the discharge hearing, however, he sought entry into the program. Concluding that the employee was seeking to avoid the discharge and was not, based upon his prior inaction, sincere in his desire to be treated, the arbitrator sustained the discharge.

Employee *C* was discharged for excessive absenteeism in accordance with the employer's progressive discipline system. The employer maintained an effective alcohol control program and frequently advertised the availability of treatment. *C* had not volunteered. However, *C*'s problem with alcohol was known to her supervisor, who on occasion had urged her to enter the treatment program. *C* denied that she was an alcoholic. At the arbitration, the union raised *C*'s alcoholism as a defense. *C*, however, continued to deny the condition. The arbitrator, finding fault with the employer's failure to condition *C*'s continued employment upon treatment at an earlier stage in the progressive discipline, ordered the employee into the program and instructed the employer to reinstate *C* at such time as it may appear that *C* has her problem under control.

Guidelines

Alcoholism will not be a sufficient defense to discharge following progressive discipline if the condition is revealed for the first time in connection with the discharge. However, if the employer had knowledge of the condition prior to the commission of the dischargeable offense and failed to condition future employment on entry into a treatment program, the defense will be effective; the employee will be given a chance to see if treatment will work.

Relevant Cases

Allegheny Ludlum Steel Corp. (Alexander), 84 LA 476
Freeman United Coal (Roberts), 82 LA 861
Youngstown Hospital Association (Miller), 82 LA 31
Bemis Co. (Wright), 81 LA 733
Asarco, Inc. (Grooms), 76 LA 163
National Gypsum Co. (Jacobs), 73 LA 228
St. Joe Minerals Corp. (McDermott), 73 LA 1193
General Electric Co. (Clark), 72 LA 355
Greenlee Brothers & Co. (Wolff), 67 LA 847
Armstrong Furnace Co. (Stouffer), 63 LA 618

4   *The employee must evidence a will and a desire to overcome the problem, and there must be a reasonable possibility of the employee's success in doing do.*

Examples

Employee *A* was discharged for intoxication on the job. There was no other record of similar conduct, but the employee's attendance and production were only marginal. *A* sought reinstatement and entry into an alcoholism treatment program. The arbitrator reinstated the employee, with the condition that she enter an alcohol rehabilitation program.

Employee *B* was discharged for excessive absenteeism after exhausting all of the steps in the progressive discipline system. During the grievance procedure and at the arbitration, the employee raised his alcoholism as a defense and offered to enter a treatment program as a condition of reinstatement. The discharge was sustained: The employee should not have waited until his discharge to reveal his problem and to offer to enroll in an alcohol program. His delay cast suspicion on the likelihood of the treatment's success.

Employee *C* was suspended for excessive absenteeism. During the disciplinary conference, *C* admitted to alcoholism. The employer recommended that the employee enter an alcohol treatment program. The employee entered a program. But, while his record improved, it was still not good enough to avoid the next step in the absenteeism control program, and he was discharged. The employee was reinstated by the arbitrator without back pay. The arbitrator found that the employee had demonstrated an honest effort to overcome his problem, even though he had not been completely successful at that time.

Employee *D* was suspended for excessive absenteeism. During the disciplinary conference, *D* admitted to alcoholism. The employer recommended an alcohol treatment program and gave *D* time off for therapy. When the absenteeism did not significantly improve, *D* was discharged. The discharge was sustained, with the arbitrator noting the apparent failure of the treatment.

Employee *E* was disciplined for excessive absenteeism. The employer, learning of *E*'s alcoholism, recommended an alcohol treatment program. The employee asked the employer to assume the cost of the program. This request was denied, and the employee did not enter a program. When her excessive absenteeism continued, *E* was discharged. *E* asked for reinstatement on the grounds that the employer would not pay for the treatment program and she was, therefore, not obligated to go. The discharge was sustained.

Guidelines

The efforts of the employee to treat his or her alcoholism must be sincere and must show a reasonable chance of success. Where the employee's dedication or progress is found to be insufficient, the employer will be entitled to terminate the employment.

Relevant Cases

Atchison, Topeka & Santa Fe Railway Co. (Johnson), 87 LA 972
Morgan Adhesives Co. (Abrams), 87 LA 1039
Freeman United Coal (Roberts), 82 LA 861
Tecumseh Products Co. (Murphy), 82 LA 420
American Ship Building Co. (Everitt), 81 LA 243
Dahlstrom Manufacturing Co. (Gootnick) 78 LA 302
Johns-Manville Products Corp. (Kates), 76 LA 845
Continental Airlines (Ross), 75 LA 896
United States Military Traffic Management Command (Friedman), 75 LA 968
Eastern Airlines (Turkus), 74 LA 316
National Gypsum Co. (Jacobs), 73 LA 228
St. Joe Minerals Corp. (McDermott), 73 LA 1193
Bordo Citrus Products Co. (Naehring), 67 LA 1145
Greenlee Brothers & Co. (Wolff), 67 LA 847
Sterling Drug (Draper), 67 LA 1296
Land O'Lakes (Smythe), 65 LA 803
United States Steel Corp. (Garrett), 63 LA 274

Alcohol-Related Conduct

Most cases involving alcohol do not involve or, at least, do not discuss alcoholism. In reviewing these cases, there are several matters which arbitrators seem to find significant.

The most serious violation is when the employee is intoxicated or drinking while on the job or premises. In such cases, the discharge will almost always be upheld.[16]

A corollary of the drinking-on-the-job issue is that, due

to the extended time effects of alcohol, drinking during an employee's lunch hour or break may be sufficient to uphold a discharge for drinking "on duty," "during working hours," or "during the workday."[17]

Another matter related to drinking on the job to which arbitrators give consideration is whether the nature of the work or operation the employee is performing is dangerous. Where such danger is substantially increased when the employee drinks, a discharge is more likely to be upheld.[18]

The plant setting may serve to mitigate a drinking-on-the-job infraction when, for example, a "holiday spirit" prevails before a holiday shutdown.[19]

Of prime significance in these cases is the existence of a company rule and its precise wording. For instance, where the company rule prohibited drinking "on-the-job," an employee, who returned to work from lunch intoxicated and was discharged, was reinstated by the arbitrator.[20] On the other hand, some arbitrators have more expansively interpreted contract language, especially where a specific employer interest, such as the safe operation of motor vehicles, is involved.[21] Employers are obliged, therefore, to insure that their rules cover all situations over which they wish to have control. As a general principle, arbitrators are unwilling to consider such issues as the degree of intoxication or impaired ability where the conduct itself is specifically prohibited.[22] A rule which prohibits "being under the influence of alcohol" or "intoxication," therefore, presents a substantially more difficult case, because it requires proof of a condition, rather than the circumstances of an event. Proof of intoxication has presented numerous and special problems for employers and arbitrators. Several cases hold that intoxication can be established through observation of the employee. The signs include the employee's speech, appearance, demeanor, walk, the smell of alcohol, etc.[23] The smell of alcohol alone, however, is insufficient to prove intoxication, especially where the employee defends on the basis that he or she was suffering from a hangover, which would explain the odor.[24]

Blood alcohol content (BAC) tests have figured instrumentally in several cases. Frequently, these cases discuss the necessary BAC level to show intoxication. Often, the level of the state's motor vehicle law will be used—.10 percent in most states.[25] One arbitrator, however, reinstated an employee with back pay where the employer had not established a standard for what BAC level would constitute "under the influence."[26]

Also, at least one arbitrator has stated that a blood alcohol test alone is not sufficient, but must be supported by observational evidence of intoxication, like that discussed above, because of the different tolerances people have to alcohol.[27]

In *Blue Diamond Coal Co.,* the arbitrator held that the refusal to submit to a BAC test, without other evidence of intoxication, was insufficient to sustain an intoxication discharge.[28] However, this arbitrator did not raise the question of insubordination that such refusal properly presents. On the other hand, in *Champion Spark Plug Co.,* the arbitrator sustained a 15-day suspension because the employee refused to submit to a search for the bottle he was seen drinking from.[29]

Key Points

1   *An appropriate rule against drinking should anticipate whether drinking during the workday, but during nonworking hours and/or off the premises, should be prohibited. A technically defective rule or too limited a rule may be broadened by an arbitrator where the conduct infringes on the employer's interest and violates the intent of the rule.*

Examples

Employee *A* went off the employer's premises for lunch and was seen by her supervisor drinking a beer. *A* was discharged for drinking during her workday. The employer's rule prohibited the consumption of alcoholic beverages during an employee's workday and stated that a violation of the rule would result in summary discharge. *A* defended on the basis that one beer would have no effect on her and that the consumption took place off the premises and "on her own time." The arbitrator denied the grievance, holding that the prohibition was against all drinking and stated he was without authority to distinguish between amounts consumed.

Employee *B* went off the employer's premises for lunch and seen by his supervisor drinking a beer. *B* was discharged for drinking during his workday. There was no company rule regarding the consumption of alcoholic beverages. *B* defended on the basis that he was off the premises and on his own time. Further, *B* said that one beer would have no effect on him. The arbitrator, noting the absence of intoxication or other infringement on the employer's interests, reinstated *B* with back pay and commuted the discipline to a warning.

Employee *C* went off the employer's premises for lunch and was witnessed by a supervisor having a beer with her sandwich. *C* was discharged for drinking during her workday. The company rule prohibited drinking on the job. *C* defended on the basis that her drinking was off the premises and on her own time. Further, *C* defended on the basis that one beer would have no effect on her. *C* was reinstated without back pay: The arbitrator found that the rule had been discriminatorily applied, because supervisors occasionally drank beer at lunch. Consequently, *C* had been misled into believing that the rule did not reach this type of conduct.

Employee *D* was discharged for drinking on the job, when it was discovered that during his lunch break he went to his car in the parking lot and drank a beer. *D* defended on the grounds that the incident occurred on his own time and that one beer had no effect on him. The discharge was sustained. While the violation was not covered by the employer's rule prohibiting the consumption of alcoholic beverages on company premises, the arbitrator construed the discharge as a reasonable extension of the employer's intent.

Employee *E* was discharged for drinking when he was seen by a supervisor consuming a beer with his lunch at a nearby restaurant. The employer's rule prohibited drinking on company premises or elsewhere while on the job. *E* was a local delivery truckdriver. The discharge was sustained. The arbitrator reasoned that *E* was in the course of making a delivery and, hence, was on the job; and because he was responsible for the truck, he was technically on the premises of the employer. The arbitrator added that the employer had an interest in the safe operation of its vehicles and in community relations. Drinking by the employee at any time during the workday placed both of these interests at risk.

Guidelines

Consuming an intoxicating beverage at any time during an employee's workday is acceptable as a cause for discipline, particularly when the prohibition is set forth in a broad rule consistently applied. Neither technically deficient rules nor the absence of rules will necessarily result in the overturning of discipline for an employee's conduct, if a specific interest of the employer is shown to have been violated or put at risk.

Relevant Cases

Foote and Davies (Wahl), 88 LA 125
Keebler Co. (Belcher), 88 LA 183
Signal Delivery Service (Weis), 86 LA 75
Durion Co. (Coyne), 85 LA 1127
American Cyanamid Co. (Fogelberg), 81 LA 630
American Transportation Corp. (Nelson), 81 LA 318
Western Paper Box (Concepcion), 81 LA 917
Browning-Ferris Industries of Ohio (Shanker), 77 LA 289
Beatrice Foods (Thornell), 73 LA 191
City of Milwaukee (Maslanka), 71 LA 329
Shaefer-Alabama Corp. (LaValley), 70 LA 956
Cal Custom/Hawk (Ross), 65 LA 723
AMF Lawn & Garden Div. (Wyman), 64 LA 988

2 *Where an employee has been discharged for drinking just prior to his or her workday, there should be some evidence that the drinking had, or could have had, an adverse effect on the employee's work performance or on the safety of the employee or others.*

Examples

Employee *A*, a third-shift employee, was seen by a supervisor in a local bar drinking beer before the start of his shift, and when he reported to work, he was discharged for having alcohol on his breath. The employee's work and attendance record was good, although he was a known troublemaker. *A* was reinstated without back pay. The arbitrator stated that the employee's lack of responsibility deserved some discipline, but without more proof of the employee's actual condition, summary discharge was too harsh.

Employee *B*, a third-shift employee, was seen by a supervisor in a local bar drinking beer before the start of his shift, and when he reported to work, *B* was discharged for drinking at a time too close to the start of his workday. Noting that the employee had a bad tardiness record and that the employer lacked a precise discipline system for tardiness, the arbitrator sustained the discharge, reasoning that the employee's lack of concern for his job duties made him an unsatisfactory employee.

Employee *C* was discharged for drinking at a time proximate to his workday when he was seen drinking beer in a bar just prior to the start of his shift. The discharge was sustained, for even though the employee's work record was good, the arbitrator held that the employee was a heavy equipment operator and should have known that any diminution of his capabilities could endanger himself as well as others.

Guidelines

An employee may be disciplined for drinking at a time proximate to his or her worktime, when the consumption of alcoholic beverages can be shown to have had a material effect on his or her work performance, caused intoxication, or created a risk to the safety of others, product, or equipment.

Relevant Cases

Apcoa, Inc. (Hewitt), 81 LA 449
Jehl Cooperage Co. (Odom), 75 LA 901
Beatrice Foods (Thornell), 73 LA 191
City of Milwaukee (Maslanka), 71 LA 329

3   *The employer must be able to prove that the employee violated the rule, i.e., intoxication, consumption, etc.*

Examples

Employee *A* was discharged under a rule which forbade drinking or intoxication on the job. *A* was reinstated with back pay when the only evidence was the smell of alcohol on his breath. The arbitrator noted that there was no evidence of either drinking on the job or intoxication.

Employee *B* was discharged under a rule which forbade drinking during the workday. The only evidence was the smell of alcohol on the employee's breath. Noting that the smell was detected six hours into the shift, the arbitrator sustained the discharge.

Employee *C* was discharged for intoxication on the job when he displayed sleepiness and had the smell of alcohol on his breath. The employee refused to take a breathalyzer test. *C* was reinstated on the grounds that there was inadequate proof of intoxication.

Employee *D* was discharged for intoxication on the job when he had the smell of alcohol on his breath at the start of the shift. When the employee refused to have blood drawn by the company nurse for analysis, insubordination was added as a reason for discharge. The arbitrator, noting a lack of evidence of intoxication, nevertheless sustained the discharge for insubordination.

Employee *E* went off the premises to have lunch. When she returned, her supervisor detected the smell of alcohol on her breath, and *E* was discharged. The employer's rule prohibited drinking, or possessing, alcoholic beverages on the premises. *E* was reinstated with back pay. The arbitrator held that there was no proof *E* had been drinking on the premises and no proof of intoxication.

Guidelines

Drinking during the workday can be proven through such external signs as appearance, odor, eyewitness accounts, or other physical evidence. Proof of intoxication on the job, however, is more difficult because, in addition to the external signs mentioned above, the proof involves the physical condition of the employee and requires evidence of extremely aberrant behavior or the results of scientific tests. The employer has the right to compel the employee to submit to reasonable tests, and an employee's refusal may constitute a separate cause for discipline, i.e., insubordination.

Relevant Cases

Foote and Davies (Wahl), 88 LA 125
Signal Delivery Service (Weis), 86 LA 75

Durion Co. (Coyne), 85 LA 1127
Georgia Pacific (King), 85 LA 542
Apcoa, Inc. (Hewitt), 81 LA 449
Farm Stores (Hanes), 81 LA 344
Trailways Southeastern Lines (Gibson), 81 LA 365
Hayes-Albion Corp. (Kahn), 76 LA 1005
General Felt Industries (Carnes) 74 LA 972
Champion Spark Plug Co. (Cassellman), 68 LA 702
Tennessee River Pulp & Paper Co. (Simon), 68 LA 421
Blue Diamond Coal Co. (Summers), 66 LA 1136
Memphis Light, Gas & Water Div. (Rayson), 66 LA 948
Northrop Worldwide Aircraft Services (Goodstein), 64 LA 742

Notes to Chapter 10

1. *Asarco, Inc.* (Grooms), 76 LA 163.
2. *See also National Gypsum Co.* (Jacobs), 73 LA 228.
3. *Standard Packaging Corp.* (Fogelberg), 71 LA 445.
4. *NCR* (Gundermann), 70 LA 756.
5. *Freeman United Coal Co.* (Roberts), 82 LA 861.
6. *Greenlee Bros. & Co.* (Wolff), 67 LA 847.
7. *Armstrong Furnace Co.* (Stouffer), 63 LA 618.
8. *Bethlehem Steel Co.* (Porter), 43 LA 1215; *see also Dahlstrom Mfg. Co.,* (Gootnick), 78 LA 302.
9. *St. Joe Minerals Corp.* (McDermott), 73 LA 1193.
10. *Youngstown Hosp. Ass'n* (Miller), 82 LA 31; *see also Morgan Adhesives Co.* (Abrams), 87 LA 1039; *Allegheny Ludlum Steel Corp.* (Alexander), 84 LA 476.
11. *General Elec. Co.* (Clark), 72 LA 355; *see also Dahlstrom Mfg. Co., supra,* note 8.
12. *Atchison, Topeka & Sante Fe Ry.* (Johnson), 87 LA 972; *Morgan Adhesives Co., supra,* note 10; *St. Joe Minerals Corp., supra,* note 9; *Greenlee Bros. & Co., supra,* note 6; *Land O'Lakes* (Smythe), 65 LA 803.
13. *Dahlstrom Mfg. Co., supra,* note 8; *Johns-Manville Prods. Corp.* (Kates), 76 LA 845; *Continental Airlines* (Ross), 75 LA 896; *U.S. Military Traffic Management Command* (Friedman), 75 LA 968; *National Gypsum Co., supra,* note 2, *Bordo Citrus Prods. Co.* (Naehring), 67 LA 1145; *Sterling Drug* (Draper), 67 LA 1296; *U.S. Steel Corp.* (Garrett), 63 LA 274.
14. *See Eastern Airlines* (Turkus), 74 LA 316.
15. *Bemis Co.* (Wright), 81 LA 733.
16. *Shaefer-Alabama Corp.* (LaValley), 70 LA 956; *Cal Custom/ Hawk* (Ross), 65 LA 723; *AMF Lawn & Garden Div.* (Wyman), 64 LA 988.
17. *Browning-Ferris Indus. of Ohio* (Shanker) 77 LA 289; *Beatrice Foods* (Thornell), 73 LA 191; *City of Milwaukee* (Maslanka), 71 LA 329.

18. *Jehl Cooperage Co.* (Odom), 75 LA 901 (punch press operator); *Beatrice Foods, supra.* note 17 (forklift operator); *City of Milwaukee, supra*, note 17 (equipment operator).

19. *Okonite Co.* (Ghiz), 74 LA 664 (insufficient to support discharge but enough to uphold suspension.)

20. *Baumfolder Corp.* (Modjeska), 78 LA 1060.

21. *Browning-Ferris Indus. of Ohio, supra*, note 17; *City of Milwaukee, supra*, note 17.

22. *City of Milwaukee, supra*, note 17.

23. *General Felt Indus.* (Carnes), 74 LA 972 (the employee was reinstated with back pay because he was only boisterous and there was no other evidence of intoxication); *Champion Spark Plug Co.* (Cassellman), 68 LA 702 (a 15-day suspension was upheld); *Tennessee River Pulp & Paper Co.* (Simon), 68 LA 421 (the discharge was upheld).

24. *Hayes-Albion Corp.* (Kahn), 76 LA 1005 (the discharge was denied); *Memphis Light, Gas & Water Div.* (Rayson), 66 LA 948 (the employee was reinstated without back pay).

25. *General Felt Indus., supra*, note 23 (reinstatement was ordered where employee's BAC was tested at .05 percent and .08 percent; the state motor vehicle law was .10 percent; *Beatrice Foods, supra*, note 17 (the suspension was sustained where BAC was .07 percent two hours after consumption and testimony accepted that BAC falls at a rate of .02 percent/hour after peak occurring about one hour after consumption); *Tennessee River Pulp & Paper Co., supra*, note 23 (the discharge was upheld where .10 percent was used); *Memphis Light, Gas & Water Div., supra*, note 24 (the employee was reinstated but without back pay where the BAC was only .01 percent, allegedly due to a hangover condition).

26. *Northrop Worldwide Aircraft Servs.* (Goodstein), 64 LA 742.

27. *Hayes-Albion Corp., supra*, note 24, (the employee's discharge was denied).

28. *Blue Diamond Coal Co.* (Summers), 66 LA 1136.

29. *Champion Spark Plug Co., supra*, note 23.

11

Poor Attitude or Disloyalty

Issue Whether an employee may be discharged or otherwise disciplined for either a poor attitude or disloyalty towards the employer.

Principle An employee may be discharged or otherwise disciplined for a poor attitude or disloyalty where there is a continuing course of conduct which results in damage to workplace morale or efficiency or which creates so serious a breach between employer and employee that a continuing relationship is impossible. If there was no other independent basis for the discipline (e.g., insubordination, inadequate job performance), the employee must have exhibited the unacceptable conduct repeatedly and failed to respond to warnings and/or counseling.

Considerations
1. Whether the employee's poor attitude causes, or is combined with, other unacceptable conduct;
2. Whether the employee's attitude affects the morale or performance of other employees;
3. Whether the employee's conduct has an adverse effect on customer relations;
4. Whether there has been progressive discipline.

Discussion In cases involving discipline for poor attitude, arbitrators appear to be heavily influenced not only by the nature of the final

192

incident resulting in the discipline, but also by the employee's entire record of performance, attitude, and conduct.

In *Uarco Co.*, for instance, an employee with six and one-half years seniority was discharged for generally unacceptable behavior resulting from a bad attitude.[1] The arbitrator noted that the employee had been counseled on numerous occasions about his attitude and concluded:

> ... In this case, the Grievant, union representatives, everyone affected, all were aware the Grievant had several warnings; that he was on probation; that if his attitude did not improve or if he violated the Company rules again within the six month period, he would be discharged.[2]

Although the employee had a good work record in some respects, the arbitrator sustained the discharge because the employee failed to respond to the progressive discipline.

In *National Council of Jewish Women*—perhaps the most extensive and unique case of this kind—the arbitrator sustained the discharge of a high seniority employee where the precipitating incident was a letter which some co-employees wrote regarding the grievant.[3] The text of the letter amply sets forth the elements of that case.

FROM: All Professional   Feb. 8, 1971
        Staff of Community
        Activities Department

TO: K— —
SUBJECT: N— —

We feel that N—'s behavior has reached the point where it cannot be tolerated. Following our meeting with you last Thursday, we are listing the reasons:

N— poses a major irritant and distraction, so that she cuts down on the productivity of both professionals and other secretaries, both in our department and in nearby departments.

She poisons the atmosphere by constantly complaining, downgrading professionals and secretaries to other professionals and secretaries.

She constantly complains about being overworked, while spending a good amount of time wandering around the office complaining and generally wasting time.

She talks incessantly and compulsively in an extraordinarily loud voice, making it impossible for anyone not to hear her, and making it extremely difficult to concentrate.

She often leaves at 4:00 p.m. if the Department Head is not in. Sometimes she lays the groundwork by complaining in the morning about being sick, and finally leaving early. At other times she simply leaves, without telling anyone. She has been seen leaving early by the mail-room elevator. Since she has usually been our only full-time secretary, this means that the professional staff then has to answer the phone and take messages, using time better spent in getting their work done.

Her work is not always of good quality. She makes minor errors in all her work, her letters must be read very carefully, as there are frequent errors. Her longer pieces of work contain major errors, such as omitting whole paragraphs, phrases, etc., in short she is very careless. If she makes an error and is asked to correct it, she spends several minutes loudly justifying the error on the basis of overexhaustion due to overwork, or to mistreatment by members of the department.

She terrorizes the secretaries whom she supervises. At least two have been reduced to tears by her browbeating and telling them loudly how stupid and inefficient they are so that no one can escape hearing. Supervision of the Day Care report temporary secretaries were taken away from her for this reason; a professional spends time breaking them in and supervising them in order to protect them from N—, hoping that they will not quit.

She is sometimes insubordinate, either refusing or loudly protesting work a professional has given her, even when the professional has not set a deadline, but in fact has asked her to do it when she has time.

She tries to order the professionals around, has even ordered one professional to retype a draft of a letter before she, N—, would copy it. She tries to summon professionals to her desk by loudly calling them across the room.

Sometimes if she is given material to do at 4:15 or 4:30, she puts it in her folder for the next morning and goes to the ladies' room to get ready to leave. Sometimes when she is given work late in the afternoon she laughs scornfully and recites the list of all the people she works for, before starting to type the work, then complains aloud while she does it.

She rewrites professionals' material according to her own ideas of grammar, punctuation and language. She has been so impolite to some people who have called on the telephone that they have stopped leaving messages with her. At the same time she objects vehemently if anyone calls in and leaves a message at the switchboard rather than with her.

She has called a professional's home to see if she had gone home instead of to the meeting she had told N— she was going to. She wastes a great deal of time by complaining loudly at her desk or by walking around and complaining loudly to anyone who will listen, even, in fact, to people who turn their back and try not to listen. She tells her personal problems loudly to anyone who will listen.

She expresses a resentment at the fact that the Assistant Head has a full-time secretary whom N— does not supervise.

She tries to act as the supervisor of the whole department, both secretaries and professionals.

Signed LW_____

JR_____

NK_____

SE_____

(Signature on ML's return)

However, in *Woodward's Spring Shop*, the arbitrator overturned a discharge because the employer had based the discharge, not upon a record of poor attitude, but upon a single incident similar to an earlier one which the employer had tolerated.[4]

Even where there is a less grievous but similarly well-established and documented pattern of consistent complaining and minor troublemaking, as in the *National Council of Jewish Women* case, arbitrators are generally willing to sustain fairly severe discipline, particularly where the poor attitude is accompanied by inadequate or borderline job performance. However, for discipline to be sustained, the employer must have adequately documented the employee's conduct and must have properly warned the employee. [5]

The factors of central importance to these types of cases are that (1) the employee's bad attitude continued over a long period of time; (2) the employer made good-faith efforts to improve the situation by less drastic measures, with no corresponding effort on the employee's part; (3) the employee's conduct continued unabated up to the time of discipline; and (4) the employee's attitude had some negative effect on the workplace, such as causing general morale to drop or creating emotional disturbances in other specified employees.[6]

In *New Plasco Co.*,[7] for instance, an employee was discharged for refusing to perform assigned work and for a bad attitude. Of particular importance to the arbitrator was that the grievant's "demeanor, at hearing, indicated by voice, and attitude relating to his manner in testifying indicated that here was a person that cared little or nothing for the well-being or success of this Company."

> This Grievant engaged in a confrontation with his Supervisor, refused to perform assigned work, loitered on the hill when, allegedly, time was of the essence and did not meet credibility standards in his demeanor at the hearing. He took matters into his own hands and violated the historical Labor-Management concept of "obey now and grieve later." The total picture is one of defiance bordering on rebellion. . . .

However, there must also be evidence to support the contention that the situation was both extreme and irremediable, that every effort had been made to resolve the problem in other ways, or that the final confrontation, or incident, was severe enough to warrant discharge. Unless there is a very substantial history of an unacceptable attitude or other behavior which would usually support discharge, arbitrators require a showing of progressive discipline before they will sustain a discharge for poor attitude.[8]

In *Wolf Baking Co.*,[9] the employee was a route salesman with five years' seniority. Due to a dispute with a customer centering on what the customer contended was an uncooperative attitude, the employee was barred by the customer from the customer's chain of stores. The employer, concluding that the employee could not service his route due to the customer's action, terminated the employee. The arbitrator sustained the grievance on the basis that the employee had not been accorded the progressive discipline to which he was entitled, even though the employer contended that a warning would have been futile, under the circumstances. Critical was that the employer apparently had made insufficient efforts to resolve the problem.

> In any event, despite the Company's strenuous argument in its brief that it would have been impossible or impracticable to resolve the problem without terminating the Grievant, such a dire predicament was not supported by the facts. The Company made no effort to persuade the customer to reconsider its hasty action, although this same thing had happened at Natchitoches some time earlier with a salesman named Jordan and the Company interceded with the customer to let the salesman back in. Moreover, the Union had proposed a viable alternative to switch part of the Grievant's route with another salesman, which would have cost the Company nothing in extra commissions or downgraded service, but the Company apparently did not even give it serious consideration. The Company suggests that such a switching of customers may have given rise to a grievance by the other salesman, but the plain answer to this is that the Union controls the prosecution of grievances and could have granted the Company immunity as part of the settlement of this grievance.
>
> The fact remains that in this case, the Company had not given the required two warning notices of a "complaint" against the Grievant; indeed, it had not given even one such warning, assuming that there had in fact been prior complaints (which the Company never proved).

Finally, evidence is frequently required showing that the employee's attitude had a demonstrably negative impact on either his own job performance, the job performance of other employees, or on some other aspect of the employer's business. In *Mead Corp.*, for instance, the employee was justifiably discharged when his discourteous conduct with customers resulted in his being barred from making any further deliveries to that location.[10] The employer had previously counseled the employee on numerous occasions about his attitude and behavior. While the terms of the discharge were stated as discourtesy to customers, it was obvious that the employee's troubles stemmed from his poor attitude and the material and adverse effect this attitude had on his job performance.[11]

It is important to note that there are only a limited number of cases on bad attitude, and as a result, arbitrators generally focus on specific testimony to support their awards. It is, therefore, hard to accurately assess how extreme an employee's attitude problems must be before he can be discharged. However, an employee's bad attitude may act effectively as an additional ground for discipline where an employee's inadequate job performance, or other undesirable conduct, alone would not sustain the discipline. Further, in dealing with a persistent attitude problem, the employer's best course would be to thoroughly document incidences where the employee's poor attitude has a demonstrably negative effect on the employer's business, as well as to document the steps taken to help the employee to improve. Where a substantial number of such occurrences exist, their cumulative effect will produce a justifiable cause for discipline.

Key Points

1   *The employee's poor attitude should have caused, or have been combined with, other unacceptable conduct.*

Examples

Employee *A*, a skilled mechanic, made frequent complaints about work assignments, the work environment, etc. He had never actually refused to do a specific project that he was ordered to do. He was discharged, during an argument with the manager, on the basis of his stated intention of refusing to do certain work in the future. The arbitrator reinstated him, but without back pay or seniority credit for the period of discharge.

Employee *B* was a machine operator who complained continually about work assignments, management, etc. He also had an above-average rate of defective output and failed to follow instructions. He was discharged without any progressive discipline or prior warning. Noting the cumulative effect of inadequate job performance and poor attitude over a period of time, the arbitrator sustained the discharge.

Employee *C* was a frequent complainer about work assignments, work environment, etc. Although a constant complainer, however, he never actually refused to do a job. *C*'s production was excellent. On a particular day *C* was directed to operate a second machine along with his original assignment, and he complained. While operating the two machines, he said to his supervisor that the next time he was told to operate two machines at the same time, he would refuse. The supervisor finally had had enough and suspended him. The arbitrator reinstated *C* on the basis that he had never actually refused to do the work and that his production appeared to be unaffected by his complaining.

Guidelines

If an employee's work record is otherwise good and the employee is not causing problems with the other employees, poor attitude alone will not support discharge, although it may justify milder forms of discipline. However, if an employee is not performing well and/or is creating substantial amounts of discontent among the other employees, more severe forms of discipline are likely to be upheld.

Relevant Cases

Day & Zimmerman, Inc.. (Dilts), 85 LA 1151
Montebello Container Corp. (Kaufman), 85 LA 1011
New Plasco Co. (Canestraight), 85 LA 787
Otero County Hospital Association (Finston), 83 LA 98
Town House Apartments (Roumell), 83 LA 538
Monarch Machine Tool Co. (Schedler), 82 LA 880
Challenge Machinery Co. (Roumell), 81 LA 865
FMC Corp. (Nicholas), 81 LA 176
Tempmaster Corp. (Kubie), 81 LA 371

Mead Corp. (Morgan), 75 LA 957
Apollo Merchandisers Corp. (Roumell), 70 LA 614
Gardner Motors (Lightner), 64 LA 428
Safeway Stores (Gould), 64 LA 563
Craftool Co. (Weiss), 63 LA 1031
Woodward's Spring Shop (Pinkus), 63 LA 367
Tex-A-Panel Manufacturing Co. (Ray), 62 LA 272
National Council of Jewish Women (Scheiber), 57 LA 980

2   *The employee's attitude must have affected the morale or performance of other employees.*

Examples

Employee *A* had a long history of continually complaining about her work; downgrading other employees; loud, constant, distracting talk; refusing to do minor tasks or doing them carelessly; being rude to superiors; and generally poisoning the atmosphere of the workplace. In addition, there was substantial testimony that the employee's attitude and conduct had a detrimental effect on the efficiency and morale of all the other employees, and even the employee who testified on her behalf characterized her behavior as abrasive. The employee's discharge for bad attitude and general misconduct was upheld in spite of the fact that she had 21 years of seniority.

Employee *B* was rude and uncooperative and was discharged on the basis that he had created friction among fellow employees. Although there was evidence of a bad attitude, the testimony of other employees failed to support the charges that *B*'s attitude had seriously affected the morale of the workplace and was the primary cause of other employees leaving, or threatening to leave, their jobs. The arbitrator, therefore, reinstated the employee.

Guidelines

Where the employee's negative attitude and behavior is extreme enough to have a detrimental effect on the work performance or morale of other employees, severe discipline may be justified. However, there must be substantial and well-documented evidence of both the employee's misconduct and its effects on other employees, and the charges must be supported by the testimony of other employees.

Relevant Cases

Mead Corp. (Morgan), 75 LA 957
Gardner Motors (Lightner), 64 LA 428
Tex-A-Panel Manufacturing Co. (Ray), 62 LA 272
National Council of Jewish Women (Scheiber), 57 LA 980
Ourisman Chevrolet (Robertson), 56 LA 512

3   *The employee's conduct should have had an effect on customer relations, where relevant.*

Examples

Employee *A*, who had a history of complaining, was fired after engaging in a loud and angry argument with the manager in front of a customer. The arbitrator reversed the discharge on the grounds that there was neither evidence of an effect on customer relations nor was there any other independent grounds for supporting the discharge. The employee, upon agreeing not to repeat the conduct in the future, was reinstated without back pay.

Employee *B*, a newspaper reporter, wrote an article for a competing magazine in which he made extensive criticisms and attacks on the newspaper which employed him. Subsequently, he repeated his negative comments about his employer on talk shows and on other public occasions. A discharge on grounds of disloyalty was upheld, because both the public nature of his attacks on the paper and the unnecessarily vindictive tone in which they were delivered made it impossible for the employer to continue in a working relationship with its employee.

Guidelines

Arbitrators consider any conflict, or poor relationship, between an employer and an employee which is made public or which otherwise affects the employer's relationship with its customers or clientele to be more serious a breach than a dispute which is contained within the workplace. Unnecessarily tarnishing the employer's public image may support more severe discipline than mere interoffice griping. The arbitrator may evaluate the employee's attitude and/or disloyalty in determining what discipline would be appropriate for this type of conduct.

Relevant Cases

City of Rochester, New York (Lawson), 82 LA 217
Nabisco Foods Co. (Allen), 82 LA 1186
San Diego Gas & Electric Co. (Johnston), 82 LA 1039
Alumax Extrusions (Miller), 81 LA 722
H. E. Miller Oldsmobile (Westbrook), 81 LA 1112
Wine Cellar (Ray), 81 LA 158
Triple L. Enterprises (Jeanney), 70 LA 97
Corley Distributing Co. (Ipavec), 68 LA 513
Elizabeth Horton Memorial Hospital (Sandler), 64 LA 96
Safeway Stores (Gould), 64 LA 563
Woodward's Spring Shop (Pinkus), 63 LA 367

4   *Progressive discipline should have been imposed and proved to be unsuccessful.*

Examples

Employee *A* had received two warning notices over a period of eight months. The first was for a bad attitude, and the second, for a specific job mistake. Her transfer to a less desirable department was not upheld by the arbitrator, because the warnings were too far apart and for two different problems. The arbitrator noted that the employer's attempts to improve her attitude and performance by less drastic measures were insufficient and that the consequences of her behavior were never made clear to her prior to the transfer.

Employee *B* had been put on probation for six months because of a bad attitude and the poor quality of his work. His supervisors attempted to counsel him repeatedly and warned him that failure to improve would result in more severe discipline. He made no effort to improve either his attitude or the quality of his work. The arbitrator sustained the discharge, since *B* had been given every chance to solve his problems, had not filed a grievance over the prior warnings, and had refused to correct his attitude.

Employee *C* was a complainer: His complaints were not focused, but everything having to do with work, the employer, the work environment, and the other employees was subject to his complaints. Disgusted with the situation, *C*'s supervisor finally called him in and told him that unless he stopped his complaining he would be discharged. *C* pointed to his perfect attendance and to his productivity as the best in the company. He added that his personal opinions were irrelevant and that he could only be disciplined for bad work. The next day he was heard complaining to another employee about the temperature in the plant. The supervisor discharged him. The arbitrator reinstated the employer, but without back pay. Although the employee had been specifically warned about the continuance of his behavior, the arbitrator found that discharge was too severe. There had been too little done by the employer to impress upon the employee the seriousness with which it viewed his conduct.

Guidelines

Arbitrators are much more willing to support the discipline imposed when the employee has been given prior warnings, counseling, and an opportunity to improve. Discharge or severe discipline is not viewed as an appropriate remedy unless there are other, independent grounds to support it; there is a long history of an unacceptable attitude; and there have been repeated attempts to solve the problem with less drastic penalties. Attitude problems must be very extreme before they will suffice to support severe disciplinary measures. Even then the offense is not that the employee exhibited a poor attitude, but that the employee obstinately refused to respond to the employer's good-faith effort to correct the situation in an affirmative way.

Relevant Cases

Day & Zimmerman Inc. (Dilts), 85 LA 1151
Wolf Baking Co. (Marlatt), 83 LA 24
Dyer's Chap House (Ray), 82 LA 198
Palmer Terrance Nursing Center (Kossoff), 82 LA 1179
Apollo Merchandisers Corp. (Roumell), 70 LA 614
Gardner Motors (Lightner), 64 LA 428
Safeway Stores (Gould), 64 LA 563
Craftool Co. (Weiss), 63 LA 1031
Woodward's Spring Shop (Pinkus), 63 LA 367
Tex-A-Panel Manufacturing Co. (Ray), 62 LA 272
Uarco Co. (Gibson), 58 LA 1021
National Council of Jewish Women (Scheiber), 57 LA 980
Ourisman Chevrolet (Robertson), 56 LA 512

Notes to Chapter 11

1. *Uarco Co.* (Gibson), 58 LA 1021.
2. *Id.*, at 1022.
3. *National Council of Jewish Women* (Scheiber), 57 LA 980.
4. *Woodward's Spring Shop* (Pinkus), 63 LA 367.
5. *See Apollo Merchandisers Corp.* (Roumell), 70 LA 614 (discharge denied); *Craftool Co.* (Weiss), 63 LA 1031 (transfer denied); *Uarco Co.*, *supra*, note 1 (discharge denied); *Ourisman Chevrolet* (Robertson), 56 LA 512 (discharge denied).
6. *See Gardner Motors*, (Lightner), 64 LA 428; *Tex-A-Panel Mfg. Co.* (Ray), 62 LA 272 (discharge sustained); *National Council of Jewish Women*, *supra*, note 3.
7. *New Plasco Co.* (Canestraight), 85 LA 787.
8. *See Mead Corp.* (Morgan), 75 LA 957 (discharge sustained); *Uarco Co.*, *supra*, note 1 (discharge sustained); *National Council of Jewish Women*, *supra*, note 3 (discharge sustained).
9. *Wolf Baking Co.* (Marlatt), 83 LA 24.
10. *Mead Corp. supra*, note 8.
11. *See also Triple L. Enters.* (Jeanney), 70 LA 97 (discharge reduced to a suspension); *Corley Distrib.* (Ipavec), 68 LA 513 (discharge sustained); *Elizabeth Horton Memorial Hosp.* (Sandler), 64 LA 96 (discharge sustained); *Safeway Stores* (Gould), 64 LA 563 (discharge denied); *National Council of Jewish Women*, *supra*, note 3.

12

Carelessness and Negligence

Issue   Whether an employee may be discharged or otherwise disciplined for carelessness and negligence.

Principle   An employee may be discharged, or otherwise disciplined, for carelessness and negligence where an employer can sustain the burden of proving that the employee's actions resulted in job performance well below that of similarly positioned co-workers. An employer does not have to have applied progressive discipline for a discharge to be sustained if the employee's act was very costly to the employer or was extremely hazardous to others.

Considerations
1. Whether the frequency and/or nature of the employee's actions reflect a job performance well below that of co-workers in similar positions;
2. Whether the performance expected of the employee was within his or her experience, training, and physical capabilities;
3. Whether the employee was made aware of his or her responsibilities by the company through prior notifications or warnings;
4. Whether the employee's actions were costly to the company; i.e., the actions resulted in damage to equipment or product, significant lost time, etc.; or

the actions created a hazardous condition for co-workers or others;

5. Whether the company has handled analogous situations in the same fashion.

Discussion   In general, careless and negligent actions by employees take three forms: negligence or carelessness which results in inefficiency or in the production of an inordinate amount of scrap; negligence or carelessness which causes damage to machinery or product; and negligence or carelessness which constitutes unsafe practices. The different forms of carelessness and negligence encountered by arbitrators have resulted in a varying emphasis placed on the several relevant considerations. In cases of this kind, the employee's prior record with the company appears to be an especially significant factor in the arbitrator's determination.

Where an employee's negligence results in inefficiency, a comparison of the employee's performance with that of others in the same job will weigh heavily in the arbitrator's decision.[1] In such a case, it is unlikely that a discharge will be sustained, however, unless the company has applied a progressive discipline system.

In *National Gypsum Co.*, for example, an employee was discharged for carelessness and negligence following his ninth accident in two and one-half years.[2] In his defense, the employee claimed that only one of the accidents was his fault. He stated that six of the accidents were clearly due to the generally unsafe working conditions and that only one accident resulted in time lost. The arbitrator found, however, that the other employees in the area had worked without accidents. Consequently, the arbitrator reasoned, the employee had been careless. Moreover, the employee had received counseling, during which he had stated that the work environment made him nervous. In a spirit of humanity, the arbitrator concluded that the discharge was for the good of the employee.

Arbitrators frequently assess the attitude of an employee when determining whether the employee would continue to be careless or negligent on the job and whether any further discipline, less than discharge, would have any beneficial effect. In *Rinker Materials Corp.*, for instance, the discharge of a truck driver was sustained following his third accident.[3] While waiting for a traffic light to change, the employee's foot slipped off the brake because something was on his shoe, and the truck rammed into the rear of a car. At the time, the truck was two feet behind the car, in violation of the company's traffic manual which specified that at least one vehicle space must be maintained between the driver's truck and a vehicle in front. During the arbitration, the employee testified that the manual was unreasonable and that he would continue to abide by its rules only on a selective basis. Further, the driver stated that having foreign substances on his shoes was not uncommon. Nevertheless, he had not checked to see if that was the case in this instance. The arbitrator, obviously alarmed by the employee's attitude, sustained the discharge on the basis that the employee's attitude evidenced a proclivity for future negligence.

In *Vulcan-Hart Corp.*, the employee had a history of many injuries to his hands, eyes, and feet, caused, primarily, by the employee's refusal to use available safety equipment. Although he had been warned that continuing to practice unsafe behavior would result in his discharge, the employee did not alter his work habits. The arbitrator, apparently concluding that the employee's attitude offered little hope for an improved work history, sustained the discharge.[4]

Although progressive discipline is usually a necessary prelude to discharge for negligence or carelessness, a very serious offense committed by an employee may abrogate the need for previous reprimands or suspensions. For example, a discharge may be sustained if the employee's carelessness or negligence seriously endangers the lives of others. Also, a discharge without prior discipline may be upheld, if an adequately trained, experienced employee damages equipment through negligence or carelessness which results in great expense to the company; this is particularly true when the amount of damage is probative of the care taken by the employee.[5]

In *Hess Oil Virgin Islands Corp.*, the arbitrator found that the employer had just cause for discharging an employee for gross negligence, even though there had been no prior discipline.[6] In that case, the employee had failed to shut off a gas valve when the flame in a heater went out, and as a result, an explosion caused substantial damage. Even though the employee had only one week's on-the-job experience, she had been trained, and the arbitrator found that she had failed to follow the prescribed emergency procedures. Her negligence not only resulted in severe property damage, but also created a potential danger to other employees. The seriousness of the gross negligence justified the summary discharge.

Similarly, the summary discharge of an employee was approved in *Rohr Industries*.[7] In that case, an employee had misdrilled a part through negligence. The part disappeared; and the arbitrator concluded that the employee had sought, through deception, to conceal his act. The arbitrator found that the negligence, combined with the dishonest act of concealment, justified the employee's dismissal without prior, intermediate disciplinary steps.

Key Points

1 *The frequency and/or nature of the employee's carelessness or negligence must be reflected in the employee's job performance and must be more excessive than that of co-workers in similar positions.*

Examples

Employee *A* failed to immediately push an emergency stop button, when trouble was encountered along a production line. Significant time was lost in rectifying the situation, and the supervisor discharged the employee. The arbitrator, noting that other employees have made similar judgmental errors, reinstated the employee.

Employee *B*, a truck driver, had nearly the worst accident record out of 20 drivers. After his third avoidable accident in the most recent three-month period, he was discharged. The arbitrator sustained the discharge.

Guidelines

To uphold disciplinary action for negligence or carelessness, the employer must show that the employee, relative to others in similar jobs, performed significantly worse than average. Negligence which has recurred frequently within a short time will strengthen the company's position.

Relevant Cases

Copperweld Bimetallics Group (Denson), 83 LA 1024
Production Steel Co. (Roberts), 82 LA 229
M.M. Sundt Construction Co. (Zechar), 81 LA 432
National Gypsum Co. (Klaiber), 78 LA 226
Vulcan-Hart Corp. (Ghiz), 78 LA 59

Beatrice Foods Co. (Gradwohl), 74 LA 1008
VRN International (Vause), 74 LA 806
Wheeling-Pittsburgh Steel Corp. (Chockley), 74 LA 793
S&T Industries (Madden), 73 LA 857
United Parcel Service (Das), 73 LA 1308
Associated School Bus Service (Krebs), 72 LA 859
Reynolds Metals Co. (Frost), 72 LA 1051
Greenlee Bros. & Co. (Rezler), 67 LA 686
Shop Rite Foods (Weiss), 67 LA 159
United Metal Trades Association (Stephen), 66 LA 1342

2   *The performance expected of the employee must have been within his or her experience, training, and physical capabilities.*

Examples

Employee *A* neglected to check a valve on a tank, and subsequently the tank collapsed. Although the valve-checking procedure did not appear in the operations manual, the employee was discharged. Finding that the employee had been adequately trained by another employee with respect to checking the valve, the arbitrator sustained the discharge.

Employee *B*, after having been promoted to a more difficult clerical position, was discharged for having a higher error ratio than employees who had previously held the position. The arbitrator reinstated the employee, finding that the company had not given the employee suitable time to adjust to the new job.

Guidelines

To sustain disciplinary action for carelessness or negligence, an employer must show that the employee was properly trained, had the job experience, and had the physical capability to do the job properly. Careless or negligent work is identified by poor job results that could have been avoided by the employee. Therefore if a poor work performance is the result of insufficient training or experience, discipline is inappropriate.

Relevant Cases

Jewish Convalescent & Nursing Home (Bowers), 85 LA 805
Allied Employers (Hedges), 83 LA 583

Wheeling-Pittsburgh Steel Corp. (Leahy), 83 LA 318
National Fire Sprinkler Corp. (Madden), 82 LA 391
Universal Foods Corp. (Belcher), 82 LA 105
Chardon Rubber Co. (Layborne), 81 LA 659
Utility Trailer Manufacturing Co. (Maxwell), 81 LA 537
National Gypsum Co. (Klaiber), 78 LA 226
Rinker Materials Corp. (Lurie), 78 LA 44
Vulcan-Hart Corp. (Ghiz), 78 LA 59
Universal Camshaft & Heat Treat (Keefe), 76 LA 808
Neville Chemical Co. (Parkinson), 74 LA 814
VRN International (Vause), 74 LA 806
S&T Industries (Madden), 73 LA 857
Hess Oil Virgin Islands Corp. (Berkman), 72 LA 81
Reynolds Metals (Frost), 72 LA 1051
Santiam Southern Corp. (Mann), 68 LA 46
Standard Oil of California (Walsh), 65 LA 829
Gates Chevrolet Co. (Coyle), 63 LA 753
Whitfield Tank Lines (Cohen), 62 LA 934

3   *The company must have warned or notified the employee of his or her responsibilities prior to the disciplinary action.*

Examples

Employee *A*, a welder, produced several bad welds and was discharged. Within the preceding two months the company had issued general warnings twice to all welders that improper welds would be cause for dismissal. The arbitrator commuted the discharge to a suspension, finding that the employee was entitled to specific warnings that his work was unsatisfactory.

Employee *B*, a clerk, made numerous errors and was discharged. Although the employee had received no prior written warnings, she had been counseled by superiors to be more attentive to her work. The arbitrator sustained the discharge.

Guidelines

An arbitrator is more likely to sustain severe discipline for negligence or carelessness if the employee has been warned or reprimanded for negligence in the past. The company's position is enhanced if the employee was found again to be in violation of the employer's standards soon after a warning had been issued.

Relevant Cases

Consolidated Coal Co. (Hoh), 85 LA 506
Lone Star Cement (Foster), 85 LA 468
W-L Molding Co. (House), 85 LA 58
Centennial One (Mittelman), 84 LA 89
Pacific Bell (Oestreich), 84 LA 710
Victory Markets (Sabghir), 84 LA 354
Gibson Greeting Cards (Singer), 83 LA 1033
Groovfold, Inc. (Morgan), 83 LA 521
Harry Davies Molding Co. (Fish), 82 LA 1024
Southeastern Trailways (Craver), 82 LA 810
Alfred M. Lewis, Inc. (Sabo), 81 LA 621
Majestic Iron Works (Fitzsimmons), 81 LA 816
Piggly Wiggly T-212 (Nelson), 81 LA 808
Telle Tire Co. (Kubie), 81 LA 789
National Gypsum Co. (Klaiber), 78 LA 226
Vulcan-Hart Corp. (Ghiz), 78 LA 59
Pet Inc. (Jason), 76 LA 292
Beatrice Foods Co. (Gradwohl), 74 LA 1008
Neville Chemical Co. (Parkinson), 74 LA 814
VRN International (Vause), 74 LA 806
FMC Corp. (Marlatt), 73 LA 705
Huntingdon Alloys (Shanker), 73 LA 1050
S&T Industries (Madden), 73 LA 857
United Parcel Service (Das), 73 LA 1308
Associated School Bus Service (Krebs), 72 LA 859
Bonded Scale & Machine Co. (Modjeska), 72 LA 520
Canron, Inc. (Marcus), 72 LA 1310
Reynolds Metals Co. (Frost), 72 LA 1051
Greyhound Lines (Larkin), 67 LA 483
Michel Warehousing Corp. (Mallet-Prevost), 67 LA 565
Station WPLG-TV (Serot), 66 LA 805
Transport Body Services (Raffaele), 65 LA 894
American Standard (Biddinger), 64 LA 159
Kelsey-Hayes (Keefe), 64 LA 740
May Dept. Stores Co. (Dean), 64 LA 122
United Metro (Schutz), 64 LA 7
West Chemical Products (Dykstra), 63 LA 610
Tex-A-Panel Manufacturing Co. (Ray), 62 LA 272
Whitfield Tank Lines (Cohen), 62 LA 934
Precision Extrusions (Epstein), 61 LA 572

4   *The employee's actions must have been costly to the company, i.e., the actions resulted in damage to equipment or product, significant lost time, etc.*

Examples

Employee *A* neglected to adjust a valve on a tank. Subsequently, the tank collapsed, resulting in the loss of the tank as well as a large quantity of valuable chemicals. *A*'s carelessness cost the company over $10,000. The employee was discharged, and the discharge was sustained by the arbitrator.

Employee *B*, a truck driver had two avoidable accidents within a six-month period, resulting in his discharge pursuant to a company policy requiring dismissal for two accidents. The arbitrator, noting that the amount of vehicle damage was minimal and expressing some question about whether the accidents had, in fact, been avoidable, reinstated the employee with back pay.

Employee *C* carelessly drove a forklift into a stack of piled skids and knocked it over. One of the falling skids narrowly missed a co-employee working in the area. *C*'s employment history was average and contained no record of any prior carelessness. Nevertheless, *C* was discharged. The arbitrator sustained the discharge, finding *C* to have been wantonly in disregard for the safety of others.

Guidelines

Discharge is more readily upheld when the employee's negligence results in great expense to the company; this is particularly so if the amount of damage is probative of the care exercised by the employee. Expense to the company can take forms other than damaged equipment or product. Lost time and the inability of other workers to perform their jobs because of the employee's negligence can be costly.

Relevant Cases

Anchor Hocking Corp. (Ruben), 85 LA 783
Stauffer Chemical Co. (Corbett), 83 LA 272
Stauffer Chemical Co. (Wren), 83 LA 533
Magma Copper Co. (Kelliher), 82 LA 895
Municipality of Anchorage (Hauck), 82 LA 256
General Services Administration (Lubic), 75 LA 1158
Hoerner Waldorf Champion International Corp. (Newmark), 75
  LA 416

Neville Chemical Co. (Parkinson), 74 LA 814
Wheeling-Pittsburgh Steel Corp. (Chockley), 74 LA 793
FMC Corp. (Marlatt), 73 LA 705
Hinckley & Schmitt (Goldberg), 73 LA 654
Hess Oil Virgin Islands Corp. (Berkman), 72 LA 81
Reynolds Metals Co. (Frost), 72 LA 1051
Rohr Industries (Lennard), 65 LA 982
United Metro (Schutz), 64 LA 7
Corns Truck & Tractor (Cowan), 63 LA 828
Gates Chevrolet Co. (Coyle), 63 LA 753
VCA of New Jersey (Aiges), 62 LA 951
Whitfield Tank Lines (Cohen), 62 LA 934
Buegers Mining & Manufacturing (Grooms), 61 LA 952
Gulf Printing Co. (Lilly), 61 LA 1174

5   *It must be shown that the employee's actions could have created a hazardous condition for co-workers or others.*

Examples

Employee *A*, a school bus driver, negligently stopped her bus on a railroad crossing to lecture unruly students. Although she had no prior serious offenses on her record, she was discharged. The arbitrator sustained the discharge.

Employee *B*, a machinist, was found sleeping on the job. The employee was discharged by the company, which claimed that the employee, by falling asleep, had created a hazard to himself and co-workers. The arbitrator commuted the discharge to a suspension, noting that the employee had been on the second leg of a double shift and had not had an opportunity to rest.

Employee *C*'s careless driving of a forklift caused a tire to puncture. The cost to the company was $50 for tire repair and one hour lost time in the use of equipment. *C* was discharged. The arbitrator reinstated *C*, noting the minimal cost created by the employee's carelessness.

Guidelines

Negligence by an employee which endangers the lives of others may be cause for discharge without progressive discipline. However, factors may be present which act to mitigate the offense, and these will be taken into account, even when the employee has created a significant hazard.

Relevant Cases

Southwest Fire Control Tax District 6 (Kanzer), 83 LA 900
CMI (Keefe), 82 LA 735
National Gypsum Co. (Klaiber), 78 LA 226
Hoerner Waldorf Champion International Corp. (Newmark), 75
    LA 416
FMC Corp. (Marlatt), 73 LA 705
Associated School Bus Service (Krebs), 72 LA 859
Bonded Scale & Machine Co. (Modjeska), 72 LA 520
Hess Oil Virgin Islands Corp. (Berkman), 72 LA 81
Standard Oil of California (Walsh), 65 LA 829

6   *The company's prior practice must have been consistent
in the handling of analogous situations.*

Examples

Employee *A*, a school bus driver, received a traffic citation
for speeding and was discharged. The arbitrator reinstated the employee, noting that two other drivers had
received traffic citations during the preceding two years
and had not been disciplined.

Employee *B*, a quality control inspector, carelessly allowed an excessive amount of scrap to be produced. He
was discharged, although the company had not discharged
two other inspectors who had permitted an excessive
amount of scrap to be produced. The arbitrator sustained
the discharge, finding that the circumstances surrounding the previous cases differed from the case in question.

Guidelines

Two elements must be analyzed when comparing
a company's present actions with its past actions in
other cases—the severity of the discipline imposed and
the circumstances accompanying the respective cases.
In general, if the circumstances are the same, discipline
which departs from past practice reflects negatively on
the company's treatment of the employee and on its
view of the severity of the offense.

Relevant Cases

Pacific Airmotive (Meiners), 81 LA 747
Safeway Stores (Yaney), 81 LA 772

Wheeling-Pittsburgh Steel Corp. (Chockley), 74 LA 793
St. John Transportation Co. (Modjeska), 73 LA 1156
Canron, Inc. (Marcus), 72 LA 1310
Reynolds Metal Co. (Frost), 72 LA 1051

Notes to Chapter 12

1. *Greenlee Bros. & Co.* (Rezler), 67 LA 686; *Shop Rite Foods* (Weiss), 67 LA 159; *United Metal Trades Ass'n* (Stephen), 66 LA 1342.

2. *National Gypsum Co.* (Klaiber), 78 LA 226.

3. *Rinker Materials Corp.* (Lurie), 78 LA 44.

4. *Vulcan-Hart Corp.* (Ghiz), 78 LA 59.

5. *See generally General Services Admin.* (Lubic), 75 LA 1158; *Hess Oil Virgin Islands Corp.* (Berkman), 72 LA 81; *Rohr Indus.* (Lennard), 65 LA 982; *Standard Oil Co. of Cal.* (Walsh), 65 LA 829; *Gates Chevrolet Co.* (Coyle), 63 LA 753; *Buegers Mining & Mfg. Co.* (Grooms), 61 LA 952; *Gulf Printing Co.* (Lilly), 61 LA 1174.

6. *Hess Oil Virgin Islands Corp., supra,* note 5.

7. *Rohr Indus., supra,* note 5.

13

Dishonesty or Falsification
of Company Records

Issue   Whether an employee may be discharged
                     or otherwise disciplined for dishonesty or
                     falsification of company records.

Principle   An employee may be discharged or oth-
                     erwise disciplined for dishonesty or falsi-
                     fication of company records where the
employer can sustain the burden of proving that the employee
acted with knowledge of the wrongfulness of the act and with
intent to defraud the company. A prior good work record may
be insufficient to mitigate a discharge, because the offense is
perceived as too serious.

Considerations   1. Whether the employee's act was a will-
                        ful, deliberate attempt to defraud the
                        company;
                     2. Whether the employee attempts to cover
                        up the conduct, or whether upon dis-
                        covery the employee denies the act or
                        intent to deceive;
                     3. Whether the employee knew when
                        committing the offense that, if caught,
                        he or she would be subject to discipline;
                     4. In cases of employment application fal-
                        sifications, whether the denial or omis-
                        sion of facts would have prevented the
                        hire of the employee, if the facts had
                        been known, or whether sufficient time

215

had elapsed between the act of falsification and its discovery to allow the employee to develop an acceptable work record, which may serve to lessen the severity of the offense;

5. Whether the dishonest act had a detrimental effect on the employer;

6. Whether the company acted expeditiously upon discovery of the falsification or dishonesty, and/or whether the company evidenced willingness to overlook the conduct under certain conditions;

7. Whether the company's past practice in handling similar cases has been applied;

8. Whether the employee's work record has been taken into consideration.

Discussion   Dishonesty, or the falsification of company records, appears to be one of those causes for discipline which are so serious that arbitrators often do not insist upon progressive discipline. In such situations, the falsification of company records is in the same class as the theft of company property. In fact, when the dishonesty involves falsification of records used in incentive systems, expense accounts, etc., the two offenses are closely related.[1]

Falsification of Company Records

As with cases of theft, the most crucial aspect of these cases is often one of proof. If the company can establish that the employee willfully committed a dishonest act for his or her own benefit and that this act had some significant adverse or detrimental effect upon the employer, the discharge will be sustained, absent a gross procedural error.

In *Pacific Telephone and Telegraph Co.*, for instance, an employee was reinstated with back pay where the employer was unable to prove that the employee acted with the intent to deceive for the purpose of obtaining a benefit to which he would have been otherwise unentitled.[2] In that case, the employee was out of the plant due to a summons for jury duty.

The employer's contract required employees to return to work upon conclusion of their jury duty, if it ended at a reasonable time prior to the end of the employees' workday. The employee was dismissed by the court and was told to go home and to remain "on call." When the employee did not report for work, stating that he was on jury duty, and later requested jury duty pay for those days, he was terminated. The arbitrator found "that, rather than trying to deceive the Company, the Grievant simply believed that he had a continuous obligation for jury service during those entire ten days."[3]

Falsification of company records may be cause for discipline, even if it has no economic effect on the employer. In *Dresser Industries, Galion Manufacturing Division*, for example, four employees were justifiably discharged for falsifying production records, even though they had not been paid for more work than they actually performed.[4] The employees were incentive workers who were required to submit their job tickets at the end of their shift. These tickets were then factored into a formula to establish the actual amount of pay for the week. Unknown to the employer, the employees were withholding job tickets and "banking" them for use at a later time. The time came just before Christmas, when the employees decided to pay themselves a "bonus." When the number of job tickets turned in produced a larger than normal payroll for the week, the employer discovered the scheme. All four employees were discharged for falsifying production records. Even though the employees' scheme had resulted in payment to them for work actually done and no more, the arbitrator sustained the discharges for falsification of records.

The employee in *Potlatch Corp.*[5] falsified a sales receipt for a pair of hunting boots to read "safety" so that he could be reimbursed by the employer. The employee argued that he was unaware that the safety shoe reimbursement policy permitted reimbursement for safety shoes only and that other employees were reimbursed for shoes other than safety shoes. The arbitrator considered both of these defenses and denied the grievance. The arbitrator held:

> The grievant must be considered to have had full knowledge of the safety shoe policies, both in regard to wearing of the shoes and the procedure for reimbursement. Testimony indicates the company policies in reference to safety shoes were well publicized in all parts of the plant. Secondly, and most important, to indicate the grievant's knowledge of these policies, he had in 1981 and 1982 followed company policy and

procedure and obtained reimbursement for his purchase of safety
shoes. In the instant case, the grievant purchased hunting boots,
which he obviously knew did not meet the safety shoe requirements. He then had the clerk make the notation "safety" on
the sales slip with the intent to deceive the employer, and collect
the reimbursement. The grievant's defense, that he believed he
was entitled to a reimbursement each year contradicts his previous actions and lacks credibility. Grievant's testimony also
indicated he would never have acted as he did had he realized
the penalty involved.

The Union President testified other employees received
reimbursement without the purchase of safety shoes, however,
there was no evidence presented to substantiate this claim. The
witness also refused to answer a question from the Employer's
Attorney when asked to name any of these employees.

The question previously posed by this arbitrator was to
the necessity placed upon the company to support its position
with a high degree of proof. Have they done so?

The Employer has had an ongoing policy covering safety
shoes, which has been adequately promulgated to all employees.
The grievant, from his past actions by following company procedure, had full knowledge of the policy. In the instant case
there is a clear intent to defraud the employer. A basic concept
in the Employer-Employee relationship is trust. The action of
the grievant betrayed or abrogated this trust that is the foundation of this relationship. The record is uncontradicted by evidence from the Employer that past disciplinary actions have
been uniformly imposed, and there has been no unequal treatment of the grievant. Based on the offense involved and the
foregoing analysis and summary it is my conclusion that the
Employer has met this degree of proof and I so find.

Unlike their treatment of theft cases, many arbitrators
appear to be less demanding in the quantum of proof required
in cases involving misrepresentation. Generally a preponderance of the evidence is acceptable, as opposed to proof beyond
a reasonable doubt.[6] However, there is significant support
amongst arbitrators for a heightened standard of burden of
proof. Arbitrator Kanowitz in *Pacific Telephone and Telegraph
Co.* for instance, stated that

> . . . the Arbitrator is in accord with the overwhelming view
> of arbitrators that an employer who discharges an employee for
> alleged dishonesty must establish the facts of that dishonesty
> by proof beyond a reasonable doubt or at least by clear and
> convincing evidence. *See, e.g., Kroger Co.,* 25 LA 906, 908 (Smith,
> 1955); *George H. Dentler & Sons,* 42 LA 954, 956 (Boles, 1964);
> *Retail Clerks International Ass'n, Local 782,* 69-ARB Par. 8552
> (Brothwell, 1969). The consequences for an employee of being
> discharged for dishonesty, not only in terms of his immediate
> loss of employment but also in terms of his future employment

prospects, are so severe, that no less stringent standard is reasonable under the circumstances. Moreover, as indicated in the course of the hearing in this case, the Company, in order to prevail, must establish that, pursuant to its heightened burden of proof, it had sufficient information at the time it discharged the Grievant for dishonesty to justify the discharge at that time.[7]

The presence of significant arbitral opinion in favor of a more stringent burden is due, primarily, to the issue's close kinship to an offense which is punishable under the criminal law.

Because arbitrators perceive the offense to be a serious one and are apparently willing to concede that progressive discipline is inappropriate in most cases of serious dishonesty, they are less likely to reinstate the employee—but, if they did, it would be without back pay or any other mitigation of the full penalty. Either the employer's disciplinary action is sustained or it is completely voided and the employee made whole.[8]

Employment Application Falsification

Employment application falsification requires special comment, not only because of its frequency, but also because the dishonesty involved differs somewhat from other types of dishonesty. The most frequent instances of application falsification involve prior records of either criminal activities or medical conditions. Employers do not normally discipline employees for employment application falsification unless the employer-employee relationship is affected or unless the employee's work performance is somehow affected by his or her moral or physical capabilities. On the other hand, it may be that other forms of falsification are simply not discovered or that unions do not contest the disciplinary action taken in other cases. Relevant cases are listed under Key Points 3 and 4.

Considerations   Employment Application Falsification

1. Whether the information concealed was important, i.e., would the employer have hired the applicant had it known the information at the time of application;
2. Whether the applicant knowingly and deliberately sought to conceal the in-

formation for the purpose of deceiving the employer;

3. Whether the length of time which passed between the application falsification and its discovery, as well as the record of the employee during the interim period, made the falsification immaterial.

Discussion A single case provides a rather comprehensive review of situations met with in dealing with falsification of employment applications, and the case deserves special note. In *Dart Industries*, Arbitrator Greene was presented with four discharges for application falsification.[9] Each of these cases involved the employees' answers, or lack of answers, to a series of questions having to do with an applicant's arrest and conviction record. Setting aside and leaving to the courts the question of whether an employer has the right to ask about arrest records, Arbitrator Greene made the following dispositions:

1. Employee *A* answered "No" to the question of whether he had ever been arrested. When approached later about a substantial arrest and conviction record, *A* denied having filled out the application and the accuracy of the record. Finding that *A* evidenced substantial untrustworthiness, Greene sustained the discharge.
2. Employee *B* left the questions on the application form which had to do with arrests and convictions blank. When confronted by the employer, *B* then denied the accuracy of the police record. Finding *B*'s answers and demeanor evasive and unreliable, Greene sustained the discharge.
3. Employee *C* answered "No" to the arrest and conviction questions. His record, however, revealed a conviction for disorderly conduct. *C* was of limited intelligence and education and had not received help in filling out the application. The company representative testified that had *C* revealed the conviction he would have nonetheless been hired. Greene reinstated *C* with partial back pay.
4. Employee *D* admitted to one arrest and conviction for nonsupport, but he failed to reveal numerous arrests. Because *D* evidenced no untrustworthiness at the arbitration and honestly believed his arrests, which ended

with dismissals on the basis of mistaken identity, did not have to be revealed, Greene reinstated *D* with partial back pay.

In cases involving the falsification of time cards or of work unit slips or other kinds of dishonesty in the workplace which closely parallel theft, arbitrators are reluctant to apply any mitigating circumstances and will sustain a discharge upon proof of a willful attempt by the employee to defraud or cheat the company. In cases involving employment application dishonesty, however, arbitrators look to the materiality of the deception and are much more likely to void the discharge. There seems to be at least a tacit understanding that progressive discipline can only play a very limited role. How, for instance, can progressive discipline be justified in the case of falsification of an employment application? The dishonest act was finite and incapable of repetition. Either the misrepresentation was material and the discharge was warranted or it was not.

Key Points

1   *The employee's act must have been a willful, deliberate attempt to defraud the company, and the employee must have had the knowledge that the deception, if discovered, would result in discipline.*

Examples

The department supervisor saw employee *A* punch in *B*'s time card. The supervisor then saw *B* come in late, look at his card, and go to his work station. At the end of the payroll period, the supervisor went to *B* and asked him if his time card was accurate. *B* said it was. *A* was discharged for punching in *B*'s card, and *B* was discharged for accepting and participating in *A*'s dishonest act. Both discharges were sustained by the arbitrator.

Employee *C*'s supervisor saw her punch in, return to the locker room, and report to her work station 5 minutes after her shift had begun. *C* was discharged. The discharge was denied. The arbitrator reinstated *C* without back pay after a three-month suspension, because there was some evidence that the employer had not always required employees to be dressed and ready for work before punching in.

Employee D had been convicted as a juvenile of breaking and entering to commit burglary. He had been put on probation and had had no further offenses. At the time, his lawyer informed him that upon a successful completion of his probation and upon reaching the age of 21, his record would be expunged. Five years later, he applied for a job with his current employer. To the question on the application "Have you ever been convicted of a crime?," he responded "No." The company discovered the juvenile conviction in its routine check of employee backgrounds three months after it had hired D. D was discharged pursuant to a contract clause providing for discharge in the event of employment application falsification. The arbitrator reinstated D with back pay, finding that the falsification was unintentional because the employee believed that his record had been expunged.

Employee E was arrested and pleaded guilty to a charge of larceny. He received a suspended sentence. Five years later, he concealed the record on an employment application, which asked, "Have you ever been convicted of a crime?." The employer learned of the record two years later when a local college professor asked to interview the employee in connection with a survey of convicted felons who had received suspended sentences. E was discharged pursuant to a contract clause authorizing discharge for falsification of the employment application. The arbitrator sustained the discharge, finding that the employee had intended to conceal his criminal record.

Employee F had made frequent reports to the Department of Transportation (DOT) about the employer's vehicle safety violations, and DOT had responded by giving the employer numerous citations, but not for all of the violations reported. When the employer discovered F to be the source of the reports, F was fired for dishonesty. The arbitrator sustained the discharge, finding that, while many reports were valid, some were obviously untrue. The arbitrator reasoned further that there was an element of maliciousness involved, since F did not use the contract machinery to report safety violations but had made reports verbally to a friend at DOT instead of through the normal channels.

Guidelines

Of necessity, disciplinary action for dishonesty or falsification requires proof of an intent to deceive. If an employee can provide a reasonable explanation for the misrepresentation, an arbitrator is less likely to sustain the discipline.

Relevant Cases

Atlanta Linen Service (Slatham), 85 LA 827
Great Lakes Container Corp. (Madden), 84 LA 451
Safeway Stores (Staudohar), 84 LA 910
Chattanooga Gas Co. (Mullin), 83 LA 48
Thomas Industries (Feegenbaum), 83 LA 118
Western Rubber Co. (Cohen), 83 LA 170
Bekins Moving & Storage Co. (Daughton), 82 LA 491
Elwell-Parker Electric Co. (Dworkin), 82 LA 327
Frontier Airlines (Watkins), 82 LA 1238
John J. Nissen Baking Co. (Chandler), 82 LA 309
Michigan Department of Mental Health (Borland), 82 LA 961
Potlatch Corp. (Kapsch), 82 LA 445
Southwest Detroit Hospital (Ellmann), 82 LA 491
Sumter Electric Cooperative (Maxwell), 82 LA 647
United States Sugar Corp. (Hanes), 82 LA 604
Illinois School Bus Co. (Cox), 81 LA 736
Linn County, Iowa (Sinicropi), 81 LA 929
Pringle Transit Co. (Duda), 81 LA 393
Topeka, Kansas (Thornell), 81 LA 579
United Carbide Corp. (White), 81 LA 864
Alco Gravure (Adler), 78 LA 368
McDonnell Douglas Electronics Co. (Fitzsimmons), 78 LA 287
Plantation Patterns (Dallas), 78 LA 647
Seaway Food Town (Belkin), 78 LA 208
Union Carbide Corp. (Teple), 78 LA 603
Dresser Industries (McIntosh), 75 LA 45
Pacific Northwest Bell Telephone Co. (Render), 75 LA 40
Pacific Telephone & Telegraph Co. (Kanowitz), 74 LA 1095
St. Johnsbury Trucking Co. (Knowlton), 74 LA 607
Confer Smith & Co. (Raymond), 73 LA 1278
Hygrade Food Products Corp. (Chiesa), 73 LA 755
General Electric Co. (MacDonald), 72 LA 391
Marine Corps Air Station (Nolan), 72 LA 28
General Electric Co. (Foreman), 71 LA 142
United States Postal Service (Krimsly), 71 LA 100
Bucyrus-Erie Co. (Gundermann), 70 LA 1017

Factory Services (Fitch), 70 LA 1088
Federal Aviation Administration (Larkin), 70 LA 1249
Hayes-Albion Corp. (Glendon), 70 LA 696
Texas Refinery (Williams), 70 LA 167
Robertshaw Controls Co. (Duff), 69 LA 887
Bi-State Development Agency (Dugan), 67 LA 231
National Vendors (Edelman), 67 LA 1042
Alberto-Culver Co. (Grant), 66 LA 736
Briggs & Stratton Corp. (Grant), 66 LA 758
Commonwealth of Pennsylvania (LeWinter), 66 LA 96
Genuine Parts Co. (O'Neill), 66 LA 1331
Hooker Chemical Corp. (Goodstein), 66 LA 140
Lone Star Beer Co. (Cowart), 66 LA 189
Pennsylvania Power Co. (Altrock), 65 LA 623
Cudahy Foods Co. (Fox), 64 LA 110
Commercial Warehouse Co. (Sater), 62 LA 1015
Price Brothers Co. (High), 62 LA 389
Whitfield Tank Lines (Cohen), 62 LA 934
Blue Chip Stamps Warehouse (Kenaston), 58 LA 148
Dart Industries (Greene), 56 LA 799

2   *The employee must either continue to deny the dishonest act or attempt to continue the deception upon discovery.*

Examples

Employee *A* called in sick for a period of three days. In fact, *A* went to a distant city to handle an emergency health and financial problem for his aged parents. Upon discovery of the falsehood, *A* did not deny the truth. The employer discharged *A*. The arbitrator, finding the employee to be contrite and seeing the value of progressive discipline in this case, commuted the discharge to a suspension.

Employee *B* was on an incentive job. The counting device is activated pneumatically. *B* placed the device in such a way as to continue the airflow through the counter while he moved another bin of incomplete work into position. Upon discovery by the foreman, *B* was discharged. The employee protested that his placement of the device was accidental. Finding that the device could only be placed in an "on" position intentionally, the arbitrator sustained the discharge.

Employee *C* had been on a light duty schedule for two years because he had a history of physical problems. The employer conducted a general layoff, and *C* was laid off despite his seniority because of his light duty status and the elimination of all light duty work. When *C* protested that he could do the available work, the employer had the company doctor examine him. The doctor gave *C* a release for full duty. *C* then asserted that the release was based upon an examination for only one problem and that the doctor had ignored a second malady. *C* further stated that if the doctor had examined him for the second problem, then his work would have been restricted to a lighter duty job which was still available. When the company doctor refused to reconsider his initial findings, *C* went to his own doctor for a modified light duty slip. The second doctor also refused. The employer, finally, discharged *C* for falsifying his medical conditions. The arbitrator sustained the discharge and stated that *C* had failed in his obligation to give an honest day's work for his pay.

Employee *D* witnessed and acted to break up a fight between *X* and *Y*. The employer saw *D*'s actions but was unable to determine the cause of the fight. All the employer knew was that *D* was present at the fight from start to finish and that he was not involved, except as a peacemaker. The employer sought to take disciplinary action against either *X* or *Y*, or both, depending upon the facts. When asked what happened, *D* denied all knowledge. *D* was given a 10-day suspension for failing to cooperate. The suspension was sustained on the basis that *D* had been dishonest in his denial and had interfered with the company's efforts to investigate the occurrence.

Guidelines

The attitude of the employee at the time the dishonest act is discovered may be relevant in cases which do not have serious economic effect on the employer. However, in most cases the discharge or discipline will be sustained where the dishonesty involved an expense account, sick leave, or a compensation system, such as an incentive pay program.

Relevant Cases

Atlanta Linen Service (Slatham), 85 LA 827
Michigan Department of Mental Health (Borland), 82 LA 961

Seaway Food Town (Belkin), 78 LA 208
Dayton Pepsi Cola Bottling Co. (Keenan), 75 LA 154
Dresser Industries (McIntosh), 75 LA 45
Morrel, John & Co. (Stokes), 74 LA 756
Super-Valu Stores (Evenson), 74 LA 939
Warner Robins Air Logistics Center (Dallas), 74 LA 710
General Electric Co. (MacDonald), 72 LA 391
Bucyrus-Erie Co. (Gundermann), 70 LA 1017
Federal Aviation Administration (Larkin), 70 LA 1249
Hayes-Albion Corp. (Glendon), 70 LA 696
Golden Pride (Jaffee), 68 LA 1232
Air Canada (O'Shea), 66 LA 1295
Genuine Parts Co. (O'Neill), 66 LA 1331
Hooker Chemical Co. (Goodstein), 66 LA 140
Lone Star Beer Co. (Cowart), 66 LA 189
Whitfield Tank Lines (Cohen), 62 LA 934
Dart Industries (Greene), 56 LA 799
Duval Corp. (Block), 55 LA 1089
Laughlin, Homer China Co. (Seinsheimer), 55 LA 360
Shop Rite Foods (Hayes), 55 LA 281
International Harvester Co. (Seinsheimer), 53 LA 1197

3   *In cases of falsification of employment applications, the information concealed must have been of such character that, if known, it would have prevented the hire of the applicant.*

Examples

Employee *A* answered "No" to an application question concerning the conviction for any crime committed by the applicant. In fact, the employee had been convicted of possessing hashish two years earlier. Upon discovery of the falsehood, *A* was discharged. During the hearing, the employer admitted that had the employee answered the question honestly, he still would have been hired. The arbitrator denied the discharge and ordered reinstatement with full back pay.

Employee *B*, when asked on the application form whether he had any physical condition which might limit or otherwise affect his ability to do the work, replied in the negative. Six months later, the employee injured his back lifting a trash barrel. A check of his medical records revealed a history of lower back trouble. *B* was discharged. At the arbitration hearing, the employer testified that had it known of the employee's back trouble, the employee would not have been hired because the job required some heavy lifting. The arbitrator sustained the discharge.

Guidelines

Where the concealment of an employment application form is of a material fact which would have prevented employment, the discharge is generally upheld. Where the employer testifies, however, that the employee would have been hired even if the information had been given, falsification by itself is generally not sufficient to justify discharge.

Relevant Cases

Morton Thiokol, Inc. (Williams), 85 LA 834
Utility Trailer Manufacturing Co. (Brisco), 85 LA 643
Owens-Illinois (Cantor), 83 LA 1265
Wine Cellar (Ray), 81 LA 158
United States Steel Corp. (Simpkings), 74 LA 354
Eaton Corp. (Atwood), 73 LA 367
Indianapolis Power and Light Co. (Kossoff), 73 LA 512
I. E. Products (Brooks), 72 LA 35
Dan-Van Rubber Co. (Rothschild), 68 LA 217
Air Canada (O'Shea), 66 LA 1295
Price Brothers Co. (High), 62 LA 389
Fruehauf Trailer Co. (Belkin), 58 LA 1169
Dart Industries (Greene), 56 LA 799

4   *In employment application cases, the employee's work record during the time between the act of falsification and discovery and the nature of information concealed may make the falsification lose its materiality.*

Examples

Employee *A* failed to disclose on his application that he had been convicted of larceny, had served time, and had been on parole for less than a week. Ten years later, the employer learned of the conviction. During the intervening years, the employee had a good employment record and had received promotions up to the top grade in his classification. The employer discharged *A* for falsification of his employment application. The arbitrator reinstated the employee with full back pay, finding that the employee's work record was proof of his rehabilitation and that his discharge would serve no useful purpose, either as a protection to the employer or as a necessary measure for the maintenance of the integrity of the employment process.

Employee *B* failed to disclose on his application that he had been convicted of larceny and had received a suspended sentence less than a week before. Two years later, the employer learned of the conviction. During the intervening years, the employee had established a good work record and was promoted to the top grade in his classification. The employer discharged *B* for falsification of his application. The arbitrator sustained the discharge.

Employee *C* failed to disclose on his application that he had been convicted for possession of hashish. Five years later, this conviction was discovered by the employer. During this time, the employee established a good work record as a tool and dye maker. The employer discharged *C*. The arbitrator reinstated *C* with back pay, finding that the information concealed was not relevant to the employment and that the work record of the employee demonstrated that the use of the drug, if continued, had had no adverse effect on work performance.

Employee *D* failed to disclose on his application that he had been convicted for possession of hashish. Three months later the employer learned of the conviction and discharged *D*. *D*'s work record had been good. The arbitrator sustained the discharge, finding that not enough time had elapsed for the employee to have established ground for mitigation.

Employee *E* tried to conceal a medical problem by answering in the negative the relevant questions on the employment application and post-employment physical form. When the falsification was discovered, the employer told *E* to get a medical certificate stating he could do the job. *E* could not produce a satisfactory certificate, and he was discharged for falsifying the application. The arbitrator held that the employer waived its right to discharge *E* for falsification of the employment application forms by giving *E* an opportunity to produce a medical certificate of fitness. The employer had to prove at the arbitration that *E* was not physically fit to do the job.

> ## Guidelines
>
> Arbitrators often base their decisions on application falsification discharges after balancing numerous factors, including length of time between the date of falsification and date of discovery, the nature of information concealed, and the work record of the employee. Employers must present evidence regarding the specifics of the employee's work record, the materiality of the information concealed to employment (security, etc.), and the importance to the employer of maintaining its unabridged right to discharge an employee for falsifying an employment application.

Relevant Cases

Owens-Illinois (Cantor), 83 LA 1265
Horizon Mining Co. (LeWinter), 72 LA 117
Texas Refinery (Williams), 70 LA 167
Dan-Van Rubber Co. (Rothschild), 68 LA 217
Commonwealth of Pennsylvania (LeWinter), 66 LA 96
Price Brothers Co. (High), 62 LA 389
Blue Chip Stamps Warehouse (Kenaston), 58 LA 148
Freuhauf Trailer Co. (Belkin), 58 LA 1169

Notes to Chapter 13

1. *See Bucyrus-Erie Co.* (Gundermann), 70 LA 1017; *City Prods. Corp.* (Goetz), 67 LA 27; *Air Canada* (O'Shea), 66 LA 1295; *Cudahy Foods Co.* (Fox), 64 LA 110; *Olin Corp.* (Martin), 63 LA 952; *Active Indus.* (Ellmann), 62 LA 985; *Belle Cheese Co.* (Torosian), 59 LA 609; *Central Motor Lines* (Carson), 56 LA 824; *Laughlin, Homer China Co.* (Block), 55 LA 1089; *International Harvester Co.* (Seinsheimer), 53 LA 1197; *Aristocrat Travel Prods.* (Koven), 52 LA 314. *Contra Shop Rite Foods* (Hayes), 55 LA 281.

2. *Pacific Tel. & Tel. Co.* (Kanowitz), 74 LA 1095.

3. *Pacific Tel. & Tel. Co., supra*, note 2, at 1100; *see also Dunlop Tire & Rubber Corp.* (Mills), 64 LA 1099; *United Parcel Serv.* (Nicholas), 63 LA 849; *Commercial Warehouse Co.* (Sater), 62 LA 1015; *Whitfield Tank Lines* (Cohen), 62 LA 934. *Contra Mallinckrodt Chem. Works* (Allen), 57 LA 709.

4. *Dresser Indus.* (McIntosh), 75 LA 45.

5. *Potlatch Corp.* (Kapsch), 82 LA 445.

6. *See Active Indus., supra,* note 1; *Justrite Super Mkts.* (Bothwell), 56 LA 152.

7. *Pacific Tel. & Tel. Co., supra,* note 2, at 1098–99.

8. *But see Pacific Nw. Bell Tel. Co.* (Render), 75 LA 40; *Kentile Floors* (Block), 57 LA 919.

9. *Dart Indus.* (Greene), 56 LA 799.

14

Dress or Grooming

Issue   Whether an employee can be discharged
                     or otherwise disciplined for poor dress or
                     grooming.

Principle   An employee can be discharged or other-
                     wise disciplined for poor dress or grooming
                     where the employer's dress and grooming
code is relevant to the legitimate interests of the employer, is
communicated to the employees, is not in conflict with the
labor agreement, and is consistently enforced.

Considerations   1. Whether the dress and grooming code
                        is reasonable and related to the work-
                        place or other legitimate interests of the
                        employer;
                     2. Whether the code has been communi-
                        cated to the employees so that they have
                        actual or constructive notice of the rule;
                     3. Whether the rule is consistent with the
                        labor agreement;
                     4. Whether the rule has been consistently
                        enforced or applied.

Discussion   Arbitrators have recognized that an em-
                     ployer's restrictions on its employees' dress
                     or grooming may restrict the individual
employee's right to freedom of expression through his or her
appearance. For employers' rules or regulations to be considered reasonable, therefore, they must be related to either the
employee's health and safety or to a legitimate business in-

terest or necessity of the employer. An employer cannot impose a dress code which is the result of an arbitrary decision
based on personal taste.[1] For example, in *Oxford Nursing Home*,
the employer had maintained the same dress code for 20 years
that required the female employees to wear white dresses,
shoes, and stockings.[2] The female employees filed a grievance
requesting that they be allowed to wear white pant suits. The
arbitrator sustained the grievance stating that the employer's
dress code was an unreasonable exercise of management rights.
He also noted that pant suits are acceptable in many medical
facilities and that the employer should keep up with the times.

In reviewing discipline cases involving violations of a dress
or grooming code, arbitrators look first to see if the rule is
reasonably related to the employer's articulated purpose and
then to see if it is consistently applied.[3] If the rule is reasonable, arbitrators still appear willing to disallow discipline if
the employee later conformed to the standard, or if the employee had a legitimate reason for refusing to conform, or if
the employee's years of service or work history entitle him or
her to another opportunity to comply with the rule. In *Allied
Chemical Corp.*, the employee refused to shave his beard after
a company rule was promulgated that all employees using
respirators could not have beards.[4] After two suspensions for
refusing to shave, he was discharged. The employee then agreed
to shave after a test fit. The arbitrator ordered reinstatement
based on the employee's 14 years of service and his present
willingness to conform with the rule. Similarly, in *Randall
Foods No. 2*, the employer made a no-beard rule and suspended
the grievant.[5] The grievant shaved, but filed a grievance to
have the suspension removed from his record. The arbitrator
sustained the grievance, finding that the employee did conform with the rule and that the employer's motivation, i.e.,
the desire for a clean-shaven staff, was inappropriate, although the rule itself was reasonable. In *Safeway Stores*, an
employee, who had worked five years for Safeway and for all
of those five years had worn a beard, was discharged when he
refused to shave after a no-beard rule was enacted.[6] The employee had a skin condition that prevented him from shaving,
and he brought two letters from his physician explaining this
to the employer. The arbitrator found that the employer's rule
was allowable, because the rule was related to the employer's
attempt to present a certain public image and to compete for
its market share of retail food business. The arbitrator also
found that the discharge of an employee whose challenge of

the rule was not based on vanity or personal preference was too harsh, and he reduced the discharge to a leave of absence.

While the focus in the enforcement of many plant rules is the degree to which the employee conforms with the rule, in the area of dress or grooming codes the primary focus is whether the rule is reasonably related to the employer's articulated purpose. Legitimate employer purposes are limited to health and safety or to company image. Though restrictions on facial hair and on certain types of clothing for health and safety reasons are fairly well accepted, the degree to which an arbitrator will accept limits on the employee's appearance for the sake of company image varies widely.

In the area of health and safety an employer's dress or grooming code must in fact be related to the health and safety reasons given as the employer's rationale. In *Allied Chemical Corp.*, the company made a no-beard rule for all employees.[7] The arbitrator found that the rule was only reasonable when applied to those employees who actually used respirators and then only when it could be shown that the facial hair obstructed the respirator seal. The arbitrator stated that the employees have certain legitimate rights and freedoms regarding their bodies and that if their jobs did not require their use of a respirator, the no-beard rule was unreasonable insofar as it applied to them. It appears a well-established principle that facial hair obstructs a respirator seal, and the arbitrator found that rules restricting facial hair for employees required to wear respirators are reasonable.[8]

Employers may restrict certain types of clothing when employees are required to operate machinery. As in the "respirator, no-beard" cases, the rule must be related to the protection of the employees and not a restriction on their dress for arbitrary reasons alone. In *Babcock & Wilcox*, the arbitrator reviewed the rules the employer had put into effect concerning its employees' dress.[9] The dress code required that the employees wear snug clothing while operating the machinery and that this same clothing be worn from the plant gate to the time clock, i.e., prior to reaching the actual work station. The rules also banned all beads, finger rings, and wigs. The arbitrator sustained only the rule requiring the wearing of snug clothing while operating the machinery and found that without supporting evidence the other rules were unreasonable. As the arbitrator stated, the requirement that an employer's dress or grooming code be reasonable implies that the employees to be protected will be in such geographic proximity to the machinery that their compliance with the rule will contribute to the reduction of risks. The requirement of reasonableness was not met when the employer placed restrictions on employees' clothing while they were not working or when the employer prohibited the wearing of jewelry or wigs without evidence that wearing these items endangered the employees' safety.

Hospitals can require certain dress standards for use in operating rooms for health and safety reasons. But, if an employee has some type of objection to a certain dress or uniform requirement, he or she should be given opportunity to present an alternative that can meet the health and safety standards. In *Hurley Hospital*, the employee was given this opportunity.[10] Her design was unsatisfactory, and the employer found the opportunity to transfer her to another department.

An employer may regulate the dress and appearance of its employees if there is a reasonable relation between its standards for dress and grooming and the public image the company hopes to communicate. It is not clear who has the burden of proof where the reasonableness of the rule is at issue. In *Blue Cross of Northern California*, the arbitrator found that the employer had a right—consistent with the management rights clause in the contract—to enforce its dress code.[11] The arbitrator did not require the employer to prove a relationship existed between its dress standards and the image it wanted to project. Similarly, in *Randall Foods No. 2*, even though the arbitrator felt the employer's motivation for his no-beard rule was inappropriate, he accepted the employer's explanation that it wanted a clean-cut, clean-shaven staff, without any proof that this image made a competitive difference in the company's market share.[12]

The arbitrators in *Big Star No. 35* and *Pacific Southwest Airlines* articulated a requirement that the employer come forward with some showing of reasonable business necessity, or evidence, that the appearance requirement (in both cases, the employer had a no-beard rule) had a rational connection with the operation of the business enterprise.[13] In *Pacific Southwest*, the arbitrator required the employer to meet the burden of proof of the public's real attitudes and reactions, as well as proof of a demonstrable relationship between those attitudes and the rules intended to nurture a positive public image. Without meeting this burden, the employer could not arbitrarily restrict its employees' right to determine their own personal appearance.

Most arbitrators do not require such a strong showing. If the employer can show that its standard applies to those employees who have public contact and that it is trying to project a particular image for competitive business reasons, an arbitrator will uphold the rule, or discipline, if the employee fails to comply.

In *Aslesen Co.*, the company had a clean-shaven rule for its drivers, who were also required to wear uniforms.[14] The grievant, a driver, had been told to shave, and he had refused. The arbitrator sustained the employee's suspension, stating that due to the driver's customer contact and the company's concern about its public image, the company had acted within its right. Similarly, in *Arden-Mayfair, Inc.*, the company had a no-beard rule that applied to employees who worked with customers.[15] The arbitrator recognized the employer's prerogative to project to the public a "clean-shaven, well-attired, clean, appealing type individual" as legitimate. The rules were reasonable and easily understood; the employees who were suspended had been given the opportunity to shave, and they had refused. In *Southern Bell Telephone & Telegraph*, the arbitrator recognized that dress and appearance regulations are not valid unless they are reasonably necessary to serve some legitimate business interest of the employer.[16] In this case, the employer's refusal to allow an employee to wear shorts when he was collecting money from pay phones was found to be an extension of the employer's legitimate desire to project an attractive public image.

In professions that have traditionally required employees to wear a uniform or to project a particular image, arbitrators uphold the rule, as well as any discipline meted out for failure to comply. In *City of Erie*, a seasoned police officer was suspended for not wearing the proper uniform.[17] In *Alameda-Contra Costa Transit District*, the arbitrator sustained the rule that bus drivers wear a particular hat, or no hat at all, and concluded that the uniform requirement established an air of authority for the bus driver.[18] The grievant had been suspended for wearing a turban, and the suspension was upheld.

Similar reasoning has been applied in cases where nurses or nurses' aides have been required to wear certain uniforms. In *Greater Harlem Nursing Home*, there were different colored uniforms for the men and women aides.[19] One of the male attendants requested permission to wear the female uniform, in psychological preparation prior to transexual surgery. The employer allowed him to do so for three years and, then, requested him to dress in the male uniform until his surgery. The employee filed a grievance over this request. The arbitrator accepted the employer's rationale that the employee's dressing as a woman confused the patients. Because the proper care of patients, with due regard for their preferences and rights, is the sole purpose of a nursing home, the arbitrator found the employer's request that the grievant dress as a male in his role as a nurses' aide, as long as he was anatomically male, to be reasonable.

Key Points

1   *The dress and grooming code must be reasonably related to the workplace or to some legitimate business of the employer.*

Examples

Employee A grieved his forced transfer out of a chemical-mixing department. The employer had established a rule that all employees would be required to wear respirators when working with loose chemicals in the mixing department. After tests, it was determined that facial hair broke the seal of the respirators, and beards were then prohibited. The employee refused to shave his beard, asserting a skin condition which prevented him from shaving. The employer transferred the employee. The arbitrator upheld the transfer.

Employee B, a female, was given a three-day suspension for refusing to wear a bra under her T-shirt. The employer asserted that such dress was inappropriate, unduly provocative to other employees, and affected their production. The arbitrator sustained the grievance, noting that the employee's attire was not shown to be reasonably related to levels of production or to the safety of other employees.

Guidelines

Dress or grooming rules must be clearly and demonstrably related to the legitimate interests of the employer. Where the dress or grooming of the employee cannot be shown to have a direct effect upon production, safety, sales, or relationships with public consumers, such limitations on dress or grooming will not be sustained by an arbitrator.

Relevant Cases

Walgreen Co. (Wies), 85 LA 1195
Bismark Food Service (Ellmann), 84 LA 870
Spartan Stores (Daniel), 84 LA 1138
Union Carbide Corp. (Goldman), 82 LA 1084
E. I. duPont de Nemours & Co. (Light), 78 LA 327
Hotel Bancroft (Wolff), 78 LA 819
International Minerals & Chemical Corp. (Jones), 78 LA 682
Pacific Southwest Airlines (Jones), 77 LA 320
Allied Chemical Corp. (Harkless), 76 LA 923
Greater Harlem Nursing Home (Marx), 76 LA 680
Alameda-Contra Costa Transit District (Randell), 75 LA 1273
Oxford Nursing Home (Wolff), 75 LA 1300
Safeway Stores (Madden), 75 LA 798
Allied Chemical Corp. (Eischen), 74 LA 412
Aslesen Co. (Fogelberg), 74 LA 1017
Randall Foods No. 2 (Sembower), 74 LA 729
Southern Bell Telephone & Telegraph (Duff), 74 LA 1115
Babcock and Wilcox (Strashofer), 73 LA 443
Big Star No. 35 (Murphy), 73 LA 850
Blue Cross of Northern California (Barrett), 73 LA 352
City of Erie (Kreimer), 73 LA 605
Pacific Southwest Airlines (Christopher), 73 LA 1209
Arden-Mayfair, Inc. (Kaufman), 71 LA 200
Hurley Hospital (Roumell), 71 LA 1013

2   *The employee must have actual or constructive notice of the dress or grooming code prior to discipline.*

Examples

Employee *A*, a retail store clerk, was issued a shirt to be worn while working in the store. On occasion, the employee would forget to have his shirt cleaned and would wear another. The store manager reminded him of the requirement to wear the shirt on each of these occasions. One day he again forgot his shirt and wore a simple, white dress shirt. The general manager for the store chain visited the store; noted the employee's violation of the dress code; and, upon being told that the employee had been warned about similar violations in the past, ordered the employee to punch out and lose the balance of the work shift. The employee grieved, and the arbitrator sustained his grievance, noting that while the employee had actual notice of the rule, he was not aware that the next violation of the code would result in a disciplinary suspension.

Employee *B* was a bus driver who was given a copy of the company's dress code at the time of his employment, which required that a uniform hat be worn at all times the drivers were on duty and which prescribed discipline for being "out of uniform." The employee was disciplined when seen driving his bus without his hat on. The employee defended by saying that his hat ruined his hair style and that he always had the hat next to him on a ledge of the bus. The discipline was sustained.

Guidelines

The dress or grooming rule must be specific, and the employee must have actual or constructive knowledge that a violation of the rule will result in discipline.

Relevant Cases

City of Cocoa, Florida (Cocalis), 81 LA 949
Hotel Bancroft (Wolff), 78 LA 819
New Cumberland Army Depot (Mount), 78 LA 630
Allied Chemical Corp. (Harkless), 76 LA 923
Greater Harlem Nursing Home (Marx), 76 LA 680
Alameda-Contra Costa District (Randall), 75 LA 1273
Oxford Nursing Home (Wolff), 75 LA 1300
Safeway Stores (Madden), 75 LA 798
Babcock & Wilcox (Strashofer), 73 LA 443
City of Erie (Kreimer), 73 LA 605
Hurley Hospital (Roumell), 71 LA 1013

3   *The dress or grooming code must be consistent with the labor agreement.*

Examples

Employee *A*, a car salesman, was given a disciplinary suspension for repeatedly reporting to work in a sport shirt rather than a coat and tie. The employer grieved on the basis that his appearance was neat and clean and that his refusal to wear a coat and tie was not just cause for discipline. The arbitrator noted the absence of any contractual language other than the "just cause" provision of the contract and found the appearance of the salesman in a coat and tie to be within the interest of the employer in maintaining a "high class" public image. The discipline was, therefore, sustained by the arbitrator.

Employee *B* was suspended for failing to wear the company shirt when making service calls. The employee defended on the basis that the employer had agreed during contract negotiations that it would provide shirts and wanted the employees to wear them, but use of the shirts would not be a condition of employment. The arbitrator sustained the grievance.

Guidelines

Even where the business necessity or legitimacy of the dress or grooming rule can be established, the labor agreement cannot be used to establish the parties' agreement that such a rule would not be created or enforced.

Relevant Cases

Walgreen Co. (Wies), 85 LA 1195
City of Cocoa, Florida (Cocalis), 81 LA 949
Hotel Bancroft (Wolff), 78 LA 819
New Cumberland Army Depot (Mount), 78 LA 630
Greater Harlem Nursing Home (Marx), 76 LA 680
Alameda-Contra Costa District (Randell), 75 LA 1273
Asleson Co. (Fogelberg), 74 LA 1017
Blue Cross of Northern California (Barrett), 73 LA 352
City of Erie (Kreimer), 73 LA 605

4 *The dress and grooming rule must be uniformly applied and enforced.*

Examples

Employee *A*, a female, grieved the disciplinary action taken against her for wearing shorts while working. Noting that male employees frequently wore shorts in hot weather, the arbitrator sustained the grievance.

Employee *B*, a male, was disciplined for having shoulder-length hair and wearing earrings. At the arbitration, *B* presented several other male employees who also had long hair and earrings. Noting that the grievant frequently dealt with the public while the other employees did not, the arbitrator sustained the discipline.

Guidelines

Like all rules, dress and grooming rules must be equally applied and enforced. Comparisons between employees must take into account the differences in the employees' jobs and responsibilities, that is, different rules may exist in the same workplace for different classes or types of employees depending upon the nature of their jobs.

Relevant Cases

New Cumberland Army Depot (Mount), 78 LA 630
Greater Harlem Nursing Home (Marx), 76 LA 680
Alameda-Contra Costa District (Randell), 75 LA 1273
Oxford Nursing Home (Wolff), 75 LA 1300
Safeway Stores (Madden), 75 LA 798
Allied Chemical Corp. (Eischen), 74 LA 412
Babcock & Wilcox (Strashofer), 73 LA 443
City of Erie (Kreimer), 73 LA 605
Arden-Mayfair, Inc. (Kaufman), 71 LA 200
Hurley Hospital (Roumell), 71 LA 1013

Special Note

An ancillary, but frequent, problem encountered in connection with dress codes and grooming is that having to do with the wearing of union insignia, or other union-related messages, on hats or other articles of clothing. This issue is raised most often in the context of union campaigns and is resolved under the Labor Management Relations Act (the Act) by the National Labor Relations Board (the NLRB, the Board). Because this question involves the application of law and is not within the primary jurisdiction of labor arbitrators, it is not precisely within the scope of this book. However, because the subject is so closely related to the issue of dress and grooming as a cause for discipline and is normally raised within the context of some disciplinary action, it deserves special mention here.

Consider, for instance, an employee who reports to work wearing clothes appropriate for his job, and otherwise acceptable, but for a slogan on his T-shirt which says "We Care" over a union insignia. Although the employer permits employees to wear T-shirts with all sorts of sayings, it considers this pro-union message to be an affront. Can the employer require the employee to remove the shirt under threat of discipline? Consider also whether an employer has the right to require an employee to remove a hat containing a union insignia, when other hats have been generally allowed.

An employee's right to wear union insignia includes wearing that insignia on a hat or T-shirt.[20] As in other union insignia cases, an employer cannot restrict or ban the wearing of such insignia, without a showing of special circumstances warranting a ban or restriction.[21] In cases where an employer asserts that the hat or T-shirt is in violation of a dress code, the employer must demonstrate that the dress code is enforced and that the rule serves a legitimate purpose.[22] The wearing of some T-shirts, while not bearing union insignia but some message relating to unions, union activity, or terms and conditions of employment, is considered a protected activity.[23] Unless the employer can demonstrate that the shirt is restricted by a valid, nondiscriminatorily enforced nonsolicitation or company uniform rule, that the message disrupts order and discipline at the plant, or that the message is obscene or offensive, the employer cannot prevent the employee from wearing the shirt.[24]

In *Singer Co. v. NLRB*, the employer maintained that shirts with union insignia had to be banned because of the interfactional hostility which existed between different unions at the factory and because the wearing of the shirts caused disruptions, affected discipline, and caused a drop in production. However, the employer was unable to produce any evidence that the drop in production or other objections raised were caused by the wearing of the shirts.[25] Accordingly, the National Labor Relations Board and the Court held that the restrictions violated §8 (a)(1) of the Act.[26]

The employer in *Honda of America* did not require its employees to wear a hat as part of the company uniform.[27] The employer did have a rule prohibiting other items from being worn with the uniform, but the rule was found by the Board to have been unevenly enforced in that the employer had permitted other nonuniform items to be worn. When one employee took to wearing a hat bearing a union insignia, he was asked to remove it and was offered a company hat instead. The employee refused. The Board found that the employer's request violated §8(a)(1) of the Act: The hat was not offensive, hats were not part of the uniform and were not required, and the employer offered no evidence to show that the wearing of the hat with the union insignia interfered with the employer's teamwork concept. Moreover, the board held that the enforcement of the rule as to this employee was selective, since the rule had not been consistently enforced in the past. Similarly, in *Dixie Machine Rebuilders*, the employer asked several employees who were wearing hats bearing union insignia to remove them, because the hats were not part of the company uniform.[28] The Board held that the employees' right to wear union insignia was protected by Section 7 and that the employer's request, without any additional evidence, violated §8(a)(1) of the Act.

In *The Nestle Company*, all employees were required to wear a uniform supplied by the company.[29] When there was an insufficient number of uniforms, however, employees were allowed to wear their own clothing. It was common at these times for the male employees to wear their own various colored T-shirts, which often bore slogans or product names. When several employees chose to wear T-shirts with union insignia, however, they were told to remove them. Although the employer's uniform rule was valid, the Board found that the employer could not apply the rule selectively to union insignia and permit breaches of the rule for other nonuniform clothing.[30]

What would seem to be a more troublesome area is whether it is protected activity to wear a T-shirt with a message arguably about union activity or about the terms and conditions of employment. The outer limit of this question seems to have been set by *Southwestern Bell Telephone Co.*[31] In that case, a group of employees arrived at work wearing T-shirts that said "Ma Bell is a Cheap Mother." The employees' stated purpose was to demonstrate support for the union during the pending contract negotiations. The employer requested the employees to either remove the shirts, cover the slogan, or leave. The Board, holding that the employer's actions were lawful, stated:

> . . . In view of the controversial nature of the language used and its admitted susceptibility to derisive and profane construction, Respondent could legitimately ban the use of the provocative slogans as a reasonable precaution against discord and bitterness between employees and management, as well as to assure decorum and discipline in the plant.[32]

In contrast, the Board found in three other cases that the wearing of T-shirts that said "Don't simonize, unionize," "Fight Speed-up," and "I'm tired of busting my ass" to be protected activity.[33]

In *Publishers Printing Co.*, the employer was found by the Board to have violated §8(a)(1) of the Act by requesting an employee to remove a T-shirt he was wearing that said "Don't simonize, unionize" (a Mr. Simon was the president of the company).[34] The Board's decision was based on the fact that the company had allowed other commercially printed T-shirts with other sayings or signs to be worn in the plant, including a T-shirt imprinted with a marijuana leaf.

In another case, *American Motors Corp.*, the union had printed and sold T-shirts that said "Fight Speed-up" and had distributed literature about wages, hours, and working conditions as well.[35] The wearing of the shirts was found to be protected activity, and the efforts of the foreman to discourage employees from wearing them were found to have violated §8(a)(1) of the Act.

The Board also held in *Borman's, Inc.* that an employee was engaged in protected activity when he wore a T-shirt that had the employer's name above a decal showing a man with a pick standing above the pieces of a donkey or jackass with the inscription "I'm tired of busting my ass."[36] The employer objected to the shirt and testified that it felt that the message on the shirt conveyed a negative impression about the company to outsiders. The administrative law judge found, with the Board's approval, that the slogan on the shirt was not an interference with the company's right to maintain order and discipline at the warehouse. Further, the judge held that the slogan did not vilify any company official and that the language was not so obscene as to be objectionable. The judge also stated that the employee had the right to use the company name on a shirt to identify their employer as the one with which they have a dispute and to advertise a grievance with that employer over working conditions.

It is clear from these cases that an employer will have a very difficult time restricting the employees' right to wear T-shirts or hats bearing union insignia, or union-related or working-condition messages. The only protection an employer may create for itself is to establish a uniform rule which is strictly and evenly enforced. Even then, employees will be permitted to wear union buttons, unless there is a reason clearly related to the employer's business interests, such as the employer's public image and personal or product safety, which would preclude the advantage gained by this form of advertising. In the absence of such a rule, the employer has to establish that the message, as distinguished in most cases from a simple union insignia, created actual, or a demonstrably high risk of, interfactional hostility; fights; loss of, or reduced, production; or that the message was intrinsically obscene or libelous.

Of course, the cases cited above in this Note only refer to issues raised when the clothing, which the employer seeks to prohibit, contains messages related to unions, unionization, grievances, terms or conditions of employment, or anything else arguably protected by §7 of the Act. All other types of messages would be subject to the grievance and arbitration procedure.

Notes to Chapter 14

1. *Big Star No. 35* (Murphy), 73 LA 850.
2. *Oxford Nursing Home* (Wolff), 75 LA 1300.
3. *Pacific Sw. Airlines* (Christopher), 73 LA 1209.
4. *Allied Chem. Corp.* (Harkless), 76 LA 923.
5. *Randall Foods No. 2* (Sembower), 74 LA 729.
6. *Safeway Stores* (Madden), 75 LA 798.
7. *Allied Chem. Corp.* (Eischen), 74 LA 412.
8. *E. I. du Pont de Nemours & Co.* (Light), 78 LA 327; *Pacific Sw. Airlines* (Jones), 77 LA 320; *Allied Chem. Corp.*, supra, note 4; *Allied Chem. Corp.*, supra, note 7. But see *International Minerals & Chem. Corp.* (Jones), 78 LA 682.
9. *Babcock & Wilcox* (Strashofer), 73 LA 443.
10. *Hurley Hosp.* (Roumell), 71 LA 1013.
11. *Blue Cross of N. Calif.* (Barrett), 73 LA 352.
12. *Randall Foods No. 2, supra*, note 5.
13. *Big Star No. 35, supra*, note 1; *Pacific Sw. Airlines, supra*, note 3.
14. *Aslesen Co.* (Fogelberg), 74 LA 1017.
15. *Arden-Mayfair, Inc.* (Kaufman), 71 LA 200.
16. *Southern Bell Tel. & Tel.* (Duff), 74 LA 1115.
17. *City of Erie* (Kreimer), 73 LA 605.
18. *Alameda-Contra Costa Transit Dist.* (Randell), 75 LA 1273.
19. *Greater Harlem Nursing Home* (Marx), 76 LA 680.
20. *Overnite Transp. Co.*, 254 NLRB No. 11, 107 LRRM 1130 (1981); *Dixie Mach. Rebuilders*, 248 NLRB 881, 104 LRRM 1094 (1980).
21. *Honda of Am. Mfg.*, 260 NLRB No. 97, 109 LRRM 1267 (1982); *Singer Co. v. NLRB*, 480 F. 2d 269, 83 LRRM 2655 (10th Cir. 1973).
22. *Honda of Am. Mfg., supra*, note 21; *The Nestle Co.*, 248 NLRB 732, 103 LRRM 1567 (1980).
23. *Borman's, Inc.*, 254 NLRB No. 130, 106 LRRM 1310 (1981); *American Motors Corp.*, 214 NLRB 455, 87 LRRM 1393 (1974).

24. *Borman's, Inc., supra*, note 23; *Publishers Printing Co.*, 246 NLRB 206, 102 LRRM 1628 (1979); *Southwestern Bell Tel. Co.*, 200 NLRB 667, 82 LRRM 1247 (1972).

25. *Singer Co. v. NLRB, supra*, note 21.

26. *See also Overnite Transp. Co., supra*, note 20 (wearing of Teamster T-shirt protected activity).

27. *Honda of Am. Mfg., supra*, note 21.

28. *Dixie Mach. Rebuilders, supra*, note 20.

29. *The Nestle Co., supra*, note 22.

30. *See also Publishers Printing Co., supra*, note 24 (employer, which allowed employees to wear commercially printed T-shirts bearing various legends in the plant, could not restrict union-related materials).

31. *Southwestern Bell Tel. Co., supra*, note 24.

32. *Id.*, at 1248.

33. *Borman's, Inc., supra*, note 23; *Publishers Printing Co., supra*, note 24; *American Motors Corp., supra*, note 23.

34. *Publishers Printing Co., supra*, note 24.

35. *American Motors Corp., supra*, note 23.

36. *Borman's, Inc., supra*, note 23.

15

Drugs: Use or Possession

Issue
Whether an employee can be discharged or otherwise disciplined for use and/or possession of drugs.

Principle
An employee may be discharged or otherwise disciplined for use and/or possession of drugs while on duty, regardless of whether the employee is on or off the premises of the employer. An employee may also be discharged or otherwise disciplined for possession of drugs with an intent to sell or for the actual sale of drugs at any time, regardless of whether the employee's conduct was detected within employment hours or whether his or her actions were connected in any way with his or her employment. As used in this chapter, the term "drugs" is intended to mean all controlled substances which, when ingested by an individual, will cause some behavioral or physical change which will affect the individual's ability to work, exercise reasoned judgement, and/or get along with peers, subordinates, or others with whom he or she comes in contact during the workday. Consequently, a "drug" may be a legally prescribed substance being taken by an employee with a legitimate physical difficulty and under a doctor's care, as well as an illegal chemical or organic product. For the purposes of this discussion, the drugs referred to, except where noted, are those generally referred to as illegal or street drugs, such as marijuana, heroin, morphine, cocaine, codeine or opium additives, LSD, DMT, STP, amphetamines, methamphetamines, and barbiturates. The term "hard" drug when used here is intended to mean all of the drugs listed above except marijuana.

Considerations

1. Whether the use or possession of drugs takes place while the employee is on the premises of the employer or within his or her workday;
2. Whether the employee is under the influence of drugs on the employer's premises or during the employee's workday;
3. Whether the employee sells or sold drugs or whether the employee has possession of drugs with an intent to sell;
4. Whether the employer maintains and has communicated its rule against use and/or possession of drugs on the work premises or during the workday.
5. Whether the drug is within the category of "hard drugs";
6. Whether a "drug problem" exists within the workplace;
7. Whether the employee's use or possession of drugs affected the orderly operation of the employer's business;
8. Whether the employee's use or possession of drugs had an adverse affect on the reputation of the employer.

Discussion

The most common circumstances presented to arbitrators involves the discharge of an employee for possession of a drug, usually marijuana, on company premises and/or while on duty. In a few of these cases, the arbitrators have reinstated employees, although without back pay, on the theory that the "mere possession" of drugs is less serious than its use[1] or on the basis that the plant rule only prohibited employees from being "under the influence."[2] However, it is more frequently the case that an arbitrator will uphold the discharge of an employee who possesses a controlled and unprescribed drug on company premises or while on duty, especially where the conduct is against a company or labor contract rule.[3]

The second largest group of cases in this area deals with employees disciplined for the use of or being under the influence of drugs on company premises and/or while on duty. Generally, arbitrators have upheld discharges for the use of controlled and unprescribed drugs, including marijuana, while on the premises of the employer, even in cases where it has been a first offense.[4] Remarkably, however, one arbitrator, noting the increasingly liberal legal treatment of marijuana, ordered an employee who smoked marijuana on the employer's premises to be reinstated without back pay.[5]

Discipline may also be warranted when the employee is under the influence of a prescribed rather than illegal drug where there is some threat to the safety and efficiency of the employee's performance.[6] In *FMC Corp.*,[7] for instance, an employer was held to have properly given an employee a three-day suspension where the employee was found to be on medication, Valium, prescribed by his physician for neck pain. The arbitrator refused to distinguish between prescribed and other drugs.

> The rule clearly makes no exception for that situation. To provide such an exception would not be appropriate in my opinion. The purpose of the rule is to safeguard the employee and fellow workers from injury which might occur as a consequence of the employee being under the influence. Whether that influence resulted from the employee taking medication as prescribed or using drugs without benefit of prescription is not relevant to the fact that the employee was under the influence and therefore a risk in the work place.
>
> An employee who is taking prescribed medication which would diminish his capacity to work safely should take sick leave rather than report to work under the influence. Even in the event there is no provision to compensate an employee who is on sick leave, it is far better to lose pay than present a dangerous hazard in the work place by being under the influence.

While arbitrators generally will uphold discharges of employees who possess or use drugs on company premises and/or during their workday, an employee may be reinstated when he or she has been discharged for use or possession off the premises. These off-the-premises use or possession cases usually arise when the employee has been arrested, and the employer then invokes discipline. Many arbitrators still cling to the belief that an employee's conduct in his or her private life is not the employer's concern, and an arrest for drug use or possession off the employer's premises, therefore, will not justify discharge, as long as the arrest does not damage the employer's public image or reduce the ability of co-workers to deal with the employee or as long as the employee's work performance is unaffected by drugs.[8]

Thus, where a nexus to the job was not proven, the suspension of an employee for off-the-job marijuana use was invalidated. In *General Telephone Co. of California*,[9] the arbitrator relied on the following criteria:

> It is widely accepted by arbitrators that in order for off-the-job misconduct to serve as a proper basis for discipline by the employer, that misconduct, whether criminal or otherwise, must have a direct relationship to the employee's job. A widely accepted three-part test of that relationship was stated by Arbitrator Kesselman in W. E. Caldwell Co., 28 LA 434 (1957): Discharge for misconduct away from the place of work has no basis unless (1) the behavior harms the company's reputation or product; or (2) the behavior renders employee unable to perform his or her duties or appear at work; or (3) the behavior leads to the refusal, reluctance or inability of other employees to work with the employee. None of these critical elements is present here. Further, any job relationship alluded to by the Company is speculative, unsupported, and, at best, *de minimis*.
>
> In *Alabama Power Co.*,[10] this nexus was found where the publication of an employee's arrest in a local newspaper was held to have an adverse effect on the employer's business interests.
>
> The effect of off-plant involvement with illegal drugs on an employer's business has been the subject of many recent arbitration cases. The adverse effects on the business have ranged from concerns about safety of employees and property to concerns about fears of other employees. Grievant was an Assistant Plant Control Operator and as such, received very minimal supervision in a very hazardous operational setting in which mistakes (from possible drug related impairments) could cause disastrous property damage or injury and death. In Arco-Polymers, Inc., 69 LA 379 (1977), Arbitrator Milentz, in upholding a discharge based on an off-site heroin involvement, stated that the employee's possession of the drug adversely affected the employer's business because it "gives rise to a legitimate fear for the safety of other employees or property". The arbitrator went on to add that the Grievant's statement that the drugs in his possession were not his, could imply that "some or all of (the drug) *could have* been destined for sale and use by employees within the plant . . . it is only logical to conclude that Grievant's criminal activity did . . . create a legitimate fear for the safety of other employees and property, especially when considering the hazardous nature of operations and the mental alertness required of all employees at all times." Grievant occupied a responsible position with the Company. Many fellow employees rely on the Plant Control personnel in the daily performance of their jobs. It is reasonable that these employees show concern about working with a convicted drug user, which Grievant was. There was evidence introduced at the hearing which convinced the arbitrator of that concern by employees. To subject these fellow employees to the realized fears of re-

placing Grievant as Assistant Plant Control Operator, would be to hamper their production and to increase the likelihood of mistakes through inattention by them. This very possible likelihood would, of course, adversely affect the Company's business. Other arbitrators have reached this same conclusion based upon the possible "detrimental effect on the employer's reputation or product", or "reluctance or inability of other employees to work with employee" . . . Thus, the adverse effects of Grievant's outside conduct did have some very real and perceived impact upon the Company. The loss of reputation from the adverse publicity and the concern over safety by both the Company and fellow employees are among some of these effects.

There is an emerging trend that where a properly negotiated drug rule covers off-premises misconduct or where the off-duty or off-premises misconduct adversely affects the employer, an employee may be disciplined or fired for violating the rule or engaging in the prohibited conduct. In *Lick Fish and Poultry*,[11] for example, an arbitrator denied a grievance on the basis of a negotiated policy:

The Grievant testified that he had been using "crank" for about two years. The Grievant considered himself a moderate user. The Grievant testified that his use of "crank" varied and occurred "maybe once a week and on weekends; on days off." Thus, the Grievant, by his own admission, did use an illegal narcotic. However, as developed through testimony, the phrase "illegal use of narcotics" meant use which occurred at work or an adverse impact upon the performance of duties by an employee who had used drugs off the job. In this case, the Grievant asserts that he did not use narcotics while at work and there is no evidence to the contrary. However, it is clear that there was an adverse impact as a result of the Grievant's use of "crank" on Saturday, June 5, 1986. The Grievant suffered amphetamine psychosis and as a result of that condition, he could not remain at work. That is, while there is no evidence of specific impairment as it relates to job performance, the Grievant's condition rendered him unfit to perform his work. The Grievant's condition was drug induced. The fact that the Grievant supposedly was trying to act responsibly toward his employer while the Grievant was engaged in the use of an illegal narcotic is not of significant mitigating value. In fact, the Grievant's particular effort to keep his drug use separate from work highlights the Grievant's knowledge of the consequences of being under the influence of drugs on the job. The Grievant thought he could consistently predict the outcome of his drug usage and he was wrong. The Grievant assumed all the risk attendant to drug usage when he elected to partake of the use of "crank" including the potential loss of employment. The Grievant cannot avoid accountability for his acts simply because he got an unexpected result. The Grievant cannot look to the unintentional nature of his problem for relief. The Grievant did violate the Company's rule against the use of illegal narcotics.

The Union contends that discharge is unfair and inappropriate to the circumstance. The thrust of the Union's position is that the Company should allow for the Grievant's rehabilitation and let him return to work. However, the latter ignores the fact that the Company bargained for and obtained the right to summarily discharge any employee who engaged in the illegal use of narcotics. That is, where warning was required, a reasonable opportunity to rectify and change the offending behavior attached; however, where no warning was required, no corrective opportunity attached. According to the testimony of the Company's Chief Negotiator, who participated in the 1973 negotiations, the Union as well as Company shared a stringent viewpoint regarding drugs and the workplace. Whether the same viewpoint is appropriate to today's setting is irrelevant. The fact of the language adopted in 1973 remains.

In *Arco-Polymers*, the arbitrator held that the employee's arrest for possession of heroin with intent to sell did raise a legitimate fear that he would sell to co-workers, and the discharge was therefore upheld.[12] Also, in *Michigan Power Co.*, the arbitrator found that the employer properly suspended an employee whose arrest for the distribution of a controlled substance adversely affected the company's reputation.[13] However, the arbitrator also held that the employee should have been reinstated after the charges were dismissed.

Cases involving the sale of drugs, either on or off the employer's premises, are handled considerably different from use and possession cases. It does not appear to matter whether the sale is on or off the premises; the offense always appears to be considered a proper subject for summary discharge. In *Eastern Airlines* and *Cerro Corp.*, where the employees were selling marijuana to their co-workers, for instance, both arbitrators upheld the discharges.[14] Also, in *State University of New York*, the arbitrator upheld the discharge of a bartender, who had sold "black mollies" to student customers of the campus bar.[15]

In *Martin-Marietta Aerospace*,[16] arbitrator Aronin summarized the positions being taken by arbitrators in cases involving the sale of drugs as follows:

> An Employer has a legitimate concern that an employee such as Grievant may continue using drugs and has just cause to anticipate that Grievant may attempt to sell drugs to other employees. Where Grievant has not changed after a prior conviction and has only escalated his problem by moving to a stronger and more expensive drug, it is reasonable for this Employer to

> anticipate a propensity exists to use and sell prohibited sub-
> stances. This is not a risk this Employer must assume under
> these circumstances. Just cause exists for a discharge under
> these facts because of the impact on the Employer's product,
> its reputation, employee safety, plant security and production
> and discipline.
>
> The fact that Grievant's activities were off the premises
> and not on company time is not relevant when a relationship
> can be established to the Employer's operations, as noted above.
> The undersigned agrees with the other arbitrators who have
> noted a distinction may be drawn between the user and the
> "pusher"—one who has sold a controlled substance. In this in-
> stance, Grievant falls into the latter category based not only
> on the single sale but on the totality of Grievant's conduct.

Where the employee was selling drugs off the premises, arbitrators still have been willing to uphold the discharge, noting the employer's concern that the employee would sell to other employees.[17] However, in one case, the arbitrator reinstated with back pay an employee who had been discharged when he pleaded guilty to a sale of methamphetamine which had occurred before his employment. The arbitrator noted that there was no evidence that either the employee's performance or the company's reputation was affected or that there was a drug problem among the other employees; such factors have been considered in the other cases as well.[18]

The existence or the lack of a clear rule prohibiting the use or possession of drugs also appears to have been significant in several arbitrations. On at least two occasions arbitrators have refused to permit the discharge of employees for first offenses for possession of marijuana, because there was no rule allowing for such serious disciplinary action. In making this conclusion, the arbitrators noted the increasingly relaxed legal treatment of marijuana and felt that, without prior notice by the employer, the mere possession of that substance on the company's property should not be cause for summary discharge.[19] However, others have found that employees need no special notice, or that they have constructive notice when the offense involves criminal conduct or something as serious as the use and possession of marijuana.[20]

The rule prohibiting the use or possession of drugs, no matter how clear, must still pass scrutiny as reasonable. A rule that requires an employee's discharge for a single instance of drug use at work but that imposes a lesser penalty for use of alcohol at work will be held unreasonable. In *Mallinckrodt, Inc.*,[21] the arbitrator stated:

I found four cases by four different arbitrators dealing specifically with the question as to whether the punishment for
drug abuse should be the same as the punishment for alcohol
abuse. All four arbitrators agreed that this should be so. All
four set aside a punishment of discharge for drug abuse where
under like circumstances some lesser penalty would be imposed
for alcohol abuse and measured the proper penalty by the alcohol standard.

. . .

I agree with what Umpire Valtin has stated in the above
excerpts from this case which represents majority arbitral thought
today. Alcoholism in industry, and as a social problem, is far
more debilitating, costly, and destructive than marijuana. There
is no rational or reasonable basis to treat them as distinct.
Therefore to treat alcohol abuse with progressive discipline and
treat drug abuse with immediate discharge is improper.

Arbitrators also give some consideration to the type of
drug involved. Generally, arbitrators will permit more severe
measures to be taken in cases involving "hard drugs." Thus,
in *Wheaton Industries*, the arbitrator upheld the summary
discharge of an employee arrested for possession with intent
to sell heroin, even though he had not yet been convicted.[22]
The arbitrator specifically noted that this case involved a "hard"
drug.[23]

Another factor sometimes considered to be relevant is
whether a general drug problem exists at the plant. Arbitrators will endorse more severe measures taken against drug
offenders when there is evidence of a more widespread drug
problem at the plant. For example, in *Arco-Polymers*, the discharge of an employee who had been arrested for possession
of heroin with intent to sell was upheld; in *Pepsi Cola Bottlers*
and in *S. F. Kennedy-New Products*, the summary discharges
of employees for the possession and sale of marijuana and
mescaline on the premises was upheld, and the drug problem
within the companies was held to justify the lack of progressive discipline.[24]

Of special note in this regard is the case of *Watauga Industries*, in which the discharges of four employees for smoking marijuana on the premises during their lunch break were
reduced to suspensions.[25] There was no problem of proof; the
employees were caught in the act. While recognizing that
smoking marijuana on the plant premises during the workday
was a legitimate cause for discharge, the arbitrator nevertheless reduced the penalty to a suspension. Apparently, reasoned the arbitrator, smoking marijuana on the premises had
been a common practice for up to five months prior to this

incident. Although just prior to the incident the company president had told his supervisors that this practice would no longer be condoned and that the supervisors were to enforce the rule against smoking marijuana, this enforcement policy had not been communicated to the employees. Consequently, the discharge penalty was found to be inappropriate, because the general drug problem in the plant made a clear rule unenforceable on its face and the employees had not been given adequate notice.

Proving the charges of drug use and/or possession present a separate but complex problem that must be noted. The problem includes the burden of proof, the type of proof, and the closely related charges of insubordination, which may result from a demand upon the employee that he or she produce the suspicious material, bag, or the like.

Two burdens of proof have been applied to the employers' cases. The first is that the employer must prove its case beyond a reasonable doubt. This criminal standard is used, because the charge is one of a criminal nature.[26] The second standard of proof used frequently in drug cases is that of "clear and convincing" proof.[27] The significance of this difference in the two standards of the burden of proof is not clear. Some arbitrators have suggested that there is little difference, if any.[28]

There is also discrepancy among arbitrators over the sort of proof or evidence that can be offered to support the discipline. One problem area is the weight to be given to the testimony and accusations of the employee's co-workers. In *Structurlite Plastics Corp.*, for instance, the arbitrator upheld the discharge of an employee for using drugs on the job upon the testimony of employees that the grievant looked like he was on drugs.[29] By contrast, in *Casting Engineers*, a suspension was not upheld, because there was no corroborating evidence of the co-worker's accusation of use of marijuana.[30] However, in *St. Joe Minerals Corp.*, the arbitrator, in upholding the discharge, gave substantial weight to the conclusion of the company doctor, who had examined the grievant and determined that he was under the influence of marijuana based on the inflammation of the grievant's eyes and his affected reactions.[31]

Arbitrator Murphy, in *Sun Chemical Corp.*,[32] applied the standard of sufficient credible evidence to persuade the arbitrator that certain conduct violative of a clear rule occurred:

> The arbitrator has concluded that the Employer has sustained its burden of proving that both Grievants were "under

the influence of . . . marijuana on Company Property" while in the electrical room during the evening of December 12-13, 1985. This conclusion is based upon:

1) the direct evidence of the behavior and physical characteristics of the Grievants immediately after their discovery in the electrical room on the night in question;

2) the direct evidence was supplied by one supervisor found to be a trained observer of persons under the influence of marijuana, and supported by the observations of another supervisor;

3) the fact that the odor of marijuana was present in the electrical room—a fact established by testimony of one Grievant, Grievant X, and both supervisors.

Arbitrator King, in *Georgia Pacific Corp.*,[33] applied the same standard of credibility:

The question of whether one has carried his burden of proof is not determined by the number of persons who have testified but rather by whether such evidence as has been presented is credible and, if believed, establishes the matter in issue. In this case, the testimony of Clinton Williams did just that. His investigative reports were precise and professionally prepared. They gave the kind of details regarding the circumstances surrounding each incident to give his presentation an unmistakable ring of truth. The arbitrator believes that each incident that he reported happened as he testified. Due to the nature of the investigation and the manner in which it had to be carried out, further corroboration of the various incidents was not possible.

While in a court of law it might be difficult to convict a person of possession of drugs or alcohol without the physical evidence being presented, convictions of being under the influence of alcohol or drugs are quite routinely based upon the uncorroborated testimony of the observance of an arresting officer.

Arbitrator Nicholas, in *Owens-Corning Fiberglas Corp.*,[34] also rejected the criminal standard, although eventually concluding that the employer failed to sustain even a lesser burden of proof.

As the parties are aware, the paramount question that serves to frame this case is this: Was the decision to terminate Grievant for just and sufficient cause based on the events of October 4, 1985? Indeed, if the action taken was not for just cause, it must be either reversed and/or modified.

In cases of this sort Arbitrators are divided as to what standard of proof that Management should have to bear in order to make for a good cause showing. Many have held that Management must meet a strict burden tantamount to the criminally imposed rule "beyond a reasonable doubt", while just as many have favored a lesser standard, i.e., that the employer's case be supported by the evidentiary standard "a preponderance of the evidence." Unless linked directly to criminal action, this Arbitrator has favored something of a middle ground. This is to say that Management must come forward and show that there is, in fact, good and sufficient evidence to support the charges made against the subject employee. Accordingly, with all things considered in the instant case, this is the standard that Company will have to meet.

Another problem confronting arbitrators is that of culpability when more than one person is in an area in which marijuana has been used or found. In *Whirlpool Corp.*, the arbitrator reinstated with back pay two employees who had been merely riders in a truck in which marijuana was later found.[35] However, in *General Foods Corp.*, the arbitrator upheld the 30-day suspension of all four employees, who had been found in a company car which smelled of marijuana.[36] The arbitrator rejected the argument that to uphold the suspensions he had to find which of the four actually possessed and smoked the marijuana.

A final problem area related to proof occurs when an employer demands that the employee produce the suspicious material or container which has been seen, the employee refuses, and the employee is then discharged for insubordination. The employer has the right to make such a demand, and there is no constitutional protection involved in the case of a private employer. The refusal to comply with such a request will sustain a discharge for insubordination.[37]

It is apparent, therefore, that there are many factors which can affect a drug-related discharge or discipline, in addition to those generally considered by arbitrators, such as the reasonableness of the rule against use and/or possession and the employee's length and quality of past service. One arbitrator set out a list of factors for drug-related cases, which can serve as a useful summary:

(1) whether possession or sale is involved; (2) the type of drug (marijuana vs. hard drugs); (3) whether the transaction was a casual sale; (4) whether the conduct occurred on the premises of the employer; (5) the presence or absence of a drug problem at the workplace; (6) impact on the reputation of the employer, and (7) effect on the orderly operation of the employer's business.[38]

Key Points

1   *Where an employee possesses drugs while at the
workplace or on duty, some discipline will be sustained.
The severity of the discipline will depend upon the
nature of the drug, the presence of a general drug
problem in the workplace, the existence of a clear rule,
and/or the work history of the employee.*

Examples

Employee *A* was discharged following a routine locker
check which revealed a quantity of marijuana in *A*'s possession. The employer's work rules stipulated that pos
session of narcotics in the workplace would be cause for
summary discharge. The discharge was sustained.

Employee *B* was discovered in the plant with a user's
quantity of cocaine in his possession. The employer had
no rule against drug possession, and the employee had an
excellent work record. *B* was discharged, and the discharge was sustained.

Employee *C* was discharged following the discovery of a
user's quantity of marijuana in his lunchbox. The employer had no rule regarding the possession of drugs, and
the search was conducted in connection with a company
program to prevent theft of product. The employee had a
marginal performance record and was also one of those
suspected of theft. The discharge was reduced to suspension.

Employee *D* was discharged following the discovery of a
user's quantity of marijuana in his lunchbox as a result
of the employer's crackdown against drug use in the workplace. The employee's work record was without blemish.
The arbitrator, recognizing the need of the employer to
control drug usage in the plant, sustained the discharge.

Employee *E* was discharged for possession of marijuana
in the plant. Company policy prohibited employees from
working while under the influence of drugs or alcohol.
The arbitrator reduced the discharge to a warning, noting
that the employer could not rely on the rule in this case
because the rule did not cover mere possession.

Guidelines

In the absence of a specific rule which makes the mere possession of drugs on the employer's premises an offense likely to result in discipline, an employee may nevertheless be disciplined for possession of drugs in the workplace, where it can be shown that a general drug problem exists in the plant, the use of drugs would present an immediate and severe safety risk to other employees, or the nature and quantity of the drugs suggests a dealer.

Where prohibited by a clear and communicated rule, the mere possession of drugs in the workplace will be sufficient cause for discipline.

Relevant Cases

Rust Engineering Co. (Whyte), 85 LA 270
Livingston Export Packing (Ives), 83 LA 270
Hussmann Refrigerator Co. (Mikrut), 82 LA 558
U.S. Aluminum Corp. (Darrow), 81 LA 174
Watauga Industries (Galambos), 78 LA 697
Brooks Foundry (Daniel), 75 LA 642
Detroit Stoker Co. (Daniel), 75 LA 816
Georgia Pacific Corp. (Vadakin), 72 LA 784
Swift & Co. (Rentfro), 72 LA 513
B. Green & Co. (Cushman), 71 LA 685
St. Joe Minerals Co. (Roberts), 70 LA 1110
Arco-Polymers (Milentz), 69 LA 379
Joseph G. Tropiano, Inc. (Belsky), 69 LA 1243
Stansteel Corp. (Kaufman), 69 LA 776
Jeep Corp. (Keefe), 67 LA 828
Abex Corp. (Rybolt), 64 LA 721
Wheaton Industries (Kerrison), 64 LA 826

2   *Where an employee uses drugs or is under their influence at the workplace or while on duty, summary discharge normally will be sustained.*

Examples

Employee *A* was discovered smoking marijuana during his lunch break. The employer had no rule against drugs. Nevertheless, *A* was discharged. The arbitrator sustained the discharge.

Employee *B* was discovered smoking marijuana during her lunch break and was discharged. The employer had no rule against drugs. The employee defended on the basis of her good work record and high productivity. The arbitrator reduced the discharge to a suspension.

Employee *C* was discharged following an accident in a forklift, which resulted in minor injuries to himself and another employee. During the investigation of the incident, the employer discovered that the employee was under medication, which had been prescribed by his doctor and which affected the employee's ability to react and to make judgments. The bottle containing the medication clearly stated that, after taking, the user should not operate machinery or drive. The employee was discharged and the arbitrator sustained the discharge, noting the employer's rule requiring summary discharge for the use of drugs in the plant.

Guidelines

Should any employee be found to be under the influence of drugs while on duty, such conduct will justify summary discharge, regardless of whether there is a rule prohibiting the use of drugs in the workplace, while on duty, or at a time proximate to the employee's work time.

The use of any controlled drug which affects behavior, or the ability of an employee to work in a safe manner, regardless of whether the drug is a narcotic or "illegal" in the common sense may be cause for discipline where the employee knew or should have known that the drug would materially diminish his or her capabilities.

Relevant Cases

Central Ohio Transit Authority (Murphy), 88 LA 633
Sun Chemical Corp. (Murphy), 88 LA 633
Owens-Corning Fiberglas (Nicholas), 86 LA 1026
Georgia Pacific (King), 85 LA 542
Kraft, Inc. (Denson), 82 LA 360
Washington Metropolitan Area Transit Authority (Bernhardt), 82 LA 150
Walker Mfg. Co. (Morgan), 81 LA 1169

FMC Corp. (Reynolds), 80 LA 1173
Mallinckrodt, Inc. (Seidman), 80 LA 1261
Combustion Engineering (Jewett), 70 LA 318
St. Joe Minerals Corp. (Roberts), 70 LA 1110
Arco-Polymers (Milentz), 69 LA 379
Pepsi Cola Bottlers of Youngstown (Klein), 68 LA 792
Monfort Packing Co. (Goodman), 66 LA 286
S. F. Kennedy-New Products (Traynor), 64 LA 880
Wheaton Industries (Kerrison), 64 LA 826
Mississippi River Grain Elevator (Marcus), 62 LA 200

3   *Where an employee uses or possesses drugs while off the employer's premises and while not on duty, neither discipline nor discharge will normally be sustained without the presence of some fact which directly impacts on the legitimate business interest of the employer, e.g., the employer's reputation, or without some other element which will justify the discipline.*

Examples

Following a minor automobile accident, employee *A* was charged with being under the influence of a controlled substance, marijuana. Upon reading an account of the occurrence in a local newspaper, the employer discharged *A*. Noting *A's* acceptable work record, the arbitrator reinstated him with back pay.

Employee *B* was suspended after his arrest for possession and for being under the influence of cocaine. Following *B's* admission into an alcohol and drug rehabilitation program, which required as a condition of entry an admission of guilt, *B* was discharged. Noting that the employer had a restaurant which catered to teenagers, the arbitrator sustained the discharge.

Employee *C* was discharged following his arrest and conviction for using illegal drugs, marijuana. The employer argued at the arbitration that it had a problem of drug use in the plant which it had been unsuccessful in solving. The arbitrator, stating that the employer's need to rout out drug users in the plant created a special circumstance, sustained the discharge.

Guidelines

The possession or use of drugs while off the employer's premises and while not on duty may be cause for discipline, up to and including discharge, where such conduct can be shown to have a direct and material adverse effect on the employer's business interests, including public image.

Relevant Cases

Alabama Power Co. (Baroni), 88 LA 425
General Telephone Co. of California (Collins), 87 LA 441
Houston Power and Light (Howell), 87 LA 478
Lick Fish and Poultry Co. (Concepcion), 87 LA 1062
University of Missouri-Kansas City (Thornell), 82 LA 112
Martin-Marietta Aerospace (Aronin), 81 LA 695
Nugent Sand Co. (Daniel), 81 LA 988
City of Wilkes-Barre (Dunn), 74 LA 33
Indian Head (Rimer), 71 LA 82
Nugent Sand Co. (Kanner), 71 LA 585
Metropolitan Atlanta Transit Authority (Anderson), 70 LA 1022
Gamble Brothers (Krislov), 68 LA 72
Emhart Manufacturing Co. (McKone), 63 LA 1265
General Portland Cement Co. (Davidson), 62 LA 377

4   *Where an employee is found to be selling drugs or in possession of drugs with the intent to sell, discharge normally will be sustained, regardless of whether or not the discovery is made on the company's premises.*

Examples

Employee *A* was discharged for possession of marijuana when a locker search turned up a quantity of the drug in excess of the normal user's amount in his locker. The employer had no rule regarding drugs. The arbitrator sustained the discharge on the grounds that the quantity discovered indicated that the employee had an obvious intent to sell.

Employee *B* was arrested and convicted for selling heroin. The sale and subsequent arrest took place away from the employer's workplace, and there was no evidence of any connection between *B*'s activity and his employer. B was discharged. The arbitrator, recognizing the employer's legitimate concern over the possibility of *B* making sales to other employees, sustained the discharge.

Guidelines

Regardless of the absence of a rule prohibiting the sale of drugs or possession with intent to sell drugs at any time or any place, such conduct will be cause for summary discharge, since it is perceived as a serious and immediate threat to the employer's business interest in that such an employee will be found to constitute a probable source for the acquisition of drugs by other employees.

Relevant Cases

Times-Mirror Cable Television (Berns), 87 LA 543
Martin-Marietta Aerospace (Aronin), 81 LA 695
Eastern Airlines (Turkus), 76 LA 961
New York City Health & Hospitals Corp. (Simons), 76 LA 387
State University of New York (Babishkin), 74 LA 299
Missouri Public Service Co. (Yarowski), 70 LA 1208
Arco-Polymers (Milentz), 69 LA 379
Cerro Corp. (Griffin), 69 LA 965
Joy Manufacturing Co. (Freeman), 68 LA 697
Michigan Power Co. (Rayl), 68 LA 183

Notes to Chapter 15

1. *B. Green & Co.* (Cushman), 71 LA 685.
2. *Joseph G. Tropiano, Inc.* (Belsky), 69 LA 1243.
3. *Brooks Foundry* (Daniel), 75 LA 642; *Detroit Stoker Co.* (Daniel), 75 LA 816; *Georgia Pac. Corp.* (Vadakin), 72 LA 784; *Stansteel Corp.* (Kaufman), 69 LA 776; *Jeep Corp.* (Keefe), 67 LA 828.
4. *Combustion Eng'g.* (Jewett), 70 LA 318; *St. Joe Minerals Corp.* (Roberts), 70 LA 1110; *Mississippi River Grain Elevator* (Marcus), 62 LA 200.
5. *Monfort Packing Co.* (Goodman), 66 LA 286.
6. *Porcelain Metals Corp.* (Roberts), 73 LA 1133 (3-day suspension upheld).
7. *FMC Corp.* (Reynolds), 80 LA 1173.
8. *City of Wilkes-Barre* (Dunn), 74 LA 33 (the employee was reinstated with back pay); *Indian Head* (Rimer), 71 LA 82 (employee was reinstated without back pay); *Nugent Sand Co.* (Kanner), 71 LA 585 (the employee was reinstated without back pay); *Metropolitan Atlanta Transit Auth.* (Anderson), 70 LA 1022 (the employee was reinstated with back pay); *Gamble Bros.* (Krislov), 68 LA 72

(the employee was reinstated without back pay); *Emhart Mfg. Co.* (McKone), 63 LA 1265 (a 6-month suspension was denied); *General Portland Cement Co.* (Davidson), 62 LA 377 (a 2-month suspension for a heroin arrest was denied). *But see National Floor Prods. Co.* (Eyrand), 58 LA 1015 (discharge sustained).

9. *General Tel. Co. of Calif.* (Collins), 87 LA 441.

10. *Alabama Power Co.* (Baroni), 88 LA 425.

11. *Lick Fish and Poultry Co.* (Concepcion), 87 LA 1062.

12. *Arco-Polymers* (Milentz), 69 LA 379.

13. *Michigan Power Co.* (Rayl), 68 LA 183.

14. *Eastern Airlines* (Turkus), 76 LA 961; *Cerro Corp.* (Griffin), 69 LA 965.

15. *State Univ. of New York* (Babishkin), 74 LA 299.

16. *Martin-Marietta Aerospace* (Aronin), 81 LA 695.

17. *New York City Health & Hosps. Corp.* (Simons), 76 LA 387 (the discharge was upheld where the employee had sold cocaine); *Joy Mfg. Co.* (Freeman), 68 LA 697 (the discharge was upheld where the employee had sold marijuana).

18. *See Missouri Pub. Serv. Co.* (Yarowski), 70 LA 1208.

19. *Swift & Co.* (Rentfro), 72 LA 513 (the employee was reinstated without back pay); *Abex Corp.* (Rybolt), 64 LA 721 (the employee's discharge was reduced to a 3-day suspension as with first alcohol offenses).

20. *St. Joe Minerals Corp., supra,* note 4; *B. Green & Co.* (Cushman), 65 LA 1233.

21. *Mallinckrodt, Inc.* (Seidman), 80 LA 1261.

22. *Wheaton Indus.* (Kerrison), 64 LA 826.

23. *See also Arco-Polymers, supra,* note 12.

24. *Arco-Polymers, supra,* note 12; *Pepsi Cola Bottlers of Youngstown,* (Klein), 68 LA 792; *S. F. Kennedy-New Prods.* (Traynor), 64 LA 880. *See also Wheaton Indus., supra,* note 22.

25. *Watauga Indus.* (Galambos), 78 LA 697.

26. *Braniff Airways* (Ray), 73 LA 304; *Todd Pac. Shipyards Corp.* (Brisco), 72 LA 1022; *Pepsi Cola Bottlers, supra,* note 24; *Whirlpool Corp.* (Gruenberg), 65 LA 386.

27. *General Tel. Co. of Calif.* (Richman), 73 LA 531; *Keystone Steel & Wire Co.* (Elson), 72 LA 780; *St. Joe Minerals Corp., supra,* note 4; *Day & Zimmerman* (Stratton), 63 LA 1289.

28. *St. Joe Minerals Corp., supra,* note 4; *Day & Zimmerman, supra,* note 27.

29. *Structurlite Plastics Corp.* (Leach), 73 LA 691.

30. *Casting Eng'rs* (Petersen), 71 LA 949.

31. *St. Joe Minerals Corp., supra,* note 4.

32. *Sun Chem. Corp.* (Murphy), 88 LA 633.

33. *Georgia Pac. Corp.* (King), 85 LA 542.

34. *Owens-Corning Fiberglas Corp.* (Nicholas), 86 LA 1026, 1029.

35. *Whirlpool Corp., supra,* note 26.

36. *General Foods Corp.* (Maslanka), 65 LA 1271.

37. *Prestige Stamping Co.* (Keefe), 74 LA 163; *Issaacson Structural Co.* (Peck), 72 LA 1075.

38. *State Univ. of New York, supra,* note 16 at 301.

16

Gambling

Issue
Whether an employee can be discharged or otherwise disciplined for gambling.

Principle
An employee may be discharged or otherwise disciplined for gambling where it is shown that the activity was on the employer's premises; that it was part of a well-established pattern which either pervaded the company or had a deleterious effect on other employees or on production; or that the employee has shown by work and/or discipline record that he or she is unlikely to reform. Discipline is more readily accepted if the activity is in violation of a company rule which is equally enforced.

Considerations
1. Whether a company rule exists prohibiting gambling and whether the employee had actual or constructive notice;
2. Whether the activity actually constituted gambling;
3. Whether gambling is a general problem in the company;
4. Whether the gambling was on company premises;
5. Whether the gambling had a detrimental effect on the productivity of the company and/or on the morale of the employees;
6. Whether the reinstatement of the employee will have a detrimental effect on the other employees;

7. Whether the employee's work record and prior history of discipline indicate a likelihood of reform;

8. Whether the rule against gambling was evenly enforced.

Discussion There appear to be no settled rules among arbitrators with respect to discharges and discipline for gambling activities. Certainly, where an employee is the principal in an organized and pervasive gambling operation—numbers writing, bookmaking, or floating crap games—and the activity has had a demonstrable effect on employee production and morale, arbitrators normally sustain the discharge of the employee as for just cause. This will occur even where the employer has no established rule against gambling, as such. However, the exceptions to this general rule are too numerous to permit an all-inclusive generalization upon which employers and employees can rely with certainty. It is in this area that the personal backgrounds and predispositions of arbitrators seem most apparent.

Nevertheless, arbitrators do recognize the severity of the problems created for a company by the gambling of employees within the plant, and clearly, gambling can constitute just cause for discharge. These problems were delineated best by Arbitrator Turkus as follows:

In-plant gambling poses a grave problem to both industry and labor. The direct and indirect deleterious effects thereof have impelled responsible Unions on a high level to institute educational programs for employees as far back as 1953 in an effort to curb and/or eliminate inplant gambling, its concomitant demoralization of plant morale and discipline, the disruption and impairment of plant productivity and enmeshment of workers in hopeless financial difficulty—the natural and inevitable corollaries of such illicit activity.

The magnitude and gravity of the misconduct of operating as a policy collector within the Company plant, taking numbers bets from employees during working hours, is of itself just and sufficient cause for his discharge. The Company had the right, indeed it would seem, the obligation to effectively and irrevocably terminate the employment status of any worker who utilized the Company's premises as a base for the operation of a policy or numbers racket.[1]

Indeed, some arbitrators view gambling on the premises of the employer as so serious that they will find just cause to exist where such an employee has been discharged without progressive discipline or where there is no company rule against such activity.

For instance, in *Sun Drug Co.*, the employee was discharged when it was discovered that he was "writing numbers."[2] The union argued that the company could not discharge the employee, because there was no provision in the "Rules and Regulations" which prohibited gambling. The arbitrator, however, held that the discharge was for just cause despite the absence of an applicable company rule.

> With respect to the Union's final contention that discharge was too severe a penalty, in view of the fact that no notices were posted by the Company, it is the considered opinion of the Arbitrator that very little consideration can be given to this position. It certainly does not seem either reasonable or necessary that the Company post notices to the effect that acts which are in violation of the State Criminal Code cannot be tolerated. The Arbitrator feels certain that [the Union] does certainly not expect the Company to become an accessory, and for the Company to impose any penalty short of outright discharge would in a sense make it an accessory, insofar as it would be condoning the matter of the booking of numbers on its premises.
>
> . . .
>
> The contract provides that discharge shall be for violation of reasonable Company rules and regulations. To say that the absence of a rule in the Company's RULES AND REGULATIONS, specifying that an act of any employee in violation of the State Criminal Code on Company time and Company property would not be tolerated, would be to imply that in the absence of such a rule, the Company would condone a criminal act on its premises, and thus make itself an accessory to it. To rule that the Company had no right to discharge for a criminal offense, because it was not spelled out in the Company's RULES AND REGULATIONS, would be writing something into the contract that neither the Company nor the Union had intended to put into it.[3]

Surprisingly, arbitrators have treated the issue of whether the employee was gambling on his or her own time or during working time with some concern. In *Bethlehem Steel Co., Sparrows Point Plant*, for instance, an employee was discharged for conducting a numbers operation.[4] The arbitrator held that the employee "was discharged for just cause for participating in unlawful gambling activities within the Plant.[5] There was no mention in the arbitrator's report of the existence or the absence of a company rule prohibiting gambling.

In that case it was argued by the employee that the discharge was unwarranted, because he was conducting the numbers game "on his own time." The arbitrator argued that this fact did not immunize the employee from discharge, for it "hardly severs the tie between his numbers activity and his employment relationship."[6] The fact that he was conducting gambling activity on company premises was sufficient.

Most commonly, however, arbitrators who sustain discharges for gambling have relied upon either a contract provision or a company rule which specifically prohibits the activity.[7]

The presence of a clear and communicated rule prohibiting gambling is not necessarily a guarantee that a discharge will be sustained or that the offense will be considered summary in nature. In fact, it would appear that most arbitrators believe gambling to be a nonsummary offense and subject to the progressive discipline system. Consequently, unless the labor agreement or company rules make gambling a summary offense, arbitrators will most likely examine the more traditional aspects of due process and employee history.

In *Black Diamond Enterprises*, for example, there was a company rule which prohibited gambling on company premises.[8] An employee was discharged for engaging in a "check pool" and for playing poker. The arbitrator noted that the purpose of the company rule was "to ensure good conduct." The arbitrator believed that the employee's conduct in participating in the check pool did not warrant discharge, because this activity was not "detrimental to the conduct of the workforce."[9] However, the company had merely issued reprimands for first violations of other rules, and the arbitrator found that this practice made it inequitable to discharge the employee for playing poker in violation of the gambling prohibition. The arbitrator held that the company must itself correct the practice by rigid enforcement of its rules, and the discharge could not stand. All violations should be treated equally, unless "of such severity as to warrant instant discharge."[10]

In *Radio Corp. of America*, an employee, who was caught gambling on employer premises and who had pleaded guilty to a criminal charge of bookmaking, was also discharged by the employer.[11] There was a company rule prohibiting gambling, which was known to the employee. Nevertheless, the arbitrator held that the discharge was not justified:

> However, gambling violations, per se, are not just cause for discharge regardless of circumstances. Gambling involves a continuum in which the seriousness of the offense and the man's record with the Company constitute important variables which must be considered in determining just cause and appropriateness of penalty.[12]

The arbitrator went on to consider the fact that the employee had a good work record. Such consideration led the arbitrator to reinstate the employee.

> On the other hand, Mr. X _____ has an unblemished 35-year record with the Company. Mr. X _____ is entitled to have his record weighed in the determination of appropriateness of penalty. . . . Under these circumstances, it is appropriate to give the individual an opportunity to reform. Clearly however, Mr. X _____ is to be penalized by denial of back pay. . . . His conduct must be above reproach in the future.[13]

It should be noted, however, that other arbitrators have sustained employee discharges for gambling, even in the face of a long and favorable employee work record.[14] In *Jenkins Brothers*, the arbitrator concluded:

> In view of the seriousness of the gambling problem in this plant and X's obvious involvement in it, [there is] no reason to mitigate the penalty imposed by the Company because of X's good work record.[15]

Thus, as appears to be the case generally in this area, arbitrators disagree as to the weight which should be given to an employee's good work record. It is unclear, therefore, whether an employee discharged for "writing numbers," or engaging in other gambling activities on company premises, would be discharged for "just cause" without a showing of other factors supporting the discharge. If there is no company rule in force, most arbitrators would probably hold that a discharge for gambling activities is unjustified. However, another arbitrator, when faced with the seriousness of a gambling charge, may feel disinclined to overturn management's decision. The result may simply depend on which particular arbitrator is hearing the case. Indeed, gambling offenses have been treated with such variety that it may serve an employer well not to rely on the offense alone as its only justification for the discipline.

In *Advertising Publishing Co.*, the employee had been ordered by the employer to cease and desist from his gambling activities, and when he failed to do so, the employee was discharged.[16] The arbitrator held that the employee's actions constituted insubordination and that the employer was justified in concluding that the employee would not reform. The arbitrator stated:

> It is clearly his duty and a part of his employment to be governed by the instructions as given him by his supervisor to refrain from gambling.[17]

Accordingly, at least one employer overcame arbitral uncertainty on the issue by ordering the employee to stop all gambling activity, and when he did not, the employer was able to discharge him for insubordination.

Key Points

1   *There should be a communicated company rule which makes engaging in gambling activity a summary offense.*

Examples

Employee *A* was discovered operating a numbers writing pool within the company and was discharged pursuant to a rule prohibiting gambling on the premises. The arbitrator, noting the employee's good work record of 10 years, reinstated the employee with full back pay. The arbitrator declared that the employee should have been accorded progressive discipline, beginning with a verbal warning.

Employee *B* was discovered operating a numbers writing pool within the company and was discharged pursuant to a contract provision, which made gambling on the premises a cause for immediate discharge. The arbitrator, while noting the unfairness in light of the employee's otherwise unblemished work history of over 20 years, sustained the discharge.

Guidelines

The rule against gambling must be clear, incapable of misunderstanding, and sufficiently broad to cover all conduct the employer seeks to prohibit. The penalty should also be specific to limit the arbitrator's authority and to avoid a requirement of progressive disciplinary action.

Relevant Cases

International Minerals & Chemical Corp. (Kulkis), 83 LA 593
Metro Contract Services (Moore), 68 LA 1048
City of Flint, Mich. (Stieber), 59 LA 370
Black Diamond Enterprises (Nicholas), 52 LA 945
Radio Corp. of America (Gershenfeld), 49 LA 1262
Sun Drug Co. (Marcus), 31 LA 191

2   *The activity must constitute actual gambling.*

Examples

Employee *A* was discharged for playing poker with three co-workers during their lunch hour. The players had been making small stake bets. The arbitrator, drawing a distinction between a friendly game of cards and gambling, reinstated the employee under a simple just cause standard and reduced the discharge to a verbal warning.

Employee *B* was discharged for conducting a craps game during his lunch break. The stakes were modest. The arbitrator sustained the discharge, refusing to distinguish between craps and other forms of gambling activity.

Employee *C* was discharged for operating a football pool. The arbitrator sustained the discharge. The arbitrator noted that the organized fashion in which the employee conducted his operation constituted gambling, while occasional pools run by other employees for the World Series and Super Bowl were not.

Guidelines

Even where a company rule is involved, the employer must be able to establish that the activity, in fact, constituted gambling, as the term is normally construed. The operation of a lottery, therefore, is distinguished from a raffle. Card games appear to fall into a grey area, and arbitrators look to the circumstances which surround the games. The difference appears to lie in the scope, intent, and organization of the operation.

Relevant Cases

International Minerals & Chemical Corp. (Kulkis), 83 LA 593
Black Diamond Enterprises (Nicholas), 52 LA 945
Bethlehem Steel Co. (Gill), 51 LA 707
Haskell Manufacturing Co. (Wood), 33 LA 174

3   *The gambling activity must be conducted on the company's premises.*

Examples

Employee *A* was convicted of running a numbers operation and was discharged by the employer. There was no evidence that the employee engaged in any such activity while on the company's property, although some of his co-workers used his service. The arbitrator reinstated the employee, noting that the necessary connection between the employee's activity and the employer's legitimate interest did not exist.

Employee *B* was discharged for running a craps game during his lunch break. *B* defended on the basis that the game took place "on his own time" and did not affect any business interests of the employer. The arbitrator sustained the discharge.

Employee *C* was discharged for numbers writing. The employee defended on the basis that all of his activities were off the premises and on his own time. The arbitrator found that some of the people using *C* were employees and that, while collection and payoffs were made off the premises, the receipt of numbers did occur on the premises, although during the employee's breaks and lunch periods. The discharge was sustained.

Guidelines

Nearly all arbitrators require the employer to prove that the gambling took place on company premises in order to justify a discharge. Evidence of gambling, which is conducted by an employee while off company premises, generally cannot be used as a basis for discharge, unless a close connection is established between the gambling activity and the employer's workplace. Whether the activity took place during working time or in work areas is generally perceived to be irrelevant.

Relevant Cases

International Minerals & Chemical Corp. (Kulkis), 83 LA 593
City of Flint, Mich. (Stieber), 59 LA 370
Bethlehem Steel Co. (Gill), 51 LA 707
Bethlehem Steel Co., Sparrows Point Plant (Porter), 45 LA 646
Bethlehem Steel Co. (Porter), 45 LA 1007
General Electric Co. (Seitz), 41 LA 823
Radio Corp. of America (Scheiber), 39 LA 621

4   *Discharge or disciplinary action is clearly warranted where the gambling activity is not an incidental occurrence, but part of a well-established pattern of gambling, especially if it is pervasive within the company.*

Examples

Employee *A* was discharged along with three others for playing pinochle for stakes. The evidence indicated that this game was the first time the employees had played at work, although they played regularly in off hours. In the absence of clear contract language to the contrary, the arbitrator reinstated all of the employees and reduced the discharge to a verbal warning.

Employee *B* was discharged for participating in a craps game. The evidence indicated that this was the first time *B* had ever engaged in this activity, that he didn't know the rules and that he lost his only bet, $5. Finding that the discharge was part of the employer's announced crackdown on all types of gambling in the plant and that this was the first time the employer had been successful in catching a game in progress, the arbitrator sustained the discharge.

Guidelines

Arbitrators are more sympathetic to discharged employees if they have participated only in isolated, infrequent gambling activities, e.g., sports "pools." If the evidence reveals that an established gambling operation with a substantial volume exists, then the arbitrator will be more likely to deny the grievance. Moreover, arbitrators consider the seriousness of a gambling problem throughout the company, when determining the propriety of an employee discharge. If it is apparent that gambling is currently widespread among the employees, an arbitrator will often realize the importance of eradicating the problem and will sustain the discharge, regardless of other mitigating circumstances which may surround an individual grievant's case.

Relevant Cases

International Minerals & Chemical Corp. (Kulkis), 83 LA 593
Bethlehem Steel Co., Sparrows Point Plant (Porter), 45 LA 646
Bethlehem Steel Co. (Porter), 45 LA 1007
Jenkins Brothers (Stutz), 45 LA 350
Haskell Manufacturing Co. (Wood), 33 LA 174

5   *The gambling activity must have had a demonstrably adverse effect on the work operations.*

Examples

Employee *A* was discharged for continuing to conduct weekly football pools after repeated warnings. Noting that every Monday morning as many as 30 employees would crowd around *A's* work station and that up to 10 minutes of work time would be lost as a result, the arbitrator sustained the discharge.

Employee *B* was discharged for running a numbers operation. At the arbitration hearing, the employee maintained that the only time he transacted business was before and after the workday in the company's parking lot and that his activity had not interfered with his work or that of his customers. The employer established that *B* frequently gave credit and carried on his collection activities during the workday, although on breaktimes. On one occasion an employee had pleaded with his supervisor to allow him more overtime because of his need to pay *B* a gambling debt. The arbitrator sustained the discharge.

Guidelines

Arbitrators have tended to sustain discharges when it is apparent that the gambling activity is harmful to the company's business. Employers have sometimes shown that the gambling activity reduced the productivity of the affected employees. Also, employers often have been able to establish that employee morale was lessened as a result of gambling losses. However, if the employee can establish that his conduct was not detrimental to work operations, an arbitrator might be less inclined to sustain a discharge.

Relevant Cases

City of Flint, Mich. (Stieber), 59 LA 370
Haskell Manufacturing Co. (Wood), 33 LA 174
Advertising Publishing Co. (Cobb), 32 LA 26
Sun Drug Co. (Marcus), 31 LA 191

6   *Whether the prior work record of the employee is good and whether there is an indication of possible reform.*

Examples

Employee *A* was discharged for participation in a craps game. The employee's work record spanned 20 years and was unblemished. The arbitrator nevertheless sustained the discharge.

Employee *B* was discharged for participation in a craps game. The employee's work record spanned 20 years and was unblemished; the arbitrator reinstated the employee.

Guidelines

Some arbitrators will not consider the employee's work record in ruling on a discharge for gambling. Others, however, will consider a long and favorable work record as a factor to be weighed against the employee's gambling activity and often will give the employee an opportunity to reform. However, if the employer can establish that an employee is unlikely to reform and to abandon his gambling activity, a discharge of that employee will probably be justified.

Relevant Cases

Black Diamond Enterprises (Nicholas), 52 LA 945
Radio Corp. of America (Gershenfeld), 49 LA 1262
Jenkins Brothers (Stutz), 45 LA 350
Radio Corp. of America (Scheiber), 39 LA 621
Advertising Publishing Co. (Cobb), 32 LA 26

7   *The gambling rule must be enforced equally.*

Examples

Employee *A* was discharged for conducting a numbers game. The arbitrator noted that gambling was one of several types of offenses, published in the company's rules, which would subject an employee to discipline. The arbitrator looked to the degree of discipline to be administered for the first violation of other types of prohibited conduct and found that the firm had a progressive discipline system. The arbitrator, therefore, ordered the reinstatement of the employee with the appropriate degree of discipline to be given as for first offenses of other types of prohibited conduct.

Employee *B* was discharged for operating a numbers game. *B* defended by presenting evidence that *M* had been given a lesser penalty when the latter was caught conducting a basketball pool. The arbitrator reinstated the employee and ordered the same discipline as was given *M*.

Employee *C* was discharged for playing poker for stakes during a lunch break. *C* complained that the other players had only been suspended. The arbitrator reinstated *C* without back pay, commuting the discharge to a suspension.

Guidelines

If the employer does not rigidly enforce work rules in other areas, it cannot selectively enforce a gambling rule. Also, if an employer generally does not discharge employees for first violations of other company rules, it cannot choose to discharge employees for first violations of a gambling rule, unless the stated and communicated rule provides for summary discharge. In addition, an employer cannot discharge one employee and take no action against other employees involved in the same gambling operation.

Relevant Cases

Metro Contract Services (Moore), 68 LA 1048
Black Diamond Enterprises (Nicholas), 52 LA 945
Radio Corp. of America (Gershenfeld), 49 LA 1262
Bethlehem Steel Co., Sparrows Point Plant (Porter), 45 LA 646
Bethlehem Steel Co. (Porter), 45 LA 1007
Lockheed Aircraft Corp. (Roberts), 37 LA 188
Haskell Manufacturing Co. (Wood), 33 LA 174

Notes to Chapter 16

1. *Charm Footwear Co.* (Turkus), 39 LA 154, 156.
2. *Sun Drug Co.* (Marcus), 31 LA 191.
3. *Id.*, at 194, 195.
4. *Bethlehem Steel Co., Sparrows Point Plant* (Porter), 45 LA 646.
5. *Id.*, at 647.
6. *Id.*, at 646.
7. *See Jenkins Bros.* (Stutz), 45 LA 350; *Haskell Mfg. Co.*, (Wood), 33 LA 174.

8. *Black Diamond Enters.* (Nicholas), 52 LA 945.
9. *Id.,* at 950.
10. *Id.,* at 951.
11. *Radio Corp. of Am.* (Gershenfeld), 49 LA 1262.
12. *Id.,* at 1264.
13. *Id.*
14. *See Advertising Publishing Co.* (Cobb), 32 LA 26.
15. *Jenkins Bros., supra,* note 7.
16. *Advertising Publishing Co., supra,* note 14.
17. *Id.,* at 27.

17

Insubordination

Issue   Whether an employee can be discharged or otherwise disciplined for refusing to perform a task or to comply with an order given to him by a supervisor.

Principle   An employee can be discharged or otherwise disciplined for insubordination where the employee not only understands the supervisor's directive, but willfully disobeys or disregards it under circumstances where the employee's behavior is neither provoked nor justified by reasonable concern over safety.

Considerations   1. Whether the employee understood or evidenced an understanding of the order or directive of the supervisor, and the employee willfully disobeyed or disregarded it;
2. Whether the behavior of the employee was provoked by supervisory misconduct;
3. Whether the refusal to obey or the disregard of the supervisor's directive was justified;
4. Whether the employee was entitled to and received progressive discipline.

Discussion   Arbitrators generally view employee compliance with reasonable management orders as essential to the functioning of the employer's business. Consequently, arbitrators consistently

279

hold that refusal to obey an order or directive of any importance warrants discipline, up to and including discharge. In fact, the generally accepted rule is that, where the employee refuses to obey or willfully disregards a direct order of significant importance, the employee will be subject to summary discharge and will be denied the rights of progressive discipline. Frequently, the gravity of the offense is defined in terms of the impact of the employee's action on the authority of the supervisory personnel and on the safety and property of the employer or others. Indeed, arbitrator response to discipline for alleged insubordination has not been to automatically sustain discharges. In this respect, the review of Arbitrator Michael Jay Jedel is particularly relevant:

> Based on an examination of Labor Arbitration Reports, Volumes 1–10 (Bureau of National Affairs, Inc.), Orme W. Phelps concluded his discussion of insubordination in his 1959 pioneering work on *Discipline and Discharge in the Unionized Firm* as follows (pp. 100, 102);
> The statistical evidence, drawn from reported arbitrations, supports the conclusion that managerial treatment of insubordination tends to exceed the bounds of propriety. The standard remedy is discharge, but the arbitrators either reversed or modified almost two-thirds of the company rulings, which meant at a minimum, reinstatement of the employee. Where the penalty was less severe, a sizable majority of the decisions were in favor of management.
> What all this means is not that the plant has become a "debating society." It is still the employee's duty to obey. However, the latitude accorded management in its demand for prompt and unquestioning obedience is considerably narrowed from the principal infinity of noncontractual times. . . . Management, as well as the work force, operates under "a higher law," consisting of limits set by the agreement, standardized practice in industry, and the general rules of fair play. . . . There is no blinking the fact that this is markedly different from the exercise of managerial authority in the absence of an agreement. However, the loss in efficiency, if any, may well be counter-balanced to a considerable extent by a better feeling, a higher morale, and eventually increasing cooperation toward common goals.

It is apparent that, although discharge is still a frequent response by management to instances of what it perceives as insubordination, that is not the only action taken, nor is discharge automatically accepted at arbitration as proper where management has chosen this action. Instead, arbitrators have looked at a variety of factors including the nature of the alleged insubordination in the specific work setting, the employee's prior record, the company's approach to discipline, how management has treated similar infractions, the existence of a specific rule or contractual language threatening discharge for insubordination, etc.[1]

In *Chromalloy Division-Oklahoma*, the arbitrator sustained the summary discharge of an employee who had refused to comply with a supervisor's direct command to return to work.[2] Likewise, in *Arcrods Plant*, the arbitrator sustained the discharge of an employee who had refused to stop burning trash.[3] On the other hand, the arbitrator in *Ohio Crankshaft Co.* refused to sustain the summary discharge of an employee who had refused to remove a painting from his work area, until after he had been accorded progressive discipline.[4] And, in *Acme Industrial Co.*, the arbitrator required progressive discipline for an employee who had refused to stop whistling and denied the employee's discharge.[5]

Frequently, discipline for abusive language is treated as insubordination, because there is an element of attack on supervisory authority. (For a discussion of this subject, see Chapter 9.)

By definition, the charge of insubordination requires that the element of willfulness be present for an employer to support disciplinary action against the employee. The offense concerns a considered and rational decision by an employee to disobey, or disregard, his or her employer's reasonable directive. Where an employee's ability to exercise self-control is substantially diminished by some outside force, however, it becomes highly questionable whether his or her actions can be considered insubordinate. Although perhaps not articulated in quite this way, it appears to be this element which causes arbitrators to question and to mitigate discipline for insubordination. This can be seen especially in cases where the employee asserts that a supervisor provoked the conduct which later resulted in the disciplinary action.[6] Provocation, however, is generally viewed as an incomplete defense; provocation may serve to mitigate, but cannot completely overcome, discipline for insubordination.[7] Provocation cases, however, refer only to abusive language situations, since an arbitrator is unlikely to find that any provocation could be sufficient to justify an employee's willful refusal to obey a reasonable order of management.

Discharges and lesser disciplinary measures for insubordination frequently involve claims by employees that they refused to perform directed tasks because it would expose them and/or others to safety risks or dangerous conditions. When this type of situation arises, there are several factors which may become involved.

First, the employee may file a grievance over discipline resulting from such an incident. At arbitration, there is a recognized justification for insubordination, where the employee refused to perform a task because of a real and reasonable fear for his or her safety. However, when the employer has taken sufficient action to avoid the danger or has made an adequate explanation of the situation to allay the fear, the employee will be subject to discipline if the employee persists in his or her refusal to obey management's instructions. For example, in *Imperial Foods*, employees, who had refused to operate a saw for which they had no training, were reinstated without back pay, because the company had made no attempt to train them or to otherwise remove their fears.[8] However, in *Dayton Tire & Rubber Co.*, the arbitrator upheld the discharge of an employee who had refused to perform a task he alleged was dangerous. There would have been no such danger, the arbitrator found, if the employee had followed the instructions of the supervisor with regard to the manner in which the task was to be performed.[9] In *United Parcel Service*, the arbitrator sustained the discipline of an employee, where he found the employee's allegation of an unsafe practice to be unreasonable.[10] In this case, the employee had refused to write receipt slips while in the process of walking back to his truck after making a delivery. Likewise, the arbitrator in *Canton Drop Forging & Manufacturing Co.* approved of the discipline given to employees who refused to cross a picket line because of an alleged fear for their safety.[11] The arbitrator held that their refusal was unprotected activity and was unreasonably based.

Significantly, the right of employees to refuse to do a job because it is unsafe exists independently of labor agreements. There are labor agreements, however, which permit employees to refuse to do unsafe work, where there exists a good-faith belief that a danger is present.[12]

Second, whether there is a contractual provision permitting refusals to do unsafe work or not, the employee's action may be deemed to be concerted, protected activity under the National Labor Relations Act (the Act), thereby making the discharge or discipline an unfair labor practice. The National Labor Relations Board and many courts have found violations of Section 8(a)(1), and occasionally Section 8(a)(3), of the Act where employees were disciplined for good-faith refusals to do unsafe work pursuant to collective bargaining agreement provisions.[13] However, at least one court has held that before there can be a Section 8(a)(1) violation, more that a single employee must refuse to work because the conditions are unsafe, even when the refusal is pursuant to an agreement provision. Criticizing and distinguishing the *Interboro* doctrine[14] in which individual action or a right secured by a labor agreement is considered concerted activity, the court denied enforcement of the Board's Section 8(a)(1) finding, because there was no concerted activity under Section 7.[15]

The Board and the courts have also found employer violations of the Act where employees have refused to perform tasks for safety reasons, even in the absence of a contractual provision securing such a right. The Board found a 8(a)(1) violation in the discharge of three employees who had refused to wear protective suits, because of the employees' good-faith belief that the suits were unsafe.[16] However, where a single employee refused to drive a truck he believed in good faith to be unsafe, no 8(a)(1) violation had been found, because there had been no concerted activity.[17] Courts of appeal have upheld unfair labor practice charges and the reinstatement of employees with back pay in cases of refusals to work for safety reasons. For example, where the employees were found to have had a good-faith belief that the radioactive material with which they were to work was unsafe and the employer's assurances had been inadequate to allay those fears the employer was found to have violated Section 8(a)(1), when it discharged those employees.[18]

It should also be noted that the Act provides for the quitting of labor in good faith because of abnormally dangerous conditions and provides that such quitting of labor cannot be deemed a strike.[19] Therefore, an employee so quitting his labor cannot be discharged for violation of an agreement's no-strike clause.

Finally, a regulation of the Occupational Safety and Health Administration provides that employees who refuse in good faith to expose themselves to a dangerous condition are protected against subsequent discrimination. Where possible, the employee must have sought to correct the condition by addressing his or her employer.[20] This regulation was upheld by the U.S. Supreme Court in a case where two employees had refused to work on a suspended wire mesh that had been the cause of past accidents.[21]

There are, therefore, several limitations upon an employer's ability to discipline an employee who refuses to perform an assigned task for safety reasons. Under each provision, however, there is the understanding that the employee must have a good-faith belief that the task involves a dangerous condition. Included in the arbitral determination of the employee's good-faith belief is an assessment of the employer's efforts to assure the employee of the safety of the situation and its efforts to make the condition safe.

The final element considered by arbitrators is the need, except in the most severe cases, for employers to demonstrate that progressive discipline had been administered prior to the discharge. In many cases arbitrators have required that employees be reinstated where there has been no prior discipline, particularly where there has been no prior suspension.[22] Conversely, where there had been prior discipline, whether for insubordination or something else, the discharges have been sustained.[23]

The extent to which arbitrators may go to modify or to void discipline for insubordination because of the lack of progressive discipline or a prior discipline record is seen in *Reynolds Metals Co.*.[24] In that case an employee, who had suffered an industrial accident, refused to complete the accident reporting forms on the basis that he could neither read nor write. The supervisor knew this was untrue. The employee then said he was sick and was leaving. The supervisor ordered him to see the company nurse. He did not, and he left the plant through a fire exit without punching out. At the arbitration, the employer presented other instances of bad attitude, erratic behavior, poor performance, and insubordination. The arbitrator refused to consider these additional occurrences, because the incidents had never been "written-up" and the employee had never been disciplined for them. Finding, therefore, a good prior work record, the arbitrator held that the employee had not received progressive discipline commensurate with that record and reduced the discharge to a disciplinary suspension.

Key Points

1   *The employee must have understood the order or directive of a supervisor, and then the employee must have willfully disobeyed or disregarded it.*

Examples

Employee A, while working, was told by a supervisor to stop smoking. When A was discovered smoking in another part of the plant while taking a part to another employee, she was disciplined by the supervisor. The supervisor's disciplinary action was revoked by the arbitrator when the employee testified that her only understanding was that she was not to smoke while at her normal work station.

Employee B was told by a supervisor not to continue to burn the trash collected in his department in an incinerator at the rear of the plant's property, but to stack it for cartage. The supervisor had told B that the scrap from his department, if burned, would give off toxic fumes. B stacked the trash next to the incinerator where the trash caught fire. The employee was discharged. The arbitrator sustained the discharge, stating that the employee should have known that the scrap, if stacked next to the incinerator, would catch fire and that the burning of the trash could have had serious consequences.

Employee C was discharged for incorrectly mixing a batch of chemicals. At the arbitration, C admitted that he was aware from the operations manual that the chemicals should have been mixed in different amounts and that his supervisor had told him to follow the manual precisely. C stated that he had run short of a particular chemical, had begun the process without checking his supplies, and rather than stopping the operations to get more of the particular chemical, chose to add only what he had. The arbitrator sustained the discharge.

Employee D had been given a package by his supervisor and had been told to deliver it to a particular address. He was not told of the extreme importance of the delivery to the intended recipient. Receiving no answer at the address, the employee left it next door with instructions to have the package taken to the proper recipient the next day. When the package disappeared, D was discharged. The arbitrator mitigated the discharge to a suspension, noting that the employee had only been negligent and did not have the intent necessary to be found insubordinate.

Employee *E*, a recent transferee to a new department, received instructions from her supervisor in the operation of various pieces of equipment and the action to take to correct errant conditions. *E* was also given an operations manual and shown by the supervisor several procedures in the manual which were no longer acceptable. The employee made several errors and was given assistance by her co-employees. When she used an obsolete correction procedure out of the manual, however, she was suspended for insubordination. The arbitrator reduced the employee's discipline to a warning, stating that the employee lacked the training necessary to justify a charge of insubordination.

Guidelines

To be able to sustain discipline or discharge for insubordination, the employer must be able to establish that (a) the employee actually knew and understood the directive of his or her supervisor, (b) the order was so clear that no reasonable person could have misunderstood it, and/or (c) the employee intentionally disobeyed, or disregarded, the instruction.

Relevant Cases

John W. Galbreath & Co. (Bolte), 85 LA 575
Minnesota Mining & Manufacturing Co. (White), 85 LA 1179
Wilton Corp. ((Smedley), 85 LA 667
Arrow Lock Corp. (Nemaizer), 84 LA 734
Fourco Glass Co. (Cantor), 84 LA 693
Illinois Power Co. (Penfield), 84 LA 586
Scovill, Inc. (Storey), 84 LA 201
Shell Oil Co. (Milentz), 84 LA 562
Transitank Car Corp. (Sartain), 84 LA 1112
Fry's Food Stores of Arizona (Weizenbaum), 83 LA 1248
Lake Park of Oakland, California (Griffin), 83 LA 27
Tenneco Oil Co. (King), 83 LA 1099
Army Armor Center (Wren), 82 LA 464
Kraft, Inc. (Denson), 82 LA 360
National Aeronautics and Space Administration (Groshoup), 82 LA 1020
Oklahoma State AFL-CIO (Yaney), 82 LA 657
Texas Utilities Generating Co. (Edes), 82 LA 6
Air Express International Corp. (Weiss), 81 LA 753
Equitable Gas Co. (Sergent), 81 LA 368

Gwaltney of Smithfield, Inc. (Bernhardt), 81 LA 24
Mitch Murch's Maintenance Management Co. (Fitzsimmons), 81
    LA 1021
Shell Oil Co. (Brisco), 81 LA 1205
Canton Drop Forging & Manufacturing Co. (Teple), 78 LA 1189
E.I. du Pont de Nemours & Co. (Light), 78 LA 327
Globe Refractories (Bolte), 78 LA 320
International Minerals & Chemical Corp. (Jones), 78 LA 682
Kay-Brunner Steel Products (Gentile), 78 LA 363
United Parcel Service (McAllister), 78 LA 836
National Gypsum Co. (Ray), 74 LA 7
Chromalloy Division-Oklahoma (Moore), 67 LA 1310
American Sugar Co. (Whyte), 52 LA 1228
Ohio Crankshaft Co. (Teple), 48 LA 558
Arcrods Plant (Bradley), 47 LA 994
Acme Industrial Co. (Updegraff), 41 LA 1176

2   *The behavior of the employee must not have been*
provoked by any action of the supervisor.

Examples

Employee *A* was discovered by his supervisor during work time, not at his work station, but talking with another employee. The supervisor called to him from a distance, "Hey, you lazy, no-good s——of-a-b——, get your bloody a—— back to work." The employee yelled back, "Up your f—— a——." and slowly returned to his work station by way of the men's room. The supervisor went to the employee's work station and discharged him for insubordination. At arbitration, the employer stated that *A* had verbally abused the authority of the supervisor and had not returned to his work station immediately as directed. The arbitrator reinstated the employee without back pay, holding that the employee's response had been provoked by the supervisor's misconduct.

Employee *B* was discovered away from the station and was seen talking with a co-employee. *B's* supervisor yelled at him from a distance, "Hey, you lazy, no-good s——of-a-b——, get your bloody a—— back to work." *B* went to the supervisor and demanded an apology. The supervisor refused and again told him to get his f——, no-good a——— back to work. The supervisor discharged the employee. The arbitrator sustained the discharge, noting that the provocation, while severe, could not justify the employee's refusal to return to work.

Guidelines

Provocation of an employee by supervisory misconduct may result in the mitigation of an employee's discipline for insubordination. However, such provocation normally will neither serve to protect an employee from all discipline nor justify an employee's total refusal to perform a directive from the employer.

Relevant Cases

Fourco Glass Co. (Cantor), 84 LA 693
Texas Utilities Generating Co. (Edes), 82 LA 6
Michigan Bell Telephone Co. (Dyke), 78 LA 896
Reynolds Metal Co. (Fasser), 78 LA 687
Williams, White & Co. (Guenther), 67 LA 1181
Leaseway of Western New York (France), 60 LA 1343
Anaconda Aluminum Co. (Erbs), 59 LA 1147
Armco Steel Corp. (Duff), 52 LA 101
Chalfant Manufacturing Co. (Nichols), 52 LA 51
Westinghouse Electric Corp. (Altrock) 51 LA 1311

3   *The conduct of the employee cannot have been justified.*

Examples

Employee *A* was instructed to go into a trench, six feet deep, and repair a broken pipe. *A* refused, asserting that the walls of the trench had been inadequately shored. The supervisor went into the trench, inspected the shoring, declared it safe, and told the employee to do the work. The employee refused and was discharged. The arbitrator, finding that the employee's fear was unreasonable, sustained the discharge.

Employee *B* was instructed to perform electrical repair work on the roof of the employer's building. *B* refused, asserting that he was not trained in electrical work and feared for his safety. The supervisor told him that the work only consisted of changing a household-type fuse. The employee still refused and was discharged. Holding that the work was not unreasonably dangerous, even for a person who had not been trained in electrical work, the arbitrator sustained the discharge.

Employee *C* was an electrician who had been instructed to make certain electrical repairs on the roof of the employer's building. While *C* was engaged in the work, it began to rain. *C* refused to complete the work in the rain without certain protective equipment. The employer told him that it did not have such equipment available and ordered *C* to complete the work without it. *C* refused and was discharged. The discharge was overturned by the arbitrator on the grounds that the refusal was justified.

Guidelines

An employee's refusal to perform a task may be justified, if the refusal is based upon a reasonable fear of personal injury or safety.

Relevant Cases

Minnesota Mining & Manufacturing Co. (White), 85 LA 1179
Wilton Corp. (Smedley), 85 LA 667
Longmont Turkey Processors (Cohen), 84 LA 638
Scovill, Inc. (Storey), 84 LA 201
Daniel International Corp. (Thornell), 83 LA 1096
Lake Park of Oakland, California (Griffin), 83 LA 27
Tenneco Oil Co. (King), 83 LA 1099
Kraft, Inc. (Denson), 82 LA 360
Glen Manor Home for the Jewish Aged (Katz), 81 LA 1178
Imperial Foods (Crawford), 69 LA 320
Dayton Tire & Rubber Co. (Ipavec), 67 LA 78
United States Steel Corp. (Garrett), 66 LA 489
See also Labor Board and Court cases cited in Text.

4   *Except in extreme cases, the employee should be accorded progressive discipline.*

Examples

Employee *A* was discharged for shouting to other employees stationed on the other side of the production floor. He had been warned previously that continuing the practice would result in his discipline. When he continued, unabated, the supervisor gave him a direct order to stop shouting. Within an hour, *A* had resumed his shouting and was discharged. The arbitrator, finding that *A* had not been accorded all of the steps in the progressive discipline system, reinstated the employee and instructed the employer to issue a written warning.

Employee *B* was found sleeping in a remote part of the plant and was ordered by his supervisor to return to his work station immediately. *B* started toward his workplace, but then went into the men's room, where he was later discovered sleeping in a toilet stall. *B* was discharged. Noting the employee's poor work record, which included a suspension for absenteeism, the arbitrator sustained the discharge, even though the employee had not been accorded progressive discipline.

Guidelines

Unless the insubordination involves an employee's complete refusal to do a job, arbitrators generally require that progressive discipline be administered by the employer in insubordination cases.

Relevant Cases

Transportation Union (Droznin), 82 LA 358
Bellingham Cold Storage (Krebs), 81 LA 1243
Mitch Murch's Maintenance Management Co. (Fitzsimmons), 81 LA 1021
E. I. du Pont de Nemours & Co. (Light), 78 LA 327
Globe Refractories (Bolte), 78 LA 320
Kay-Brunner Steel Products (Gentile), 78 LA 363
Pepsi Cola Bottlers Co. of Canton, Ohio (Keenan), 78 LA 516
Reynolds Metals Co. (Fasser), 78 LA 687
United Parcel Service (McAllister), 78 LA 836
National Gypsum Co. (Ray), 74 LA 7
Bethlehem Steel Corp. (Harkless), 58 LA 363
San Francisco Redevelopment Agency (Koven), 57 LA 1149
Ohio Crankshaft Co. (Teple), 48 LA 558
Arcrods Plant (Bradley), 47 LA 994
Acme Industrial Co. (Updegraff), 41 LA 1176

Notes to Chapter 17

1. *Prismo-William Armstrong Smith Co.* (Jedel), 73 LA 581, at 584–585.
2. *Chromalloy Div.-Okla.* (Moore), 67 LA 1310.
3. *Arcrods Plant* (Bradley), 47 LA 994.
4. *Ohio Crankshaft Co.* (Teple), 48 LA 558.

5. *Acme Indus. Co.* (Updegraff), 41 LA 1176.

6. *See National Gypsum Co.* (Ray), 74 LA 7 (employee was reinstated without back pay); *Ekstrom, Carlson & Co.* (Davis), 55 LA 764.

7. *See American Sugar Co.* (Whyte), 52 LA 1228.

8. *Imperial Foods* (Crawford), 69 LA 320.

9. *Dayton Tire & Rubber Co.* (Ipavec), 67 LA 78.

10. *United Parcel Serv.* (McAllister), 78 LA 836.

11. *Canton Drop Forging & Mfg. Co.* (Teple), 78 LA 1189.

12. *United States Steel Corp.* (Garrett), 66 LA 489.

13. *City Disposal Sys.*, 256 NLRB No. 73, 107 LRRM 1267 (1981) (the employee refused to drive a vehicle; the discipline was found to have violated §8(a)(1) of the Act); *Mclean Trucking Co.*, 252 NLRB No. 104, 105 LRRM 1558 (1980) (an employee refused to drive a truck; the discharge violated §8(a)(1) and (3) of the Act); *United Parcel Serv.*, 241 NLRB No. 166, 101 LRRM 1067 (1979) (an employee refused to drive a truck and a §8(a)(1) violation arose from the discharge); *Wheeling-Pittsburgh Steel Corp.*, 241 NLRB No. 198, 101 LRRM 1070 (1979), *enforced sub nom.*, *Wheeling-Pittsburgh Steel Corp. v. NLRB*, 618 F.2d 1009, 104 LRRM 2054 (3d Cir. 1980) (an employee refused to operate a crane and a violation of §8(a)(1) and (3) of the Act was found to exist when the employee was suspended); *Roadway Express v. NLRB*, 532 F.2d 751, 91 LRRM 2239 (4th Cir. 1976), *enforcing*, 217 NLRB No. 49, 88 LRRM 1503 (1975) (an employee refused to drive a truck and a finding of a violation of §8(a)(1) of the Act was upheld and the employee was reinstated with back pay).

14. *Interboro Contractors*, 157 NLRB 1295, 61 LRRM 1537 (1966).

15. *Kohls v. NLRB*, 629 F.2d 173, 104 LRRM 3049 (D.C. Cir. 1980).

16. *E. R. Carpenter Co.*, 252 NLRB No. 5, 105 LRRM 1492 (1980).

17. *Washington Cartage*, 258 NLRB No. 93, 108 LRRM 1144 (1981).

18. *NLRB v. Modern Carpet Indus.*, 611 F.2d. 811, 108 LRRM 2167 (10th Cir. 1979). *See also NLRB v. Service Mach. & Shipbldg. Corp.*, 662 F.2d 1125, 108 LRRM 3235 (5th Cir. 1981) (reinstatement of four welders who refused to operate electrical equipment in the rain).

19. 29 U.S.C. §143.

20. 29 C.F.R. §1977.12(b)(2).

21. *Whirlpool Corp. v. Marshall*, 445 U.S. 1 (1980).

22. *San Francisco Redev. Agency* (Koven), 57 LA 1149; *Ohio Crankshaft Co., supra,* note 4; *Acme Indus. Co., supra,* note 5; *National Gypsum Co.. supra,* note 6.

23. *Bethlehem Steel Corp* (Harkless), 58 LA 363; *Arcrods Plant, supra,* note 3.

24. *Reynolds Metals Co.* (Fasser), 78 LA 687.

18

Medical Disability

Issue Whether an employee may be discharged or otherwise disciplined because of a medical disability.

Principle The existence of a medical disability cannot be a cause for discipline, except in cases of fraud, because the necessary element of employee volition of fault is missing. Employees can be terminated, however, where their medical disabilities prevent them from performing their jobs, or attending work regularly; where the disability places the employees themselves or their co-workers in danger; where reasonable accommodation for the disabilities is not possible; and where there is little, or uncertain, hope for improvement of the medical conditions within a reasonable period of time.

Considerations 1. Whether the medical condition prevents the employee from performing the tasks of the job;
2. Whether the medical condition causes the employee to be excessively absent;
3. Whether the medical condition presents a danger to the employee or to co-workers;
4. Whether the medical condition prevents the employee from comporting himself or herself with the needs of the workplace;
5. Whether the medical condition is work related;

6. Whether there is a likelihood of improvement within a reasonable period of time;
7. Whether there are suitable alternative positions available.

Discussion
Although the flexibility of most employers in dealing with employees suffering from medical disabilities has been substantially limited by the various discrimination statutes, issues concerning employee terminations due to such conditions still frequently reach arbitrators. The issue is normally raised in the context of an employee who has suffered an injury or illness during his or her term of employment and then has sought to return to the workplace in some fashion unsatisfactory to the employer. Apart from the ability of the employer under the law to reinstate the employee (or to terminate, after reinstatement) following a leave of absence, the question addressed by arbitrators is, "Does the condition of the employee constitute just cause for severing the employment relationship?" More appropriate in many cases, the question is not "Should employment have been terminated?", but "When is the employer justified in terminating what appears to be an almost hopeless situation?" or "At what point is an employer entitled to declare an employee a hopeless situation and terminate the relationship?"

The most common cases of this kind involve heart conditions, back problems, and mental illness. A complete review of these cases, as decided by arbitrators, does permit several dependable generalizations. Where, for instance, an employee is demonstrably no longer able to perform the tasks of his or her job due to some medical disability, arbitrators consistently recognize the right of the employer to discharge that individual. In allowing for the termination of such employees, arbitrators have generally relied on the fact that one of the primary conditions of a person's employment is the ability of the person to do the work.[1] Arbitrator Roumell, in *Plastomer Corp.*,[2] summarized the operative principles in this type of case:

> Under a just or proper cause standard, the ultimate question is the reasonableness of the Company's action in light of the facts of the case. An extensive review of cases on discharge for excessive absences due to illness is contained in Huskey Oil Co., 65 LA 47 (Richardson, 1975). Arbitrator Richardson's conclusions at 56 may be profitably applied to this case:

From the foregoing decisions and cases, which have been presented mainly in abstract form, it can be readily seen that: (1) Discharge for excessive absenteeism is not an unusual penalty. (2) Where excessive absenteeism is present and other requirements for discharge are met, the fact that sick leave is excused or not completely used up is not controlling. (3) In addition to showing that absenteeism is excessive, an employer must also meet certain requirements of 'just cause', i.e. (a) progressive discipline prior to discharge in the form of advance warning and/or disciplinary action (b) a clear warning to the employee that continued excessive absenteeism will result in discharge, (c) evidence that after receiving warnings the employee continues to abuse leave privileges and/or to create problems for the employer by exceeding what might be considered a normal use of leave, (d) evidence that there is little to indicate that the excessive leave behavior of the employee will be corrected in the future, (e) evidence that the employer has tried to assist the employee to resolve the problem, (4) evidence that discharge has not involved bias, discrimination or anything which might constitute arbitrariness or capriciousness.

The principles of excessive absence as grounds for discharge even if due to illness or other excused reasons is the law of the contract between these parties.

In his Opinion of June 29, 1972, concerning grievances C-106446 and C-106445, Arbitrator E. V. Ott concluded:

[I]t has long been decided in arbitral law that 'Just cause for discharge may exist without fault on the part of the employee'. I am inclined to go along with this line of reasoning. It appears to me that one of the obligations of employment is that the employee will regularly come to work. Successful operation of a plant depends on regular attendance. Frequent absences may cause a loss of production, a disruption of work schedules, a decline in efficiency; all of these occur whether or not there is a good reason for the employee's absence. The interests of the employees and the Company must outweigh the personal interests of these aggrieved employees. It is obvious that if all other employees were so unfortunate as to be unable to work at the same extent as the aggrieved employees, that the Company could not continue production, and that the economic well-being of all concerned would be defeated.

These principles were reaffirmed in this Arbitrator's Opinion of June 11, 1982, concerning grievance number EA0625, David Jones, wherein it was stated:

It is well established that excessive absenteeism can be grounds for a just cause termination. (Citations omitted). Even if absenteeism is caused by genuine illness, this may be a grounds for discharge if the illness prevents the employees from regular attendance.

There are also several cases, however, where arbitrators have considered other factors and have not upheld discharges, because they have not found the appearance of an employee's immediate inability to do the work to be conclusive *per se.* Prior satisfactory service contributed to the reinstatement order for an employee suffering from severe, but not permanent, back pain.[3] Ten years of prior service was also a major factor in an arbitrator's order for a six-month trial return to work for a schizophrenic employee whose illness was in remission.[4] Finally, in *Reynolds Metals-Sherwin Plant*, the arbitrator denied the discharge and ordered a review to determine whether the employee, who had had back surgery, was eligible for a disability pension.[5]

Arbitrators have upheld discharges where an employee failed, or refused, to return to work after his medical disability had ceased to exist. In *National Can Corp.*, the arbitrator upheld the discharge of an employee who had insisted on being given light duty upon his return to work, even though his doctors had placed no such restrictions on his performance.[6] A discharge was also upheld where the employee, after being given a medical release to return to work, did not report to work for some six weeks.

Arbitrators have also recognized the employer' right to expect regular attendance from their employees, regardless of the medical condition of the employees. The attitude appears to be that, while an employee may be entitled to some adjustment to the nature of the work to be performed due to a disability, the employee must be capable of coming to work and being on time. As a result, arbitrators have sustained the discharges of employees whose whose medical conditions have resulted in excessive absenteeism.[7] For example, in *Automotive Distributors*, the absences of the employee were due to a sinus condition about which the employee had done nothing; in *Monsanto Co.*, the absences of the employee were due to a post-Vietnam stress disorder; in *Asarco, Inc.*, the employee had had many absences over several years due to hepatitis; in *Scott & Fetzer Co.*, the employee had missed over 75 percent of his work time in one year; in *American Broadcasting Companies*, the employee had sought a second leave within one year for hypertension; and, in *Kimberly-Clark Corp.*, the employee had missed 60 to 100 percent of his work time during the previous four years.[8]

In *Newport News Shipbuilding & Dry Dock Co.*, the discharge of an employee for excessive absenteeism was sustained where the employee claimed he was unable to work due to a chronic back problem.[9] The arbitrator found a lack of evidence to substantiate a serious problem and found no evidence to support the employee's claim that he could not do any work. The arbitrator noted that the employee could have done light work, at least, and did not evidence a desire to get better by doing exercises prescribed by his doctors.

Arbitrators also will sustain the discharges of employees where their disabilities make their continued employment a danger to themselves or to others. However, the danger must be real and not merely hypothesized, and there must be evidence that the danger cannot be avoided or reduced in the future. For example, the discharges of heavy equipment operators suffering from epilepsy—where there was no guarantee of their not having future seizures and the risk posed by their continued employment was great—have been sustained on these grounds.[10] Similarly, where an employee's mental condition presented a danger to other employees, his discharge was sustained because there was no evidence that his antisocial behavior would not recur.[11]

By comparison, employees have been reinstated, although without back pay, where there was no evidence of future danger,[12] or where the employee has been able to compensate for his condition and, thereby, reduce the danger[13] created by his or her continued employment.

Another situation in which an arbitrator may sustain a discharge is where the employee cannot adjust his or her conduct to the needs of the workplace due to some mental disability. An employee, who had used profane language, had shoved a supervisor, and had been otherwise disruptive in his behavior, was properly discharged, since there was no prognosis for improvement of the employee's diagnosed mental illness.[14] An employee who had destroyed company property while suffering from a mental disorder was also found to have been properly discharged.[15] In another case, an arbitrator denied the discharge of a schizophrenic employee, who had made threats and the like, pending the employee's entry into treatment. However, while ordering an indefinite suspension, the arbitrator acknowledged the ultimate right to discharge such an employee if the treatment was unsuccessful.[16]

In contrast to the preceding cases, at least one arbitrator has reduced a discharge to a one-year suspension for a disruptive and insubordinate employee, because the behavior was not willful, but rather the result of a mental disorder.[17] However, this case was also complicated by the company's failure to follow the grievance procedure.

A factor which arbitrators consider, although it is certainly not controlling, is whether the injury giving rise to the disability was work related. There is some indication in the holdings and dicta of arbitration decisions that work-related injuries, and any attendant disabilities, will be dealt with more leniently than those which are not work related. In *Truck Transport*, for instance, the discharge of an employee, who would have been required to miss over nine months due to a nonwork injury, was upheld.[18] The arbitrator suggested that the outcome would have been different if the injury had been work related.[19] However, as suggested, this factor is not controlling, or dispositive. For example, in one case the discharge of an employee for absenteeism caused by a work-related injury was upheld, and the fact that the injury resulted from the employee's job made no apparent difference.[20]

Another factor which arbitrators consider relevant in reviewing discharges for medical disabilities is the outlook for improvement in the employee's condition. Where the employee is responding to treatment and has a likelihood of improving, discharges are generally denied.[21] On the other hand, where there is little likelihood of improvement in the employee's condition, the employee's discharge will generally be sustained.[22]

A final factor which arbitrators consider is the availability of alternate jobs with the employer which the disabled employee could perform. Where no such position is available, arbitrators have upheld discharges, even in the face of a contractual obligation to seek an alternative position.[23] An obligation to seek an alternative position has not included, or been found to include, requiring an employer to create a job to fit the employee's condition. In this respect, arbitrators do not appear ready to require job accommodations for these situations, as have equal employment offices. By contrast, in *West Penn Power Co.*, the arbitrator ordered a lineman, who suffered from acrophobia, to be reclassified pursuant to the contract where there were other suitable positions for the employee.[24]

Key Points

1   *The medical disability must substantially prevent the employee from performing the normal tasks of his or her job or from attending work regularly.*

Examples

Employee *A* had a coronary bypass operation. His physician certified that he could return to work provided it was light-duty work and did not involve lifting more than 25 pounds at a time or exerting more than 50 pounds of force. The employer had no job within those limitations, and the employee was terminated. The termination was sustained by the arbitrator.

Employee *B* had a back fusion operation and was permitted to return to work by his physician under the condition that he only do light work. The employer asked the physician if the employee could push trucks weighing up to 200 pounds without danger. The physician said that if the employee felt he could do it without hurting himself, he should be allowed to do so. The employer, nevertheless, transferred *B* to a lower-paying, but less strenuous job. The employee grieved. At the arbitration, the employer asserted that it had forced the transfer to protect itself from a potentially higher workers' compensation rate. The grievance was sustained, and the employee was ordered back into his original job.

Employee *C* suffered from migraine headaches. As a result, her absenteeism became excessive under the company's absenteeism-control policy. *C* was terminated. The arbitrator commuted the termination to a leave of absence for treatment purposes.

Employee *D* suffered from a deep depression which periodically caused her to be absent from work for periods of up to one month. She had had six such bouts and one two-month leave of absence for treatment. Even though under treatment *D* had been told on several occasions that the employer could not continue to put up with her absenteeism and that she must become regular in her attendance. After her second absence of two weeks within the last four months of her employment, *D* was terminated. Noting that even a long-suffering employer has a right to cry, "Enough," the arbitrator sustained the termination.

Employee *E* had an industrial accident and acquired epilepsy. Although assured by *E*'s doctor that the condition would be controllable, the employer terminated *E*, explaining that it could not take a chance that *E* might hurt himself on a machine if he should have a seizure while working. The arbitrator reinstated the employee, finding the employer's fears to be unreasonable.

Guidelines

After taking into consideration all of the capabilities of the employee, an employer may terminate an employee with a medical disability if the disability acts to destroy the ability of the employee to be of any value to the employer.

Relevant Cases

Great Lakes Container Corp. (Madden), 84 LA 451
Emhart Corp. (Katz), 83 LA 907
Porritts & Spencer, Inc. (Byars), 83 LA 1165
Linn County, Iowa (Sinicropi), 81 LA 929
Plastomer Corp. (Roumell), 81 LA 700
Newport News Shipbuilding & Dry Dock Co. (Garrett), 78 LA 202
Central Telephone Co. (Mead), 76 LA 1137
Zellerbach Paper Co. (Stashower), 68 LA 69
National Steel Corp. (Traynor), 66 LA 533
B.F. Goodrich Chemical Co. (Kimsly), 65 LA 1213
Reynolds Metals-Sherwin Plant (Caraway), 65 LA 678

2 *Termination may be justified where the employee's disability creates an unusual danger to the employee or others.*

Examples

Employee *A* acquired epilepsy because of a fall. While *A*'s physician stated that the condition would be controllable if the employee took the medicine as prescribed, the physician would not commit himself to an unequivocal assurance. The employer, fearing that the condition might not be totally controllable and that the employee might fail to take his medicine, transferred the employee from his regular job of driving a forklift truck into a lower-rated, general warehouseman classification. The arbitrator sustained the transfer.

For years employee *B* had missed time from work due to a weak back. After a spinal fusion operation, *B* returned to work and sought to resume his former job. The employer sent the job specifications to the employee's physician, who stated that the work was too strenuous. The employee continued to demand the job. When the employer stood firm, *B* grieved the issue, asserting that he should be allowed to assume the risk. The arbitrator sustained the employer's action, stating that while an employee may be unconcerned about his or her own health, the employer has a legitimate business interest to protect, i.e., worker's compensation insurance costs.

Employee *C* suffered from a disease which caused her to suddenly and unpredictably fall asleep for a short period of time. The condition can be controlled by medication, which the employee had. On occasion *C* forgot to take the medication and suffered a sleeping attack. Fortunately, these ocurrences took place while *C* had been on breaks. The employer refused her bid upward into the position of machine operator on the grounds that the employee might have an attack while operating a machine and be injured. The arbitrator overruled the employer, finding that the possibility of any danger by the employee's failure to take her medicine was no greater than that presented by any other machine operator who might be negligent and therefore, *C's* condition did not constitute an unusual danger.

Guidelines

Where an employee's disability or medical condition creates a danger to the employee or to others, the employer may terminate the employee provided the danger is greater than that which normally exists in the workplace.

Relevant Cases

Alton Packaging Corp. (Talent), 83 LA 1318
Appleton Electric Co. (Roomkin), 76 LA 167

City of Fenton (Roumell), 76 LA 355
Samuel Bingham Co. (Cohen), 67 LA 706
Weber Manufacturing Co. (Yeager), 63 LA 56
Acme Galvanizing (Moberly), 61 LA 1115

3   *Termination generally will not be justified if an
    employee's condition is likely to improve within a
    reasonable period.*

Examples

Employee *A* suffered from phlebitis for many years. Gradually the condition made it impossible for her to continue
her regular job, which involved standing for substantial
periods of time. *A* took a leave of absence to have an
operation. At the conclusion of the three-month leave, *A*
was still unable to return to work, and her physician could
not give an estimate of when she would be able to return,
beyond "within the next year." The employer terminated
C but told her that, when she was able, she should reapply
for a position. The arbitrator sustained the termination.

Employee *B* was an alcoholic. After the condition was
discovered because of *B*'s absenteeism record, the employer gave him a leave of absence for treatment. Following his leave, *B* returned to work under the condition that
he continue treatment as an outpatient. After a few months,
B began to drink again and was terminated. The arbitrator found that there was insufficient evidence to support
a belief that *B* could get his condition under control within
the reasonable future and sustained the discharge.

Employee *C* had a knee condition, which caused him pain
when he stood for long periods of time. As a result of *C*'s
complaints and other agitation, the employer allowed the
employee to construct a seat-like structure near his machine. The employee then requested a two-month leave
of absence for corrective surgery. The employer, noting
that company policy only permitted medical leaves of up
to one month, allowed *C* only one-half the time he requested. After the one month, *C* attempted to return to
work, but left after one day due to excessive pain. The
employer terminated him. The arbitrator reinstated the
employee, stating that the condition would heal in a reasonably short time and that the employer's action had

been unreasonable, without other reasons for the termination of substantial weight.

Guidelines

Absent contract language to the contrary, an employer cannot be compelled to keep a job open and available to an employee for an indefinite, or overly long, period of time. What is overly long will depend upon what the employer evidences is reasonable by its existing leave-of-absence policy and the nature of the job itself. The employer's legitimate need to be able to plan and to regulate the workplace will normally be honored.

Relevant Cases

City of Fenton (Roumell), 76 LA 355
City of Hartford (Mallon), 69 LA 303
Scott & Fetger Co. (Chattman), 69 LA 18

4   *The employer must have made good-faith efforts to find alternative work which the employee could do and to make some accommodations for the employee's special circumstances. However, the employer is not required to create a new job just to fit an employee's special condition.*

Examples

Employee *A* suffered from lower back pain and, as a result, lost sufficient time from his job to justify discipline under the employer's absenteeism-control policy. The employee requested a light-duty job. The request was persistently denied, and the employee was ultimately discharged for excessive absenteeism. The arbitrator, finding that the employer had not made a good-faith effort to find light work for the employee, sustained the grievance.

Employee *B*, a secretary, suffered a concussion, which resulted in a substantial hearing loss. As a result, *B* was terminated. The arbitrator reinstated the employee upon a showing that the employer had not investigated devices which could be put on the telephone to enable the hearing-impaired employee to use it.

Employee *C* lost an arm in an accident. The employee could still perform all the functions required in his job, except for the carting of unfinished material to and from his workstation. The employer determined that *C* could not do his regular job, and the employee was transferred to a lower-rated position. The arbitrator ordered *C's* reinstatement to his former position and required the employer to accommodate the employee by having one of the other workers assist *C* with the carts.

Employee *D* suffered a heart attack, and his doctor limited him to light-duty work. The employer, not having such work available terminated the employee. The arbitrator sustained the termination.

Guidelines

The employer must make a good-faith effort to accommodate the employee's condition by finding a suitable, alternative job or by making nonessential changes to the employee's regular job. Where such reasonable accommodation is not possible and a wholly new job must be created, a termination will be sustained.

Relevant Cases

Zellerbach Paper Co. (Stashower), 68 LA 69
West Penn Power Co. (Blue), 67 LA 1085
Weber Manufacturing Co. (Yeager), 63 LA 56

Notes to Chapter 18

1. *Zellerbach Paper Co.* (Stashower), 68 LA 69; *see also Central Tel. Co.* (Mead), 76 LA 1137.
2. *Plastomer Corp.* (Roumell), 81 LA 700.
3. *B.F. Goodrich Chem. Co.* (Kimsly), 65 LA 1213.
4. *National Steel Corp.* (Traynor), 66 LA 533.
5. *Reynolds Metals-Sherwin Plant* (Caraway), 65 LA 678.
6. *National Can Corp.* (Turkus), 68 LA 351.
7. *Los Angeles Die Casting Co.* (Rose), 61 LA 1218.
8. *Automotive Distrib.* (Eisler), 76 LA 552; *Monsanto Co.* (Thomson), 76 LA 509; *Asarco, Inc.* (Bothwell), 74 LA 1024; *Scott & Fetzer Co.* (Chattman), 69 LA 18; *American Broadcasting Co.* (Gentile), 63 LA 278; *Kimberly-Clark Corp.* (Shieber), 62 LA 1119.
9. *Newport News Shipbldg. & Dry Dock Co.* (Garrett), 78 LA 202.

10. *Weber Mfg. Co.* (Yaeger), 63 LA 56; *Acme Galvanizing* (Moberly), 61 LA 1115.

11. *Appleton Elec. Co.* (Roomkin), 76 LA 167.

12. *City of Fenton* (Roumell), 76 LA 355 (a police officer had suffered from a mental disorder).

13. *Samuel Bingham Co.* (Cohen), 67 LA 706 (an epileptic employee was able to avoid tasks that could create a danger, and the potential for danger was further reduced by the fact that seizures came with several minutes' warning).

14. *Babcock & Wilcox Co.* (Duff), 75 LA 12.

15. *Allis-Chalmers Corp.* (Goetz), 73 LA 1230.

16. *Johns-Manville Perlite Corp.* (Traynor), 67 LA 1255.

17. *Marion Power Shovel Co.* (McDermott), 69 LA 339.

18. *Truck Transp.* (Seidman), 66 LA 60.

19. *See also Scott & Fetzer Co., supra,* note 8 (dicta indicating that the arbitrator was intentionally more lenient when the injury was job related); *Ryerson & Son* (Zack), 61 LA 977 (reinstatement without back pay was ordered in a situation where the employee was discharged for excessive absenteeism resulting in large part from a work-related injury).

20. *Kimberly-Clark Corp., supra,* note 8.

21. *City of Fenton, supra,* note 12; *City of Hartford* (Mallon), 69 LA 303.

22. *Scott & Fetzer Co., supra,* note 8.

23. *Zellerbach Paper Co., supra,* note 1; *Weber Mfg. Co., supra,* note 10.

24. *West Penn Power Co.* (Blue), 67 LA 1085.

19

Misconduct, Horseplay, and Fighting

Issue   Whether an employee can be discharged
             or otherwise disciplined for misconduct,
             horseplay, or fighting.

Principle   An employee can be discharged or other-
             wise disciplined for misconduct where the
             employee has performed an intentional act
which caused, or had the potential of causing, physical injury
or property damage; the employee can be discharged or otherwise disciplined for misconduct where the employee committed an act which, although unintentional, was in wanton
disregard for the safety of others or of property; an employee
can be disciplined, but not discharged for horseplay (unless
the discharge is a final step in progressive discipline), where
the employee has performed a childish act which has unin-
tentionally caused injury or embarrassment to a person or
damage to property; and, an employee can be discharged or
otherwise disciplined for fighting where it appears that the
employee was the aggressor, or a willing participant, in a fight
with the apparent intent to injure another employee.

Considerations   Misconduct or Horseplay

             1. Whether the actions of the employee
                were intentional and were committed
                with the apparent purpose of wrong-
                doing;
             2. Whether the actions of the employee
                had the potential for physical injury or
                property damage;

305

3. Whether the tone of the workplace or the general behavior of employees in the workplace created an atmosphere which condoned such behavior;
4. Whether the employee is contrite to such an extent that the employer can expect that the conduct, or similar conduct, will not be repeated in the future.

Fighting

1. Whether the employee was the aggressor or a willing participant in the fight;
2. Whether the employee was provoked;
3. Whether the employee used an instrument in the fight with an apparent intent to do serious bodily harm to the other employee;
4. Whether the work history of the employee indicates a likelihood of peaceful behavior in the future.

Discussion Arbitrators distinguish between misconduct and horseplay when reviewing cases of discipline for employee misconduct. Misconduct is defined as those incidents which have "the potential for physical injury and property damage," and are the result of "intentional acts of wrongdoing."[1] Horseplay is generally viewed as behavior which is essentially without malice, but childish and infantile behavior, resulting from "uncurbed impulse," "yielding once to such a temptation," or the "fallible nature of the human condition."[2]

An employer can punish employee misconduct by taking severe disciplinary action, even discharging the employee, while horseplay usually does not warrant the same serious punishment.

In discipline cases involving misconduct, it is not uncommon for the grievant to raise a defense that his or her behavior should be classified as horseplay, rather than as misconduct and, thereby, escape a harsher punishment.[3]

This general distinction between misconduct and horseplay is indicative of the two themes to be found in this area. The first is that arbitrators recognize the employer's right to expect reasonable social behavior from its employees in their relationships between each other, toward their supervisors, and if a service enterprise, toward the public.[4] This expectation is coupled with an employer's responsibility to its employees to provide a safe workplace and with its legitimate interest in protecting its property.[5]

The second theme, which adds some balance to the rights and expectations of the employer, is the arbitrator's awareness of the human element in the workplace or the inevitable consequences when any group of people are thrown together. Arbitrators look to any fact that might explain, rationalize, or lend insight to the employee's behavior. Some of these factors have been recognized as "normal human frailty"; reactions to stress, tension, or fatigue; the tone the employer has set for the workplace, which either condones mischievous behavior or refuses to diffuse hostile situations; and, an employee's misunderstanding of the effects of his or her behavior.[6]

An arbitrator will often reduce the punishment meted out to an employee, if the arbitrator makes the determination that the behavior was a result of one or more of these factors and that the employer overreacted in disciplining the employee, i.e., the punishment did not fit the crime.[7] In *Perfection American Co.*, a 58-year-old male employee with 14 years of service went into the ladies' locker room at the plant.[8] He was seen by a female employee in the locker room at the time. He made no offensive or suggestive moves toward her, but she later testified she heard him say to himself that he had always wanted to see what it looked like in there. The company discharged him for violating a rule prohibiting any conduct which violates common decency or morality. The arbitrator reduced the discharge to a suspension, finding that discharge for this behavior was too severe. Similarly, in *Southeast Container Corp.*, the arbitrator reduced the immediate discharge of an employee, who had smeared red paint on the handle of a press machine, to a suspension.[9] The arbitrator held that horseplay is a fact of industrial life and that this action did not warrant by-passing the progressive discipline system. In *W-L Molding Co.*, an employee had been discharged for yelling at the representative of a vending machine company, after the employee had lost money in the machine.[10] The employee's discharge was for aggressive behavior and abusive language. The arbitrator found that the company failed to show that the employee, who had used words like "punk" and "clown" toward the representative, was more angry or more abusive than any other employee similarly frustrated. The arbitrator stated, "Vending machines being what they are and people being what they are, Grievant's offense cannot be viewed as overly serious." The discharge was reduced to a two-week suspension.

Arbitrators will often specify which of the two types of action—misconduct or horseplay—the employee has been accused of committing. Arbitrators generally refuse to allow an employer to augment the nature of a minor incident by coupling it with a serious incident of misconduct. For instance, in *Chatham Supermarkets*, an employee was discharged for waving a five-inch knife that he used in his job and for saying, "Don't say s—— to me, bitch," to a fellow employee.[11] The arbitrator held that the employee's language was not sufficient to warrant discharge and the employee's action with the knife had not been proven to be an assault with a weapon. Similarly, in *Kroger Co.*, an employee was discharged for urinating, or pretending to urinate, on the shop floor; then, calling out for the U.S. Department Agriculture inspector; and for throwing a potato at another employee.[12] The arbitrator found that throwing the vegetable was not a dischargeable offense; but, the urinating incident, even if a ruse, did warrant discharge, because the employee created the risk of causing a plant shutdown.

Many misconduct cases result from the use of a racial slur, the use of a racial epithet, or the eruption of racial hostility. Arbitrators are sensitive to the use of racial slurs in the workplace and approve disciplinary action against the use of such language. In *Memorial Hospital*, a white employee received a three-day suspension for failure to show respect for her fellow employees, when she said she was being "worked like a nigger."[13] In *Bowman Transportation*, the arbitrator upheld a 14-day suspension for an employee who had said over a radio dispatch, "Get those niggers off the radio."[14] The arbitrator found that "under any circumstances, and most particularly in the present industrial climate, remarks tending toward racial antagonism cannot be tolerated."

Arbitrators attempt to diffuse the tension created by the underlying racial hostilities which are to be found in some cases involving fights and threats by not condoning the language or the violence, by encouraging employers to assume the primary responsibility for monitoring this behavior, and by giving employees a second chance to curb their physical reactions to such language.

In *Union Camp Corp.*, the arbitrator reduced the employee's discharge for fighting with a fellow employee over a racial slur to a suspension and warned the employee that a similar incident in the future would warrant discharge.[15] The employee in *LTV Aerospace Corp.* received a two-week suspension for threatening to cause bodily harm to employees who had used racial slurs.[16] The arbitrator held that threats of physical violence cannot be condoned and warned the employee that it was his responsibility to inform the company of the use of racial slurs, not to take justice into his own hands. In *Kaiser Foundation Health Plan*, the arbitrator held the employer to be responsible, when physical violence erupted between a supervisor and an employee, for failing to respond to employees' complaints about the racially derogatory comments used by a supervisor about the employees under his direction.[17] This may have been part of the arbitrator's reasoning in *Cavalier Corp.*, when he reinstated a young black employee who had been discharged for hitting an older, white female employee on the back of the head after an exchange of expletives.[18] Though the arbitrator clearly warned the employee that he must rework his attitude, the discussion at the hearing of the blatant hostility which existed between the two employees may have been a suggestion to the employer that it has a responsibility to be aware of and diffuse this type of hostility.

Arbitrators appear to minimize the racial overtones when an argument erupts between a white and a black employee. In *Alvey, Inc.* two employees, one white and one black, were discharged for fighting.[19] The employees ran a "jackpot" lottery each week and got into an argument over a procedural aspect of the drawing. During the argument, the white employee called the other a "dumb nigger." The white employee then challenged the other to a fight in the parking lot. The arbitrator found the name calling sufficient provocation for the black employee to agree to fight. He reinstated both employees because the prospects of industrial harmony were good, especially since the employees had a history of friendship. Similarly, in *Tyrone Hydraulics*, a white employee, while intoxicated, kicked his black foreman.[20] In reducing the discharge to a suspension, the arbitrator found that the employee had a great deal of respect for his foreman, had gone to his house to apologize, and had not meant to demean the foreman.

Another consequence of combining random groups of people is the conflict, or continuing saga of the relationship, between the sexes. Though some cases involve incidents of attempted rape and sexual harassment, arbitrators are wary of attempts to characterize normal shop behavior as something other than horseplay just because it involves a man and a woman. The arbitrator in *Chatham Supermarkets* expressed this concern, finding that the employer had overreacted to a male meat cutter's use of language and his motion with a knife because the other employee involved was new and a woman.[21] Similarly, the arbitrator in *Powermatic/Houdaille* refused to sustain a discharge for immoral conduct, where the male employee had attracted the attention of a female employee, had put his finger through or by the fly of his pants, and had said, "Hey, big mama, look what I have for you."[22] The arbitrator found this type of behavior distasteful, but not immoral. Arbitrators appear to be interested in developing an atmosphere of peaceful coexistence, requiring both sexes to make some modification in their expectations of each other at the workplace.

Arbitrators are less tolerant, however, when there is evidence of physical assault and threats of rape. In *St. Regis Paper Co.*, for instance, a male employee for 13 months was discharged for threatening to rape a female employee.[23] On two prior occasions, he physically assaulted her, touched her, tried to kiss her, and picked her up. In *Monsanto Chemical Intermediates Co.*, the arbitrator upheld a 30-day suspension for two male employees, who had locked a female employee in a supply room, wrestled her to the couch, and attempted to take her clothes off.[24] In both of these cases, the male employees had maintained a defense that their behavior was merely horseplay. In neither case did the arbitrators agree. Rather, they determined that the threat posed by the male employees was real and that the company had a responsibility to maintain a workplace free from fears of threats and intimidation.

Arbitrators also appear cautious when the issue is the occurrence or appropriateness of disciplinary action in cases involving sexual harassment. Part of this caution would seem to be a recognition that definitions of sexual harassment and classifications of conduct as sexual harrassment are subjective determinations which vary from individual to individual. As stated by the arbitrator in *Godchaux-Henderson Sugar Co.*, a case involving a charge of immoral behavior, "When the Company brings a young female employee into the plant and allows her unsupervised freedom to invite male employees to her workplace for conversation and play, trouble is inevitable."[25]

In *University of Missouri*, for example, the discharge of a housekeeping supervisor was primarily sustained because his conduct created an atmosphere of stress and anxiety amongst female employees and because there was a fear of the consequences if the behavior continued.[26] The employee had a habit of putting his arms around females, smacking his lips at them, commenting on their attractiveness and the attractiveness of other employees, and looking at them in a way which made them "feel undressed." The employees testified that his conduct affected their mental health and job performance.

As mentioned earlier, arbitrators, in cases which involve misconduct, also look to a variety of facts and circumstances that may serve to mitigate the punishment. Disciplinary action for misconduct or horseplay can be sustained without a specific company rule governing the situation. If the company is enforcing a particular rule, however, the usual rule analysis is utilized. This analysis examines whether it is a reasonable rule, whether it has been communicated to employees, and whether it is consistently enforced.[27]

In *Rochester Methodist Hospital*, the arbitrator revoked the three-day suspension given to an employee and granted her back pay, when he found that the employees had had no advance notice of the rules and found that the employer's disciplinary system did not follow customary standards of just cause and due process.[28] The arbitrator in *Kraft Foods*, when discussing the employer's rule against fighting, noted "the implementation of the rule, however, must meet the accepted test of reasonableness and any abuse of management discretion should be avoided."[29] In *Welch Foods*, the arbitrator reduced the discharge of an employer to a suspension, basing his decision in part on his sense that the employer had treated the two employees involved in the incident differently.[30]

Arbitrators also look to determine whether or not the employees had notice of the behavior expected of them, be it a specific rule or an understood policy. In *Mobil Oil*, the arbitrator questioned the publication of the employer's policy that employees are to avoid conflict and walk away from any threat or potential confrontation.[31] Similarly, in *Flat River Glass Co.* the employee testified that he did not know that his horseplay would be cause for discipline and that the behavior he had indulged in was a way of life on his shift.[32] So also, the arbitrator in *New York Air Brake Co.* refused to sustain the employer's discipline of two employees, because their behavior occurred within a context of poor supervision, leadership, and discipline.[33] However, the arbitrator in *Midland Ross Corp.* dismissed the employee's contention that he was unaware of a rule against exploding firecrackers at his work station.[34] The arbitrator found that the employee's knowledge of the rule was irrelevant and that the employee's common sense should have told him that shooting firecrackers was an improper activity.

Arbitrators also look to other factors that may serve to mitigate the punishment, e.g., the employee's length of service, work record, general relationship with other employees, and the likelihood of a reoccurrence of the incident.[35]

In cases of fighting or of threats, however, arbitrators may examine whether any provocation may have caused the fight or whether the employee's actions were in self-defense, but they rarely accept provocation as justification for physical violence.[36] Self-defense is regarded as a valid defense, particularly if the employee did not provoke the initial violence.[37]

The employee's attitude about his or her behavior may be the most important factor in mitigating discipline for misconduct or horseplay. If an employee is contrite and recognizes the negative aspects of his behavior, arbitrators allow for a lesser discipline, and in the case of discharge, reduce it to a suspension. In *General Electric Co.*, the arbitrator commented on the demeanor of the grievant.[38] The arbitrator found the employee to be an unusually candid witness who recognized the unacceptable nature of his actions and exhibited a sincerely contrite manner. The employee in *Ozark Lead Co.* did not try to avoid the responsibility for his wrongful act: the insertion of a waterhose into the vertical exhaust pipe of a tractor.[39] The arbitrator found the employee's admission of responsibility for the act to be a reflection of the employee's sincerity and forthrightness. In contrast, the arbitrator was disappointed with the employees in *Monsanto Chemical Intermediates Co.* who, when contesting their suspension for attempted rape, were evasive and flippant in the manner in which they provided information.[40]

The initial determination the arbitrator makes in these cases is whether or not the employee is guilty of the conduct with which he had been charged. As a result, many of these cases turn on the credibility of the witnesses and on the facts pleaded by both sides. Some arbitrators have suggested the use of a "clear and convincing" standard of proof as to the guilt of the employee; one arbitrator has applied a "high degree of certainty" test.[41]

Arbitrators often base their credibility findings on the choice of the witnesses and their testimony. In *VA Medical Center*, the arbitrator questioned the employer's selection of three mental patients as its key witnesses, when it was clear that the testimony of other staff personnel would deserve more weight.[42] The arbitrator in *Gateway United Methodist Youth Center* made similar remarks, when the employer based its disciplinary decision and its case on the testimony of two female residents who were receiving psychiatric counselling and who had been responsible for the termination of another employee under similar allegations.[43] The employee in this case had a clean work record, and there was no reason not to believe his testimony.

The most common type of employee misconduct is fighting, or the use of physical violence against another employee, and in most cases it warrants severe discipline, especially where a weapon is used. In *General Electric Co.*, the discharge of an employee, who had hit another employee with a machete, was sustained.[44] Arbitrators will also sustain discharges where employees fight without weapons, if there is the risk of severe personal injury. In *General Electric Co.*, for instance, one employee hit another so hard that the force of the blow caused the employee to knock several compressors weighing 80–90 pounds each to the floor.[45] Also, when the fighting presents a grave and serious threat to the safety and security of other company employees, terminations for fighting have been upheld.[46]

Arbitrators will also look to the reason for the altercation. If it is slight or insubstantial when compared to the reaction, the arbitrator will not allow the reasons for the fight to mitigate the discipline, especially in the presence of a plant rule prohibiting fighting. For example, the arbitrator found the company to be within its rights when it strictly enforced the prohibition against fighting and suspended an employee for striking and threatening another in *Mobay Chemical Corp.* In that case the employee thought the other was driving his tow motor too fast, followed him into the break room, grabbed him, hit him, and told him that if he drove that way again he would kill him. The arbitrator concluded that, even if the other's tow motor had been driven too fast, the employee could not be exonerated.[47]

Nevertheless, arbitrators tend to give employees who have

engaged in fighting a second chance if the fight caused no lasting injury and if the arbitrator, given the facts of the case, feels discharge is too severe a penalty.[48] In *General Electric Co.*, for instance, an employee had been discharged for striking another employee.[49] The employee, who had struck the first blow, became angered when the other employee started to give him instructions regarding his machine. The arbitrator found that the employee was understandably offended by the supervisory airs of his fellow employee; he was contrite; his attack on the employee was not violent or depraved; and, with respect to his work record, discharge was too severe. Similarly, in *Alvey, Inc.*, two employees, who were friends, got into a fight over a lottery which they ran at the plant.[50] The arbitrator held that discharge was too severe a penalty for these individuals, noting the past peaceful history between the two men and the favorite outlook for industrial harmony.

Next in frequency of misconduct cases are threats of physical harm, with and without weapons. Threats made with weapons are viewed as more serious infractions than mere threats. The discharge of an employee with 30 years of service was sustained in a case where the employee pulled a knife on a fellow employee, held it to his stomach, and threatened to cut the employee to pieces.[51] Similarly, in *Mobil Oil Corp.* a 10-day suspension for an employee who had pulled a knife on another employee was upheld.[52] The arbitrator found that the employee, by his actions and language, had created a threat of physical harm to the other employee and warranted discipline.

Unlike most cases involving threats with weapons, arbitrators must determine whether a threat has actually been made in cases where a weapon is not present. Calling someone a "dodo" or a "turkey" for example, has not been considered a threat.[53] However, when an employee, soliciting for the union, told another employee "Big Daddy will get you" for refusing to join, the arbitrator held that the employee could have reasonably believed he was threatened and, therefore, discipline was warranted. In *Emery Industries*, the arbitrator found that the employee's comment, "I hope your truck blows up," to a subcontractor was intended to be perceived as a legitimate threat, given the circumstances of the case, and warranted discipline.[54] And, in *LTV Aerospace Corp.*, the arbitrator sustained a two-week suspension for an employee's threat of physical harm simply on the basis that threats of physical violence cannot be condoned in a company plant.[55]

Misconduct which involves the use of fire normally warrants discharge, apparently because of the high risk of personal injury and property damage. For example, in *Abbott & Co.* the discharge of an employee for starting a fire in the ladies room to set off the smoke alarm was sustained. The arbitrator reasoned that, even if the employee's behavior was intended as a prank or could be categorized as horseplay, such conduct cannot be condoned.[56] Similarly, the discharge of the employee in *Kroger Co.* was sustained.[57] He was discharged for sprinkling lighter fluid on another employee's apron and setting it on fire. The arbitrator found no corroboration of the employee's contention that setting fire to aprons was a common act of horseplay. Also, in *Russer Foods* the discharge of an employee was sustained where the employee had placed lighted cigarettes in the pockets of another employee and, then, had started a fire under the employee's chair.[58]

Other types of conduct that arbitrators have found to be so outrageous as to warrant severe discipline include calling a bomb threat to the plant, making an obscene phone call to a company official's wife, and creating an incident that could have caused the shutdown of the employee's facility.[59] In *Union Commerce Bank*, the arbitrator upheld the discharge of an employee for his steadfast refusal to cooperate and work with his co-workers. The company made several attempts to get the employees to work together harmoniously, and in spite of all such attempts, negative forms of behavior continued. In sustaining the discharge, the arbitrator noted that an employee must act in the best interests of the employer and that those interests included employees who can work in harmony with others.[60]

Horseplay, as discussed previously, is usually the result of unbridled enthusiasm and is characterized as conduct that causes no harm and is undertaken without malice. The arbitrator in *Clay Equipment* used this concept in the plant when he held that the presence of horseplay indicated that there was room for a little fun and found that this prevailing attitude was the reason for the excellent relationship between employees and management. "A good healthy laugh between friends and among acquaintances may some day prove to be one of the best indicators of good health in a management/union relationship."[61] In this case, the employee had been discharged for throwing a pie at a management consultant. The arbitrator reinstated him, without back pay and without seniority.

In reviewing cases where employees have been disciplined for horseplay, arbitrators look to the severity of the incident, whether anyone was injured, whether or not the potential for serious injury was present, whether the employee's attitude throughout the incident indicated that the employee had acted without malice, and whether the employee was contrite after the incident. Accordingly, in *Ozark Lead Co.*, the discharge of an employee who had placed a hose in the exhaust pipe of a tractor was not sustained.[62] At the hearing, the employee confessed to being responsible for the incident, maintained that he did not know the water would damage the machine, and apologized for his behavior. In *Flat River Glass Co.*, an employee was discharged for sliding a hot bottle down the floor to the cold end of the plant. The arbitrator revoked the discharge, reasoning that no one had been seriously hurt, the employee had confessed he had not been aware that such behavior was susceptible to discipline, and that the employee's "insane, stupid bit of senseless horseplay" could not be compared to other intentional acts of wrongdoing which had been the basis of the company's discipline policy.[63] Similarly, the disciplinary actions taken in *Bechtel Corp.*, where an employee had driven a truck too fast to an intersection, slammed on the brakes, and left a skid mark and in *Southeast Container Corp.*, where an employee had put red paint on the handle of a press, were reduced.[64]

In *Kroger Co.* the arbitrator found that "mooning"—in Arbitrator Sabella's words, "an exposure of one's 'butt' to another person"—was not a matter for summary discharge.[65] Reducing the discharge to a suspension, the arbitrator held that, although an employee has an obligation to conduct himself with respect to fellow employees, the employee in this case had accidently been seen by a female employee, and no harm had been done. Similarly, in *United States Internal Revenue Service* the arbitrator refused to uphold the one-day suspension given to two revenue agents for "mooning" a group of women who had been joking with them while off duty.[66] One of the women had seen their car and had reported the license number. The arbitrator found that although "it was a foolish and totally sophomoric display," he did not see how the agency's reputation had been jeopardized by the fact that two agents "with some degree of at least imagined goading decided as a practical joke to bare their bottoms to a lady in the isolation of a garage passageway, without more."

Misconduct or Horseplay

Key Points

1   *The conduct of the employee must have been intentional and must have had the apparent purpose of causing injury to a person or damage to property.*

Examples

Employee *A* was discharged for misconduct; he had been caught putting water into spare gasoline containers, which were kept in the employer's garage, for the groundskeepers' use. *A* defended his action by stating that he had only been retaliating against one of the groundskeepers who had struck *A*'s parked car with a lawnmower. The arbitrator sustained the discharge and noted that, no matter how good *A*'s work record may have been, his record could not serve to mitigate his action.

Employee *B* was discharged for jamming a potato into the exhaust pipe of a jeep used by another employee to carry small parcels between plant buildings. As a result of *B*'s action, the muffler on the tailpipe exploded. At the hearing, the employer argued that the act was obviously intentional and, as any reasonable person would have known, could have caused much more damage than it did. The arbitrator, however, held that discharge was too severe a penalty for such childishness and reinstated *B* without back pay, while ordering him to pay the employer for the damage.

Employee *C* was discharged for throwing a smoke bomb into the window of the ladies' room, which set off the fire alarm and brought the local fire department out to the company. The arbitrator reinstated the employee without back pay.

Employee *D* was discharged for spreading a thin coat of grease on the floor around another employee's machine. Finding that someone could have been reasonably expected to suffer serious injury had they slipped on the grease, the arbitrator sustained the discharge.

Employee *E* was discharged for throwing a whipped cream

pie into the face of an outside efficiency expert while the expert was touring the plant. The arbitrator reinstated the employee with back pay for all but one day of the time lost and noted that the incident, while reprehensible, was not without humor.

Employee *F* was discharged following an incident with a female employee in which he grabbed her, pulled her to a couch, and attempted to kiss her. Categorizing the act as an indecent assault, the arbitrator sustained the discharge.

Employee *G* was discharged following an incident in which he exposed himself to two female employees in the lunchroom. The arbitrator, finding the act to be repugnant and deserving of punishment, nevertheless held that discharge was too severe.

Guidelines

Where an employee's conduct demonstrates a wanton disregard for the safety of others or of property, misconduct will be sufficient to warrant discharge, even though the harm caused thereby may have been unintentional.

Where an employee's conduct has a racial or sexual tone and is directed toward someone of that race or sex, the conduct will deserve a more severe penalty than if it had not.

Relevant Cases

Alumax Extrusions (Miller), 81 LA 722
University of Missouri (Yarowsky), 78 LA 417
United States Internal Revenue Service (Edes), 77 LA 19
Abbott & Co. (Dworkin), 76 LA 339
Flat River Glass Co. (Newmark), 76 LA 946
Godchaux-Henderson Sugar Co. (Barnhart), 75 LA 377
Kroger Co. (Berns), 75 LA 290
Monsanto Chemical Intermediates Co. (Penfield), 75 LA 592
Ralston Purina Co. (Brown), 75 LA 313
Russer Foods (Grant), 75 LA 305
Union Commerce Bank (Ipavec), 75 LA 1246
Hilo Coast Processing Co. (Tanaka), 74 LA 236
Kroger Co. (Doering), 74 LA 785

St. Regis Paper Co. (Kaufman), 74 LA 1281
Clay Equipment (Carter), 73 LA 817
Perfection American Co. (Flannagan), 73 LA 520
Kroger Co. (Sabella), 72 LA 540
Pioneer Transit Mix Co. (Darrow), 72 LA 206
W-L Molding Co. (Howlett), 72 LA 1065
Bechtel Corp. (Raffaele), 71 LA 1049
Bowman Transportation (Goodman), 71 LA 342
Memorial Hospital (Sinicropi), 71 LA 1252
Powermatic/Houdaille (Cocalis), 71 LA 54
Union Camp Corp. (Hardy), 71 LA 886
Ozark Lead Co. (Belcher), 69 LA 1227
Southeast Container Corp. (Scidenberg), 69 LA 884
LTV Aerospace Corp. (Moore), 65 LA 195

2   *The atmosphere of the workplace must not be such that the activity appears to be condoned or tolerated.*

Examples

Employee *A* was discharged for fighting, after he had knocked an employee into a machine which caused severe lacerations in the employee's arm. *A* claimed that the accident took place during the course of a friendly wrestling match with another employee. The other employee testified that *A* had assaulted him during the course of an argument about a local sports team. Other evidence was presented showing that arguments, bantering, and playful pushing were common occurrences in the workplace. The arbitrator reinstated the employee and remarked that, as the employer had tolerated similar activity in the past, it could not base its disciplinary action solely upon the outcome of one incident.

Employee *B* was given a three-day suspension for making obscene gestures and comments to a female employee. Noting that the employer apparently condoned such conduct in the plant because it allowed the employees to post lewd pictures and cartoons in their work areas, the arbitrator ordered the reduction of the penalty to a warning.

Employee *C* was discharged for placing a dead rat in the ladies' restroom. Finding that practical jokes were common in the workplace, the arbitrator ordered reinstatement with back pay.

Guidelines

The employer has an obligation to control employee conduct within the workplace. When its failure to exercise adequate control results in behavior which it considers to be reprehensible only in degree and not in kind, the employee cannot be severely disciplined.

Relevant Cases

University of Missouri (Yarowsky), 78 LA 417
Cavalier Corp. (Haemmel), 75 LA 253
Godchaux-Henderson Sugar Co. (Barnhart), 75 LA 377
New York Air Brake Co. (McDonnell), 75 LA 875
Alvey, Inc. (Roberts), 74 LA 835
Mead Packaging Co. (Ziskind), 74 LA 881
Kaiser Foundation Health Plan (Herring), 73 LA 1057
Viewpoint Nursing Home (Bard), 72 LA 1240

3   *The demeanor of an employee, following the misconduct and his or her apparent contrition, may indicate the appropriateness of the degree of discipline.*

Examples

Employee *A* was discharged for setting the apron ties of another employee on fire, which resulted in the employee's clothes becoming inflamed; the employee suffered severe burns and had to be hospitalized. Although concluding that *A*'s act was a wanton disregard for the other employee's safety, the arbitrator ordered reinstatement without back pay, upon *A*'s expression of deep regret and his assurance that such acts would not be committed in the future and that the result in this case was unintended.

Employee *B* was discharged, after he had put sugar in the gas tank of another employee's car which resulted in $750 in damages to the car. Although *B* admitted to his act and agreed to pay the damage, the arbitrator sustained the discharge on the grounds that the conduct was so completely calculated to cause damage that it indicated an unstable and undependable personality.

Guidelines

Where the arbitrator believes the conduct to have been isolated and there is a strong probability that it will not be repeated in the future, the arbitrator will not accept discharge as an appropriate form of disciplinary action.

Relevant Cases

Flat River Glass Co. (Newmark), 76 LA 946
Monsanto Chemical Intermediates Co. (Penfield), 75 LA 592
Tyrone Hydraulics (Murphy), 75 LA 672
Alvey, Inc. (Roberts), 74 LA 835
Perfection American Co. (Flannagan), 73 LA 520
General Electric Co. (Foreman), 71 LA 441
Bechtel Corp. (Raffaele), 71 LA 1049
Union Camp Corp. (Hardy), 71 LA 886
Ozark Lead Co. (Belcher), 69 LA 1227
Southeast Container Corp. (Seidenberg), 69 LA 884

Fighting

Key Points

1   *Where there is no rule against fighting or where the rule does not mandate discharge in all cases, discipline will depend upon whether the employee is the aggressor or a willing participant in the fight.*

Examples

Employees *A* and *B* were discharged for fighting where, following a quarrel about the nonpayment of a debt to *A* by *B*, *A* struck *B* with his fist. *B* retaliated and, when the fight was over, was the clear victor. Although *A* was the aggressor, the arbitrator sustained the discharge of both. Employees *C* and *D* were discharged for fighting where, following a quarrel about the nonpayment of a debt to *C* by *D*, *C* struck *D* with his fist. *D* grabbed *C* in defense and wrestled him to the ground. When the two combatants were separated, *C* went after *D* as he fled. Finding that *D* had acted in self-defense and had only repelled *C*'s attack, the arbitrator sustained the discharge of C but reinstated D.

Employees E and F were discharged for fighting where, following a quarrel, E struck F with his fist. F grabbed E and wrestled him to the ground, where they both struck each other until separated by other employees. The arbitrator found that, while E was the aggressor, F did not try to escape when the chance was presented. The arbitrator sustained the discharge of E and reinstated F without back pay, which was effectively a three-month suspension for F.

Guidelines

The employee who was struck first must act only in self-defense and only with enough force to repel the aggressor, if the employee is to avoid all discipline.

Relevant Cases

Stedman Machine Co. (Keenan), 85 LA 63
Marco Manufacturing Co. (Richman), 84 LA 134
Coca Cola Bottling Co. (Bickner), 83 LA 1172
G. Heilman Brewing Co. (Hilgert), 83 LA 829
General Dynamics (Kaufman), 81 LA 855
Nitec Paper Co. (Goodman), 75 LA 1
General Electric Co. (King), 73 LA 1248
Kraft Foods (Rose), 73 LA 493
Mobil Oil Corp. (Fox), 73 LA 993
Welch Foods (Gootnick), 73 LA 908
General Electric Co. (Foreman), 71 LA 441

2   *Fighting is not justified by provocation, but provocation may serve to reduce the degree of disciplinary action.*

Examples

Employee A was discharged for striking another employee. The employee had made a remark about a birthmark to be found on A's wife and indicated a knowledge of A's wife which exceeded normal expectations. The arbitrator, finding that A had been provoked, reduced the discharge to a suspension.

Employee B, a black, was discharged for striking another employee who had called him a "dumb nigger." The arbitrator elicited facts which indicated that the other employee had harassed *B* on other occasions as well. Concluding the *B* had been provoked, the arbitrator reduced the discharge to a suspension.

Employee *C* was discharged for striking an employee who had called him a "turkey." Finding that *C* had not been sufficiently provoked to justify his action, the arbitrator sustained the discharge.

Guidelines

The provocation must be great enough to result in a finding that the employee may have been momentarily driven to irrational action. Slight provocation will normally not be sufficient to mitigate the employer's disciplinary action.

Relevant Cases

Toledo Edison Co. (Duda), 84 LA 1289
G. Heilman Brewing Co. (Hilgert), 83 LA 829
Interstate Brands Corp. (Richman), 83 LA 497
San Diego Transit Corp. (Gentile), 83 LA 224
Apex International Alloys (Wright), 82 LA 747
Eagle Ottawa Leather Co. (Jason), 82 LA 493
Marion Power Shovel Division (Kates), 82 LA 1014
U.S. Stove Co. (Rothschild), 82 LA 965
Imperial Chevite (Hill), 81 LA 1083
Nitec Paper Co. (Goodman), 75 LA 1
Mobay Chemical Corp. (Weitzman), 74 LA 1113
General Electric Co. (King), 73 LA 1248
General Electric Co. (Foreman), 71 LA 441

3   *Where an employee uses, or threatens to use, a weapon in a fight with or an assault upon another employee, discharge is almost always warranted.*

Examples

Employee *A* was discharged, following a quarrel with another employee in which *A* had brandished a wrench and swore he would bash the other's head in. The arbitrator, finding the threat with a lethal weapon to be extreme as well as dangerous, sustained the discharge.

Employee *B*, a black, was discharged after he had thrown a tire iron at another employee who had called him a "half-civilized ape man." Even though *B* may have missed the other employee and even though he may have been greatly provoked, the arbitrator held that *B*'s action had been so life threatening that discharge was warranted.

Employee *C* was discharged following an argument with another employee during which *C* had waved a wrench. The wrench was a tool used by *C* in his work. The arbitrator, noting that there was no proof that *C* had been threatening the other employee with the wrench, reinstated *C*.

Guidelines

The use or threatened use of a weapon reveals an aspect of the character of the assailant which is so severe and predictable that an employer has the right, if not the duty, to terminate the employee summarily for the protection of all employees.

Relevant Cases

Eagle Ottawa Leather Co. (Jason), 82 LA 493
Nitec Paper Corp. (Goodman), 75 LA 1
Emery Industries (Gentile), 72 LA 110
Chatham Supermarket (Roumell), 71 LA 1084
General Electric Co. (Abrams), 71 LA 884

4   *Good work histories or other outside factors may mitigate severe discipline.*

Examples

Employees *A* and *B* were discharged for fighting after a quarrel about a debt. Neither could be found to have been the aggressor and both had been willing participants. It appeared, however, that both *A* and *B* had good work histories and, in fact, were friends. The arbitrator, noting that the two did not present a future threat to the peace of the workplace, reduced the discharges to suspensions.

Employees *C* and *D* became intoxicated at an impromptu party at the workplace on Christmas Eve. They began to argue and, then, to fight. Both were discharged. Noting the special circumstances created by the party, the arbitrator reduced the discharges to suspensions.

Employees *E* and *F* were both maintenance men, who had been called in by the employer to shore up an area along a stream in advance of an anticipated flood. They had worked 12 hours in the rain without a significant break. A quarrel broke out and ended in a fight; *E* and *F* were both discharged. The arbitrator found that the irrational behavior was caused by fatigue and the unusual working conditions and mitigated the discharges to suspensions.

Guidelines

Special circumstances, which involve unusual tension or fatigue, may serve to mitigate the discipline. It must appear that lessening the discipline will not cause, or stimulate, additional breaches of the peace at the workplace. In this respect, the totality of the situation must be examined.

Relevant Cases

ITT Higbie Manufacturing Co. (Shanker), 85 LA 859
Toledo Edison Co. (Duda), 84 LA 1289
Dole Can Plant (Tsukiyama), 83 LA 253
Lucky Stores (Sabo), 83 LA 760
Marion Power Shovel Division (Kates), 82 LA 1014
Transportation Labor (Sheehan), 76 LA 1249
Cavalier Corp. (Haemmel), 75 LA 253
Tyrone Hydraulics (Murphy), 75 LA 672
Alvey, Inc. (Roberts), 74 LA 835
Mobay Chemical Corp. (Weitzman), 74 LA 1113
Clay Equipment (Carter), 73 LA 817
Kraft Foods (Rose), 73 LA 493
Nickles Bakery (Letson), 73 LA 801
Chatham Supermarkets (Roumell), 71 LA 1084
General Electric Co. (Craver), 71 LA 337

Notes to Chapter 19

1. *Flat River Glass Co.* (Newmark), 76 LA 946; *Ozark Lead Co.* (Belcher), 69 LA 1227.

2. *United States Internal Revenue Serv.* (Edes), 77 LA 19; *Clay Equip.* (Carter), 73 LA 817; *Bechtel Corp.* (Raffaele), 71 LA 1049.

3. *University of Mo.* (Yarowsky), 78 LA 417; *Kroger Co.* (Berns), 75 LA 290; *Hilo Coast Processing Co.* (Tanaka), 74 LA 236.

4. *University of Mo., supra,* note 3; *Delaware River Port Auth.* (Raffaele), 76 LA 350; *General Servs. Admin.* (Avins), 76 LA 118; *Gateway Methodist Youth Center* (Miller), 75 LA 1177; *Alumax Foils* (Hilgert), 73 LA 250; *Kroger Co.* (Sabella), 72 LA 540; *Bowman Transp.* (Goodman), 71 LA 342.

5. *Monsanto Chem. Intermediates Co.* (Penfield), 75 LA 592; *General Elec. Co.* (King), 73 LA 1248; *Chatham Supermkts.* (Roumell), 71 LA 1084; *Midland Ross Corp.* (Dallas), 65 LA 1151.

6. *University of Mo., supra,* note 3; *Godchaux-Henderson Sugar Co.* (Barnhart), 75 LA 377; *New York Air Brake Co.* (McDonnell), 75 LA 875; *Alvey, Inc.* (Roberts), 74 LA 835; *Mead Packaging Co.* (Ziskind), 74 LA 881; *Kaiser Found. Health Plan* (Herring), 73 LA 1057; *Viewpoint Nursing Home* (Bard), 72 LA 1240.

7. *Perfection Am. Co.* (Flannagan), 73 LA 520; *W-L Molding Co.* (Howlett), 72 LA 1065; *Southeast Container Corp.* (Seidenberg), 69 LA 884.

8. *Perfection Am. Co., supra,* note 7.

9. *Southeast Container Corp., supra,* note 7.

10. *W-L Molding Co., supra,* note 7.

11. *Chatham Supermkts., supra,* note 5.

12. *Kroger Co.* (Doering), 74 LA 785.

13. *Memorial Hosp.* (Sinicropi), 71 LA 1252.

14. *Bowman Transp., supra,* note 4.

15. *Union Camp Corp.* (Hardy), 71 LA 886.

16. *LTV Aerospace Corp.* (Moore), 65 LA 195.

17. *Kaiser Found. Health Plan, supra,* note 6.

18. *Cavalier Corp.* (Haemmel), 75 LA 253.

19. *Alvey, Inc., supra,* note 6.

20. *Tyrone Hydraulics* (Murphy), 75 LA 672.

21. *Chatham Supermkts., supra,* note 5.

22. *Powermatic/Houdaille* (Cocalis), 71 LA 54.

23. *St. Regis Paper Co.* (Kaufman), 74 LA 1281.

24. *Monsanto Chem. Intermediates Co., supra,* note 5.

25. *Godchaux-Henderson Sugar Co., supra,* note 6.

26. *University of Mo., supra,* note 3.

27. *Kraft Foods* (Rose), 73 LA 493; *Mobil Oil Corp.* (Fox), 73 LA 993; *Rochester Methodist Hosp.* (Heneman), 72 LA 276.

28. *Rochester Methodist Hosp., supra,* note 27.

29. *Kraft Foods, supra,* note 27.

30. *Welch Foods* (Gootnick), 73 LA 908.

31. *Mobil Oil Corp., supra,* note 27.

32. *Flat River Glass Co., supra* note 1.

33. *New York Air Brake Co., supra,* note 6.

34. *Midland Ross Corp., supra,* note 5.

35. *Alvey, Inc., supra,* note 6; *Perfection Am. Co., supra,* note 7; *General Elec Co.* (Craver), 71 LA 337; *Union Camp Corp., supra,* note 15.

36. *Mobay Chem. Corp.* (Weitzman), 74 LA 1113 (provocation

does not exonerate the employee for his actions); *General Elec. Co.,
supra* note 5 (verbal provocation may be a reason for physical violence, but not a justification).

37. *Nitec Paper Corp.* (Goodman), 75 LA 1 (behavior might have
been justified if for self-defense); *General Elec. Co.* (Foreman, 71 LA
142 (both employees claimed self-defense; both provoked the fight;
and both discharges were sustained).

38. *Nitec Paper Corp., supra* note 37; *General Elec. Co., supra,*
note 37.

39. *Ozark Lead Co., supra,* note 1.

40. *Monsanto Chem. Intermediates Co., supra,* note 5.

41. *Gateway United Methodist Youth Center, supra,* note 4; *Godchaux-Henderson Sugar Co., supra,* note 6; *Ralston Purina Co.*
(Brown), 75 LA 313.

42. *VA Medical Center* (Ludolf), 74 LA 830.

43. *Gateway United Methodist Youth Center, supra,* note 4.

44. *General Elec. Co.* (Abrams), 71 LA 884.

45. *General Elec. Co., supra,* note 5.

46. *General Elec. Co., supra,* note 37.

47. *Mobay Chem. Corp., supra,* note 36.

48. *Transportation Labor* (Sheehan), 76 LA 1249; *Nickles Bakery* (Letson), 73 LA 801.

49. *General Elec. Co., supra,* note 35.

50. *Alvey, Inc., supra,* note 6.

51. *Nitec Paper Corp., supra,* note 37.

52. *Mobil Oil Corp., supra,* note 27.

53. *General Elec. Co., supra,* note 37; *General Elec. Co., supra,*
note 5.

54. *Emery Indus.* (Gentile), 72 LA 110.

55. *See also LTV Aerospace Corp., supra,* note 16.

56. *Abbott & Co.* (Dworkin), 76 LA 339.

57. *Kroger Co., supra,* note 3.

58. *Russer Foods* (Grant), 75 LA 305.

59. *Ralston Purina Co., supra,* note 41; *Kroger Co.* (Doering),
74 LA 785; *Pioneer Transit Mix Co.* (Darrow), 72 LA 206.

60. *Union Commerce Bank* (Ipavec), 75 LA 1246.

61. *Clay Equip., supra,* note 2.

62. *Ozark Lead Co., supra,* note 1.

63. *Flat River Glass Co., supra,* note 1.

64. *Bechtel Corp., supra,* note 2; *Southeast Container Corp.* (Seidenberg), 69 LA 884.

65. *Kroger Co., supra,* note 4.

66. *United States Internal Revenue Serv., supra,* note 2.

20

Moonlighting

Issue   Whether an employee may be discharged or otherwise disciplined for moonlighting in the absence of a specific prohibition against outside employment in the collective bargaining agreement or in written company policy.

Principle   When the collective bargaining agreement or company policy manual is silent on the issue, an employee may not be discharged or otherwise disciplined merely because he or she has obtained outside employment. For discipline to be sustained, the moonlighting must have resulted in some independent grounds for discharge or disciplinary action. An employer may discipline an employee who has an otherwise unobjectionable outside job, however, if the employee has attempted to deceive the employer on the issue. The employer, nevertheless, cannot discharge an employee for the deception, except in extreme cases amounting to gross dishonesty.

Considerations   1. Whether the outside job leads to excessive absenteeism, tardiness, or decreased work efficiency or otherwise interferes with the employee's duties at the workplace;
2. Whether the outside job places the employee in a position of competing with the primary employer or gives rise to a conflict of interest;
3. Whether the employee acts dishonestly toward the employer either to conceal

328

his or her employment elsewhere or to enable the employee to perform the obligations of the other job.

Discussion Generally speaking, an employee's off-duty activities are not open to question by an employer. Arbitrators consistently reaffirm the principle that, absent a prohibition against moonlighting in the collective bargaining agreement or in a policy manual, an employee who obtains outside employment cannot be discharged or otherwise disciplined for the fact alone.[1]

The primary focus in each case is on what, if any, was the adverse effect of the employer's second job on the legitimate interests of the primary employer. Discipline has been found to be justified where the employer has been able to show a direct relation between the second job and the employee's absenteeism or lateness or in the employee's reduced efficiency or poor job performance. Or, the employer must be able to show that the second job is in competition with the primary one.[2] Discharge is the most common penalty imposed. As is generally the case with disciplinary measures, issues such as the prior record of the employee, prior warnings to the employee, and consistency in the employer's application of discipline for the given offenses are important to arbitrators.

It is not uncommon for employees who hold two jobs to obtain a leave of absence or to take sick leave from the one employer, rather than simply not showing up for work, while continuing to work for the other. When the employer learns of such an employee's deception, it typically fires the employee. In cases of this kind which reach arbitration, an employee will be reinstated where it appears the employee is physically unable to work on his or her primary job but because of differing responsibilities is able to continue at the second job or where it does not appear that continuing the second job will prolong the employee's leave. However, if the employee has deceived the employer with regard to the secondary employment, a suspension rather than a discharge will be generally approved, absent prior discipline for similar causes which would justify discharge.[3]

An employer may unilaterally adopt a company policy against secondary employment by a competitor or against activities which might compromise with the company's best interests, so long as the policy is reasonable and not in conflict with the collective bargaining agreement. Violations of such rules generally will be considered "just cause" for discharge; however, the adoption of such a policy is not a prerequisite to a valid discharge when the employee holds a job which is in direct competition with the employer.[4]

Key Points

1   *The outside job must have led to excessive absenteeism, tardiness, decreased efficiency on the job, or some other work deficiency.*

Examples

Employee *A* obtained a second full-time job. His foreman reported that *A* is a good worker and appeared to be neither sleepy nor fatigued. Approximately seven weeks later *A* was involved in two incidents leading to spoilage of company goods. The employer admitted at arbitration that the incidents would not have lead to discharge were it not for the second job. The arbitrator reinstated the employee with full back pay, citing the employer's failure to establish a causal relationship between the moonlighting and the spoilage incidents.

Employee *B* operated a side business on his own which did not compete with that of the employer. During his six years of employment with his primary employer, *B* was absent from work 137 full days and 89 partial days. He was discharged following several warnings and one suspension for excessive absenteeism and tardiness. The grievance was denied by the arbitrator.

Guidelines

To sustain discipline, the employer must show that the action against the employee was for just cause due to a violation of some other rule of conduct. The fact that the precipitating cause was the employee's moonlighting can be used as a reason to deny mitigation on the grounds that the employee did not have the requisite loyalty to the primary employer or adequate concern for the job, which any employer may expect.

Relevant Cases

> *Microdot, Inc.* (Kelliher), 66 LA 177
> *Randle-Eastern Ambulance Service* (Sherman), 65 LA 394
> *Gas Service Co.* (Bronson), 63 LA 293
> *W. R. Grace & Co.* (Boals), 62 LA 779

2 *The employee cannot deceive the primary employer by misusing the benefits, such as sick time or leaves of absence, accorded the employee by the primary employer.*

Examples

Employee *A* was a gravedigger and held a second job as a bartender. He called in sick to his gravedigger job, complaining of an injured arm, but worked that night as a bartender. He was discharged. The arbitrator reinstated *A* with full back pay, noting that the employee did, in fact, have an injured arm, which prevented him from doing his normal work but not from performing his second job.

Employee *B* received an annual leave of absence to leave town because of severe hay fever. One year he remained in town for part of the time and continued to work at a part-time job, but had lied to his employer about it. He was discharged. The arbitrator reinstated the employee, finding that the part-time job did not prolong the employee's leave of absence. Back pay was denied, however, because of the employee's deception.

Employee *C* was scheduled to work on Saturday because of a shipping emergency at the primary employer's plant. *C* called in sick but worked at his second job. He was discharged. At the arbitration *C* defended the deception by saying that he would have lost his second job had he not reported to work and that he did not seek to be relieved from his Saturday assignment for fear his primary employer would have fired him. The arbitrator reinstated the employee without back pay and warned him that a second incident of favoring the second job over the primary one would be cause for discharge.

Employee *D* had a second job in the evenings. He had told his primary employer that his wife was partially disabled and for that reason he could never work overtime. As a result, other employees were compelled to work more overtime than they desired. When the deception was discovered, the employee was discharged. The arbitrator sustained the discharge.

Guidelines

An isolated occurrence of an employee's deception may be a cause for discipline but not for discharge. However, a prolonged pattern of deception which has an adverse effect on other employees or which abuses a benefit, such as sick leave, may be cause for summary discharge.

Relevant Cases

Consumer Plastics Corp. (Talent), 83 LA 870
Microdot, Inc. (Kelliher), 66 LA 177
Rock Hill Printing & Finishing (Whyte), 64 LA 856
Mercoid Corp. (Kossoff), 63 LA 941
I. B. Goodman Manufacturing Co. (Geissinger), 62 LA 732
Rowe International (Turkus), 55 LA 1298
Cincinnati Tool Co. (Kates), 52 LA 818
Harvard Manufacturing Co. (Kates), 51 LA 1098
Danbury Cemetery Association (Stutz), 42 LA 447
United Engineering & Foundry Co. (Kates), 37 LA 1095
Janitorial Service (Whelan), 33 LA 902

3   *The second job cannot place the employee in a position of competing with the primary employer or give rise to a conflict of interest.*

Examples

Employee *A* operated a business in his home where he provided on a private basis the same services as his employer. The employer issued a warning to *A* to cease the operation of his private business. The warning went unheeded, and *A* was discharged. The arbitrator denied the grievance.

Employee *B's* primary employment was with a company which sold new machines. On the side, he purchased and repaired used machines of the same sort for resale. Following two warnings the employee was discharged. The arbitrator reinstated the employee with full back pay, stating that the employee was not in direct competition with the primary employer because the markets were sufficiently distinct.

An employer, engaged in the sale and repair of televisions, had attempted unsuccessfully to have inserted into the collective bargaining agreement a provision which prohibited employees from competing with the firm by working with other similar employers when not directly rendering services to it. It also had unsuccessfully solicited pledges from employees not to engage in similar activities either on their own or for another company in competition with it. Employee *C* was discharged for competing with the company by repairing televisions in his home for which he would charge. The discharge was sustained on the basis that the employee's conduct was so destructive to the employer that the prior unsuccessful attempts to obtain agreements were not indicative of an agreement by the employer to allow such conduct. The arbitrator held that there would have to be a specific and clear agreement to the contrary before the employer's primary interest could be overridden.

Guidelines

An employee may be discharged for taking steps to form a business which would compete with his or her employer, if the field is a highly competitive one or involves trade secrets.

Relevant Cases

Country Club Markets (Bognanno), 85 LA 286
Jacksonville Shipyards (Taylor), 74 LA 1066
Alaska Sales & Service Co. (Axon), 73 LA 164
I. B. Goodman Manufacturing Co. (Geissinger), 62 LA 732
Sperry Rand Co. (Koven), 57 LA 68
Heppenstall Co. (Shister), 55 LA 1044
United Fuel Gas Co. (Whyte), 54 LA 942
Utility Tree Service (Karasick), 53 LA 1176
Phillips Petroleum (Caraway), 47 LA 372
Pipe Coupling Manufacturers (McCoy), 46 LA 1009
Janitorial Service (Whelan), 33 LA 902

Notes to Chapter 20

1. *See Albertson's, Inc.* (Christopher), 65 LA 1042; *Randle-Eastern Ambulance Serv.* (Sherman), 65 LA 394; *Rock Hill Printing & Finishing Co.*, (Whyte), 64 LA 856; *Gas Serv. Co.* (Bronson), 63 LA 293.

2. *See Microdot, Inc.* (Kelliher), 66 LA 177; *Gas Serv. Co., supra,* note 1; *W. R. Grace & Co.* (Boals), 62 LA 779 (discharge denied).

3. *See Microdot, Inc., supra,* note 2; *Rock Hill Printing & Finishing Co., supra,* note 1; *Mercoid Corp.* (Kosoff), 63 LA 941; *I. B. Goodman Mfg. Co* (Geissinger), 62 LA 732; *Rowe Int'l* (Turkus), 55 LA 1298; *Harvard Mfg. Co.* (Kates), 51 LA 1098.

4. *See Jacksonville Shipyards* (Taylor), 74 LA 1066; *Alaska Sales & Serv. Co.* (Axon), 73 LA 164; *I. B. Goodman Mfg. Co., supra,* note 3; *Sperry Rand Corp.* (Koven), 57 LA 68; *Heppenstall Co.* (Shister), 55 LA 1044; *United Fuel Gas Co.* (Whyte), 54 LA 942; *Utility Tree Serv.* (Karasick), 53 LA 1176.

21

Poor Performance

Issue Whether an employee may be discharged or otherwise disciplined for poor performance.

Principle An employee may be discharged or otherwise disciplined for poor performance where the employer has established and communicated a reasonable performance standard prior to the date of the discharge or discipline, where there is evidence that the employee failed to meet the standard, and where the employee was accorded progressive discipline.

Considerations
1. Whether the employer had established a reasonable performance standard prior to the discipline of the employee;
2. Whether the standard of performance was adequately communicated to the employee;
3. Whether the employee's performance failed to meet the standard;
4. Whether the employee was accorded progressive discipline.

Discussion Generally, arbitrators will uphold discipline for poor productivity only if the employer had established a standard, prior to the disciplinary action, by which the employee's productivity can be measured. At least one arbitrator, however, has held that if the labor agreement does not require a standard, the employer may discipline an employee for poor productivity without showing that the employee failed to meet a pre-established norm.[1]

Arbitrators generally recognize that management has an inherent right to set reasonable production standards and to discipline an employee for failure to meet them.[2] Only clear language in the labor agreement prohibiting the establishment of standards or of quotas can prevent an employer from doing so.[3]

Arbitrators tend to prefer productivity standards which are based on objective, measurable criteria.[4] At least one arbitrator, however, has approved somewhat subjective standards: In *International Shoe Co.*, Arbitrator Roberts noted that under the express terms of the labor agreement the employer could not establish production quotas for its employees, but he stated that the employer could, nevertheless, demand that its employees do an "honest, fair day's work."[5] Recognizing a need, however, for some objective way to judge an employee's performance, Roberts also stated that the employer could determine if an employee had put in a "fair day's work" by comparing that individual employee's production with the production of other employees (taking into account the normal variations among individual workers). Emphasizing that this method of measuring an employee's production was not the same as establishing a quota, he held that the employer had acted permissibly in concluding that an employee had not put in a fair day's work and, subsequently, suspending him for three days.

It should be noted that not all arbitrators approve of productivity standards based on the total average production of all employees. For example, in *Union Carbide Corp.*, the arbitrator refused to uphold such a standard, stating that the standard was invalid because it did not take into consideration individual work problems, such as those which employees had with machines or casings.[6]

Arbitrators will decline to uphold discipline for poor production, if the employee is unaware of the performance standard. The issue which has periodically arisen, therefore, is what constitutes the proper communication of the standard. In *A. P. Green Refractories*, the employer conducted a time study after there had been a decrease in the productivity of a group of brick hackers.[7] After finishing the study, a supervisor met with the four-member hacking crew and told them that productivity had been set at 884 bricks per work hour. Four days later, the employer sent a letter to the union detailing the new standard. After an additional three days, the productivity level of the hacking crew did not improve, and the employer discharged all of its members. Despite the union's contention that the time study and the resulting production standard were not adequately communicated to the union, the arbitrator held that the company had properly communicated the standards to the employees and to the union and upheld the discharges. The arbitrator did not indicate whether the oral communication to the crew or the written notices to the union constituted the proper method of notifying the employees of such a standard.

As might be expected, arbitrators have an easier time upholding discipline where the employer can document, through extensive record keeping, an employee's consistent failure to meet productivity standards. For example, in *Florsheim Shoe Co.*, the company maintained a weekly "point system" indicating the amount of piecework done by employees, and the discharge of an employee, who had consistently failed to meet the standard each week for six and one-half months, was upheld.[8]

Other types of evidence, however, are considered to be less reliable. In this connection, one recurring problem is whether a supervisor's testimony constitutes sufficient evidence to support disciplinary action. The predominant view appears to be that whereas the judgment or opinions of supervisors deserve consideration, they are not of much evidentiary value without the support of accompanying objective evidence.[9] However, at least one arbitrator has upheld a discharge based solely on a supervisor's testimony that the grievant was the worst performer in the entire work force.[10]

Several arbitrators have noted that where discharge or other discipline for poor production arises, not because an employee is guilty of fault or wrongdoing, but because the employee is not adequately efficient, it is incumbent upon management to warn the employee about his or her shortcomings.[11] Accordingly, in these cases, the issue often arises whether the employee has been adequately warned about his or her poor productivity. Generally, and particularly in the case of long-time employees, arbitrators insist that prior to being discharged, an employee must at least have been warned several times about poor productivity.[12]

One sub-issue which has arisen in these cases is whether the individual employee has been personally warned about his or her shortcomings. In *Canron, Inc.*, the employer sent two general notices in pay envelopes to welders, warning them that employees who made defective welds would be subject to discharge.[13] After an employee had made a defective weld, the employer discharged him. The arbitrator converted the discharge into a one-month suspension, holding that although the grievant had clearly violated the welding standard, he had been inadequately warned. The arbitrator stated that the general notice to all the employees did not sufficiently warn the grievant that he would be discharged if he made a defective weld.

In *Montague Machine Co.*, the arbitrator reduced a discharge to a suspension where the evidence showed several previous warnings about poor performance.[14] The arbitrator concluded, however, that these warnings could have been construed by the employee to have been nothing more than casual conversations. Accordingly, the arbitrator found that the employee had not been given sufficient notice of his poor performance to justify a discharge.[15]

A different view was taken in *City of Toledo*, where the arbitrator stated that a personal knowledge of shortcomings can be imputed to an employee.[16] In this case, the police department directed its accident investigation officers to issue more traffic citations, and when three officers failed to increase their number of citations, they were transferred. Although the arbitrator reinstated two of the transferred officers, concluding that they had been inadequately warned, he upheld the transfer of a third officer. That officer, stated the arbitrator, had issued so few citations that he had to have been aware that his performance was substandard.[17]

In only one recent case has an arbitrator held that notice of poor productivity need not be given prior to discharge. In *Tex-A-Panel Manufacturing Co.*, the employer discharged a machine operator without having previously warned him of his poor performance.[18] The arbitrator upheld the discharge, emphasizing that nothing in the labor agreement required previous notice of poor performance.

Several arbitrators have emphasized that in addition to providing adequate notice to an employee whose productivity is substandard, an employer must counsel the employee. The rationale is that the employee has committed no infraction and can be trained to improve his or her performance.[19] In one case, the arbitrator reinstated a discharged employee, finding that the employer had made no attempt to counsel and to rehabilitate the employee.[20]

In *City of Toledo*, the arbitrator found that one of the discharged police officers had responded to counseling, and noted that, although the officer had not quite met the established standard for the number of traffic citations to be issued, he had responded well enough to the counseling that discharge was unwarranted.[21]

Consequently, in order that disciplinary action for poor performance be upheld in arbitration, it appears vital that the employee be subject to progressive discipline. This, in part, follows naturally from the need to apprise the employee of the level of production expected of him or her. However, it is also necessary to put the employee on notice that if his or her production does not come up to standard, the employee will be terminated or otherwise disciplined. Arbitrators place great emphasis upon the need for progressive discipline, and they will often allow reinstatement of an employee, who they acknowledge is a poor performer, because of the lack of such discipline.[22] A feature closely related to progressive discipline is the arbitrators' consideration of the employee's prior work record. In this respect, a discharge may be upheld where there have been numerous prior problems—not necessarily all the same problems as that which caused the discharge—even though the final cause cited would not warrant discharge by itself.[23] Conversely, a lengthy record of good performance and conduct will make a discharge less likely to be sustained.[24]

Key Points

1   *The employer must have established a reasonable performance standard prior to the discipline of the employee.*

Examples

Employee *A* was disciplined for deburring 20 percent fewer gears than the average of the other employees in his work area. The discipline was sustained, when it was shown that, although there was no actual performance standard, the employee's substantial deviation from the norm had been noted for some time and had been a subject of discussion with the employee.

Employee *B* was disciplined for failing to meet an established productivity standard. At the arbitration, it was shown that the average performance of most of the employees was below the standard, and an expert testified that the level of production demanded by the employer exceeded the reasonable capabilities of employees working under the present conditions in the company. Although the performance of *B* was significantly below the average, the discipline was voided by the arbitrator on the basis that the standard was unreasonable.

Employee *C* was disciplined for failing to meet an established performance standard. The arbitrator sustained the grievance when the employer could not establish the objective and rational basis for the standard and could not show that the performance of the other two employees subject to the standard was not due to unusual or special abilities.

Employee *D* was disciplined for poor performance when he failed to meet an established standard of production. The arbitrator voided the discipline on the basis that the standard had been established only one week prior to the discipline and appeared to have been established for the sole purpose of justifying the disciplinary action. The arbitrator held that the employee was not given sufficient opportunity to bring his performance up to the employer's new standard.

Guidelines

The employer must be able to show that its performance standard has been based upon some rational determination of normal capabilities of other employees working under the existing conditions and that the standard is objective. Further, the standard must have been established sufficiently in advance of its enforcement to permit employees to adjust their work habits and techniques to meet the standard.

Relevant Cases

Adams Print Works (Sachs), 84 LA 443
Rockwell International Corp. (Feldman), 84 LA 496
Tribune-Star Publishing Co. (Seidman), 82 LA 714
National Fire Sprinkler Corp. (Madden), 82 LA 391
General Electric Co. (Moore), 74 LA 1278
City of Toledo (Heinsz), 70 LA 216
Union Carbide Corp. (Jones), 70 LA 201
Eaton Corp. (Kasper), 69 LA 71
Great Atlantic & Pacific Tea Co. (Seidenberg), 68 LA 485

Stoppenbach, Inc. (Lee), 68 LA 553
Associated Grocers of St. Louis (Dugan), 66 LA 55
Allied Employers (Hedges), 65 LA 270
Northern Telecom (Sembower), 65 LA 405
A. P. Green Refractories Co. (Williams), 64 LA 885
King's Command Meats (Kleinsorge), 60 LA 491
Houston Publishers Assoc. (Duff), 58 LA 321
Varbros Tool & Die Co. (Kabaker), 42 LA 440

2 *The employee must have been made aware of the standard.*

Examples

Employee *A* was disciplined for having a production level of 20 percent below that of other employees involved in deburring gear blanks. The employer had no published production standard, and *A* only learned of his below average performance at the time of his discipline. The grievance was sustained by the arbitrator.

Employee *B* was a pieceworker with a guaranteed base wage. Each week she was paid the higher of either her piece-based rate or her guaranteed wage and, when paid the guaranteed wage, was given a note with her pay indicating what her piece-based wage would have been. After receiving a guaranteed wage four weeks in a row, *B* was disciplined. The discipline was sustained. The arbitrator noted that the notice in the pay envelope was sufficient for any reasonable person to know that her or his performance was substandard and that such a performance could not be acceptable to the employer over a sustained period.

Employee *C* was given a three-day suspension for poor production. Although the employer did not have a published performance standard, the arbitrator sustained the suspension and held that, as the employee had received two warnings for low productivity before the suspension, she had received proper notice of her poor performance.

Guidelines

There must be a reasonable basis for an arbitrator to conclude that the employee knew or had to have known that his or her productivity was below what the employer reasonably expected.

Relevant Cases

Adams Print Works (Sachs), 84 LA 443
Tribune-Star Publishing Co. (Seidman), 82 LA 714
Fort Wayne Community Schools (Deitsch), 78 LA 928
Montague Machine Co. (Bornstein), 78 LA 172
County of Santa Clara (Concepcion), 76 LA 7
Florsheim Shoe Co. (Roberts), 74 LA 705
Lash Distribution (Darrow), 74 LA 274
VRN International (Vause), 74 LA 806
Interstate Brands Corp. (Hamby), 73 LA 771
Canron, Inc. (Marcus), 72 LA 1310
Eaton Corp. (Kasper), 69 LA 71
Stoppenbach, Inc. (Lee), 68 LA 553
Associated Grocers of St. Louis (Dugan), 66 LA 55
Midwest Telephone Co. (Witney), 66 LA 311
West Chemical Products (Dykstra), 63 LA 610
Uarco Co. (Gibson), 58 LA 1021
Varbros Tool & Die Co. (Kabaker), 42 LA 440

3   *The employee's performance must be proven to have been below the productivity standard.*

Examples

Employee *A* was disciplined for poor performance when his production fell below the standard for the second week in three months. The arbitrator, stating that the poor performance of the employee was too occasional to justify discipline, voided the employer's disciplinary actions.

Employee *B* was disciplined for poor performance on the basis that his production in the polishing department of a striking-tool manufacturing plant was 20 percent below that of other employees in the department. Noting that there was a possibility that the tools polished by the grievant were significantly more difficult than those of other employees during the same period, the arbitrator sustained the grievance for lack of proof.

Employee *C* was disciplined for poor performance when her production records showed that in six of the prior eight weeks she fell below the standard by an average of 2 percent. Holding that the variance was *de minimis* and possibly due to legitimate reasons, the arbitrator voided the discipline.

Employee *D* was given a three-day disciplinary suspension when her production was shown to have averaged 2 percent below the standard in six of the prior eight weeks. The employee defended on the basis that the deviation was *de minimis.* The employer presented evidence that throughout her term of employment *D's* performance had always been marginal, and that the discipline had followed only after the employer had exhausted other remedial measures. Further, the arbitrator found that *D* spent an inordinate amount of time on the telephone and had an unsatisfactory attendance and tardiness record. The discipline was sustained.

Guidelines

Discipline may not be sustained if the poor performance was only occasional or was de minimis, except where other facts demonstrate that the employee had a poor attitude.

Relevant Cases

Day & Zimmerman, Inc. (Dilts), 85 LA 1151
Adams Print Works (Sachs), 84 LA 443
Dresser Industries (Harrison), 83 LA 577
Oklahoma State AFL-CIO (Yaney), 82 LA 657
Tribune-Star Publishing Co. (Seidman), 82 LA 714
Universal Foods Corp. (Belcher), 82 LA 105
Pet, Inc. (Jason), 76 LA 292
Florsheim Shoe Co. (Roberts), 74 LA 705
Midwest Telephone Co. (Witney), 66 LA 311
King's Command Meats (Kleinsorge), 60 LA 491
Houston Publishers Assoc. (Duff), 58 LA 321
United States Plywood-Champion Papers (Amis), 56 LA 165
Jonco Aircraft (Merrill), 22 LA 1819

4   *The employee must have been accorded progressive discipline.*

Examples

Employee *A* was discharged for insubstantial production. Previously, *A* had been warned and told to increase his production. When he did not improve within the month after the warning, he was discharged. The arbitrator reinstated the employee, because *A* had not been accorded the full progressive system.

Employee *B* was discharged after repeated warnings about poor production. The employee was reinstated without back pay on the grounds that his most recent warning did not adequately put the employee on notice that he would be discharged, unless his productivity improved.

Guidelines

The employee's discipline will not be sustained unless he has been warned, given an adequate opportunity to improve, and advised of the effects of not satisfying the employer's standards.

Relevant Cases

Adams Print Works (Sachs), 84 LA 443
Oklahoma State AFL-CIO (Yaney), 82 LA 657
Tribune-Star Publishing Co. (Seidman), 82 LA 714
Los Angeles Judicial District (Draznin), 81 LA 463
Fort Wayne Community Schools (Deitsch), 78 LA 928
Montague Machine Co. (Bornstein), 78 LA 172
County of Santa Clara (Concepcion), 76 LA 7
Florsheim Shoe Co. (Roberts), 74 LA 705
City of Toledo (Heinsz), 70 LA 216
Eaton Corp. (Kasper), 69 LA 71
Stoppenbach, Inc. (Lee), 68 LA 553
Midwest Telephone Co. (Witney), 66 LA 311
Bethlehem Steel Corp. (Harkless), 58 LA 363
San Francisco Redevelopment Agency (Koven), 57 LA 1149
Varbros Tool & Die Co. (Kabaker), 42 LA 440

Notes to Chapter 21

1. *Eaton Corp.* (Kasper), 69 LA 71 (suspension upheld of employee who deburred clutches too slowly).

2. *City of Toledo* (Heinsz), 70 LA 216, 220; *Great Atl. & Pac. Tea Co.* (Seidenberg), 68 LA 485, 488; *Allied Employers* (Hedges), 65 LA 270, 273.

3. *See International Shoe Co.* (Roberts), 68 LA 444.

4. *See, e.g., Northern Telecom* (Sembower), 65 LA 405 (assembly worker standards were based on a methods-time-measurement system developed at a university); *A. P. Green Refractories Co.* (Wil-

liams), 64 LA 885 (brick workers' productivity standard was established by long-term detailed study).

5. *International Shoe Co., supra,* note 3.

6. *Union Carbide Corp.* (Jones), 70 LA 201.

7. *A. P. Green Refractories Co., supra,* note 4.

8. *Florsheim Shoe Co.* (Roberts), 74 LA 705.

9. *Midwest Tel. Co.* (Witney), 66 LA 311; *see also Jonco Aircraft* (Merrill), 22 LA 1819.

10. *Pet, Inc.* (Jason), 76 LA 292.

11. *See, e.g., Florsheim Shoe Co., supra,* note 8.

12. *Florsheim Shoe Co., supra* note 8 (the discharge of a 10-year employee was upheld); *West Chem. Prods.* (Dykstra), 63 LA 610 (the discharge of a 25-year employee was upheld where he had received at least six warning letters of a seven-year period).

13. *Canron, Inc.* (Marcus), 72 LA 1310.

14. *Montague Mach. Co.* (Bornstein), 78 LA 172.

15. *See also Fort Wayne Community Schools* (Deitsch), 78 LA 928.

16. *City of Toledo, supra,* note 2.

17. *See West Chem. Prods., supra,* note 12.

18. *Tex-A-Panel Mfg. Co.* (Ray), 62 LA 272.

19. *See County of Santa Clara* (Concepcion), 76 LA 7; *Florsheim Shoe Co., supra,* note 8.

20. *Midwest Tel. Co., supra,* note 9 at 315.

21. *City of Toledo, supra,* note 2.

22. For example, *see Eaton Corp., supra,* note 1 (the suspension was upheld, because the employee had been warned that he would face suspension if his production did not improve); *Stoppenbach, Inc.* (Lee), 68 LA 553 (the arbitrator emphasized the employee's prior suspension and warning about discharge in denying the grievance over the discharge); *San Francisco Redev. Agency* (Koven), 57 LA 1149 (a record which the arbitrator stated was "ordinarily a clear justification for discharge" did not support a discharge in that case, because there was a lack of progressive discipline).

23. *Bethlehem Steel Corp.* (Harkless), 58 LA 363.

24. *Varbros Tool & Die Co.* (Kabaker), 42 LA 440.

22

Work Slowdowns and Stoppages

Issue Whether an employee may be discharged or otherwise disciplined for engaging in a work slowdown or stoppage.

Principle An employee may be discharged or otherwise disciplined for engaging in a work slowdown or stoppage where it is established that an interruption to production in fact occurred; that the employee participated in, led, or attempted to cause the interruption; and, that there are no mitigating circumstances which either justify the conduct or warrant a lessening of the penalty.

Considerations

1. Whether the work slowdown or stoppage (or attempted work slowdown or stoppage) and the employee's participation is established to the extent that substantial weight is given the credible evidence;
2. Whether the employee was justified in participating in or causing the slowdown or stoppage;
3. Whether the employee was disciplined to the same degree as all other similarly situated employee-participants;
4. Whether there are circumstances which would warrant a lessening of the penalty.

Discussion Most collective bargaining agreements explicitly prohibit the conducting of, causing of, or participating in a work slowdown or stoppage as part of the contract's No Strike-No Lockout provision. Nevertheless, a careful review of the arbitration decisions in this area reveal that the discharge of an employee for such conduct is not always simple.

Where there is no collective bargaining agreement and, under certain circumstances, even where such an agreement exists, this kind of activity is usually within the realm of concerted activity protected by the National Labor Relations Act. Violations of the NLRA are not within the scope of this discussion. However, a review of the bases upon which arbitrators have held that such conduct constitutes just cause for discipline is appropriate.

It appears that the participation in or stimulation of a work slowdown is generally accepted by arbitrators as a serious, direct assault on the essence of economic enterprise and, as such, warrants summary discharge, absent special circumstances. In most of the cases reviewed, the problem of proving the offense has been the dominant issue. Once this problem is resolved, the decision of the arbitrator appears, in most cases, to be a foregone conclusion. In this connection, arbitrators recognize a difference between employee discipline for poor productivity, the major element of which is a nonintentional failure to perform up to the employer's standards, and employee discipline involving a work slowdown, the major element of which is an intentional and concerted refusal to perform the work available. Consequently, the issue often arises as to whether the disciplined employee or employees exhibited the necessary intent. Also, where an employee has not acted in concert with others, the issue is usually restricted to a charge of insubordination and not of a work slowdown or a stoppage.

Obviously, where the employee or employees admit to the slowdown, the problem of intent does not exist. However, wherever the employee or employees deny the existence of a slowdown, or a scheme to conduct a slowdown, the issue of intent becomes central. On the other hand, it seems that in all cases where an arbitrator has construed the evidence as establishing that there was a slowdown, the intent of the employees ceases to be an issue. The inference, in fact, is quickly made and the subject of intent is frequently not discussed or even acknowledged; the occurrence of a slowdown is enough, apparently, to establish the requisite intent, and employee intent is assumed to be a part of the finding of a slowdown.

In *Mueller Co.*, for example, the arbitrator upheld the five-day layoff of a drill press operator, whose productivity dropped for a month after new incentive rates had been introduced.[1] The operator had averaged 120 pieces per hour before the new rate was set, but only 72 pieces per hour afterwards. The arbitrator noted that "On its face, the sharp, unexplained, and long-continued drop in the grievant's productivity strongly suggests a conscious curtailment of effort" and held that the employer was justified in suspending the employee.[2]

In *United States Steel Corp.*, the issue of whether a group of employees had engaged in a slowdown was resolved through a similar analysis.[3] In that case, the company announced a "tightening" of production rates, and the output of an entire mill subsequently decreased from 50 to 20 units per hour. The decrease in output lasted for about a month, when the company decided to halt operations. The arbitrator rejected the union's contention that the company had caused a "lockout," finding that the employees had engaged in an illegal work slowdown. He stated,

> Proof of the slowdown did not lie in overt acts, observed and recorded, so much as in the simple fact that output was running at about one-third the rate reasonably expected. . . . [T]here was reason to believe the low output resulted from concerted action. . . .[4]

In at least one case, however, an arbitrator found that, although productivity was not what the employer thought it should be, the employees had not engaged in a slowdown. In another *United States Steel Corp.* case, the employer had suspended an entire shipping crew for engaging in a slowdown.[5] The suspended employees did not grieve at that time. For several days after the crew returned to work, its productivity increased, but not enough for the employer, which again suspended all of the crew members. The arbitrator set aside this second suspension and held that, although a higher level of production may have been possible, there was not enough evidence to establish that the crew members, who had substantially improved their production, had continued to engage in a slowdown.

Significantly, in cases of alleged slowdowns, arbitrators prefer that an employer show that an employee, or the employees, fell below an established productivity standard; but, there appears to be no insistence that the standard applied be a formal, implemented one.[6]

An important issue, akin to those found in cases involving concerted actions by employees and recognized as such under the National Labor Relations Act, is that having to do with an alleged justification for a slowdown. In this regard, the fact that the disciplined employee may be the union steward is central. While several arbitrators have stated that an employer has the right to discipline a union official who instigates or participates in a work slowdown, others have stated that union officials enjoy some degree of protected status and should not be harshly disciplined, if acting in good faith.

In *Inglis Limited*, for example, the employer discharged the grievant, a press operator and chief steward, for directing employees to produce pieces at a slower rate than that at which they were capable.[7] The grievant had been upset over the employer's new, but unofficial, production rate. Although he found that the grievant's behavior was unwarranted, the arbitrator nonetheless reinstated him, emphasizing that the grievant had been acting in his capacity as a union official and not out of self-interest. The proper penalty, the arbitrator held, was to strip the grievant of his union job and to reduce the discharge to a suspension, running from the day of the discharge to the day of the award.

In *Granite City Steel Co.*, however, the employer discharged a crane operator with 21 years' seniority for engaging in a slowdown to protest the bumping of another employee.[8] Throughout the grievance procedure, the grievant never claimed that he had been acting in his capacity as a union committeeman, and the arbitrator, emphasizing this fact, declined to reinstate him. Rather, the arbitrator upheld the discharge, stressing that this was not a case involving the discipline of a union official, who had acted in that capacity.

In *Pullman, Inc.*, the arbitrator took a different view on the culpability of a union official.[9] In that case, the grievant was discharged for directing several employees to slow down so that more senior employees would not look bad. The labor agreement contained a "no strike" clause, which specifically prohibited slowdowns. The arbitrator upheld the discharge, emphasizing that a union official should be more familiar with the violations set forth in the agreement and should conduct himself or herself accordingly.

One rather strange, but noteworthy, case is *Stevens Air Systems*, which involved the reinstatement of a discharged shop committee member.[10] In that case, a production worker, who was a union committeeman, directed the other 24 members on his production line to slow down. The line was scheduled to be shut down, and he apparently wanted the job to be stretched out. The labor agreement stated, in pertinent part, "[N]o work stoppages, strikes or slowdowns shall be caused or sanctioned by the Union." Finding that the grievant had acted on his own and that the slowdown tactic had not been sanctioned by the union, the arbitrator held that the labor agreement had not been violated. The arbitrator also noted that the grievant had never been warned about engaging in slowdowns, and he therefore reinstated him.

A review of the dominant cases in this area indicates that the *Stevens Air Systems* case is not within the mainstream, which suggests that factors not appearing in the written opinion may have been operating which caused the arbitrator to rule in the fashion he did. For the most part, causing a work slowdown is generally recognized as a legitimate reason for summary discipline, regardless of the technicalities of contract language.

Typically, these cases involve groups of employees who act in concert. As a consequence, the employer's treatment of the entire group comes under scrutiny in many cases, especially when it is suspected that a single employee has been treated too harshly because of some alleged or actual leadership role. In this respect, several arbitrators have had to struggle with the problem of whether to uphold discipline for all or for many of the members of a group which has engaged in a slowdown, where it is difficult to determine the role each employee played.

At least one arbitrator has stated that where several employees participate in a slowdown, the employer must administer discipline on an equal basis.[11] A more difficult problem arises, however, where all employees may not have been equally culpable.

In *United States Steel Corp.*, the employer placed written reprimands in the files of each of 26 employees in coke oven crews who had engaged in a slowdown.[12] The employer relied on a theory of "collective responsibility" in imposing discipline. The arbitrator rejected this theory, however. He concluded that similar discipline for all employees was unjustified, because the composition of the crews shifted from day to day and some crews performed worse than others. Further, the arbitrator held that, in order to reprimand individual employees, the employer did not necessarily have to produce evidence tying each employee to a precise slowdown action and only needed to show that an individual grievant had worked regularly in crews which showed a consistent reduction in productivity. Accordingly, the arbitrator divided the grievants into four categories: those definitely not engaged in slowdown; those probably not engaged; those probably engaged; and, those definitely engaged. As to employees in the second and third groups, he considered evidence against individual grievants.

In the same case, Arbitrator McDermott upheld the suspension of several crew leaders, finding that they had contributed more significantly to the slowdown. Suspending the crew leaders and not other employees, he concluded, did not amount to discrimination.

A different approach was taken by Arbitrator Richard McIntosh in *Buddy L. Corp.* There, the arbitrator held that the employer had been justified in warning several employees and in suspending all the employees who had worked on an assembly line which suffered a slowdown.[13] Such a manner of punishment, he stated, does not amount to guilt by association where production amounts to joint effort by all employees.

In several cases, arbitrators have held that, although an employee was involved in a work slowdown, mitigating circumstances warranted a decrease in punishment.

In *Library of Congress*, for instance, the arbitrator found that a supervisor, who had wanted another supervisor to look bad, had condoned a slowdown and that not all employees who had engaged in the slowdown had been disciplined.[14] He, therefore, reduced a suspension from two weeks to five days.

In *Chromalloy American Corp.*, the arbitrator reduced the suspension of two employees from five days to two days, emphasizing that both employees—each of whom had been suspended for working too slowly—had good work records and had been told by the company president that their discipline would be light.[15]

However, in several cases arbitrators have found that there were no mitigating circumstances and have upheld discharges.[16]

Key Points

1   *The work slowdown or stoppage must be proven by the substantial weight of the evidence to have been an intentional act.*

Examples

Employee *A*, along with six other employees in the same department, was discharged for conducting a work slowdown. The employer presented evidence demonstrating that *A*, the shop steward, and all of the others in his department had been upset over the employer's decision to go onto a rotating shift the following month. The contract clearly allowed the employer to make unilateral shift changes. The employer also showed that, after the announcement of rotating shifts, within 24 hours production had fallen by 30 percent and stayed that way for three weeks, when the new shift schedule went into effect. The employees denied the slowdown but acknowledged the accuracy of the employer's production figures. They contended, however, that the loss in production was due to equipment failure and lack of raw materials. Finding that there had been a higher frequency of equipment failure, a shortage of raw materials due to breakdowns in lift trucks, and no proof that these malfunctions were due to sabotage, the arbitrator reinstated all employees with full back pay.

Employee *B*, along with six others, was discharged for engaging in a work slowdown. The employer asserted that production fell by 30 percent immediately after a rotating shift was announced. The employer also showed that production returned to normal levels after the discharges. The employees defended by denying that there had been an intentional slowdown and argued that numerous equipment failures and the lack of supplies had caused production to drop. The employer acknowledged the equipment failures; but it also presented evidence showing, in nearly all instances that the failures had been due to human failure, or acts of possible sabotage. The arbitrator sustained the discharges, noting the suspicious coincidence between the announcement of the rotating shifts and the questionable equipment failures.

Employee *C* was suspended, along with three of the other four employees on the same job crew, for engaging in a work slowdown. The employer presented to the arbitrator the production records of all employees for a one-month period. They were all roughly the same. The employer then presented the production record of a new employee for the same period. It was 30 percent higher. A supervisor testified that he had observed arguments between *C* and the new employee, although the supervisor did not hear the subject in dispute. He also said that none of the suspended employees had had anything to do with the new employee. However, about one month before the disciplinary action there had been an obvious attitude change toward the new employee, and the older employees appeared to accept and to include him as "one of the boys." The employer's records showed that the production of the new employee fell drastically one month before the discipline to a level about equal to that of the other employees. The arbitrator sustained the discipline and ordered that a time study be conducted on the job to determine an appropriate production level.

Employee *D* was discharged after a new employee had reported to his supervisor that *D* had told him to slow down to keep from making it "bad for the rest of us." The new employee refused to testify at the hearing. The production records showed the production of the new employee to be significantly higher than that of the others. A time study showed production levels of other employees to be below a reasonable standard. The arbitrator reinstated the employee, but without back pay. The arbitrator also suggested that the new employee should have been disciplined for refusing to testify.

Guidelines

An admission of guilt is not a necessary requirement for sustaining disciplinary action against an employee for participating in or causing a work stoppage or slowdown. Intent will normally be inferred from the absence of other factors explaining a drop in production.

Relevant Cases

Thermal Science (Nitka), 85 LA 1017
Mann Packing Co. (Concepcion), 83 LA 552
Detroit Edison Co. (Jones), 82 LA 226
Georgia Pacific Corp. (Szollosi), 81 LA 179
Premier Industries (Murphy), 81 LA 183
Inglis Limited (Shime), 66 LA 812
United States Steel Corp. (Dybeck), 58 LA 977

United States Steel Corp. (Miller), 53 LA 1140
Mueller Co. (Porter), 52 LA 162
Buddy L. Corp. (McIntosh), 49 LA 581

2   *The purpose of the slowdown or stoppage cannot justify the act.*

Examples

Employee *A*, a union steward, was discharged for calling for a work stoppage, after he learned that the employer had subcontracted work in violation of the collective bargaining agreement. Noting that the issue in dispute was grievable and that a work stoppage was not justified, the arbitrator sustained the discharge.

Employee *B*, a crew leader, asserted that the working conditions were unsafe and urged the other employees to stop all work. Although the employer argued that the conditions were not unsafe, the crew stopped. *B* was discharged. The arbitrator found that the working conditions were not unsafe but also that *B* had been honestly mistaken. Consequently, he ordered that *B* be reinstated with three days loss in pay as discipline for not accepting the employer's evidence of safety.

Employee *C* was discharged following her statements to other employees that the employer's new production standards were unreasonable and that they should be disregarded. Finding that the employer's standards were a grievable issue, the arbitrator sustained the discharge. *C*'s lack of success in achieving concerted action did not change the fact that she had attempted to get others to join her and she had cut her own production.

Guidelines

A normally grievable or bargainable issue cannot be used as justification for a work slowdown or stoppage, absent an issue involving a threat to employee safety.

Relevant Cases

Thermal Science (Nitka), 85 LA 1017
Army (Armor) Center (Wren), 82 LA 464

Detroit Edison Co. (Jones), 82 LA 226
Georgia Pacific Corp. (Szollosi), 81 LA 179
Inglis Limited (Shime), 66 LA 812
Stevens Air Systems (Stashower), 64 LA 425
Granite City Steel Co. (Belshaw), 58 LA 69
Pullman, Inc. (Dworet), 41 LA 607

3   *All persons participating in a work slowdown or
stoppage to the same or similar degree must receive the
same disciplinary action, regardless of theoretic
differences due to positions or responsibilities.*

Examples

Following an announcement by the employer that rotating shifts would begin the following month in a particular department, production fell by 30 percent. Two years earlier, the employer had attempted to do the same thing. Following a wildcat strike, the employer had withdrawn the plan. The employer responded this time by discharging *A*, who was the union steward in the department, and by suspending all others in the department for 10 days. The suspensions were sustained, but the discharge was reduced to a similar suspension.

Following an announcement by the employer that rotating shifts would begin the following month in a particular department, production fell by 30 percent. Two years earlier, the employer had attempted the same thing. Following a wildcat strike, the employer had withdrawn the plan. When the employer announced its plan this time, *B*, the department's union steward, told the production manager that he had stopped the company before, and he would stop it again. As soon as the slowdown became apparent, the employer discharged *B* and suspended all others in the department. The arbitrator noted the increased culpability of the steward and upheld the suspensions and the discharge.

Following the imposition of new shift schedules and production standards, all of the employees in the plant walked out on a wildcat strike. Following their return to work after an injunction under *Boys Markets*, the employer suspended six local union officers and discharged *C*, the local union president. The grievants argued that the employer was required to take the same disciplinary action against everyone the same or it could take none at all. The arbitrator rescinded the suspensions of two officers because their involvement in the walkout had been restricted to participation, and the arbitrator held that these two should have been treated like all of the other undisciplined employees. *C*, as well as the other officers, had instigated the walkout, and the arbitrator sustained their discipline with the exception of *C*'s, whose discharge was reduced to a suspension.

Guidelines

Where one individual is proven by independent evidence to be particularly culpable, more severe discipline may be justified.

Relevant Cases

Schnadig Corp. (Seidman), 85 LA 692
Thermal Science (Nitka), 85 LA 1017
Detroit Edison Co. (Jones), 82 LA 226
Georgia Pacific Corp. (Szollosi), 81 LA 179
Library of Congress (Rothman), 62 LA 1289
Buddy L. Corp. (McIntosh), 49 LA 581
United States Steel Corp. (McDermott), 49 LA 1236

4   *Mitigation of a discharge is warranted only where the effects of the employee's action were minimal and where some other factor, such as a good work record or outrageous affront to the employee's principles, created an aura of injustice.*

Examples

Employee *A* was discharged for leading a work slowdown to protest what he believed to be illegal subcontracting by the employer. Although the evidence was clear that *A* had endeavored to get other employees to reduce production, little, if any, production time was lost. The subcontracting was grieved, and the employer, at arbitration, agreed to discontinue the practice. The employee's work record was good. The arbitrator reduced the discharge to a suspension.

Employee *B*, a crew leader, had stopped his crew from working at the construction site, because *B* believed that some of the working conditions were unsafe. *B* had asked for an engineer to examine it; the request had been denied. *B* refused to allow the crew to continue to work, and *B* and the crew were discharged. Another crew was brought in and they completed the work without incident. The arbitrator held that, although the condition was clearly safe, the employer had no right to deny *B*'s request for an inspection,·and the arbitrator mitigated the discharge to a warning.

Employee *C* was discharged after a new employee reported that he had been told by *C* to slowdown so "the rest of us won't look bad." The arbitrator, stating that discharge was too severe for the one isolated instance, mitigated the discharge to a suspension.

Guidelines

Generally, the stimulation of or participation in an unprotected work stoppage will justify discipline at any level chosen by the employer. The degree of discipline will not be subject to mitigation except in unusual cases.

Relevant Cases

Detroit Edison Co. (Jones), 82 LA 226
Universal Studios (Steese), 72 LA 84
Library of Congress (Rothman), 62 LA 1289
Chromalloy American Corp. (Hon), 61 LA 246
Granite City Steel Co. (Belshaw), 58 LA 69
Collis Co. (Doyle), 50 LA 1157

Notes to Chapter 22

1. *Mueller Co.* (Porter), 52 LA 162.
2. *Id.*, at 164.
3. *United States Steel Corp.* (Miller), 53 LA 1140.
4. *United States Steel Corp., supra*, note 3, at 1142; *see also Buddy L. Corp.* (McIntosh), 49 LA 581, for a similar analysis.
5. *United States Steel Corp.* (Dybeck), 58 LA 977.
6. *See, e.g., Inglis Ltd.* (Shime), 66 LA 812.
7. *Id.*
8. *Granite City Steel Co.* (Belshaw), 58 LA 69.
9. *Pullman, Inc.* (Dworet), 41 LA 607.
10. *Stevens Air Sys.* (Stashower), 64 LA 425.
11. *See Library of Congress* (Rothman), 62 LA 1289.
12. *United States Steel Corp.* (McDermott), 49 LA 1236.

13. *Buddy L. Corp., supra,* note 4.

14. *Library of Congress, supra,* note 11.

15. *Chromalloy Am. Corp.* (Hon), 61 LA 246.

16. *Universal Studios* (Steese), 72 LA 84 (a steward truck driver demanded greater pay and caused many employees to stop work while he created an uproar); *Granite City Steel Co., supra,* note 8 (a discharged employee never invoked his union status); *Collis Co.* (Doyle), 50 LA 1157 (a union steward, upset about incentive pay rates, told the employees to "work accordingly").

23

Union Activity/Steward Abuse

Issue   Whether an employee, who is a union steward, may be discharged or otherwise disciplined for actions taken allegedly within the scope of his or her union duties.

Principle   A union steward may be discharged or otherwise disciplined for actions taken as a steward where the employee abuses the grievance procedure; disrupts production; abuses privileges accorded him or her as a steward; and is insubordinate in the exercise of a steward's duties; and, where there is no evidence of union animus on the part of the employer.

Considerations
1. Whether the actions of the steward simply constituted a zealous representation of his or her constituents;
2. Whether the actions of the steward were inconsistent or otherwise clearly demonstrated an intent to harass the employer;
3. Whether the actions of the steward intentionally, and unnecessarily, disrupted production or operations;
4. Whether the steward had actual control over the employees or the situation when the disruption in production or operations occurred;
5. Whether the steward's action took place during a formal grievance, arbitration, or negotiation meeting.

6. Whether the disciplinary action taken against the steward was due to his or her position in that the steward was held accountable to a standard different from that of other employees.

Discussion   Due to their concern about employer actions motivated by union animus, arbitrators treat discharges and other disciplinary actions taken against union officials with circumspection. The question of whether a steward was disciplined simply because of his or her position as a union official or because of the steward's union activity is properly treated by the National Labor Relations Board under the Labor Management Relations Act. This issue, however, can be deferred to arbitration, or "Collyerized." Nevertheless, there are several circumstances where discipline will be considered independently of the union animus issue. Of necessity, however, the question of whether the discipline was merely a subterfuge for discrimination based upon the steward's union activity is almost always present.

Under some circumstances, a steward can be disciplined for abusing his or her authority as a steward. For instance, union officials may be properly disciplined for abusing the grievance procedure. A discharge of a union steward was upheld where he had filed many grievances which were illogical and contradictory. He had also engaged in other actions whereby he harassed the company and its management.[1] At least one other decision recognized that proper discipline could arise from a union officer's use of the grievance procedure for purposes of harassment. On the other hand, the arbitrator in *Carborundum Co.* sustained the grievance, because there was no evidence that multiple grievances had been filed to harass the employer.[2]

Interference with the employer's operations or production is a more frequently cited basis for disciplining union officials. Within this category one of the most common incidents is where the union official instigates, encourages, or otherwise participates in a work stoppage which violates a no-strike clause. In such cases, a discharge will almost always be upheld in the absence of extenuating circumstances. Furthermore, a union official who merely takes part in the strike will usually be found to have thereby encouraged the strike.[3] In *Quanex,* however, the arbitrator ordered an eight-month disciplinary suspension instead of discharge, because after initially encouraging the wildcat strike, the steward tried to get employees to return to work.[4]

Similarly, discharge has been held to be appropriate discipline for union officials who failed to adequately discourage an illegal strike, even if they did not originally instigate it. It is part of the responsibility of their positions to prevent the violation of the collective bargaining agreement.[5] In such cases, the key to deciding whether a union official encouraged, or failed to discourage, employees is whether the union official was in such a position that his or her actions would have the effect of leading the employees to illegally strike.[6] For example, in *Koehring Co.*, the arbitrator found that union trustees did not occupy such positions of leadership and ordered the employer to reduce the discipline to a suspension.[7]

Actions by union officials which are less likely to result in discharge, but will certainly result in discipline, are to encourage slowdowns, to refuse overtime, or to take other actions which interrupt production. Among these actions, the instigation of a slowdown appears to be the most likely to result in discharge. In *Dover Corp.*, the arbitrator upheld the discharge of a union steward who had encouraged the night shift to slow down production to comport with the day shift.[8] And, in *Inglis Limited*, the arbitrator reinstated a steward without back pay who had told employees to work more slowly.[9] The arbitrator cited extenuating circumstances and also stipulated that the steward could not hold union office upon his return. Encouraging employees to refuse overtime will also result in discipline. In *Central Illinois Public Service Co.*, the arbitrator noted that he would ordinarily have upheld the discharge of the steward, who had posted a notice for employees to refuse voluntary overtime, had it not been for extenuating circumstances.[10] Instead, the steward was reinstated without back pay. In *Zellerbach Paper Co.*, the arbitrator upheld the three-month suspensions of a local union president and recording secretary.[11] The arbitrator found that their encouragement of employees not to work voluntary overtime violated the no-strike clause. In *Vernitron Piezoelectric Division*,[12] Arbitrator Abrams upheld the discharge of a union steward following what the employer believed were efforts of the steward to create a slowdown by "advising" probationary employees not to work so fast. The arbitrator examined the facts and analyzed the issue as follows:

P. and H. were concerned because they were on probation; they were concerned that if they didn't produce enough they might lose their jobs without recourse; they were concerned because B. was trying to get them to slow down. They testified in no uncertain terms that this is precisely what B. repeatedly told them to do. They were new in the shop, and didn't know precisely how to take the repeated "advice" of the Union steward who had been there a long time.

To establish a charge of attempting to impede work—inducing a concerted slowdown—requires compelling proof. See, White Engines Inc., 83-1 ARB par. 8126 (Abrams, 1983). At times, arbitrators find the proof in the record insufficient to establish the charge. Compare, Premier Industries, Inc., 81 LA 183 (Murphy, 1983) (no slowdown found), with Toshiba America Inc., 78 LA 812 (Flannagan, 1982) (slowdown proven). In its closing remarks, the Union cited Pantry Pride Enterprises, Inc., 79 LA 883, 888 (Carson, 1982), to remind the Arbitrator that a deliberate intent to restrict production must be found and should be distinguished from mere "poor work habits" (as in that case), or an attempt to improve quality (as the Union claims occurred here). But this is neither a case of poor work habits nor a case of an attempt to improve quality. The Company here has established in a clear and convincing fashion that T. B. attempted to impede production. That he was only marginally successful in his efforts with P. and H. does not excuse his activities in any way.

The Union argues that discharge was too harsh a penalty, but Article VII of the parties' Agreement mandates discharge in these circumstances. This type of insidious behavior is simply intolerable in the work place, and management must act to deter others from similar misconduct by imposing discharge when allegations such as these are proven.

Discipline has also been imposed where a union official directed an employee not to fill in at a nonunit position.[13] The arbitrator found that this did not constitute a work stoppage and, therefore, that discharge was too severe. However, the arbitrator reinstated the employee without back pay, which effectively resulted in a nine-month suspension. Accordingly, it is apparent that discipline can be severe when union officials interfere with the production operations of a plant.

Another set of circumstances which occasions disciplinary actions against union officials is where the officials have abused privileges extended to them by virtue of their position. However, these cases usually involve lesser penalties and discharges are rarely sustained. One typical scenario in this category involves a steward, or other union official, who exceeds time allotted to attend to union business or who does not return to work after attending a union business meeting. In these cases, lesser discipline has been sustained.[14]

In *Kay-Brunner Steel Products*, however, the discharge of a steward was sustained where he continued to argue loudly and insistently about the employer's use of a different canteen truck, even after his break had ended and after he had been ordered to return to work.[15] The steward's overly aggressive actions and refusal to obey his supervisor's order amounted to gross insubordination.

Similarly, discipline has been upheld where union officials attended to union business without asking for the time off or without having it granted. In *Greif Bros. Corp.*, the arbitrator reinstated without back pay a local union president who had been discharged for attending a meeting for which the company had denied him the time off.[16] The arbitrator stated that the obey and grieve rule did not apply here, because the employee's disobedience involved union business and, consequently, a discharge was not appropriate. In *Golden Foundry*, a three-day suspension was upheld against a union vice president, who had frequently left his work station without approval.[17] The arbitrator stated that this conduct could not be condoned, whether it is characterized as insubordination or self-help.

Union officials can also be disciplined for using abusive language or for other actions taken in the course of performing their general duties. However, a different rule seems to apply to actions taken by union officials during the course of grievance procedures, collective bargaining negotiations, or the performance of similar duties.

Discipline, including discharge, has been sustained where union officials directed abusive language toward their supervisors in the presence of other employees while discussing disputes with the supervisors or employees. The fact that the union officials were acting in their capacity as union representatives did not immunize them from discipline for such actions.[18]

Frequently, overly aggressive representation by union stewards gives rise to disciplinary action. Stewards are expected to be aggressive in the performance of their duties, but arbitrators draw a line beyond which their conduct should not go if discipline is to be avoided. In *Kay-Brunner Steel Products*, a steward's discharge was sustained when he continued to argue past the time to return to work, refused to obey a supervisor's order to go to work, and created such a stir that other employees stopped work, or failed to go to their stations, while the arguing continued.[19] The arbitrator specifically identified the steward's conduct as overly aggressive and held the discharge to be proper.

In *Universal Steel Co.*, the issuance of a warning to a steward was found to be improper when his conduct, which consisted of finger pointing and arguing loudly in the presence of other employees, was not found to have been overly aggressive when taken in light of the employee's usual type of behavior.[20] However, in the same case, the arbitrator sustained a steward's discipline where the employee had threatened a supervisor, placing him in fear of his physical safety.

Profanity and verbal abuse figured also in *Jones & Laughlin Steel Corp.* In that case the steward protested his overtime assignment and the use of an outside contractor in a profane and abusive manner to a supervisor.[21] This conduct, found the arbitrator, was beyond the bounds of appropriateness, and a suspension was sustained.

When the union official makes the same abusive statements in the course of collective bargaining sessions or grievance arbitrations, however, discipline is usually not appropriate. In these situations, the representatives of the union and the company are equals and, therefore, there can be no insubordination.[22]

Discipline has also been applied for various other actions taken by union officials in their capacity as union representatives. In *Bakery and Confectionery Workers*, a union steward was reinstated without back pay when he had refused to sign an evaluation form in an effort to bring the dispute over the evaluations to a head.[23] In *Potlatch Corp.*, the arbitrator upheld the discharge of a local vice president who had harassed other employees for not joining the union.[24] His actions exceeded the range of reasonable conduct. A similar standard of conduct was applied in *Union Fork & Hoe Co.* The arbitrator upheld the discharge of a steward who took an employee's time slip, which had been the subject of a meeting in the superintendent's office, and would not return it.[25]

Finally, a union official can be disciplined, up to and including discharge, for just cause, where there is no antiunion motivation on the part of the employer. Union officials have no special immunity from disciplinary action where the alleged cause is not just a pretext.[26]

Arbitrators will also look at the relative treatment of

union officials and regular employees. If there is evidence of disparate treatment, arbitrators will assume that an anti-union motive exists and grant the grievance.[27]

Key Points

1 *Where there is evidence of an intent to harass an employer, as distinguished from an aggressive representation of the legitimate interests of the employees, a union steward may be disciplined.*

Examples

Employee *A*, a union steward representing 250 employees, filed numerous grievances, most of which appeared to be clearly without merit and were withdrawn just prior to arbitration. A few proceeded to arbitration but were denied. Of the 100 grievances filed in one year, none was successful in arbitration: 86 were withdrawn prior to arbitration and 14 were settled. The employer discharged the steward after several warnings on the grounds that the steward had abused the system. The arbitrator sustained the grievance—giving the steward his first win—and ordered reinstatement with full back pay. There was no evidence of anything but a zealous representation of the employees.

Employee *B*, a union steward representing 250 employees, filed numerous grievances, most of which were of dubious merit and some of which had conflicting claims. Of the 100 grievances filed in one year none was successful in arbitration: 86 were withdrawn prior to arbitration and 14 were settled. After a single warning, the employer discharged the steward for misuse of the system and harassment. Noting that on six occasions the steward had filed conflicting grievances interpreting the same contract provisions in opposite fashions, the arbitrator concluded that steward abuse and harassment could be inferred from the facts, and the discharge was sustained.

Guidelines

The steward must be found to have done something more than merely file numerous grievances to sustain disciplinary action. There must be some evidence of actions which imply an intent to harass the employer.

Relevant Cases

Schnadig Corp. (Seidman), 85 LA 692
Southern Indiana Gas & Electric Co. (Nathan), 85 LA 716
Vernitron Piezoelectric Div. (Abrams), 84 LA 1315
Edward Draemer & Sons, Inc. (Rezler), 81 LA 821
Jim Walter Resources (Williams), 81 LA 1115
Carborundum Co. (Altrock), 72 LA 118
Robintech, Inc. (Block), 65 LA 221

2   *The steward must be found to have been in a position of sufficient control and/or influence over the employees to have been able to cause or to instigate a disruption of the employer's production.*

Examples

Employee *A*, a steward, protested vehemently against the establishment of rotating shifts by the employer. A grievance over the right of the employer to institute rotating shifts was arbitrated and denied. After the arbitrator's award, the steward told the employer that this was not the last word on the issue. Immediately thereafter, the employees refused all overtime assignments, and production dropped 30 percent. The steward was discharged. The discharge was sustained.

Employee *B*, a steward, was discharged when he refused to "order" the employees to return from a wildcat strike. Noting that the steward apparently did not instigate the walkout and did not participate in the picketing, the arbitrator doubted whether the steward's order would have meant anything and reinstated him with back pay up to the day the strike ended.

Employee *C*, a steward, was suspended for one week for telling a new employee not to work in excess of a certain speed, because it would "make it bad" for the rest of the employees. The arbitrator found that this constituted an attempted instigation of a slowdown in violation of the labor agreement and sustained the suspension.

Guidelines

The evidence of the steward's improper conduct must show that the steward actually did, or attempted to, interfere with the employer's production for the purpose of obtaining a personal, or group, benefit or concession from the employer.

Relevant Cases

Schnadig Corp. (Seidman), 85 LA 692
Central Illinois Public Service Co. (Kossoff), 76 LA 300
Dover Corp. (Kaut), 74 LA 675
Mark Twain Marine Industries (Guenther), 73 LA 551
Quanex (McDonald), 73 LA 9
Zellerbach Paper Co. (Sabo), 73 LA 1140
Clinton Corn Processing Co. (Madden), 71 LA 555
Bucyrus-Erie Co. (Lipson), 69 LA 93
Dravo Corp. (McDermott), 68 LA 618
Herrud & Co. (Keefe), 66 LA 682
Inglis Limited (Shime), 66 LA 812

3 *The steward is expected not to abuse privileges accorded him or her as a union officer, and discipline will be sustained for proven abuse.*

Examples

Employee *A*, a steward, obtained time off to travel into the center of town to confer with the union's attorney in connection with an upcoming arbitration. A supervisor saw *A* going into a theater four hours before the end of his scheduled shift. The steward was discharged. The arbitrator, while acknowledging that such abuse is just cause for discipline, mitigated the discharge to a disciplinary suspension.

Employee *B*, a steward, had been warned repeatedly that he was not to leave his work station to talk to other employees unless he had the prior permission of his supervisor and unless the subject was a grievance which had already been filed. The employer suspended *B* for not being at his work station because of union business. The steward's discipline was voided when the arbitrator learned that the business involved an employee emergency and that the supervisor had not been in the department when the issue arose.

> ### *Guidelines*
>
> Except as permitted by specific language in the collective bargaining agreement, the union activities of the steward cannot unreasonably interfere with his or her normal job duties.

Relevant Cases

Edward Draemer & Sons, Inc. (Rezler), 81 LA 821
H.P. Smith Paper Co. (Lieberman), 81 LA 888
Jim Walter Resources (Williams), 81 LA 1115
Reichold Chemicals (Hon), 73 LA 636
Ward LaFrance Truck Co. (Levy), 69 LA 831
American Hoechst Corp. (Purcell), 68 LA 517
Golden Foundry (Fitch), 67 LA 887
Greif Bros. Corp. (Flannagan), 67 LA 1001

4   *The steward cannot conduct himself or herself in a fashion which demonstrates contempt for supervisors or which is otherwise insubordinate.*

Examples

Employee *A*, a union steward, discovered that a supervisor had offered overtime to a junior employee in violation of the negotiated procedure. Irate at yet another occasion of what he believed to be the third such mistake within the last month by the same supervisor, the steward ripped the assignment sheet off the bulletin board, stormed across the production floor, creating a commotion, and approached the supervisor, who was in the process of giving instructions to two other employees. *A* broke into the conversation and said, "You are a flaming a——h——. I don't know how someone so stupid could ever have become a supervisor. How many times do I have to show you how this system works?" The steward was discharged, and the arbitrator sustained the discharge.

Employee *B*, a union steward, was chairman of the grievance committee. During the course of a grievance meeting, *B* called the personnel director a flaming a——h—— and told him he was too stupid to talk to. *B* was discharged. The arbitrator found that, while the conduct was reprehensible, it was protected in that the behavior occurred during the course of a heated argument over a grievance in a closed meeting between grievance committee members and company representatives. The discharge was commuted to a warning.

Guidelines

A steward's conduct is judged according to the same standards as other employees, except during collective bargaining sessions or formal grievance meetings. At these times, the steward is regarded as being equal to the company's representatives, and any behavior exhibited by the steward during these sessions is, therefore, incapable of being judged as anything more blameworthy than extreme rudeness.

Relevant Cases

Dalfort Corp. (White), 85 LA 70
Southern Indiana Gas & Electric Co. (Nathan), 85 LA 716
Consolidation Coal Co. (Rubin), 78 LA 473
Jones & Laughlin Steel Corp. (Cook), 78 LA 566
Kay-Brunner Steel Products (Gentile), 78 LA 363
Universal Steel Co. (Daniel), 78 LA 148
Zell Brothers (Mayer), 78 LA 1012
Krauth & Benninghofen Corp. (Imundo), 73 LA 1243
Owens-Illinois, Inc. (Witney), 73 LA 663
General Electric Co. (Maroney), 71 LA 164
Tobyhanna Army Depot (McLeod), 69 LA 1220
St. Joe Paper Co. (Klein), 68 LA 124

5   *Although technically an issue to be treated under the National Labor Relations Act, discipline based on an employee's union status or on his or her union activities, rather than on the employee's conduct alone, will not be sustained by arbitrators.*

Examples

Employee *A*, a union steward, was disciplined for poor production. The supervisor, when meting out the discipline, stated that he was disappointed in *A* because, as the steward, he should set an example for the others. In fact, the arbitrator found that *A*'s production was no worse than at least one other employee who had not been disciplined. The arbitrator voided the discipline.

Employee *B*, a union steward, participated in a wildcat strike. When the strike was over, six of the employees were given two-week disciplinary suspensions. *B* was discharged on the theory that his culpability was greater than the others because of his position as steward. *B*'s discharge was reduced by the arbitrator to a two-week suspension.

Guidelines

A union steward can be held to no higher standard of conduct than other employees, unless the steward's responsibilities are increased by specific language in the collective bargaining agreement.[28]

Relevant Cases

Devon Apparel (Rock), 85 LA 645
Schnadig Corp. (Seidman), 85 LA 692
Southern Indiana Gas & Electric Co. (Nathan), 85 LA 716
Bethlehem Steel Corp. (Sharnoff), 76 LA 480
Rock Creek Plaza (Richter), 76 LA 1113
Sun Furniture Co. (Ruben), 73 LA 335
Furr's Inc. (Leeper), 72 LA 960
American Dairy of Evansville (Doering), 67 LA 1140
Emery Air Freight Corp. (Darrow), 67 LA 541
Humko Sheffield Chemical (Ross), 66 LA 1261

Notes to Chapter 23

1. *Robintech, Inc.* (Block), 65 LA 221.
2. *Carborundum Co.* (Altrock), 72 LA 118.
3. *Clinton Corn Processing Co.* (Madden), 71 LA 555; *Bucyrus-Erie Co.* (Lipson), 69 LA 93; *Dravo Corp.* (McDermott), 68 LA 618; *Herrud & Co.* (Keefe), 66 LA 682.
4. *Quanex* (McDonald), 73 LA 9.
5. *Clinton Corn Processing Co., supra,* note 3; *ITT Thompson Indus.* (Seifer), 70 LA 970.
6. *Koehring Co.* (Boals), 69 LA 459.
7. *See also Fournelle v. NLRB,* 670 F.2d 331, 109 LRRM 2441 (D.C. Cir. 1982), and cases cited therein.
8. *Dover Corp.* (Kaut), 74 LA 675.
9. *Inglis Ltd.* (Shime), 66 LA 812.
10. *Central Ill. Pub. Serv. Co.* (Kossoff), 76 LA 300.

11. *Zellerbach Paper Co.* (Sabo), 73 LA 1140.

12. *Vernitron Piezoelectric Div.* (Abrams), 84 LA 1315.

13. *Mark Twain Marine Indus.* (Guenther), 73 LA 551.

14. *Reichhold Chem.* (Hon), 73 LA 636 (warning); *Ward La-France Truck Co.* (Levy), 69 LA 831 (three-day suspension); *American Hoechst Corp.* (Purcell), 68 LA 517 (one-day suspension).

15. *Kay-Brunner Steel Prods.* (Gentile), 78 LA 363.

16. *Greif Bros. Corp.* (Flannagan), 67 LA 1001.

17. *Golden Foundry* (Fitch), 67 LA 887.

18. *Jones & Laughlin Steel Corp.* (Cook), 78 LA 566 (suspension sustained); *Krauth & Benninghofen Corp.* (Imundo), 73 LA 1243 (discharge upheld); *General Elec. Co.* (Maroney), 71 LA 164 (upheld warning notice); *Tobyhanna Army Depot* (McLeod), 69 LA 1220 (discharge upheld). *But see General Elec Co.* (Bridgewater), 72 LA 654 (grievance sustained where abuse provoked).

19. *Kay-Brunner Steel Prods., supra*, note 15.

20. *Universal Steel Co.* (Daniel), 78 LA 148.

21. *Jones & Laughlin Steel Corp., supra*, note 18.

22. *Owens-Illinois, Inc.* (Witney), 73 LA 663; *Tobyhanna Army Depot, supra*, note 18 (dicta). *See also St. Joe Paper Co.* (Klein), 68 LA 124 (suspension denied for official who wrote safety letter to management rather than grieve).

23. *Bakery & Confectionery Workers* (Robertson), 74 LA 1297.

24. *Potlatch Corp.* (Leeper), 72 LA 583.

25. *Union Fork & Hoe Co.* (Ipavec), 68 LA 432.

26. *Bethlehem Steel Corp.* (Sharnoff), 76 LA 480 (the arbitrator upheld the discharge where the union officer accosted a foreman); *Sun Furniture Co.* (Ruben), 73 LA 335 (the arbitrator reinstated without back pay a steward who had disparaged the company and its product before a customer); *Furr's, Inc.* (Leeper), 72 LA 960 (the arbitrator upheld the discharge of a steward, who had struck the manager, where there was no evidence of an antiunion motive on the part of the employer); *American Dairy of Evansville* (Doering), 67 LA 1140 (a steward was properly discharged for poor performance where there was no evidence of an antiunion motive); *Emery Air Freight Corp.* (Darrow), 67 LA 541 (the arbitrator upheld the discharge where there was no evidence of antiunion motive); *Humko Sheffield Chem.* (Ross), 66 LA 1261 (the arbitrator upheld a written warning for insubordination). *Compare Rock Creek Plaza* (Richter), 76 LA 1113 (the discharge was reduced to a three-day suspension where there was evidence of antiunion motive).

27. *Boise Cascade Corp.* (Richardson), 66 LA 1302.

28. Recent Labor Board and Court decisions appear to create an additional requirement that the steward must also have a contractual duty to prevent or halt an illegal strike if he is treated differently from other participants in a strike. *See Fournelle v. NLRB, supra*, note 7.

Appendix

Guide for Interviewing

Interviewing today is a whole new process. Many of today's applicants are as aware of the interviewing process as the company interviewer. Smart applicants are well prepared for the interview, and often it is difficult to get all the information needed to make a wise hiring decision.

Because interviewing has become such a widely practiced skill, there is a need for interviewers to learn and apply new techniques constantly.

Principles of a Good Selection Interview

- Really know the job for which individual is needed.
- Understand what characteristics you are looking for.
- Plan the interview in order to obtain the information you need.
- Establish a comfortable conversational style to build rapport.
- Maintain objectivity about the applicant as the interview progresses.
- Remain flexible, and guide the conversation from general to specific and from harmless to sensitive areas.
- Pace the interview and apportion interview time appropriately. Don't permit the applicant to spend too much time on one area, which results in your rushing to complete the interview in a timely fashion, thus covering other important areas incompletely.
- Listen. Concentrate on what the applicant is saying and respond appropriately.
- Structure the interview so that you use a variety of questioning techniques. Use open-ended questions rather than questions that can be answered "yes" or "no".
- Don't ask questions that could be considered discriminatory.
- Use silence to obtain more information. If the applicant seems

373

to run out of things to say, let the silence build up for a minute. The applicant probably will offer more information.

- If there are statements you'd like the applicant to expand on, repeat them in another way. This is called "echoing" and is an effective information-gathering technique.
- Watch for the "halo" effect! This is a situation where an interviewer permits an applicant's one or two favorable traits, such as a good appearance or ability to speak well, to influence the interviewer's overall impressions. The halo effect can work in reverse, biasing the interviewer unfavorably because of one or two bad impressions.
- Don't talk too much, but do show energy and enthusiam. A stiff, formal interviewer will turn off most applicants.
- Follow up hunches and unusual statements. If the applicant says, "I don't get along with certain kinds of people," you will want to find out what those kinds of people are.
- Close the interview in a reasonable period of time. Close on a positive note, but don't lead an applicant on or promise anything you can't deliver.
- As soon as the interview is over, write down the facts and your impressions of the interview.

Listening

Active listening is hard work! As an animated listener, the interviewer controls the interview, *but* the applicant should be doing the majority of the talking. If the interviewer talks less than 10 percent of the time, he is probably not active enough in the conversation. If he talks more than 25 percent of the time he's talking too much. The interviewer should be listening about 75 percent of the time. *As long as the interviewer talks, he is not learning about the candidate.*

The interviewer should sit up straight and concentrate on the applicant. Erect posture conveys attentiveness and interest. He should look pleasant or neutral, even when negative information is offered. Often a quizzical look will gain additional information.

As humans, we get much of our information nonverbally through observing the actions and reactions of others. The interviewer should be watching for nonverbal clues, such as:

- Posture in the chair (relaxed or stiff)
- Eye contact or avoidance
- Use of hands (gestures)
- Color of hands or face (flushing)
- Tapping with hands or feet
- Position of arms
- Change in tone of voice

- Involuntary reactions to questions in sensitive areas (lip biting)
- Ability to enjoy humor

It is a good idea to ask a friend or co-worker if you (the interviewer) have any annoying habits or nervous actions. These can come out in the stress of an interview and can distract or mislead the applicant.

Questions That Avoid Pitfalls and Elicit Honest Answers

A number of questions that follow will be non-directive in nature, and quite simple. They permit the applicant to discuss those subjects with which he is more familiar or that he feels are most important. From this point, the interviewer can guide the interview into such areas as he deems advisable.

Certainly, a person's work experience is important and is a natural and easy place to start the interview. Some key questions here might be:

1. One of the things we want to talk about today is your work experience; would you tell me about your present job?
2. What do you feel were your major responsibilities in your last job?
3. In your last job, what were some of the things that you spent the most time on, and how much time did you spend on each?
4. What are some of the things on your job you feel you have done particularly well, or in which you have achieved the greatest success, and why do you feel this way?
5. What were some of the things about your job that you found difficult to do, and why do you feel this way about them?

How Does the Applicant Feel About His Job?

In addition to knowing what the applicant does on the job, it is vital to know how he feels about what he does. The response of the applicant to the type of questions that follows may well reveal such feelings and attitudes.

Proper Inquiries   *Improper Inquiries*

Describe your current job.

Describe the type of company for whom you work.

How much time is spent on each of your job duties?

Proper Inquiries	*Improper Inquiries*
What do you like about your current job?	
What are some problems you encounter in doing your job? Which frustrate you the most? What do you do about them?	
How do you feel about the progress you have made with your present company?	
How are you viewed by the company?	
Was your departure from the prior job voluntary (quit) or involuntary (discharge)?	
If voluntary, what were your reasons for leaving?	
If involuntary, what caused you to be terminated?	
What were some of the things you liked about your last job?	
Most jobs have pluses and minuses—what were some of the negatives?	
How many hours per week should a person devote to his or her job?	
Can you work overtime?	Are you a member of any religious group which would prohibit you from working on any days or at any time?
Can you work weekends?	
Are there any shifts which you can't work?	
What do you feel is a satisfactory attendance record?	
Is there anthing which will prevent you from reporting to work on a regular basis?	Do you have a stable homelife? Does your spouse work?
Do you have a means of getting to work on time each day?	Do you own a car?
Describe your activities in outside groups or organizations	List all clubs, societies and lodges to which you belong.

Proper Inquiries

which you feel illustrate your qualifications for this job? (We are not requesting you to list any group which may reveal your race, religion or national origin.)

Improper Inquiries

Are you active in any church organizations?

How Does the Applicant Feel About People?

The way the applicant feels about people—co-workers and supervisors—plays an important part in determining job success. Here are the kind of questions that will help the interviewer explore this important area.

What kind of person is your current supervisor? (If applicant is unemployed, you can discuss his/her supervisor at prior job.)

What are some of the things about which you and your supervisor disagreed?

What do you feel were your supervisor's greatest strengths? Weaknesses?

In what areas do you feel your supervisor could have done a better job?

How do you feel about the way you and others in your department were treated by your supervisor?

Do you think your supervisor rated your job performance fairly? Explain.

What did he/she feel you did particularly well? What were his/her major criticisms? How do you feel about these criticisms?

What kind of people do you like working with?

Proper Inquiries	*Improper Inquiries*
What kind of people do you find it most difficult to work with? What do you do to enable yourself to work successfully with these people?	

The Applicant's Job Objectives

It is necessary for the interviewer to know what the applicant's job objectives are—what the applicant is looking for or wishing to avoid in a job or career. Here, again, proper questions can be of great help in obtaining such information. For example:

What are some things in a job that are important to you? Why?

What are some things you would like to avoid in a job? Why?

What do you want from your next job (that you are not getting from your present job)?

To what kind of position would you expect to progress in five years? Ten years?

What is your current wage/salary expectation? How did you arrive at this figure? What would you consider a satisfactory wage/salary progression from this point?

How Do Applicants View Themselves?

It is valuable to know how a person regards himself or herself. To learn more about this, the interviewer might ask such questions as:

How would you describe yourself?

What do you describe as your greatest strength?

Proper Inquiries

Are there certain things you feel more confident in doing than others? What are they? Why do you feel the way you do?

What are some of the things that motivate you?

Improper Inquiries

Gathering Information on Other Topics

Subject	Proper Inquiries	Improper Inquiries
Military Experience	Were you in the Armed Services of the United States, or in the National Guard? Which branch?	Were you in the Armed Services of any country other than the United States? Type of discharge from military (whether U.S. or otherwise)?
References	May I have the names of several business references?	Names of clergy? Names of religious references?
Handicaps	Do you have any *current* condition which would prevent you from performing all of the duties of the job for which you are applying? If so, please explain and describe whether anything could be done to enable you to overcome the condition?	Do you have any physical disabilities?
Arrests and Convictions	Have you ever been convicted of a crime involving theft/dishonesty or a crime involving the use of physical force? If so, please explain.	Have you ever been arrested? Have you ever been convicted of a crime?

Subject	Proper Inquiries	Improper Inquiries
Age	If someone looks very young, you may ask if he/she is over the minimum age for employment specified in the state in which employment will be performed.	What is your age? Date of birth? (Can be asked *after* hiring if such is necessary for a legitimate reason such as insurance application.)
Eligibility to Work in the United States	Are you eligible to work in the U.S.? Can you verify your legal right to work in the U.S. by providing a birth certificate, proof of U.S. citizenship, by some other means?	Of what country are you a citizen? Are you a naturalized citizen or a native-born citizen of U.S.? Date when you acquired U.S. citizenship? Are your parents citizens of the U.S.? Date when they became citizens? Of what country are they citizens?
National Origin		Your citizenship? Your parent's citizenship? Birthplace? What is your original name if your name has been changed by court order or otherwise according to law?
Foreign Languages		Do you read, write, or speak a foreign language (unless relevant to job for which applicant is applying)? How did you acquire your ability to read, write, or speak a foreign language?

Subject	Proper Inquiries	Improper Inquiries
Name		What is your original name (If name has been changed by court order or otherwise)?
Birthplace		Where were you born?
		Birthplace of your parents, spouse, or other relatives?
Financial/Credit Information		What is your credit rating (unless specifically relevant to the job)?
Sexual Preferences		What is your sexual preference?
Sex/Marital Status		What is your marital status?
		How many children do you have?
		Who will care for your children while you are at work?
Religion	Is there any reason you cannot work on any day of the week or of the year?	What is your religion or religous affiliation?
		Name of the house of worship to which you belong?
		Which religious holidays do you observe?
		Do you regularly attend a house of worship?
Photograph		Under no circumstances should a photograph be requested before hiring. (Do not request a photograph following the decision to hire without approval of your superior.)

382 *Employee Discipline: Policies and Practices*

Subject	*Proper Inquiries*	*Improper Inquiries*
Notice in Case of Emergency		Preferable to wait until the candidate is hired before asking for name of person to notify in case of emergency.

Table of Cases

A

A. P. Green Refractories Co. (Williams), 64 LA 885 70, 336, 341, 344, 345
Abbott & Co. (Dworkin), 76 LA 339 315, 318, 327
Abex Corp. (Rybolt), 64 LA 721 258, 263
Acme Galvanizing (Moberly), 61 LA 1115 301, 304
Acme Indus. Co. (Updegraff), 41 LA 1176 281, 287, 290, 291
Active Indus. (Ellmann), 62 LA 985 229, 230
Adair v. United States, 208 U.S. 161 (1908) 97, 130
Adams Print Works (Sachs), 84 LA 443 340, 342, 343, 344
Admiral Merchants v. Department of Labor, 149 Mich. App. 344, 386 N.W.2d 193 (Mich. Ct. App. 1986) 132
Advertising Publishing Co. (Cobb), 32 LA 26 270, 275, 276, 278
Agriss v. Roadway Express, 334 Pa. Super. 295, 483 A.2d 956 (1984) 18
Air Can. (O'Shea), 66 LA 1295 226, 227, 229
Air Express Int'l Corp. (Weiss), 81 LA 753 286
Alabama Power Co. (Baroni), 88 LA 425 261, 263
Alameda-Contra Costa Transit Dist.

—(Koven), 76 LA 770 70, 139, 149, 153
—(Randell), 75 LA 1273 235, 237, 238, 239, 240, 244
Alaska Sales & Serv. Co. (Axon), 73 LA 164 333, 334
Alberto-Culver Co. (Grant), 66 LA 736 224
Albertson's, Inc. (Christopher), 65 LA 1042 334
Alco Gravure (Adler), 78 LA 368 223
Alexander v. Gardner-Denver, 415 U.S. 36, 7 FEP 81 (1974) 114, 115, 132
Alfred M. Lewis, Inc. (Sabo), 81 LA 621 210
Allegheny Ludlum Steel Corp. (Alexander), 84 LA 476 181, 190
Allied Chem. Corp.
—(Eischen), 74 LA 412 233, 237, 240, 244
—(Harkless), 76 LA 923 232, 237, 238, 244
Allied Employers
—(Hedges), 65 LA 270 341, 344
—(Hedges), 83 LA 583 208
Allis-Chalmers Corp.
—v. Lueck, 471 U.S. 202, 118 LRRM 3345 (1985) 113, 132
—(Goetz), 73 LA 1230 304
Alton Packaging Corp. (Talent), 83 LA 1318 300
Alumax Extrusions (Miller), 81 LA 722 168, 201, 318

Alumax Foils (Hilgert), 73 LA 250   326
Alvey, Inc. (Roberts), 74 LA 835   309, 314, 320, 321, 325, 326, 327
AMAX Coal Co. (Kelroy), 85 LA 225   152
American Broadcasting Cos. (Gentile), 63 LA 278   295, 303
American Cyanamid Co. (Fogelberg), 81 LA 630   187
American Dairy of Evansville (Doering), 67 LA 1140   370, 371
American Hoechst Corp. (Purcell), 68 LA 517   368, 371
American Mfg. Co. (Speroff), 82 LA 36   150
American Motors Corp., 214 NLRB 455, 87 LRRM 1393 (1974)   243, 244, 245
American Packaging Corp. (Laybourne), 83 LA 369   166
American Ship Bldg. Co. (Everitt), 81 LA 243   183
American Standard (Biddinger), 64 LA 159   210
American Sugar Co. (Whyte), 52 LA 1228   287, 291
American Transp. Corp. (Nelson), 81 LA 318   187
AMF Harley-Davidson Motor Co. (Christenson), 61 LA 162   167
AMF Lawn & Garden Div. (Wyman), 64 LA 988   187, 190
Anaconda Aluminum Co. (Erbs), 59 LA 1147   288
Anaconda Copper Co. (Cohen), 78 LA 690   156, 169
Anchor Hocking Corp. (Ruben), 85 LA 783   211
Apcoa, Inc. (Hewitt), 81 LA 449   188, 190
Apex Int'l Alloys (Wright), 82 LA 747   323
Apollo Merchandisers Corp. (Roumell), 70 LA 614   199, 202, 203
Appleton Elec. Co. (Roomkin), 76 LA 167   300, 304
Arch of Ill. (Feldman), 84 LA 185   150
Arco-Polymers (Milentz), 69 LA 379   251, 253, 258, 260, 262, 263

Arco Precision Gear & Mach. Corp. (Young), 31 LA 575   38
Arcrods Plant (Bradley), 47 LA 994   281, 287, 290, 291
Arden-Mayfair, Inc. (Kaufman), 71 LA 200   235, 237, 240, 244
Aristocrat Travel Prods. (Koven), 52 LA 314   229
Arkansas Glass Container Corp. (Teple), 76 LA 841   71, 150, 153
Armco Steel Corp. (Duff), 52 LA 101   288
Armstrong Furnace Co. (Stouffer), 63 LA 618   175, 177, 181, 190
Armstrong Rubber Co. (Williams), 74 LA 362   152
Army Armor Center (Wren), 82 LA 464   286, 354
Arrow Lock Corp. (Nemaizer), 84 LA 734   286
Asarco, Inc.
—(Bothwell), 74 LA 1024   295, 303
—(Grooms), 76 LA 163   172, 180, 181, 190
Aslesen Co. (Fogelberg), 74 LA 1017   235, 237, 239, 244
Associated Grocers of St. Louis (Dugan), 66 LA 55   341, 342
Associated School Bus Serv. (Krebs), 72 LA 859   208, 210, 213
Atchison, Topeka & Santa Fe Ry. Co. (Johnson), 87 LA 972   183, 190
Atlanta Linen Serv. (Slatham), 85 LA 827   223, 225
Atlantic Richfield Co.
—(Gibson), 84 LA 257   149, 153
—(Heinsz), 81 LA 1193   149
Automotive Distribs. (Eisler), 76 LA 552   140, 153, 295, 303

B

B. Green & Co.
—(Cushman), 65 LA 1233   263
—(Cushman), 71 LA 685   258, 262
B. F. Goodrich Chem. Co. (Kimsly), 65 LA 1213   299, 303
Babcock & Wilcox Co.
—(Duff), 75 LA 12   304
—(Dworkin), 41 LA 862   38, 51, 70
—(Strashofer), 73 LA 443   233, 237, 238, 240, 244

Baker v. Lafayette College, 504 A.2d 247 (Pa. Super. Ct. 1987), *aff'd*, 532 A.2d 399   11, 18

Bakery and Confectionery Workers (Robertson), 74 LA 1297   364, 371

Banas v. Matthews Int'l Corp., 502 A.2d 637, 121 LRRM 2515 (Pa. Super. Ct. 1985)   18, 30, 39

Barrentine v. Arkansas-Best Freight Sys., 450 U.S. 728 (1981)   132

Baumfolder Corp. (Modjeska), 78 LA 1060   191

Beatrice Foods Co.
—(Gradwohl), 74 LA 1008   208, 210
—(Thornell), 73 LA 191   187, 188, 190, 191

Bechtel Corp. (Raffaele), 71 LA 1049   316, 319, 321, 325, 327

Eckins Moving & Storage Co. (Daughton), 82 LA 491   223

Belle Cheese Co. (Torosian), 59 LA 609   229

Bellingham Cold Storage (Krebs), 81 LA 1243   290

Bemis Co. (Wright), 81 LA 733   176, 181, 190

Bethlehem Steel Corp.
—(Fishgold), 74 LA 507   70, 148, 149, 152, 153
—(Gill), 51 LA 707   272, 273
—(Harkless), 58 LA 363   290, 291, 344, 345
—(Porter), 43 LA 1215   175, 177, 190
—Sparrows Point Plant (Porter), 45 LA 646   267, 273, 274, 277
—(Porter), 45 LA 1007   273, 274, 277
—(Sharnoff), 76 LA 480   370, 371

Big Star No. 35 (Murphy), 73 LA 850   234, 237, 244

Bismark Food Serv. (Ellmann), 84 LA 870   237

Bi-State Dev. Agency (Dugan), 67 LA 231   224

Black Diamond Enters. (Nicholas), 52 LA 945   268, 271, 272, 276, 277, 278

Blue Chip Stamps Warehouse (Kenaston), 58 LA 148   224, 229

Blue Cross of N. Cal. (Barrett), 73 LA 352   234, 237, 239, 244

Blue Diamond Coal Co. (Summers), 66 LA 1136   185, 190, 191

Boeing Servs. Int'l (Kramer), 75 LA 967   141, 153

Boise Cascade Corp. (Richardson), 66 LA 1302   71, 371

Bon Secours Hosp. (Feldsman), 76 LA 705   146, 152

Bonded Scale and Mach. Co. (Modjeska), 72 LA 520   210, 213

Bordo Citrus Prods. Co. (Naehring), 67 LA 1145   183, 190

Borg-Warner Corp. (Neas), 78 LA 985   156, 164, 169

Borman's, Inc., 254 NLRB 1023, 106 LRRM 1310 (1981)   243, 244, 245

Bowman Transp. (Goodman), 71 LA 342   308, 319, 326

Braniff Airways (Ray), 73 LA 304   263

Briggs & Stratton Corp.
—(Grant), 66 LA 758   224
—(Gundermann), 57 LA 441   169

Brooks Foundry (Daniel), 75 LA 642   258, 262

Browning-Ferris Indus. of Ohio (Shanker), 77 LA 289   187, 190, 191

Bruffett v. Warner Communications, 692 F.2d 910, 115 LRRM 4117 (3d Cir. 1982)   131

Bucyrus-Erie Co.
—(Gundermann), 70 LA 1017   223, 226, 229
—(Lipson), 69 LA 93   367, 370

Buddy L. Corp. (McIntosh), 49 LA 581   351, 354, 356, 357, 358

Buegers Mining & Mfg. Co. (Grooms), 61 LA 952   212, 214

Bunker Ramo Corp. (Somers), 62 LA 18   164, 166, 168, 169

Burns Int'l Sec. Servs. (Kelliher), 78 LA 1163   148, 149, 150, 152

Burton Mfg. Co. (Holley), 82 LA 1228   164

C

Cadillac Plastic & Chem. Co. (Kates), 58 LA 812   164, 166, 168, 169

Cal Custom/Hawk (Ross), 65 LA 723   187, 190
Callahan v. Scott Paper Co., 541 F. Supp. 550 (E.D. Pa. 1982)   131
Cameron Iron Works (Milentz), 84 LA 936   147, 149
Canron, Inc. (Marcus), 72 LA 1310   70, 210, 214, 337, 342, 345
Canteen Corp. (Keefe), 52 LA 781   165, 168
Canton Drop Forging & Mfg. Co. (Teple), 78 LA 1189   282, 287, 291
Carborundum Co.
—(Altrock), 72 LA 118   360, 366, 370
—(Millious), 71 LA 802   71, 139, 146, 150, 152, 153
Care Inns (Taylor), 81 LA 687   164
Casting Eng'rs (Petersen), 71 LA 949   254, 263
Caterpillar, Inc. v. Williams, 482 U.S. —, 125 LRRM 2521 (1987)   132
Cavalier Corp. (Haemmel), 75 LA 253   309, 320, 325, 326
Centennial One (Mittelman), 84 LA 89   210
Central Illinois Pub. Serv. Co. (Kossoff), 76 LA 300   361, 367, 370
Central Motor Lines (Carson), 56 LA 824   229
Central Ohio Transit Auth. (Murphy), 88 LA 633   259
Central Tel. Co. (Mead), 76 LA 1137   299, 303
Cerro Corp. (Griffin), 69 LA 965   251, 262, 263
Chalfant Mfg. Co. (Nichols), 52 LA 51   165, 167, 169, 288
Challenge Mach. Co. (Roumell), 81 LA 865   198
Champion Int'l (White), 74 LA 623   141, 152, 153
Champion Spark Plug Co. (Cassellman), 68 LA 702   185, 190, 191
Chardon Rubber Co. (Layborne), 81 LA 659   209
Charm Footwear Co. (Turkus), 39 LA 154   277
Chatham Supermkts. (Roumell), 71 LA 1084   308, 310, 324, 325, 326
Chattanooga Gas Co. (Mullin), 83 LA 48   223

Chromalloy Am. Corp. (Hon), 61 LA 246   351, 357, 358
Chromalloy Div.-Okla. (Moore), 67 LA 1310   281, 287, 290
Cincinnati Tool Co. (Kates), 52 LA 818   332
Circus, Circus (Kotin), 52 LA 1071   165, 166, 167, 168, 169
Cisco v. UPS, 476 A.2d 1340 (Pa. Super. Ct. 1984)   18
City Disposal Sys., 256 NLRB No. 73, 107 LRRM 1267 (1981)   291
City of, *see* name of particular city
City Prods. Corp. (Goetz), 67 LA 27   229
Claim of, *see* name of particular claim
Clay Equip. (Carter), 73 LA 817   315, 319, 325, 327
Clinton Corn Processing Co. (Madden), 71 LA 555   367, 370
CMI (Keefe), 82 LA 735   213
Coca-Cola Bottling Co.
—Chauffeurs, Teamsters and Helpers Local 878 v., 613 F.2d 716, 103 LRRM 2380 (1980)   54, 70
—(Berger), 81 LA 56   146
—(Bickner), 83 LA 1172   322
Cocoa, Fla., City of (Cocalis), 81 LA 949   238, 239
Collis Co. (Doyle), 50 LA 1157   357, 358
Combustion Eng'g (Jewett), 70 LA 318   260, 262
Commercial Warehouse Co. (Sater), 62 LA 1015   224, 229
Commonwealth of Pa. (LeWinter), 66 LA 96   224, 229
Confer Smith & Co. (Raymond), 73 LA 1278   223
Consolidated Coal Co. (Hoh), 85 LA 506   210
Consolidation Coal Co. (Rubin), 78 LA 473   369
Consumer Plastics Corp. (Talent), 83 LA 870   332
Continental Airlines (Ross), 75 LA 896   183, 190
Continental Fire Drum (Yaney), 83 LA 1197   164
Copperweld Bimetallics Group (Denson), 83 LA 1024   207

Corley Distrib. Co. (Ipavec), 68 LA 513   201, 203
Corns Truck & Tractor (Cowan), 63 LA 828   212
Craftool Co. (Weiss), 63 LA 1031   199, 202, 203
Country Club Mkts. (Bognanno), 85 LA 286   333
County of Santa Clara (Concepsion), 76 LA 7   342, 344, 345
Cudahy Foods Co. (Fox), 64 LA 110   224, 229

D

D&D Poultry (Nelson), 81 LA 553   164
Dahlstrom Mfg. Co. (Gootnick), 78 LA 302   183, 190
Dalfort Corp. (White), 85 LA 70   369
Danbury Cemetery Ass'n (Stutz), 42 LA 447   332
Daniel Int'l Corp. (Thornell), 83 LA 1096   289
Dan Van Rubber Co. (Rothchild), 68 LA 217   227, 229
Dap, Inc. (Shieber), 84 LA 459   146, 147, 149, 153
Dart Indus. (Greene), 56 LA 799   220, 224, 226, 227, 230
Day & Zimmerman, Inc.
—(Dilts), 85 LA 1151   198, 202, 343
—(Stratton), 63 LA 1289   263
Dayton Pepsi Cola Bottling Co. a/k/a/ Holiday Gen. Corp. (Keenan), 75 LA 154   226
Dayton Tire & Rubber Co. (Ipavec), 67 LA 78   282, 289, 291
Decor Corp. (Kates), 44 LA 389   39
Delaware River Port Auth. (Raffaele), 76 LA 350   326
DeLuca v. Reader, 227 Pa. Super. 392, 323 A.2d 309 (1974)   18
Dempster Bros. (Haemmel), 57 LA 1279   164, 168
Detroit, City of (Coyle), 75 LA 1045   70, 139, 149, 153
Detroit Edison (Jones), 82 LA 226   353, 355, 356, 357
Detroit Stoker Co. (Daniel), 75 LA 816   258, 262

Devon Apparel (Rock), 85 LA 645   370
Dixie Mach. Rebuilders, 248 NLRB 881, 104 LRRM 1094 (1980)   242, 244, 245
Dobbs House (Hilgert), 78 LA 49   156, 164, 169
Dole Can Plant (Tsukiyama), 83 LA 253   325
Dominquez v. Babcock, 696 P.2d 338, (Colo. App. 1985), *cert. granted*, 727 P.2d 362 (Colo. 1986)   18
Dover Corp. (Kaut), 74 LA 675   361, 367, 370
Dravo Corp. (McDermott), 68 LA 618   367, 370
Dravo Doyle Co. (Jones), 73 LA 649   70, 139, 146, 149, 152, 153
Dresser Indus.
—(Harrison), 83 LA 577   343
—Galion Mfg. Div. (McIntosh), 75 LA 45   217, 223, 226, 229
du Pont, E. I., de Nemours & Co. (Light), 78 LA 327   237, 244, 287, 290
Dunlop Tire & Rubber Corp.
—(Mills), 64 LA 1099   229
—(Williams), 76 LA 1228   138, 150, 152, 153
Durion Co. (Coyne), 85 LA 1127   187, 189
Duval Corp. (Block), 55 LA 1089   226
Dyer's Chap House (Ray), 82 LA 198   202

E

E. I. du Pont, *see* du Pont, E. I., de Nemours & Co.
E. F. Hauserman Co. (Gibson), 64 LA 1065   164, 166, 167, 168
E. R. Carpenter Co., 252 NLRB No. 5, 105 LRRM 1492 (1980)   291
Eagle Ottawa Leather Co. (Jason), 82 LA 493   323, 324
East Ohio Gas Co. (Michelstetter), 78 LA 71   152

Eastern Airlines
—(Turkus), 74 LA 316   177, 183, 190
—(Turkus), 76 LA 961   251, 262, 263
Eaton Corp. (Kasper), 69 LA 71   340,
    342, 344, 345
Eaton Corp., Cutler-Hammer Group,
    Bowling Green Plant (Atwood), 73
    LA 367   227
Eaton, Yale & Towne (Kates), 56 LA
    1037   164, 168
Economy Forms Corp. (Sembower),
    55 LA 1039   164, 166, 168, 169
Edward Draemer & Sons, Inc. (Re-
    zler), 81 LA 821   366, 368
Ekstrom, Carlson & Co. (Davis), 55
    LA 764   164, 167, 291
Elizabeth Horton Memorial Hosp.
    (Sandler), 64 LA 96   201, 203
Elwell-Parker Elec. Co. (Dworkin),
    82 LA 327   223
Emery Air Freight Corp. (Darrow),
    67 LA 541   370, 371
Emery Indus. (Gentile), 72 LA
    110   314, 324, 327
Emhart Corp. (Katz), 83 LA 907   299
Emhart Mfg. Co. (McKone), 63 LA
    1265   261, 263
Equitable Gas Co. (Sergent), 81 LA
    368   286
Erie, City of (Kreimer), 73 LA
    605   235, 237, 238, 239, 240, 244
Ernst v. Indiana Bell Tel. Co., 475
    N.E.2d 351 (Ind. 1985)   18

F

Factory Servs. (Fitch), 70 LA
    1088   224
Farm Stores (Hanes), 81 LA 344   190
Federal Aviation Admin. (Larkin),
    70 LA 1249   224, 226
Fenton, City of (Roumell), 76 LA
    355   301, 302, 304
Flat River Glass Co. (Newmark), 76
    LA 946   311, 316, 318, 321, 325,
    326, 327
Flint, City of, Mich. (Stieber), 59 LA
    370   271, 273, 275
Florsheim Shoe Co. (Roberts), 74 LA
    705   337, 342, 343, 344, 345

FMC Corp.
—(Doering), 74 LA 1185   141, 152,
    153
—(Marlatt), 73 LA 705   210, 212,
    213
—(Nicholas), 81 LA 176   164, 198
—(Reynolds), 80 LA 1173   248, 260,
    262
Foote & Davis (Wahl), 88 LA
    125   187, 189
Fordham Univ. (Irsay), 85 LA
    293   164
Fort Wayne Community Schools
    (Deitsch), 78 LA 928   67, 71, 342,
    344, 345
Fourco Glass Co. (Cantor), 84 LA
    693   286, 288
Fournelle v. NLRB, 670 F.2d 331,
    109 LRRM 2441 (D.C. Cir.
    1982)   370, 371
Fred Rueping Leather (Jacobowski),
    83 LA 644   147
Freeman United Coal Co. (Roberts),
    82 LA 861   173, 181, 183, 190
Frontier Airlines (Watkins), 82 LA
    1238   223
Fruehauf Trailer Co. (Belkin), 58 LA
    1169   227, 229
Fry's Food Stores of Ariz. (Weizen-
    baum), 83 LA 1248   286
FSC Paper Corp. (Marshall), 65 LA
    25   164, 167, 168
Furr's, Inc. (Leeper), 72 LA 960   370,
    371

G

G. Heilman Brewing Co.
—(Hilgert), 83 LA 829   322, 323
—(Solomon), 54 LA 1   164, 168, 169
Gamble Bros. (Krislov), 68 LA
    72   261, 262
Garcia, Claim of, 479 N.Y.S. 2d 594,
    104 A.D. 675 (N.Y. App. Div.
    1984)   132
Gardner Motors (Lightner), 64 LA
    428   199, 200, 202, 203
Garibaldi v. Lucky Food Stores, 726
    F.2d 1367, 115 LRRM 3089 (9th
    Cir. 1984), *cert. denied*, 471 U.S.

1099, 119 LRRM 2248 (1985)   104, 131
Gas Serv. Co. (Bronson), 63 LA 293   331, 334
Gates Chevrolet Co. (Coyle), 63 LA 753   209, 212, 214
Gateway United Methodist Youth Center (Miller), 75 LA 1177   313, 326, 327
General Dynamics (Kaufman), 81 LA 855   322
General Elec. Co.
—(Abrams), 71 LA 884   313, 324, 327
—(Abrams), 74 LA 847   38, 39
—(Bridgewater), 72 LA 654   166, 169, 371
—(Clark), 72 LA 355   181, 190
—(Craver), 71 LA 337   314, 325, 326, 327
—(Foreman), 71 LA 142   223, 312, 321, 322, 323, 327
—(King), 73 LA 1248   313, 322, 323, 326, 327
—(MacDonald), 72 LA 391   223, 226
—(MacDonald), 72 LA 809   70, 138, 148, 149, 152, 153
—(Maroney), 71 LA 164   369, 371
—(Moore), 74 LA 1278   340
—(Seitz), 41 LA 823   273
General Felt Indus. (Carnes), 74 LA 972   190, 191
General Foods Corp. (Maslanka), 65 LA 1271   256, 264
General Mills Fun Group (Martin), 72 LA 1285   71, 137, 150, 152, 153
General Portland Cement Co. (Davidson), 62 LA 377   261, 263
General Portland, Inc. (Flannagan), 81 LA 230   164
General Servs. Admin.
—(Avins), 76 LA 118   326
—(Lubic), 75 LA 1158   211, 214
General Tel. Co. of Cal.
—(Collins), 87 LA 441   249, 261, 263
—(Richman), 73 LA 531   263
Gengler v. Phelps, 589 P.2d 1056 (N.M. 1978)   18
Genuine Parts Co. (O'Neill), 66 LA 1331   224, 226
Georgia Pac. Corp.

—(Imundo), 71 LA 195   137, 150, 152, 153
—(King), 85 LA 542   190, 255, 259, 263
—(Szollosi), 81 LA 179   353, 355, 356
—(Vadakin, 72 LA 784   258, 262
Gibson Greeting Cards (Singer), 83 LA 1033   210
Gill Studios (Goetz), 78 LA 915   57, 65, 71
Glass Container Mfrs. Inst. (Dworkin), 53 LA 1266   164, 168, 169
Glen Manor Home for the Jewish Aged (Katz), 81 LA 1178   289
Globe Refractories (Bolte), 78 LA 320   287, 290
Godchaux-Henderson Sugar Co., (Barnhart), 75 LA 377   310, 318, 320, 326, 327
Golden Foundry (Fitch), 67 LA 887   363, 368, 371
Golden Pride (Jaffee), 68 LA 1232   226
Granite City Steel Co. (Belshaw), 58 LA 69   349, 355, 357, 358
Great Atl. & Pac. Tea Co. (Seidenberg), 68 LA 485   310, 344
Great Lakes Container Corp. (Madden), 84 LA 451   223, 299
Great Midwest Mining Corp. (Mikrut), 82 LA 52   149
Great Plains Bag Corp. (Leach), 83 LA 1281   149
Greater Harlem Nursing Home (Marx), 76 LA 680   235, 237, 238, 239, 240, 244
Green v. Oliver Realty, 526 A.2d 1192 (Pa. Super. Ct. 1987)   104, 131
Greenlee Bros. & Co.
—(Rezler), 67 LA 686   208, 214
—(Wolff), 67 LA 847   174, 177, 180, 181, 183, 190
Greif Bros. Corp. (Flannagan), 67 LA 1001   363, 368, 371
Greyhound Lines (Larkin), 67 LA 483   210
Grief Bros. Cooperage Corp. (Daugherty), 42 LA 555   39
Groovfold, Inc. (Morgan), 83 LA 521   210

Gulf Printing Co. (Lilly), 61 LA 1174   212, 214
Gwaltney of Smithfield, Inc. (Bernhardt), 81 LA 24   287

H

H. E. Miller Oldsmobile (Westbrook), 81 LA 1112   161, 168, 169, 201
H. P. Smith Paper Co. (Lieberman), 81 LA 888   368
Harris v. Iannaccone, 487 N.Y.S.2d 562, 107 A.D. 429 (N.Y. App. Div.), *aff'd*, 496 N.Y.S.2d 948 (N.Y. 1985)   132
Harry Davies Molding Co. (Fish), 82 LA 1024   210
Hartford, City of (Mallon), 69 LA 303   302, 304
Harvard Mfg. Co. (Kates), 51 LA 1098   332, 334
Haskell Mfg. Co. (Wood), 33 LA 174   272, 274, 275, 277
Hawaii Transfer Co. (Tsukiyama), 74 LA 531   152
Hayes-Albion Corp.
—(Glendon), 70 LA 696   224, 226
—(Kahn), 76 LA 1005   190, 191
Heppenstall Co. (Shister), 55 LA 1044   333, 334
Herrud & Co. (Keefe), 66 LA 682   367, 370
Hess Oil Virgin Islands Corp. (Berkman), 72 LA 81   206, 209, 212, 213, 214
Hilo Coast Processing Co. (Tanaka), 74 LA 236   318, 325
Hinckley & Schmitt (Goldberg), 73 LA 654   212
Hoerner Waldorf Champion Int'l Corp. (Newmark), 75 LA 416   211, 213
Honda of Am. Mfg., 260 NLRB No. 97, 109 LRRM 1267 (1982)   241, 244, 245
Hooker Chem. Corp. (Goodstein), 66 LA 140   224, 226
Horizon Mining Co. (Le Winter), 72 LA 117   229

Hotel Bancroft (Wolff), 78 LA 819   237, 238, 239
Houston Power & Light (Howell), 87 LA 478   261
Houston Publishers Ass'n (Duff), 58 LA 321   341, 343
Humko Sheffield Chem. (Ross), 66 LA 1261   370, 371
Hunter v. Port Auth. of Allegheny County, 277 Pa. Super. 419 (1980)   18
Huntingdon Alloys (Shanker), 73 LA 1050   210
Hurley Hosp. (Roumell), 71 LA 1013   234, 237, 238, 240, 244
Hussmann Refrigerator Co. (Mikrut), 82 LA 558   258
Hussmann Refrigerator Co. (Mikrut), 82 LA 558   258
Hyatt Hotel Palo Alto (Oestreich), 85 LA 11   169
Hygrade Food Prods. Corp. (Chiesa), 73 LA 755   223

I

I. B. Goodman Mfg. Co. (Gessinger), 62 LA 732   332, 333, 334
I. E. Prods. (Brooks), 72 LA 35   227
Ideal Elec. Co. (Martin), 77 LA 123   146, 152
Illinois School Bus Co. (Cox), 81 LA 736   223
Illinois Power Co. (Penfield), 84 LA 586   286
Imperial Chevite (Hill), 81 LA 1083   323
Imperial Foods (Crawford), 69 LA 320   282, 289, 291
Indal Aluminum Gulfport (Nicholas), 84 LA 124   166
Indian Head (Rimer), 71 LA 82   261, 262
Indianapolis Power and Light Co. (Kossoff), 73 LA 512   227
Inglis Ltd. (Shine), 66 LA 812   349, 353, 355, 357, 361, 367, 370
Interboro Contractors, 157 NLRB 1295, 61 LRRM 1537 (1966)   283, 291

Internal Revenue Serv. (Edes), 77 LA 19   316, 318, 325, 327

International Harvester Co. (Seinsheimer), 53 LA 1197   226, 229

International Minerals & Chem. Corp.
—(Jones), 78 LA 682   237, 244, 287
—(Kulkis), 83 LA 593   271, 272, 273, 274

International Paper Co. (Jaffe), 56 LA 558   169

International Shoe Co. (Roberts), 68 LA 444   336, 344, 345

Interstate Brands Corp.
—(Hamby), 73 LA 771   342
—(Richman), 83 LA 497   166, 167, 323

Irwin-Willert Home Prods. Co. (Maniscalco), 77 LA 146   150, 152, 153

Issaacson Structural Co. (Peck), 72 LA 1075   264

ITT Gen. Controls (Bickner), 76 LA 1258   140, 150, 152, 153

ITT Higbie Mfg Co. (Shanker), 85 LA 859   325

ITT Thompson Indus. (Seifer), 70 LA 970   370

J

Jacksonville Shipyards (Taylor), 74 LA 1066   333, 334

Janitorial Serv. (Whelan), 33 LA 902   332, 333

Jeep Corp. (Keefe), 67 LA 828   258, 262

Jehl Cooperage Co. (Odom), 75 LA 901   188, 191

Jenkins Bros. (Stutz), 45 LA 350   269, 274, 276, 277, 278

Jersey City Educ. Ass'n v. Jersey City Bd. of Educ., 527 A.2d 84, 44 FEP 1750 (N.J. Sup. Ct. App. Div. 1987)   132

Jewish Convalescent & Nursing Home (Bowers), 85 LA 805   208

Jim Walter Resources (Williams), 81 LA 1115   366, 368

John J. Nissen Baking Co. (Chandler), 82 LA 309   223

John W. Galbreath & Co. (Bolte), 85 LA 575   286

Johns-Manville Perlite Corp. (Traynor), 67 LA 1255   71, 304

Johns-Manville Prods. Corp. (Kates), 76 LA 845   141, 142, 153, 183, 190

Johnson v. City of Buckner, 610 S.W.2d 406 (Mo. Ct. App. 1980)   18

Jonco Aircraft (Merrill), 22 LA 1819   343, 345

Jones & Laughlin Steel Corp. (Cook), 78 LA 566   155, 164, 168, 169, 364, 369, 371

Joseph G. Tropiano, Inc. (Belsky), 69 LA 1243   258, 262

Joy Mfg. Co. (Freeman), 68 LA 697   262, 263

Justrite Super Mkts. (Bothwell), 56 LA 152   230

K

Kaiser Found. Health Plan (Herring), 73 LA 1057   309, 320, 326

Kalman v. Grand Union Co., 183 N.J. Super. 153, 443 A.2d 728 (1982)   131

Kast Metals Corp. (Moore), 61 LA 87   167, 168, 169

Kay-Brunner Steel Prods. (Gentile), 78 LA 363   287, 290, 363, 369, 371

Keebler Co. (Belcher), 88 LA 183   187

Kelsey-Hayes (Keefe), 64 LA 740   210

Kentile Floors (Block), 57 LA 919   230

Keystone Steel & Wire Co. (Elson), 72 LA 780   263

Khalifa v. Henry Ford Hosp., 401 N.W.2d 884 (1986), *appeal denied*, June 3, 1987   112, 131

Kimberly-Clark Corp. (Shieber), 62 LA 1119   295, 303, 304

King's Command Meats (Kleinsorge), 60 LA 491   341, 343

Knauf Fiber Glass (Abrams), 81 LA 333   142, 152, 153

Koehring Co. (Boals), 69 LA 459
361, 370
Kohls v. NLRB, 629 F.2d 173, 104
LRRM 3049 (D.C. Cir. 1980)   291
Kraft Foods (Rose), 73 LA 493   311,
322, 325, 326
Kraft, Inc. (Denson), 82 LA 360   259,
286, 289
Krauth & Benninghoffen Corp.
(Imundo), 73 LA 1243   369, 371
Kroger Co.
—(Berns), 75 LA 290   315, 318, 325,
327
—(Doering), 74 LA 785   308, 318,
326, 327
—(Sabella), 72 LA 540   316, 319,
326, 327

L

Lake Park of Oakland, Cal. (Griffin),
83 LA 27   286, 289
Land O'Lakes (Smythe), 65 LA
803   183, 190
Lash Distribution (Darrow), 74 LA
274   342
Laughlin, Homer China Co.
—(Block), 55 LA 1089   229
—(Seinsheimer), 55 LA 360   226
Le Blond Mach. Tool (Keenan), 76
LA 827   146, 152
Lear Siegler, Inc. (Rothschild), 85 LA
411   149
Leaseway of Western N.Y. (France),
60 LA 1343   164, 167, 168, 169,
288
Library of Congress (Rothman), 62
LA 1289   351, 356, 357, 358
Lick Fish & Poultry Co. (Concep-
cion), 87 LA 1062   250, 261, 263
Lime Register Co. (Heinsz), 76 LA
935   152
Linn County, Iowa (Sinicropi), 81 LA
929   223, 299
Litton Microwave Cooking Prods.
(Bognanno), 84 LA 761   149
Livingston Export Packing (Ives), 83
LA 270   258
Local No., *see* name of opposing party
Lockheed Aircraft Corp. (Roberts),
37 LA 188   277

Lockheed Corp. (Taylor), 83 LA
1018   167
Lone Star Beer Co. (Cowart), 66 LA
189   224, 226
Lone Star Cement (Foster), 85 LA
468   210
Longmont Turkey Processors
(Cohen), 84 LA 638   289
Los Angeles, City of (Tamoush), 64
LA 751   168
Los Angeles Die Casting Co. (Rose),
61 LA 1218   303
Los Angeles Judicial Dist. (Draz-
nin), 81 LA 463   344
Louisville Gas & Elec. (Stonehouse),
81 LA 730   158, 164, 169
LTV Aerospace Corp. (Moore), 65 LA
195   309, 314, 319, 326, 327
Lucky Stores
—(Darrow), 78 LA 233   57, 71, 148,
149
—(Sabo), 83 LA 760   325
Ludington News Co. (Platt), 78 LA
1165   148, 149, 150, 152

M

M. M. Sundt Constr. Co. (Zechar), 81
LA 432   207
Magma Copper Co. (Kelliher), 82 LA
895   211
Majestic Iron Works (Fitzsimmons),
81 LA 816   210
Mallinckrodt Chem. Works (Allen),
57 LA 709   229
Mallinckrodt, Inc. (Seidman), 80 LA
1261   252, 260, 263
Mann Packing Co. (Concepcion), 83
LA 552   353
Marco Mfg. Co. (Richman), 84 LA
134   322
Marine Corps Air Station (Nolan),
72 LA 28   223
Marion Power Shovel Co.
—(Kates), 82 LA 1014   323, 325
—(McDermott), 69 LA 339   304
Mark Twain Marine Indus. (Guenther),
73 LA 551   367, 371
Marley Cooling Tower Co. (Sergent),
71 LA 306   137, 148, 152

Martin-Marietta Aerospace (Aronin), 81 LA 695   251, 261, 262, 263
May Dept. Stores Co. (Dean), 64 LA 122   210
McDonald v. City of West Branch, Mich., 466 U.S. 284, 115 LRRM 3646 (1984)   132
McDonnell Douglas Elecs. Co. (Fitzsimmons), 78 LA 287   223
McGraw-Edison (Role), 81 LA 403   148
McLean Trucking Co., 252 NLRB No. 104, 105 LRRM 1558 (1980)   291
Mead Corp. (Morgan), 75 LA 957   197, 199, 200, 203
Mead Packaging Co. (Ziskind), 74 LA 881   320, 326
Meiger, Inc. (Ellmann), 83 LA 570   166
Memorial Hosp. (Sinicropi), 71 LA 1252   308, 319, 326
Memphis Light, Gas & Water Div. (Rayson), 66 LA 948   190, 191
Menasha Corp. (Roumell), 71 LA 653   71, 140, 141, 152, 153
Mercoid Corp. (Kosoff), 63 LA 941   332, 334
Mesker Indus. (Mikrut), 85 LA 921   146
Metro Contract Servs. (Moore), 68 LA 1048   271, 277
Metropolitan Atlanta Transit Auth. (Anderson), 70 LA 1022   261, 262
Metropolitan Transit Auth. (King), 82 LA 141   149
Michel Warehousing Corp. (Mallet-Prevost), 67 LA 565   210
Michigan Bell Tel. Co. (Dyke), 78 LA 896   164, 166, 169, 288
Michigan Dept. of Mental Health (Borland), 82 LA 961   223, 225
Michigan Power Co. (Rayl), 68 LA 183   251, 262, 263
Microdot, Inc. (Kelliher), 66 LA 177   331, 332, 334
Midland Ross Corp. (Dallas), 65 LA 1151   312, 326
Midwest Tel. Co. (Witney), 66 LA 311   342, 343, 344, 345
Military Traffic Management Command (Friedman), 75 LA 968   183, 190

Milwaukee, City of (Maslanka), 71 LA 329   187, 188, 190, 191
Minnesota Mining & Mfg. Co. (White), 85 LA 1179   286, 289
Mississippi River Grain Elevator (Marcus), 62 LA 200   260, 262
Missouri Pub. Serv. Co. (Yarowski), 70 LA 1208   262, 263
Mitch Murch's Maintenance Management Co. (Fitzsimmons), 81 LA 1021   287, 290
Mitsubishi Motors Corp. v. Soler Chrysler-Plymouth, 473 U.S. 614 (1985)   115, 132
Mobay Chem. Corp. (Weitzman), 74 LA 1113   313, 323, 325, 326, 327
Mobil Oil Corp. (Fox), 73 LA 993   311, 314, 322, 326, 327
Modern Carpet Indus.; NLRB v., 611 F.2d 811, 108 LRRM 2167 (10th Cir. 1979)   291
Monarch Mach. Tool Co. (Schedler), 82 LA 880   198
Monfort Packing Co. (Goodman), 66 LA 286   260, 262
Monsanto Chem. Intermediates Co. (Penfield), 75 LA 592   310, 312, 318, 321, 326, 327
Monsanto Co. (Thomson), 76 LA 509   150, 153, 295, 303
Montague Mach. Co. (Bornstein), 78 LA 172   57, 70, 93, 338, 342, 344, 345
Montebello Container Corp. (Kaufman), 85 LA 1011   164, 198
Morgan Adhesives Co. (Abrams), 87 LA 1039   183, 190
Morrel, John, & Co. (Stokes), 74 LA 756   226
Morton-Norwich Prods. (Nitka), 74 LA 202   141, 152, 153
Morton Thiokol, Inc. (Williams), 85 LA 834   227
Moses Lt. Cone Memorial Hosp. v. Mercury Constr. Corp., 460 U.S. 1 (1983)   115, 132
Mueller Co. (Porter), 52 LA 162   348, 354, 357
Multiplex Co. (Smith), 81 LA 625   148, 149
Municipality of Anchorage (Hauck), 82 LA 256   211

Murray v. Commercial Union Ins. Co., 782 F.2d 432, 121 LRRM 3073 (3d Cir. 1986)   131

N

Nabisco Foods Co. (Allen), 82 LA 1186   201
National Aeronautics & Space Admin. (Groshoup), 82 LA 1020   286
National Can Corp. (Turkus), 68 LA 351   295, 303
National Council of Jewish Women (Scheiber), 57 LA 980   193, 195, 199, 200, 202, 203
National Fire Sprinkler Corp. (Madden), 82 LA 391   209, 340
National Floor Prods. Co. (Eyrand), 58 LA 1015   263
National Gypsum Co.
—(Jaccobs), 73 LA 228   173, 181, 183, 190
—(Klaiber), 78 LA 226   205, 207, 209, 210, 213, 214
—(Ray), 74 LA 7   287, 290, 291
National Steel Corp. (Traynor), 66 LA 533   299, 303
National Supermkts. (Ross), 79 LA 523   93
National Vendors (Edelman), 67 LA 1042   224
NCR (Gundermann), 70 LA 756   173, 180, 190
Nestle Co., The, 248 NLRB 732, 103 LRRM 1567 (1980)   242, 244, 245
Neville Chem. Co. (Parkinson), 74 LA 814   209, 210, 212
New Castle Hospital (Witney), 74 LA 365   38
New Cumberland Army Depot (Mount), 78 LA 630   238, 239, 240
New Indus. Techniques (Gray), 84 LA 915   157, 169
New Plasco Co. (Canestraight), 85 LA 787   195, 198, 203
New York Air Brake Co. (McDonnell), 75 LA 875   311, 320, 326
New York City Health & Hosps. Corp. (Simons), 76 LA 387   262, 263
New York News (Berkowitz), 58 LA 835   164, 167, 168

Newport News Shipbldg. & Dry Dock Co. (Garrett), 78 LA 202   295, 299, 303
Niagara Mach. & Tool Works (Grant), 76 LA 160   136, 140, 152, 153
Nickles Bakery (Letson), 73 LA 801   325, 327
Niles, Shepard Crane & Hoist Corp. (Alutto), 71 LA 828   71
Nitec Paper Co. (Goodman), 75 LA 1   322, 323, 324, 327
NLRB, *see* name of opposing party
Norfolk Shipbldg. & Drydock Corp. v. Local No. 684, 671 F.2d 797, 109 LRRM 2329 (4th Cir. 1982)   39
Northern Telecom (Sembower), 65 LA 405   341, 344
Northrop Worldwide Aircraft Servs.
—(Goodstein), 64 LA 742   190, 191
—(Mewhinney), 75 LA 1059   70, 139, 140, 148, 149, 152, 153
Novosel v. Nationwide Ins. Co., 721 F.2d 894, 114 LRRM 3105, *reh'g denied en banc*, 115 LRRM 2426 (3d Cir. 1983), *on remand*, 118 LRRM 2779 (W.D. Pa. 1985)   103, 104, 131
Nugent Sand Co.
—(Daniel), 81 LA 988   261
—(Kanner), 71 LA 585   261, 262
Nuturn Corp. (Seidman), 84 LA 1058   149

O

Ogden Food Serv. Corp. (Kelman), 75 LA 805   141, 152, 153
Oglebey Norton Co. (Duda), 82 LA 652   148
Ohanian v. Avis Rent A Car Sys., 779 F.2d 101, 121 LRRM 2169, *modified*, 121 LRRM 2229 (2d Cir. 1985)   131
Ohio Crankshaft Co. (Teple), 48 LA 558   281, 287, 290, 291
Ohio River Co. (Hewitt), 83 LA 211   180
Oklahoma State AFL-CIO (Yaney), 82 LA 657   286, 343, 344
Okonite Co. (Ghiz), 74 LA 664   191
Olin Corp. (Martin), 63 LA 952   229

O'Neal Steel (King), 55 LA 402 164
O'Sullivan v. Mallon, 390 A.2d 149, 115 LRRM 5064 (N.J. Super. 1978) 131
Otero County Hosp. Ass'n (Finston), 83 LA 98 198
Ourisman Chevrolet (Robertson), 56 LA 512 200, 202, 203
Overnite Transp. Co., 254 NLRB No. 11, 107 LRRM 1130 (1981) 244, 245
Owens-Corning Fiberglas Corp. (Nicholas), 86 LA 1026 255, 263
Owens-Illinois
—(Cantor), 83 LA 1265 227, 229
—(Witney), 73 LA 663 369, 371
Oxford Nursing Home (Wolff), 75 LA 1300 232, 237, 238, 240, 244
Ozark Lead Co. (Belcher), 69 LA 1227 312, 316, 319, 321, 325, 327

P

Pacific Airmotive (Meiners), 81 LA 747 213
Pacific Bell (Oestreich), 84 LA 710 210
Pacific Nw. Bell Tel. Co. (Render), 75 LA 40 223, 230
Pacific Sw. Airlines
—(Christopher), 73 LA 1200 234, 237, 244
—(Jones), 77 LA 320 237, 244
Pacific Tel. & Tel. Co. (Kanowitz), 74 LA 1095 216, 218, 223, 229, 230
Palmer Terrance Nursing Center (Kossoff), 82 LA 1179 202
Pantasote, Inc. (Seinsheimer), 82 LA 665 146
Park Poultry (Hyman), 71 LA 1 146, 152
Pennsylvania Power Co. (Altrock), 65 LA 623 224
Pepsi Cola Bottlers Co.
—Canton, Ohio (Keenan), 78 LA 516 290
—Youngstown (Klein), 68 LA 792 253, 260, 263
Perfection Am. Co. (Flannagan), 73 LA 520 307, 319, 321, 326

Permatex Co. (Goetz), 54 LA 546 164, 168, 169
Pet Inc. (Jason), 76 LA 292 210, 343, 345
Pete Pasquinelli Co. (Jones), 68 LA 1068 93
Peterman v. Teamsters Local 396, 174 Cal. App.2d 184, 344 P.2d 25 (1959) 131
Phillips Petroleum (Caraway), 47 LA 372 333
Pickands Mather & Co. (Witt), 76 LA 676 70, 139, 149, 152, 153
Piggly Wiggly T-212 (Nelson), 81 LA 808 210
Pioneer Transit Mix Co. (Darrow), 72 LA 206 319, 327
Pipe Coupling Mfrs. (McCoy), 46 LA 1009 333
Plantation Patterns (Dallas), 78 LA 647 39, 64, 71, 223
Plastomer Corp. (Roumell), 81 LA 700 293, 299, 303
Porcelain Metals Corp. (Roberts), 73 LA 1133 262
Porritts & Spencer, Inc. (Byars), 83 LA 1165 299
Postal Serv. (Krimsly), 71 LA 100 223
Potlach Corp.
—(Kapsch), 82 LA 445 223, 229
—(Leeper), 72 LA 583 217, 364, 371
Powermatic/Houdaille (Cocalis), 71 LA 54 310, 319, 326
PPG Indus. (Coburn), 57 LA 866 164, 167, 168
Precision Extrusions (Epstein), 61 LA 572 210
Premier Indus. (Murphy), 81 LA 183 353
Prestige Stamping Co. (Keefe), 74 LA 163 264
Pretty Prods. (Stouffer), 51 LA 688 93
Price Bros. Co. (High), 62 LA 389 224, 227, 229
Pringle Transit Co. (Duda), 81 LA 393 223
Prismo-William Armstrong Smith Co. (Jedel), 73 LA 581 38, 290
Production Steel Co. (Roberts), 82 LA 229 207

Prophet Foods Co. (Howlett), 55 LA 288 168, 169
Publishers Printing Co., 246 NLRB 206, 102 LRRM 1628 (1979) 243, 245
Pullman, Inc. (Dworet), 41 LA 607 349, 355, 357

Q

Quanex (McDonald), 73 LA 9 360, 367, 370

R

Radio Corp. of Am.
—(Gershenfeld), 49 LA 1262 268, 271, 276, 277, 278
—(Scheiber), 39 LA 621 273, 276
Ralston Purina Co. (Brown), 75 LA 313 318, 327
Randall Foods No. 2 (Sembower), 74 LA 729 232, 234, 237, 244
Randle-Eastern Ambulance Serv. (Sherman), 65 LA 394 331, 334
Ranni, Claim of, 58 N.Y.2d 715, 444 N.E.2d 1328 (1982) 132
Rawson v. Sears, Roebuck & Co., 615 F. Supp. 1546, 38 FEP 1392 (D. Colo. 1985) 131
Reichold Chems. (Hon), 73 LA 636 368, 371
Reid v. Sears, Roebuck & Co., 790 F.2d 453, 122 LRRM 2153 (6th Cir. 1986) 131
Rettinger v. American Can Co., 574 F. Supp. 806, 115 LRRM 2011 (W.D. Pa. 1983) 131
Reuther v. Fowler & Williams, 255 Pa. Super. 28, 386 A.2d 119 (1978) 131
Reynolds Metals Co.
—Sherwin Plant (Caraway), 65 LA 678 295, 299, 303
—(Fasser), 78 LA 687 284, 288, 290, 291
—(Frost), 72 LA 1051 208, 209, 210, 212, 214
Rinker Materials Corp. (Lurie), 78 LA 44 205, 209, 214
Roadway Express v. NLRB, 532 F.2d 751, 91 LRRM 2239 (4th Cir. 1976),

enforcing, 217 NLRB No. 49, 88 LRRM 1503 (1975) 291
Robertshaw Controls Co. (Duff), 69 LA 887 224
Robintech, Inc. (Block), 65 LA 221 366, 370
Rochester Methodist Hosp. (Heneman), 72 LA 276 70, 311, 326
Rochester, N.Y., City of (Lawson), 82 LA 217 201
Rock Creek Plaza (Richter), 76 LA 1113 370, 371
Rock Hill Printing & Finishing Co. (Whyte), 64 LA 856 332, 334
Rockwell Int'l Corp.
—(Feldman), 84 LA 496 340
—(Feldman), 85 LA 246 166
Rohn Indus. (Sabo), 78 LA 978 30, 39
Rohr Indus. (Lennard), 65 LA 982 207, 212, 214
Rowe Int'l (Turkus), 55 LA 1298 332, 334
Royal Indus. Union (Johnson), 51 LA 642 167, 169
Royer v. Steinberg, 153 Cal. Rptr. 499 (1979) 18
Russer Foods (Grant), 75 LA 305 315, 318, 327
Rust Eng'g Co. (Whyte), 85 LA 270 258
Ryerson & Son (Zack), 61 LA 977 304

S

S. F. Kennedy-New Prods. (Traynor), 64 LA 880 253, 260, 263
S&T Indus. (Madden), 73 LA 857 208, 209, 210
Safeguard Scientifics (Gallagher), 82 LA 945 148
Safeway Stores
—(Gould), 64 LA 563 199, 201, 202, 203
—(Madden), 75 LA 798 232, 237, 238, 240, 244
—(Staudohar), 84 LA 910 223
—(Winograd), 75 LA 430 71, 140, 152, 153
—(Yaney), 81 LA 772 213

Samuel Bingham Co. (Cohen), 67 LA 706 301, 304

San Diego Gas & Elec. Co. (Johnston), 82 LA 1039 201

San Diego Transit Corp. (Gentile), 83 LA 224 323

San Francisco Redev. Agency (Koven), 57 LA 1149 290, 291, 344, 345

Santiam S. Corp. (Mann), 68 LA 46 209

Sanyo Mfg. Corp.
—(Kelliher), 85 LA 707 149
—(Nicholas), 84 LA 169 146

Schnadig Corp. (Seidman), 85 LA 692 356, 366, 367, 370

Schnelting v. Coors Distrib. Co., 729 S.W.2d 212, 125 LRRM 3367 (Mo. Ct. App. 1987) 113, 132

Scott Air Force Base (Fitzsimmons), 76 LA 46 152

Scott & Fetzer Co. (Chattman), 69 LA 18 295, 302, 303, 304

Scovill, Inc. (Storey), 84 LA 201 286, 289

Seaway Food Town (Belkin), 78 LA 208 223, 226

Service Mach. & Shipbldg. Corp.; NLRB v., 662 F.2d 1125, 108 LRRM 3235 (5th Cir. 1981) 291

Shaefer-Alabama Corp. (LaValley), 70 LA 956 187, 190

Sharon Steel Corp. (Klein), 71 LA 737 152

Shearson/Am. Express v. McMahon, 482 U.S. ___, 55 USLW 4757 (1987) 115, 132

Shell Oil Co.
—(Allen), 83 LA 787 146, 150, 152
—(Brisco), 81 LA 1205 287
—(LeBaron), 85 LA 769 149
—(Milentz), 84 LA 562 286

Shepard Niles Crane & Hoist Corp. (Alutto), 71 LA 828 150, 153

Shop Rite Foods
—(Hayes), 55 LA 281 226, 229
—(Weiss), 67 LA 159 208, 214

Signal Delivery Serv. (Weis), 86 LA 75 187, 189

Singer Co. v. NLRB, 480 F.2d 269, 83 LRRM 2655 (10th Cir. 1973) 241, 244, 245

Sobel v. Wingard, 531 A.2d 520 (Pa. Super. Ct. 1987) 18

Social Sec. Admin.
—(Cox), 81 LA 459 168
—(Muessing), 81 LA 1001 167

Southeast Container Corp. (Seidenberg), 69 LA 884 307, 316, 319, 321, 326, 327

Southeastern Trailways (Craver), 82 LA 810 210

Southern Bell Tel. & Tel. (Duff), 74 LA 1115 235, 237, 244

Southern Ind. Gas & Elec. Co. (Nathan), 85 LA 716 366, 369, 370

Southland Corp. v. Keating, 465 U.S. 1 (1984) 132

Southwest Detroit Hosp. (Ellmann), 82 LA 491 152, 223

Southwest Fire Control Tax Dist. 6 (Kanzer), 83 LA 900 213

Southwest Forest Indus. (Cromwell), 81 LA 1234 148

Southwestern Bell Tel. Co., 200 NLRB 667, 82 LRRM 1247 (1972) 242, 245

Spartan Stores (Daniel), 84 LA 1138 237

Sperry Rand Corp. (Koven), 57 LA 68 333, 334

St. Joe Minerals Corp.
—(McDermott), 73 LA 1193 175, 177, 181, 183, 190
—(Roberts), 70 LA 1110 254, 258, 260, 262, 263

St. Joe Paper Co. (Klein), 68 LA 124 369, 371

St. John Transp. Co. (Modjeska), 73 LA 1156 214

St. Johnsbury Trucking Co. (Knowlton), 74 LA 607 223

St. Regis Paper Co.
—(Anderson), 75 LA 737 140, 152, 153
—(Kaufman), 74 LA 1281 310, 319, 326

Standard Oil of Cal. (Walsh), 65 LA 829 209, 213, 214

Standard Packaging Corp. (Fogelberg), 71 LA 445 173, 180, 190

Stanley v. Sewell Coal Co., 285 S.E.2d 679 (W.Va. 1981) 131

Stansteel Corp. (Kaufman), 69 LA
   776 258, 262
State Univ. of N.Y. (Babishkin), 74
   LA 299 251, 262, 263, 264
Station WPLG-TV (Serot), 66 LA
   805 210
Stauffer Chem. Co.
—(Corbett), 83 LA 272 211
—(Wren), 83 LA 533 211
Steck v. Smith Barney, Harris
   Upham & Co., 661 F. Supp. 543,
   43 FEP 1736 (D. N.J. 1987) 132
Stedman Mach. Co. (Keenan), 85 LA
   63 322
Steiger Tractor (Jacobowski), 83 LA
   966 159, 167, 169
Sterling Drug (Draper), 67 LA
   1296 183, 190
Stevens Air Sys. (Stashower), 64 LA
   425 349, 350, 355, 357
Stockham Pipe Fittings Co. (McCoy),
   1 LA 160 30, 39
Stoppenbach, Inc. (Lee), 68 LA
   553 341, 342, 344, 345
Structurlite Plastics Corp. (Leach),
   73 LA 691 254, 263
Sumter Elec. Coop. (Maxwell), 82 LA
   647 223
Sun Chem. Corp. (Murphy), 88 LA
   633 254, 259, 263
Sun Drug Co. (Marcus), 31 LA
   191 267, 271, 275, 277
Sun Furniture Co.
—(Ruben), 73 LA 335 370, 371
—(Szollosi), 71 LA 928 71, 139, 150,
   152, 153
Suncrete Ready Mix (Cloke), 84 LA
   613 147
Super-Valu Stores (Evenson), 74 LA
   939 226
Swenson v. CDI Corp., 670 F. Supp.
   1438, 44 FEP 1743 (D. Minn.
   1987) 132
Swift & Co. (Rentfro), 72 LA
   513 258, 263

T

Tameny v. Atlantic Richfield Co., 27
   Cal.3d 167, 610 P.2d 1330 (1980)
   131

Tecumseh Prods. Co. (Murphy), 82
   LA 420 183
Telle Tire Co. (Kubie), 81 LA 789
   210
Tempmaster Corp. (Kubie), 81 LA
   371 164, 198
Tenneco Oil Co.
—(King), 83 LA 1099 286, 289
—(Marlatt), 71 LA 571 164, 167,
   168, 169
Tennessee River Pulp & Paper Co.
   (Simon), 68 LA 421 190, 191
Tex-A-Panel Mfg. Co. (Ray), 62 LA
   272 199, 200, 202, 203, 210, 338,
   345
Texas City Ref. (King), 83 LA
   923 150
Texas Int'l Airlines (Dunn), 78 LA
   893 65, 71
Texas Refinery (Williams), 70 LA
   167 224, 229
Texas Utils. Generating Co. (Edes),
   82 LA 6 286, 288
Thermal Science (Nitka), 85 LA
   1017 353, 354, 356
Thiokol Chem. Corp. (Williams), 52
   LA 1254 169
Thomas Indus. (Feegenbaum), 83 LA
   418 223
Thornton v. Potamkin Chevrolet, 44
   N.J. 92, 219 A.2d 505 (1983) 132
Times-Mirror Cable Television
   (Berns), 87 LA 543 262
Tobyhanna Army Depot (McLeod),
   69 LA 1220 369, 371
Todd Pac. Shipyards Corp.
—(Brisco), 72 LA 1022 263
—(Jones), 81 LA 1095 146
Toledo, City of (Heinsz), 70 LA
   216 70, 338, 340, 344, 345
Toledo Edison Co. (Duda), 84 LA
   1289 323, 325
Topeka, Kan. (Thornell), 81 LA
   579 223
Toussaint v. Blue Cross & Blue Shield
   of Mich., 408 Mich. 579, 292
   N.W.2d 880 (1980) 104, 112, 131
Town House Apartments (Roumell),
   83 LA 538 198
Trailways Southeastern Lines (Gib-
   son), 81 LA 365 190

Transitank Car Corp. (Sartain), 84 LA 1112 286

Transport Body Servs. (Raffaele), 65 LA 894 210

Transportation Labor (Sheehan), 76 LA 1249 325, 327

Transportation Union (Droznin), 82 LA 358 290

Tribune-Star Publishing Co. (Seidman), 82 LA 714 340, 342, 343, 344

Triple L. Enters. (Jeanney), 70 LA 97 201, 203

Trombetta v. Detroit, Toledo & Ironton R.R., 81 Mich. App. 489, 265 N.W.2d 385 (1978) 131

Truck Transp. (Seidman), 66 LA 60 297, 304

Tyrone Hydraulics (Murphy), 75 LA 672 309, 321, 325, 326

U

Uarco Co. (Gibson), 58 LA 1021 193, 202, 203, 342

Underwood Glass Co. (Hon), 58 LA 1139 166, 168, 169

Union Camp Corp. (Hardy), 71 LA 886 309, 319, 321, 326

Union Carbide Corp.
—(Goldman), 82 LA 1084 237
—(Jones), 70 LA 201 336, 340, 345
—(Teple), 78 LA 603 223
—(White), 81 LA 864 223

Union Commerce Bank (Ipavec), 75 LA 1246 315, 318, 327

Union Fork & Hoe Co. (Ipavec), 68 LA 432 364, 371

United Elec. Supply Co. (Madden), 82 LA 921 169

United Eng'g & Foundry Co. (Kates), 37 LA 1095 332

United Fuel Gas Co. (Whyte), 54 LA 942 333, 334

United Metal Trades Ass'n (Stephen), 66 LA 1342 208, 214

United Metro (Schutz), 64 LA 7 210, 212

United Parcel Serv.
—214 NLRB No. 166, 101 LRRM 1067 (1979) 291

—(Das), 73 LA 1308 208, 210
—(McAllister), 78 LA 836 282, 287, 290, 291
—(Nicholas), 63 LA 849 229

United States Plywood-Champion Papers (Amis), 56 LA 165 343

Universal Camshaft & Heat Treat (Keefe), 76 LA 808 209

Universal Foods Corp. (Belcher), 82 LA 105 209, 343

Universal Steel Co. (Daniel), 78 LA 148 364, 369, 371

Universal Studios (Steese), 72 LA 84 357, 358

University of Chicago (Seitz), 57 LA 539 167, 168, 169

University of Mo.
—Kansas City (Thornell), 82 LA 112 261
—(Yarowsky), 78 LA 417 32, 39, 311, 318, 320, 325, 326

U.S., *see* name of particular agency

U.S. Aluminum Corp. (Darrow), 81 LA 174 258

U.S. Steel Corp.
—(Dybeck), 58 LA 977 348, 353, 357
—(Garrett), 63 LA 274 183, 190
—(Garrett), 66 LA 489 289, 291
—(McDaniel), 53 LA 1210 169
—(McDermott), 49 LA 1236 350, 356, 357
—(McDermott), 55 LA 990 169
—(Miller), 53 LA 1140 348, 354, 357
—Fairless Works (Simpkings), 74 LA 354 227

U.S. Stove Co. (Rothschild), 82 LA 965 323

U.S. Sugar Corp. (Hanes), 82 LA 604 223

Utility Trailer Mfg. Co.
—(Brisco), 85 LA 643 227
—(Maxwell), 81 LA 537 209

Utility Tree Serv. (Karasick), 53 LA 1176 333, 334

V

VA Medical Center
—(Dallas), 82 LA 25 169
—(Ludolf), 74 LA 830 313, 327

Vander Toorn v. City of Grand Rapids, 348 N.W.2d 697 (1984), *appeal denied*, Feb. 25, 1986   131
Varbros Tool & Die Co. (Kabaker), 42 LA 440   71, 341, 342, 344, 345
VCA of N.J. (Aiges), 62 LA 951   212
Vernitron Pitzoelectric Div. (Abrams), 84 LA 1315   169, 361, 366, 371
Victory Mkts. (Sabghir), 84 LA 354   210
Viewpoint Nursing Home (Bard), 72 LA 1240   320, 326
VRN Int'l (Vause), 74 LA 806   208, 209, 210, 342
Vulcan-Hart Corp. (Ghiz), 78 LA 59   206, 207, 209, 210, 214

W

W-L Molding Co.
—(House), 85 LA 58   210
—(Howlett), 72 LA 1065   307, 319, 326
W. R. Grace & Co. (Boals), 62 LA 779   331, 334
Walgreen Co. (Weis), 85 LA 1195   237, 239
Walker Mfg. Co. (Morgan), 81 LA 1169   259
Ward LaFrance Truck Co. (Levy), 69 LA 831   368, 371
Warner & Swasey (Siegel), 71 LA 158   141, 152, 153
Warner Robins Air Logistics Center (Dallas), 74 LA 710   226
Washington Cartage, 258 NLRB 701, 108 LRRM 1144 (1981)   291
Washington IGA Foodline (O'Reilly), 78 LA 391   163, 164, 168, 169
Washington Metropolitan Area Transit Auth. (Bernhardt), 82 LA 150   259
Washington Scientific Indus. (Kapsch), 83 LA 824   167
Watauga Indus. (Galambos), 78 LA 697   57, 70, 253, 258, 263
Weber Mfg. Co. (Yeager), 63 LA 56   301, 303, 304

Welch Foods (Gootnick), 73 LA 908   311, 322, 326
Werner-Continental (LeWinter), 72 LA 1   70, 138, 146, 149, 152, 153
West Chem. Prods. (Dykstra), 63 LA 610   210, 342, 345
West Penn Power Co. (Blue), 67 LA 1085   297, 303, 304
Western Gear Corp. (Sabo), 74 LA 641   141, 153
Western Paper Box (Concepcion), 81 LA 917   187
Western Rubber Co. (Cohen), 83 LA 170   223
Westinghouse Elec. Corp. (Altrock), 51 LA 1311   288
Weyerhaeuser Co. (Shearer), 83 LA 365   147
Wheaton Indus. (Kerrison), 64 LA LA 826   253, 258, 260, 263
Wheeling-Pittsburgh Steel Corp.
—241 NLRB No. 198, 101 LRRM 1070 (1979), *enforced sub nom.*, Wheeling-Pittsburgh Steel Corp. v. NLRB, 618 F.2d 1009, 104 LRRM 2054 (3d Cir. 1980)   291
—(Chockley), 74 LA 793   208, 212, 214
—(Leahy), 83 LA 318   209
Whirlpool Corp.
—v. Marshall, 445 U.S. 1 (1980)   291
—(Gruenberg), 65 LA 386   256, 263
—(Williams), 54 LA 576   164, 169
Whitfield Tank Lines (Cohen), 62 LA 934   209, 210, 212, 224, 226, 229
Wilkes-Barre, City of (Dunn), 74 LA 33   261, 262
Williams, White & Co. (Guenther), 67 LA 1181   288
Wilmington v. J.I. Case Co., 793 F.2d 909, 40 FEP 1833 (8th Cir. 1986)   132
Wilson Paper Co. (Rose), 73 LA 1167   70, 138, 146, 148, 149, 152, 153
Wilton Corp. (Smedley), 85 LA 667   286, 289
Wine Cellar (Ray), 81 LA 158   201, 227
Witco Chem. (Light), 71 LA 919   70, 139, 149, 152, 153

Wolf Baking Co. (Marlatt), 83 LA
  24   196, 202, 203
Wolf Mach. Co. (High), 72 LA
  510   39, 93
Wolk v. Saks Fifth Ave., 728 F.2d
  221, 115 LRRM 3064 (3d Cir.
  1984)   131, 132
Woodward's Spring Shop (Pinkus),
  63 LA 367   195, 199, 201, 202, 203

Y

Youngstown Hosp. Ass'n (Miller), 82
  LA 31   175, 181, 190

Z

Zell Bros. (Mayer), 78 LA 1012   369
Zellerbach Paper Co.
—(Sabo), 73 LA 1140   361, 367, 371
—(Stashower), 68 LA 69   299, 303,
  304
Zipf v. American Tel. & Tel. Co., 799
  F.2d 889 (3d Cir. 1986)   132

Index

A

Abrams, Roger I.   35, 361–362
Absenteeism (*see* Attendance rule)
Absolute privilege   11
Abusive, profane, or obscene
      language   154–169
  directed toward customers   161–
      163
  as disrespect or insubordination
      to supervisor   155–156,
      158, 163–165, 167–168,
      179, 281, 287, 363, 368
  general exclamations   163, 164
  just cause for discharge   154
  obscene phone calls   315
  as provoking fights   157
  racial or ethnic slurs   156, 157,
      166, 308–309
  as response to tense
      situation   154, 159–161,
      166–167, 307–308
  sexual harassment   156–157
  "shop talk" defense   154, 157–
      158, 165
  steward's use of   363, 364, 368–
      369
  in supervisor's presence
      only   156, 167, 168
  supervisor's use of   154, 158,
      165
  within hearing of
      customers   154–155, 163,
      168, 178
  work record considerations   155
Age discrimination   97–98, 102

Age Discrimination Act of
      1967   97–98
Alcohol-related conduct   183–190
  drinking prior to workday   171,
      187–188
  just cause for discipline   170,
      171
  nature of work   184
  notice of rule   171
  plant setting   184, 324–325
  proof of intoxication   171, 184–
      185, 188–190
  workday/nonworking hours, on/
      off premises   171, 183–
      187
Alcoholism defense   170–183
  drug abuse, offenses
      compared   252–253
  employee participation in
      treatment program   171,
      175–176, 181–183, 301
  employer knowledge of
      problem   175, 180–181
  nature and effectiveness
      of   170–172, 176–177
  overriding egregious
      behavior   172–174, 177–
      180
  time of raising   171, 172, 174–
      175, 180–181
American Arbitration
      Association   120
Amoco Co.   81
Appeal procedures   111–124
  arbitration   120–121
  chosen officer   117–118

Appeal procedures—*con't.*
　designated officer　116–117
　development　111–112, 115–
　　116, 127–128
　due process right　33–34, 67–68
　employee arbitrator　119–120
　employee representation　121–
　　124
　judicial perspectives　112–114
　officer review panel　118
　ombudsperson　122
　peer review　119
　private courts　120–121
　statutory claim cases　114–115
Appearance standards (*see* Dress
　　and grooming code)
Arbitration　112
　decisions, judicial consideration
　　of　114–115
　employee arbitrators　119–120
　employee right　34, 67
　NLRB deferral　360
　nonunion employees　120–121
Arrest and conviction records　13,
　　219, 220, 222, 226–228
AT&T　81
Attendance rule　135–153
　alcoholism defense　172, 177,
　　180, 182
　consistent enforcement　136,
　　137, 149–150
　employee manipulation of　142–
　　144
　just cause for discharge　26, 51–
　　52, 135
　management right　137
　medical disability　292–296,
　　298, 302
　mitigating circumstances　136,
　　139–142, 150–152
　moonlighting　328, 330–331
　notice of effect of violating
　　standard　58–61, 135–
　　136, 138–139, 148–149
　notice of standard　58, 135, 137,
　　138, 146–148
　progressive discipline　52
　reasonableness
　　requirement　135–137,
　　144–146
　reasons for violating　23
Attitude problems　192–203

carelessness and
　　negligence　205–206
causes　22, 23
combined with poor work
　　record　192, 197–199
customer relations effect　192,
　　196–197, 200–201
detrimental effect on workplace
　　morale　192–195, 199–
　　200
employer proof
　　requirements　195–196
just cause for discharge　192
progressive discipline　192, 193,
　　195, 201–202
At-will employment (*see*
　　Employment at will)

B

Background checks　8–14
Baseball pools (*see* Gambling)
Beards　232–233, 235, 236
Blood alcohol content (BAC)
　　test　184–185
Blue Cross and Blue Shield　104
Bomb threats　315
Burden of proof (*see* Proof
　　requirements)
Bus drivers　212, 213, 235, 238

C

California　98
Candidate pools　7–8
Card games (*see* Gambling)
Carelessness and negligence　204–
　　214
　consistency of discipline　205,
　　213–214
　danger to co-workers　205, 212–
　　213
　employee attitude　205–206
　forms and consequences　204–
　　207
　just cause for discharge　204
　notice of effect of violating
　　standard　59, 61
　notice of standard　204, 209–
　　210, 285

severity of damage 204, 210–212
substandard job
      performance 204, 207–208
sufficient training 204, 208–209
Chief executive officers (CEOs) 40
Chosen officers 117–118
Civil Rights Act of 1964, Title
      VII 97, 114, 157
Clothing standards (*see* Dress and
      grooming code)
Collier doctrine 360
Common law 97
Company records,
      falsification 64–65, 215–219, 221–226
Concerted activity 22, 97
Conditional privilege 9, 11
Conflict of interest 328, 332–333
Contract interference 103
Contract law 98–102, 104, 116
Corrective discipline (*see*
      Progressive discipline;
      specific bases for
      discipline)
Counseling requirement 338–339
Counseling system (*see*
      Nonpunitive discipline)
Courts
   consideration of arbitration
      decisions 114–115
   resolution of workplace
      disputes 120–121
Criminal records 13, 219, 220,
      222, 226–228
Customers, profane language
      directed at or within
      hearing of 154–155, 161–163, 168, 178

D

Damage awards 103
Daugherty, Carroll R. 31, 36–38
Decisional conferences 88–91
Defamation 8–9, 30, 103
Designated officers 116–117
Destruction of company property
      (*see also* Carelessness and
      negligence) 26

Disability (*see* Medical disability)
Discharge
   employee obligation to
      grieve 110
   just cause (*see also* specific bases
      for discharge) 35–38
   wrongful (*see* Employment at
      will)
Discipline programs and policies
      (*see also* Employee due
      process rights)
   bundling of offenses 61
   context and focus of 3–5
   employer and employee
      expectations 20–25, 95
   failures and problems of 72–80,
      94–97
   just cause standard 35–38
   nonpunitive system (*see*
      Nonpunitive discipline)
   progressive discipline 34–35, 51
   punitive system 52–54
Discrimination
   discipline and discharge 22,
      97–98
   dual forums 114
   employment tests 16
   racial or ethnic slurs 156, 157,
      166, 308–309, 318, 322,
      324
   remedies 102
   sexual harassment and
      threats 156–157, 310–311, 316, 318, 319
Dishonesty or records
      falsification 215–230
   company records 64–65, 215–219, 221–226
   employment applications 215–216, 219–221, 226–229
Disloyalty (*see* Attitude problems)
Dispute resolution (*see* Appeal
      procedures; Arbitration;
      Grievance procedures)
Documentation (*see* Proof
      requirements)
Dress and grooming code 231–245
   consistency with labor
      agreement 231, 238–239
   just cause for discharge 231
   notice of standard 231, 237–238

Dress and grooming code—*con't.*
  reasonable relation to business
      interest   231–237
  uniform enforcement   231, 232,
      239–240
  union insignia   240–244
Drug use or possession   246–264
  on company premises or while on
      duty   247–248, 257–260
  culpability of co-workers   256
  drug problem at plant   247,
      253–254, 260
  "hard drug" offenses   247, 253
  insubordination problem   256
  job nexus requirement   247,
      248, 250–251, 260
  just cause for discharge   246,
      256
  notice of rule   57, 247, 252, 254
  off-duty conduct   248–251, 260–
      261
  pre-employment tests   15
  prescribed drugs   246, 248, 259
  proof requirements   254–256
  reasonable rule
      requirement   252–253
  sale or intent to sell   247, 251–
      252, 261–262
  substances considered   246
Due process (*see* Employee due
      process rights)
Dworkin, Harry J.   51–52

E

Emotional distress   103
Employee arbitrators   119–120
Employee Discipline (Stessin)   3
Employee due process rights   25–
      35, 51–71
  adequate documentary
      evidence   28–30, 61–63
  appeal right (*see* Appeal
      procedures)
  consideration of mitigating
      circumstances   35
  credibility issues   94–97
  equal treatment   27, 29–30, 54,
      68–69
  grievance procedures   67, 107–
      111
  hearing right   30–33, 63–66
  importance in workplace   124–
      125, 129
  knowledge of charge   32, 63
  notice of effect of violating
      standards   58–61
  notice of standards   25–27, 55–
      58
  overview   54–55, 69–70
  progressive discipline   34–35,
      51–54
  representation right   33, 66–67
  system development   125–129
Employee notice (*see* Notice
      requirements; specific
      bases for discipline)
Employee selection (*see*
      Recruitment and selection)
Employment ads   99
Employment applications
  at-will employment
      statements   100
  falsification   215–216, 219–221,
      226–229
Employment at will   23, 97–106
  implied contract exception   98–
      102, 116
  legal encroachment on   97–98
  public policy exception   102–103
  tort of wrongful discharge   103–
      106
Employment discrimination (*see*
      Discrimination)
Employment testing   15–16
Equal treatment (*see also* specific
      bases of discipline)   27,
      29–30, 54, 68–69
Europe   103
Evidence (*see* Proof requirements)
Exxon Corp.   81

F

Facial hair   232–233, 235, 236
Fact-finding   28–29
Fair Labor Standards Act   98
Federal Arbitration Act   114
Fighting
  just cause for discharge   305,
      306, 313, 321–322
  likelihood of future peaceful

behavior 306, 314, 324–325
mitigating factors 313–314, 325
notice of rule 311
provocation defense 306, 312, 322–323
racial hostilities 309, 322, 324
rule requirements 311
self-defense 312, 322
severity of injury 313
weapons use 306, 313, 323–324
workplace atmosphere 319
Fire pranks 315
First Amendment (*see* Free speech right)
Football pools (*see* Gambling)
Free speech right
dress and grooming preferences 231
wrongful discharge for exercising 102–105

G

Gambling 265–278
activities constituting 265, 271–272
adverse effect on performance or morale 265, 275
gambling problem at plant 265, 273–274
insubordination issues 270
just cause for discharge 265–267
notice of standard 268
rule or contract requirements 265, 268–271
rules, uniform enforcement 268, 276–277
work record considerations 266, 269, 270, 275–276
workday/nonworking hours, on/off premises 265, 267–268, 272–273
General Electric Co. 81
Georgia 97
Good faith and fair dealing 98
Greene, J.G. 220
Grievance procedures 101, 127
employee right 67

nonunion employees 107–111
obey and grieve rule 363
steward abuse of 359, 360, 365–366
Grooming standards (*see* Dress and grooming code)

H

Hair length 239
Handicap discrimination 97, 102
Hats 235, 238, 241–242
Hearing right 30–33, 63–66
High, Theodore K. 31–32
High-tech industry 24
Hiring procedures (*see* Recruitment and selection)
Horseplay (*see* Misconduct or horseplay)
Hospitals, dress standards 234

I

Illness (*see* Medical disability)
Immoral or indecent
behavior 310–311, 316, 318, 319
Implied contract exception 98–102, 104, 116
Information disclosure
arrest and conviction
records 13, 219, 220, 222, 226–228
employee work records 8–14
medical problems 226, 228
Insubordination 279–291
drug use 256
gambling 270
just cause for discharge 26, 279–281
profane language 155–156, 158, 163–165, 167–168, 281, 287
progressive discipline
requirement 279, 281, 284, 289–290
provocation defense 279, 281, 287–288
reasons 23

Insubordination—*con't.*
  refusal to perform unsafe
      work   279, 281–284, 288–
      289
  refusal to take BAC test   185,
      189
  by union stewards   359, 363,
      368
  willfulness requirement   279,
      281, 284–287
  work slowdown compared   347
Interviewing skill   15, 373
Intoxication (*see* Alcohol-related
      conduct; Alcoholism
      defense)

J

Jedel, Michael Jay   280–281
Jewelry   233–234, 239
Jury duty   102, 216–217
Just cause (*see also* specific bases
      for discipline)
  actions justifying summary
      discipline   26
  standard defined   35–38

K

Kanowitz, L.   218
King, Otis H.   255

L

Labor Management Relations Act
      (LMRA) (*see also* National
      Labor Relations Act)
  Sec. 301, contract
      enforcement   113–114
Labor shortages   106
Language (*see* Abusive, profane, or
      obscene language)
Leaves of absence   329, 331
Lockouts   348
Lotteries   272

M

McCoy, Whitley P.   30
McDermott, T.J.   351

McIntosh, Richard   351
Malice liability   8–10
Malinowski, A.A.   34
Medical disability   292–304
  available alternate jobs   293,
      297, 302–303
  as creating unsafe working
      conditions   292, 296, 299–
      301
  drug use on company
      premises   246, 248, 259
  as excusing profane
      language   159–161
  improvement likelihood   293,
      297, 301–302
  inability to adjust to workplace
      needs   292, 296–297
  just cause for discharge   292–
      296, 298–299
  refusal to return to work
      after   295
  work-related injuries   292, 297
Medical records falsification   225,
      226, 228
Medical tests   15
Mental disability   296–297
Michigan   104
Misconduct or horseplay   305–321
  employee regret   306, 312, 320–
      321
  examples   315–316
  fighting (*see* Fighting)
  intent or purpose   305, 317–319
  just cause for discharge   305–
      307
  mitigating factors   307–308, 312
  notice of standard   311–312
  offenses distinguished   306, 308
  proof requirements   312–313
  racial hostilities   308–309, 318
  rule requirements   311–312
  severity of injury or
      damage   305, 317
  sexual harassment and
      threats   310–311, 318
  threats, with and without
      weapons   314
  workplace atmosphere   306,
      319–320
Misrepresentation (*see* Dishonesty
      or records falsification)
Montana   98

"Mooning" 316
Moonlighting 328–334
  as causing absenteeism,
      tardiness, or poor job
      performance 328, 330–
      331
  competition with employer 328,
      329, 332–333
  deception of employer 328–329,
      331–332
  just cause for discharge 328–
      329
  rule against, reasonableness
      requirement 329–330
Murphy, John J. 254–255

N

Narcotics (*see* Drug use or
      possession)
National Labor Relations Act
      (NLRA) 240
  employee representation
      right 67
  Sec. 7, employee rights 97, 242
  Sec. 8(a)(1), employer
      interference with
      employee §7 rights 241–
      243, 282–283
  Sec. 8(a)(3), employer
      discrimination
      encouraging or
      discouraging union
      membership 282
  union steward discipline 360
  work slowdowns and
      stoppages 347
National Labor Relations Board
      (NLRB) 240, 282–293,
      360
Negligence (*see* Carelessness and
      negligence)
Nicholas, Samuel J., Jr. 255–256
Nonemployee representatives 124
Nonpunitive discipline 80–93
  focus and objectives 81–84
  implementation/case study 84–
      92
  supervisor role 81, 92–93
  system overview 52–54, 80–81
Nonunion employees (*see also*

Appeal procedures;
      Employment at will)
  credible due process system 94–
      97, 124–129
  grievance procedure 107–111
Northern States Power Co. 81
No-strike agreements 283, 347
Notice requirements (*see also*
      specific bases for
      discipline)
  notice of effect of violating
      standards 58–61
  notice of standards 25–27, 52,
      55–58, 81

O

Obey and grieve rule 363
Obscene language (*see* Abusive,
      profane, or obscene
      language)
Obscene phone calls 315
Occupational Safety and Health
      Act 98
Occupational Safety and Health
      Administration 283
Off-duty activities
  drug use, possession, or
      sale 246, 248–252, 260–
      262
  gambling 265, 267–268, 272–
      273
  indecent behavior 316
  moonlighting 328–334
Officer review panels 118
Ombudspersons 122
Orientation program 16–18
Overtime 22, 361

P

Peer review 119
Pennsylvania 11
Phelps, Orme W. 280
Physical disability (*see* Medical
      disability)
Picket lines, refusal to cross 282
Police officers 235, 338–339
Policy manuals 99–102, 104
Polygraph tests 16, 98

Poor attendance (*see* Attendance rule)
Poor attitude (*see* Attitude problems)
Poor performance (*see also* Carelessness and negligence) 335–345
  causes 23
  good work record considerations 339
  just cause for discipline 335–336
  moonlighting as causing 328, 330–331
  notice of effect of violating standard 57
  notice of standard 335, 336, 341–342
  progressive discipline requirement 335, 337–339, 343–344
  proof requirements 335, 337, 342–343
  reasonable rule requirement 335, 336, 339–341
  work slowdown compared 347
"Positive Discipline," (Performance Systems Corp.) 76
Pre-employment testing 15–16
Prince George Pulp and Paper Co. 81
Productivity problems (*see* Carelessness and negligence; Poor performance)
Profane language (*see* Abusive, profane, or obscene language)
Progressive discipline (*see also* specific bases for discipline)
  nonpunitive (*see* Nonpunitive discipline)
  punitive 52–54, 72–80
  system defined 34–35, 51
Proof requirements
  alcohol intoxication 171, 184–185, 188–190
  dishonesty cases 218–219
  drug use or possession 254–256
  implied employment contract 99–102
  misconduct cases 312–313
  poor performance 335, 337, 342–343
  reasonableness of dress code 234–235
  recordkeeping requirements 28–29, 61–63
Property right of job 103
Protected activity
  concerted activities 22, 97
  wearing of union insignia 240–244
Psychological tests 15, 16
Public policy exception 102, 104
Punitive discipline 52–54, 72–80

Q

Quantum of proof (*see* Proof requirements)

R

Racial or ethnic slurs 156, 157, 166, 308–309, 318, 322, 324
Raffles 272
Rape 310
Recordkeeping requirements 28–29, 61–63
Records falsification (*see* Dishonesty or records falsification)
Recruitment and selection 6–19
  background checks, problems in obtaining 8–14
  candidate pool, development of 7–8
  interview training 15, 373
  multiple-step procedure 14
  orientation program 16–18
  pre-employment testing 15–16
  of supervisors 40–43
  typical problems 6–7
Refusals
  to cooperate 315
  to perform unsafe work 281–284, 288–289, 354, 357
  to testify 353
Rehabilitation Act of 1973 97

Rehabilitation programs 175–176, 260
Releases or waivers 10–12
Representation right 33, 66–67, 121–124, 127
Respirators 232, 233, 236
Retirement plan documents 99
Roberts, R.R. 336
Roumell, George 293–294

S

Sabella, Anthony J. 316
Safety issues
  medical disability, as creating unsafe working conditions 292, 296, 299–301
  refusal to perform unsafe work 281–284, 288–289, 354, 357
School bus drivers 212, 213
Sears, Roebuck and Co. 100, 103
Securities Exchange Act 115
Selection of employees (*see* Recruitment and selection)
Sexual harassment and threats 102, 156–157, 310–311, 316, 318, 319
Shell Oil Co. 81
Sherman Act 115
Shisler, Joseph 52
Shop talk (*see* Abusive, profane, or obscene language)
Sick leave abuse 23, 328
Sickness (*see* Medical disability)
Skills testing 15–16
Sleeping on job 65
Slowdowns (*see* Work slowdowns and stoppages)
Speech right (*see* Free speech right)
Sports pools (*see* Gambling)
Stessin, Lawrence 3–4
Steward discipline 359–371
  abuse of grievance system 360, 365–366
  abuse of official privileges 362–363, 367–368
  abusive or profane language 363, 364, 368–369
    aggressive representation of employee interests 359, 363–364
  conduct warranting, examples 364
  just cause 359
  overtime refusals 361, 366
  union animus concerns 360, 364–365, 369–370
  work slowdowns or stoppages 349 350, 354, 360–362, 366–367
Steward responsibilities 33, 67
Strikes (*see* Work slowdowns and stoppages)
Subcontracting 354, 356
Substance abuse (*see* Alcohol-related conduct; Alcoholism defense; Drug use or possession)
Substance tests 15
Successor employers 104
Supervisors (*see also* Abusive, profane, or obscene language) 22
  appeal procedures role 123–124
  due process system development 125–126
  employee conduct information 13, 15, 29
  hearings role 63–64
  insubordination provoked by 279, 281, 287–288
  nonpunitive discipline system role 81–93
  performance evaluations by 42, 337
  punitive discipline system role 77, 79–80
  responsibilities summarized 43–44
  selection and training 40–43, 60, 70, 73
  sources of power 44–47
Suspension 53, 72, 75–77, 80

T

Taft-Hartley Act (*see* Labor Management Relations Act; National Labor Relations Act)

Tardiness (*see* Attendance rule)
Tests   15–16
Theft   26
Threats   310, 314, 364
Time studies   336–337
Tort of wrongful discharge   103–
    106, 113–114
Training
   employees   204, 208–209
   interview training   15, 373
   supervisors   40–47, 60, 70, 73
Turkus, Burton   266

U

Uniform clothing   235–236
Union animus   359, 360, 364–365,
    369–370
Union Carbide Corp.   81
Union insignia   240–244
Union officials, discipline of (*see*
    Steward discipline)
Unions
   appeal of   94, 129
   high-tech industry   24

V

Verbal abuse (*see* Abusive, profane,
    or obscene language)

W

Waivers   10–12
Weapons use   306, 313, 314, 323–
    324
Whistling   281
Wigs   233–234
Work performance (*see*
    Carelessness and
    negligence; Poor
    performance)

Work record or history
   disclosure problems   8–14
   as mitigating circumstance
      alcoholism   174
      attendance problems   140, 151
      attitude problems   198
      drug use   248, 259, 260
      fighting   306, 314, 324–325
      gambling   266, 269, 270, 275–
          276
      poor performance   339
      profane language   155
      work slowdowns   356
Work slowdowns and
          stoppages   346–358
   insubordination compared   347
   intent   347–349, 351–354
   just cause for discipline   346,
       347
   justification for   346, 349–350,
       354–355
   mitigation of penalty   346, 351,
       356–357
   NLRA protection   347
   no-strike/no-lockout
          clauses   283, 347
   poor productivity compared   347
   refusal to perform unsafe
          work   283, 354, 357
   striker replacements   23
   uniform discipline
          requirement   346, 350–
          351, 355–356
   union steward
          responsibility   349   350,
          354, 360–362, 366–367
Workers' compensation
       claims   102

Y

Yarowsky, S.M.   32
Young, Dallas M.   27

About the Author

JAMES R. REDEKER is chairman of the Labor Law and Employee Relations department of the law firm of Wolf, Block, Schorr and Solis-Cohen with offices in Philadelphia, Pa., Great Valley, Pa., West Palm Beach, Fla., and Boca Raton, Fla. Mr. Redeker received a B.A. degree, *cum laude*, from the Central University of Iowa, an M.A. degree with honors from the University of Arkansas, and a J.D. degree from the University of Pennsylvania School of Law. In addition to his direct practice of law and representation of clients in labor matters, Mr. Redeker has written and lectured extensively in all areas of employer-employee relations and is author of *Discipline: Policies and Procedures* (1983). He is listed in *Who's Who in American Law, The Dictionary of Distinguished Americans*, and *International Men of Achievement*.